Rights, Democracy, and Fulfillment in the Era of Identity Politics

New Critical Theory
General Editors:
Patricia Huntington and Martin J. Beck Matuštík

The aim of *New Critical Theory* is to broaden the scope of critical theory beyond its two predominant strains, one generated by the research program of Jürgen Habermas and his students, the other by postmodern cultural studies. The series reinvigorates early critical theory—as developed by Theodor Adorno, Herbert Marcuse, Walter Benjamin, and others—but from more decisive post-colonial and post-patriarchal vantage points. *New Critical Theory* represents theoretical and activist concerns about class, gender, and race, seeking to learn from as well as nourish social liberation movements.

Phenomenology of Chicana Experience and Identity:
  Communication and Transformation in Praxis
    by Jacqueline M. Martinez
The Radical Project: Sartrean Investigations
    by Bill Martin
From Yugoslav Praxis to Global Pathos: Anti-Hegemonic
  Post-post-Marxist Essays
    by William L. McBride
Unjust Legality: A Critique of Habermas's Philosophy of Law
    by James L. Marsh
New Critical Theory: Essays on Liberation
    edited by William S. Wilkerson and Jeffrey Paris
The Quest for Community and Identity: Critical Essays in
  Africana Social Philosophy
    edited by Robert E. Birt
After Capitalism
    by David Schweickart
The Adventures of Transcendental Philosophy: Karl-Otto
  Apel's Semiotics and Discourse Ethics
    by Eduardo Mendieta
Love and Revolution: A Political Memoir: People's History
  of the Greensboro Massacre, Its Setting and Aftermath
    by Signe Waller
Beyond Philosophy: Ethics, History, and Liberation Theology
    by Enrique Dussel
    edited by Eduardo Mendieta
From Class to Race: Essays in White Marxism and Black Radicalism
    by Charles W. Mills
Rights, Democracy, and Fulfillment in the Era of Identity Politics:
  Principled Compromises in a Compromised World
    by David Ingram

Rights, Democracy, and Fulfillment in the Era of Identity Politics

Principled Compromises in a Compromised World

David Ingram

ROWMAN & LITTLEFIELD PUBLISHERS, INC.
Lanham • Boulder • New York • Toronto • Oxford

ROWMAN & LITTLEFIELD PUBLISHERS, INC.

Published in the United States of America
by Rowman & Littlefield Publishers, Inc.
A wholly owned subsidiary of The Rowman & Littlefield Publishing Group, Inc.
4501 Forbes Boulevard, Suite 200, Lanham, Maryland 20706
www.rowmanlittlefield.com

PO Box 317
Oxford
OX2 9RU, UK

Copyright © 2004 by Rowman & Littlefield Publishers, Inc.

All rights reserved. No part of this publication may be reproduced, stored in a retrieval system, or transmitted in any form or by any means, electronic, mechanical, photocopying, recording, or otherwise, without the prior permission of the publisher.

British Library Cataloguing in Publication Information Available

Library of Congress Cataloging-in-Publication Data

Ingram, David, 1952-
  Rights, democracy, and fulfillment in the era of identity politics : principled compromises in a compromised world / David Ingram.
    p. cm. — (New critical theory)
   ISBN 0-7425-3347-6 (cloth : alk. paper) — ISBN 0-7425-3348-4 (pbk. : alk. paper)
  1. Human rights. 2. Democracy. 3. Group identity. I. Title. II. Series.
   JC571.I4893 2004
   323--dc22   2003020461

Printed in the United States of America

∞™ The paper used in this publication meets the minimum requirements of American National Standard for Information Sciences—Permanence of Paper for Printed Library Materials, ANSI/NISO Z39.48-1992.

To Max

All is politics, philosophy as well as the philosophies, and the only "philosophy" is history in action, life itself.

—Antonio Gramsci, *Prison Notebooks*, 1926–1937

Contents

Acknowledgments	ix
Introduction: New Critical Theory: Taking Rights, Democracy, and Identity Politics Seriously	1
1 Human Rights and Differends: The Fragmentation of Reason and Identity in the (Post)modern Age	29
Part I IDENTITY	51
2 White Man's Burden? Ethnicity and Race in the Era of Identity Politics	53
3 Identity Politics and the Law: Reflections on Disability	91
Part II DELIBERATIVE DEMOCRACY	117
4 Democracy and Racial Identity: Reconsidering Representation	119
5 Democracy and the Rule of Law: Differends and Crises in Postliberal Capitalism	143
Part III RIGHTS	175
6 Toward a Pragmatist and Perfectionist Theory of Rights	177
7 Human Rights and International Justice	203
Concluding Remarks: Achieving Global Harmony through Transformative Dialogue	239
Bibliography	245
Index	257

Acknowledgments

I wish to acknowledge the use of previously published articles in the following chapters. Chapter 1 contains portions of "Can Groups Have Rights? What Postmodern Theory Tells Us about Inclusive Democracy in the Era of Identity Politics," *Democracy and Nature* 7, no. 1 (March 2001): 134–58; chapter 4 contains portions of "The Dilemmas of Racial Redistricting," *The Philosophical Forum* 31, no. 2 (June 2000): 131–44; and chapter 5 contains portions of "The Sirens of Pragmatism versus the Prophets of Proceduralism," in *Habermas and Pragmatism*, ed. M. Aboulafia, M. Bookman, and C. Kemp (New York: Routledge, 2002): 83–112. Chapter 7 contains portions of "Immigration and Social Justice: Cosmopolitan and Communitarian Appeals to the Challenge of Globalization," *Peace Review* 14, no. 4 (2002): 403–13; and "Between Political Liberalism and Post-National Cosmopolitanism: Towards an Alternative Theory of Human Rights," *Political Theory* 31, no. 3 (June 2003): 359–91. Chapters 2, 3, 6, the introduction, and the conclusion appear here for the first time.

I would like to thank Martin J. Beck Matuštík and Patricia Huntington for inviting me to publish this book in their series. Special thanks are also owed to the anonymous readers for useful criticism, and to Michael Marino, Eve DeVaro, John Wehmueller, and Stefano Giacchetti for assistance in editing and producing the book.

I also wish to express my gratitude to Russ Powell, for teaching me the finer points of Islamic natural law theory; and to the students who attended the 2001 graduate seminar on disability rights, which I taught with my life partner, Jennifer Parks. Last but not least, I thank Jenny and my daughter Sabina, for teaching me *la meravigliosa arte della vita e dell'amore*.

Introduction

New Critical Theory: Taking Rights, Democracy, and Identity Politics Seriously

> In the eighteenth century the conviction that man is endowed with certain rights was not a repetition of beliefs that were held by the community, nor even a repetition of beliefs handed down by forefathers. It was a reflection of the situation of the men who proclaimed these rights; it expressed a critique of conditions that imperatively called for change, and this demand was understood by and translated into philosophical thought and historical actions. The pathfinders of modern thought did not derive what is good from the law—they even broke the law—but they tried to reconcile the law with the good.
>
> —Max Horkheimer, "Means and Ends" (1947)

In the wake of the recent war in Iraq, commentators pondered whether the good that resulted from overthrowing an evil regime could compensate for the apparent lawlessness of a war that, in retrospect, looks more like a war of aggression than a war of self-defense. Leaving aside the final outcome of the war, which might conceivably bring freedom, democracy, and prosperity to the Iraqi people and greater security to the citizens of the United States, one wonders whether this war was right, or at the very least a compromise that was in some sense principled.

In my opinion, it was neither. The good end—should it miraculously come about—will not justify the means taken to achieve it. Not just fedayeen thugs but coalition forces violated the rights of innocent Iraqis when they targeted strategic sites near civilian neighborhoods, knowing full well that some people would be killed, injured, and left homeless. This suffering cannot be redeemed as if by some providential history. Furthermore, by deciding not to get clearance from the UN Security Council for a war resolution, coalition forces effectively ignored, or disingenuously "misinterpreted," over fifty years of international law. This was especially bad, since international law and international governing bodies such as the UN were instituted by the United States and its allies to provide an equal and impartial forum for debating rights violations and their legitimate remedies. The irony of a rogue state's dismissing democracy at the international level to impose it elsewhere on a less-than-willing people has not been lost on the rest of the world. To paraphrase Horkheimer, law can only be reconciled with a good that embodies lawfulness, or respect for rights and the democratic processes by which rights are enacted into law.

Acknowledging that vigilante justice is wrong and that selective appeals to democracy are unprincipled does not, however, solve the daunting problem of getting the nations of the world to act democratically in agreeing on pressing issues of world security and safety. The Cold War conflicts that made bipolar multilateralism possible have been replaced by North–South conflicts that pit rich nations against poor ones. Here, one fact about globalization looms far above all others. Citizens of the United States can afford to make the fight on terrorism our single-minded obsession in a way that the rest of the world cannot. For "us," justice boils down to punishing terrorists. For most everyone else, it is an ongoing struggle against the poverty, malnutrition, disease, ignorance, and countless other forms of oppression and domination (some of which undoubtedly spawn terrorism).

Rights, Democracy, and Fulfillment in the Era of Identity Politics is devoted to examining the impact of this economic conflict on other conflicts, such as those we find in the Middle East. These conflicts no doubt have multiple causes, and one that has been frequently mentioned in the aftermath of the war pertains to the rise of Islamic fundamentalism and the "clash of civilizations," as Samuel Huntington (1996) famously put it. However, the question whether Muslim civilization is compatible with Western ideals of liberalism and democracy is really part of a larger question that has dominated recent debates among democratic theorists. That question involves the problematic intersection of democracy and multiculturalism.

Why is this intersection problematic? According to some critics, the infusion of identity politics into democratic life supposedly undermines the solidarity requisite for maintaining the rule of law. In my opinion, these critics are mistaken. What is necessary for legitimate government and the rule of law is that the democratic process be fair and embedded in social conditions that provide both formal and substantive equality of opportunity for the development of capabilities and motivations requisite for democratic citizenship. Democratic fairness does not require that laws and policies advance the interests of everyone equally or identically—although it does require spreading risks and benefits fairly. Just as important, it requires that all legitimate groups have an equal voice in the process of deliberation leading up to a decision. From this perspective, special rights that exempt particular groups from duties borne by others can be legitimate, so long as they compensate for differences in social standing that prevent these groups from having an equal opportunity for influencing democratic outcomes.

Now it is clear from what I have just said that the defense of group rights proposed here would be unthinkable without taking into account both normative political theory and social science. This is one feature of the critical social theory approach I have adopted in this volume. The other is a synthesis of utopianism and pragmatism. The utopianism of critical theory harks back to the eudaimonistic humanism of the early Marx. It criticizes the way in which capitalism—or, for that matter, any undemocratic system of ownership and economic production—alienates us from our human capacities, thwarting the full realization of our freedom, individuality, and sociality. The pragmatism of critical theory, by contrast, criticizes societal injustice—above all, the failure to respect the rights of all citizens equally and to realize democratic ideals.

The chapters I have collected in this book bring these two sides together. Combining *eudaimonism* (reflection on the good) with *deontologism* (reflection on the right) in the manner proposed here is compelling for the simple reason that neither the good nor the right can be adequately specified independently of each other. In specifying the subject matter of human rights, reference must be made to fundamental human capacities and goods that any person needs to live a minimally decent life.

Talk of human rights and human capabilities is taken for granted by most mainstream social theorists. The same, however, cannot be said for critical theorists. It was Marx, after all, who alerted us to the potentially reactionary and ideological uses to which abstract concepts such as "humanity" and "universal rights" might be put. Marx, of course, was thinking about the way in which the ruling classes try to dupe the masses into believing that there are no classes, no social conflicts—just one happy community of human beings who all possess the same humanity and the same rights. Today critical theorists are more likely to voice concern over the denial of basic rights in the name of a parochial interpretation of humanity, against which some persons are deemed deficient. Some critical theorists respond to this exclusion by insisting on the unconditional universality of human rights; others of postmodern bent—and here I have in mind such notable French philosophers as Jean-François Lyotard, Michel Foucault, and Jacques Derrida—respond to it by reaffirming Marx's own criticism of humanism in ways he would never have imagined possible. These critical theorists have gone beyond Marx in dividing humanity into "subject positions" that transcend those of economic class, including social groupings based on gender, (dis)ability, race, sexual orientation, ethnicity, nationality, and religion—all of whom demand special rights in recognition of the special circumstances in which they are situated.

Postmodernists are right—up to a point. Our humanity has indeed become lost in the jungle of "identity politics." Each of us is positioned with respect to numerous points of view reflecting numerous group and individual identifications. One implication of this perspectivalism is a growing acceptance of standpoint ethics, in which questions of justice and happiness are interpreted in ways that are relative to each person's utterly singular horizon of identifications. The universal language of humanism would appear to have no standing in this ethics.

Yet I maintain that critical theorists are compelled to use this language by dint of their own utopian and pragmatic orientations. The argument in support of this contention can be summarized as follows: Since Marx, critical theorists have long insisted that the "truth" of any critical theory is at least partly a function of its capacity to resonate with the practical needs of real human beings to live in freedom and solidarity. Left to its own devices, capitalism frustrates the fulfillment of these needs. Therefore, citizens should try to reform and replace it. But they will do this only if they are enlightened about their needs. Enlightenment cannot come from a vanguard elite who are presumed to have privileged access to the truth, because this would violate citizens' need for self-determination and presumes that the vanguard are themselves untainted by the system. Citizens must therefore enlighten themselves through their own activity.

For critical theorists like myself, who draw from the work of Jürgen Habermas, enlightenment comes from open democratic debate between free and equal persons. Such debate remains effective only when it is embedded in popular culture and other information media. Embedding them in this way presupposes, among other things, a framework of civil rights and public policy incentives that both protect and promote such things as freedom of speech, freedom of association, and civic education. Because civil rights and policies are shaped by legislators, judges, and administrators, it is imperative that they remain accountable to public opinion. Liberal democratic institutions—including elections, parliamentary procedures, administrative hearings, and forms of judicial oversight—are thus important mechanisms for preserving and protecting a vibrant political culture in which critical enlightenment can occur. But unless these institutions are designed to foster rational deliberation among all sectors of the population, granting each of them an "equal" voice, there is a danger that democracy will degenerate into tyranny rather than become the vehicle of enlightenment that populists have long proclaimed it to be.

Now, it is precisely this danger that points us back to the utopian, eudaimonistic strand of critical theory. Critical theorists maintain that the contradictions of a capitalist economy distort and endanger democracy in multiple ways. Since Marx, they have bemoaned the fact that the rich use their wealth to gain political power by bribing elected officers, threatening investment strikes, and controlling mass media. The advent of the social welfare state has no doubt mitigated this tyranny somewhat, at least to the extent that the working class has organized itself as a political counterforce. But the system works to thwart labor militancy in countless other ways. Leaving aside legal impediments to unionization, the system encourages political apathy and discourages activism. The demands of work and consumption increasingly dominate our lives; the sheer technicality of public policy debate intimidates us; the ideology of economism—that the only thing that matters is sustaining high levels of profitability whose "trickle down" effects will ensure steady employment—blinds us to the realities of class; and the authoritarian organization of a mechanically segmented labor force encourages mental stultification and passivity. As for the victims of uneven growth, those for whom there are no sustainable jobs, the therapeutic and punitive administration of workfare may well perpetuate—rather than alleviate—their dependency.

In short, the injustice of a capitalist economic system—whose market lotteries create large disparities in educational and employment opportunities for vast segments of the population—and its stultification of the needs, capacities, and attitudes essential to a vibrant democratic culture work to reinforce one another. Pathologically disabled citizens are easily manipulated into making irrational choices that serve to perpetuate their own domination and oppression. They are easily pitted against one another by the powers that be, diverted from the primary sources of their oppression, and thus unable to perceive their common interests.

The problem of social division brings us back to the importance of identity politics in democratic theory. Here in the United States, race has traditionally been the most powerful tool for dividing the masses. This is not accidental. Capitalism by its nature creates social divisions, and the exploitation of a white working class could not have been made so tolerable had it not been for the compensatory benefits of white privilege. Indeed, I would venture that identity politics—and racial politics in particular—is structurally embedded within capitalism. To be sure, such a politics is no stranger to socialism, despite its celebration of working-class solidarity. And whatever its economic origins might have been, racial thinking and other forms of identity politics have proven to be remarkably resilient across economic, political, and social contexts. In affluent Western democracies, conflicts pertaining to identity politics and to related issues concerning moral values and social status have become increasingly visible, to the point where they sometimes eclipse older class struggles (Smith and Tatalovich 2003, 11–46). Of course, some of these new conflicts—especially the ones gravitating toward social status—have been compared to older civil rights struggles, which still retain a connection to earlier class struggles despite their focus on racial and gender discrimination. However, in many cases, such comparison is strained to the point where any connection to economic oppression is all but occluded. Witness, for instance, the remarkable way in which militant advocates of deaf culture appropriate the language of racial distinction in defending deafness against the disabling discrimination of the hearing. For them, eliminating this discrimination by "mainstreaming" deaf children into the hearing culture through cochlear implantation is no different than eliminating racial discrimination by "assimilating" blacks into white society through skin "whitening." Be that as it may, this analogy is nonetheless overdrawn, since, in sharp contrast to disability discrimination, racial discrimination served—and was intended to serve—very obvious economic functions.

Of course, the mere fact that social divisions can be manipulated and even fabricated for purposes of diverting attention away from older—but still salient—class-related struggles does not make them less real and legitimate. To think that it would is to presume that concepts such as "the masses" or "the working class" are intrinsically more real—more determined by the objective structures of "the system"—than social groupings based on (dis)ability, race, culture, and gender. These "subjective" affinities, however, often emerge in response to systematic realities. In any case, it is wrong to think that their reality and legitimacy must be tied to something as systematic as a market economy. If most of these latter subdivisions are indeed real and legitimate—and not all of them are—then critical theorists will have to explain how they can be harnessed to progressive democratic struggle without transforming the latter into a divisive, and often reactionary, politics of identity.

RIGHTS

The chapters in this volume attempt to do just that. It might be useful to think of them as developing three ideas central to progressive identity politics: rights, democracy, and identity. As noted, critical theorists since Marx have been suspicious of rights. Early on in his career Marx addressed his doubts about the capacity of rights to provide genuine freedom within the context of a debate over religious freedom. In doing so, he expressly rebutted Bruno Bauer's extreme solution to the "Jewish Question," which called for the abolition of all publicly exercised religious "privileges" (such as the Jewish community's demand to be exempted from work on the day of the Jewish Sabbath) as a precondition for receiving full civil and political rights. According to Marx, Bauer's demand was excessively illiberal because he misconceived the basic function of such rights, which is precisely to protect the freedom of persons to be different and even anticivil. If Marx is right that protecting religious freedom sometimes entails extending exemptions and privileges to particular groups in ways that apparently contradict the universal humanistic basis underlying "human rights"—a view that conforms to the position I'm defending in this book—it is equally true, according to him, that all rights permit privileges, implicitly, if not explicitly. This fact about rights, however, is taken by Marx in the negative sense intended by Bauer: because all rights permit privileges that contradict their humanistic justification, they are ipso facto "limited" in their capacity to bestow genuine freedom.

No doubt, the emancipation from ecclesiastical and secular authority wrought by the classical rights celebrated in the American founding documents and in the French Declaration of the Rights of Man and Citizen represents "a great step forward" compared to the inherited privileges of rank and occupation that narrowly circumscribed one's freedom under feudalism (Marx 1994, 10). Nevertheless, this political emancipation "is not the final form of universal human emancipation." For, by freeing individuals from the religious and caste requirements imposed on them in virtue of their incorporation within narrowly defined ranks and occupations, it unleashes social conflicts in which one's freedom is opposed to and limited by the freedom of others. This is indeed a contradictory freedom insofar as the very humanity (species being) that enjoins universal respect for each individual's rights in the name of a higher social solidarity is violated in the actual exercise and application of such rights.

> The so-called rights of man . . . are only the rights of the member of a civil society, that is of egoistic man, man separated from other men and from the community . . . . This is liberty of man viewed as an isolated monad, withdrawn into himself . . . . The practical application of the right of liberty is the right of private property . . . . [This right] is the right to enjoy and dispose of one's possessions as one wills, without regard for other men and independently of society. (16)

In making possible a civil society of property owners, "civil" rights transform human beings into uncivil, self-centered egoists. They endow individuals with the "negative" freedom to think and act without interference from state or society, and so they are regarded by them in a proprietary and possessive way, as setting up "hedges" (as Locke puts it) excluding others. In the meantime, democratic politics—the sphere wherein, according to Rousseau, we put aside selfish interest for the sake of enacting laws that express our social interdependency and good will toward our fellow citizens—is inverted. Far from being suppressed or suspended, the privileges of property and power conspire to ensure that the laws express a particular will, one that tyrannizes over those who do not share it.

> Man proclaims that private property is overcome politically once he abolishes the property qualification for active and passive voting as has been done in the many North American states . . . . Nevertheless the state permits private property, education, and occupation to act and manifest their particular nature as private property, education, and occupation in their own ways (8) . . . . The citizen thus is proclaimed to be the servant of egoistic man. (18)

Here the contradiction within the concept of rights assumes its most palpable form. Formal rights that theoretically guarantee citizens equality before the law in practice sanction inequality among individuals in their everyday lives. This inequality belies the ostensible fairness of a democratic process that defines the legal scope of our rights. For Marx, the only way to resolve this contradiction is to change the very nature of civil society by eliminating those economic presuppositions that generate conflict, privilege, and possessive individualism in the first place. "Only when the actual, individual man has taken back into himself the abstract citizen and in his everyday life, his individual work, and his individual relationships has become a species being, only when he has recognized and organized his own powers as social powers so that social force is no longer separated from him as political power, only then is human emancipation complete" (21). In sum, complete emancipation would require a new social organization in which social solidarity and individual freedom have become so essentially identified—in consciousness and in reality—that the need for a coercive legal order of protective and exclusionary rights no longer obtains.

I have more to say about the supreme importance—stressed by Marx—of bringing the citizen into the (democratic) workplace, in chapter 5. For now, however, I want to extend Marx's critique of rights beyond that developed here, which focuses mainly on the dehumanization of rights holders, to include his discussion of the inherent inability of rights to guarantee equal treatment, as set forth in his *Critique of the Gotha Programme*. Criticizing Ferdinand Lassalle's failure to adequately address the problem of distributive justice in postcapitalist society, Marx has this to say about the right of an individual in the transitional socialist society to draw from the general store of consumer goods an amount equivalent to the labor she or he has contributed:

> This right is still encumbered by a bourgeois limitation. The right of producers is proportional to the labour they supply; the equality consists in the fact that measurement is made with an equal standard, labour. But one man is superior to

another physically or mentally and so supplies more labour in the same time, or can work for a longer time; and labour, to serve as a measure, must be defined by duration or intensity; otherwise it ceases to serve as a standard of measurement. This right is an unequal right for unequal labour. It recognizes no class distinctions, because everyone is only a worker like everyone else; but it tacitly recognizes the unequal individual endowment and thus productive capacity of workers as natural privileges. It is, therefore, a right of inequality, in its content, like every other right. Right by its nature can exist only as the application of an equal standard; but unequal individuals (and they would not be different individuals if they were not unequal) are measurable by an equal standard only insofar as they are made subject to an equal criterion, are taken from a certain side, for instance, in the present case, are regarded only as workers and nothing more is seen in them, everything else being ignored . . . . [Only after the division of labor has been abolished and abundance achieved] can the narrow horizon of bourgeois right be crossed in its entirety and society inscribe on its banners: From each according to his abilities, to each according to his needs! (321)

Marx's argument can be summarized accordingly: Endowing individuals with equal formal rights—that is, permitting them to act without interference—does not guarantee them the material capacities and substantive opportunities necessary for acting. The unjust distribution of material capacities and substantive opportunities would be mitigated—but not eliminated—under socialism. On the one hand, giving everyone the same material entitlement, or guaranteeing everyone at least a minimum entitlement, still discriminates against the specially needy (Marx 1994, 321). On the other hand, protecting the specially needy involves imposing a uniform measure of normalcy that still discriminates by defining their difference from the norm as intrinsically disabling.

The theory of rights defended in this volume concedes Marx's point about supplementing formal rights with substantive entitlements. It also affirms his mature view that some kind of democratic empowerment is necessary for ensuring that all needs are met. Hence, no single category of need—whether it be a need to security, freedom, empowerment, subsistence, or cultural identity—can be satisfied without satisfying others, and part of guaranteeing their satisfaction will be a corresponding system of rights.

The insensitivity of rights to differences in needs is likewise accidental. The problem is showing how difference-sensitive rights can be derived from more primary human rights that apply uniformly to abstract individuals in virtue of their common humanity. I argue that group-specific rights compensate for disadvantages that prevent certain groups of individuals from enjoying the equal protection of their basic human rights. Humanity is itself an abstract standard of uniformity that permits standards of normalcy and capability to be articulated in ways that are sensitive to cultural and experiential context.

These responses do not address all of Marx's concerns about rights. Human rights that are believed to have their sole justification and definition in unchanging nature are regarded by him as "ideological." The force of this objection is directed against the notion that human nature is static and uniform across different sociohistorical groups. Given that different sociohistorical groups have different needs relative to their peculiar economic circumstances, no system of rights can be fair for all (as Marx notes in the *Communist Manifesto,* "The interests of Human Nature, of man in general, who belongs to no class, has no reality . . . exists only in the misty realm of philosophical fantasy" [180]). Coupled with his view that rights reflect a bourgeois bias, Marx maintained that the constitutional frameworks within which rights are entrenched act as a conservative drag on popular democratic reform. (Marx accordingly asserts in the *German Ideology* that the "doctrine of the separation of powers" merely expresses a political modus vivendi in which different classes—for example, the aristocracy and bourgeoisie—check or prevent a change that might endanger their power [129–30]). Indeed, rights and egoism are virtually synonymous for him. Hence, he could not but conclude that with the emergence of communism—and the abolition of scarcity, need, and possessiveness—rights and the political life they protect would cease to exist.

Let me begin by responding to this last objection. Rights would be necessary even under communism, since many social conflicts are driven by noneconomic factors that have little or nothing to do with scarcity and egoism. Furthermore, decisions regarding the coordination and regulation of complex economic activities would still have to be made, and such decisions—as well as the power and knowledge to make them—would be contested by persons who feel that they have something to gain or lose. Indeed, any modern, complex society will be mediated by hierarchies of decision making whose potential for abuse will call forth protective rights.

Marx's other objections against the incoherence and conservatism of rights are equally inconclusive. Marx rightly rejected natural law justifications of rights, but the justification of rights I propose here—following Habermas—is pragmatic and postmetaphysical. Although there are relatively universal normative principles regarding reciprocity and freedom that are embedded in our communicative expectations as a matter of historical fact, these do not provide a certain foundation from which we might deductively infer any particular right. Combined with modern legal conventions, such expectations might imply general categories of rights. But prescriptive and enforceable rights are entirely the outcome of legislative and judicial processes.

This applies to human rights as well. By definition, human rights refer to the protection and cultivation of basic human capacities. But this fact alone does not justify them. Additional arguments are needed to show why their protection and cultivation ought to command the highest level of importance. Furthermore, so long as they are not embedded in international conventions (such as the UN Universal Declaration of Rights) and further elaborated in constitutions and concrete statutes, they remain but vapid abstractions lacking prescriptive force.

To be sure, legal conventions are not self-justifying. They need to be processed through democratic channels in which legislators and ordinary citizens present convincing arguments in their support. This applies no less to human rights legislation. Our reasons for accepting these rights need not be metaphysical or transcendental; nor need they privilege any particular comprehensive moral doctrine—utility, divinity, legality, practicality, tradition, and rationality are all acceptable grounds for affirming rights. The main thing is that we accept them and know that others accept them for these kinds of reasons.

The reasoned justification of rights constitutes a powerful impetus against conservatism. To begin with, constitutionally entrenched rights must be susceptible to emendation and reinterpretation in response to evolving conceptions of morality and changing social conditions. Courts as well as legislatures must be responsive to these changes in public opinion. On one hand, the conservative weight of precedent is not something critical theorists should necessarily rue. Constitutional safeguards and precedents sometimes act as a counterweight to reactionary tendencies that threaten democracy. Despite its romantic charm, revolutionary anarchism is no stranger to totalitarianism. On the other hand, progressive populist mandates should constrain judges in overturning obstructive precedents, even when doing so effects revolutionary changes in constitutional paradigm (Ackerman 1991).

But how can populist mandates be generated from within a divided society? And how can they be generated rationally in a way that holds out hope for genuine progress? The lack of consensus regarding the interpretation of rights and democratic procedures threatens a legitimacy crisis. Given the trenchancy of social divisions in capitalist society, this crisis is unlikely to disappear without reforming the system. But reforming the system might not be enough, either.

DELIBERATIVE DEMOCRACY

The idea of deliberative democracy is intended to address this problem. This is not the idea of democracy held by mainstream democratic theorists, who view democracy as protection against tyranny or as procedure for aggregating preferences. In my opinion, neither of these aims can be fulfilled without reforming electoral and legislative procedures (the formal institutions anchoring democratic processes) and regulating information media, political campaigns, and educational fora (the informal public spheres). Reform and media regulation should be targeted toward the creation of a more just and consensual process of deliberation and decision; and even workplaces should be restructured to reflect values commensurate with stakeholder democracy.

With this aim in mind we arrive at a fundamentally different view of democracy, understood as a way of life that promotes the authentic self-realization and fulfillment of citizens as free, social beings. For a better assessment of this claim, it might be useful to distinguish three levels of democracy: *formal* processes encompassing legislation, adjudication, and administration; *informal* processes of public opinion formation and workplace democracy; and *quasi-formal* processes, such as elections, hearings, intermediary associations (such as NGOs) and other media that link formal and informal processes. Formal institutions both deliberate and decide, with the quality of decision making being dependent on the quality of deliberation. Much of what gets discussed concerns the aggregation of diverse voter preferences. Rational choice theorists have well documented the obstacles that legislatures, judges, and administrators encounter when trying to aggregate raw votes into coherent rank orderings of policy preferences. Deliberation among legislators, judges, and administrators can partially circumvent these obstacles by striking compromises and by balancing competing interests. But compromises must fairly factor in all interest positions in ways that show equal respect and concern for each citizen. Here, electoral laws must ensure that each voter's preferences are represented by some elected candidates. They must ensure that each voter can cast a ballot having equal weight and equal impact; over a wide range of choices expressing widely divergent perspectives, ideologies, and policy preferences; sufficient to elect at least one candidate of his or her choice who will represent his or her most important values, interests, opinions, and perspectives in parliamentary bargaining. In sum, formal and quasi-formal institutions must aggregate (or distribute) equal opportunities for exercising free choice so that interests can be reciprocally balanced.

But no matter how fair and rational the process of formal aggregation might be, it will not yield rational results unless the process of formal deliberation that accompanies it is equally rational. Ideals of freedom, equality, and reciprocity must also be extended to the qualitative parameters governing rational discussion. For formal democratic institutions to satisfy criteria of discursive freedom, equality, and reciprocity, parliamentary rules and court proceedings must permit the relevant players to have equal opportunities to speak freely and openly and in such a way that there are equally powerful incentives for them to be heard by and acted upon by others.

Formal democratic institutions must therefore allow the strategic pursuit of partial interests to be balanced against the consensual pursuit of the common good. This endeavor is frustrated whenever the interest positions that legislators, judges, and administrators are given to compromise are themselves tyrannical or contrary to the common good. Legislators, judges, and administrators discount the irrational preferences of their constituents at the risk of their own commitment to democracy, and trying to alter these preferences through efforts of paternalistic education and manipulation is hardly more satisfactory. Therefore, aggregative and deliberative ideals of autonomy, equality, and reciprocity must also be realized at the informal level of public opinion formation. Citizens should have reasonably equal opportunities to speak freely and openly in venues where they will be heard and taken seriously. And they should have ample opportunities and incentives to engage in grassroots activism, to initiate and become involved in social movements, and to form coalitions by strategically exchanging mutual favors. Above all, for aggregative and deliberative ideals to be realized, the background conditions for a vibrant public sphere must also be in place—equal opportunity education for all, broad and equal access to health and welfare services, full employment for everyone in enterprises that encourage workplace democracy, and the decentralized dissemination and ownership of media across all relevant interest groups.

In sum, the public sphere must be structured in such a way that average citizens have incentives to participate in grassroots politics. The institutions of family and civil society—above all businesses—must be structured so as to foster the development of critical faculties and other capacities. At the same time, neither the state nor the economic institutions of civil society should overly influence the spontaneous cultivation of autonomous public opinion. Last but not least, the terms of political discussion and bargaining should be sensitive to cultural and ideological differences so as to avoid what Jean-François Lyotard calls *differends*, or injustices involving the linguistic suppression of certain viewpoints.

I will argue that the design of formal and quasi-formal institutions can have a powerful impact on the aggregative and deliberative quality of public opinion formation and grassroots politics. For example, distributing legislative seats in multiseat districts with cumulative or alternative voting mechanisms might encourage candidates to reach out, appeal to, and bargain with constituencies they might otherwise have ignored. This system might be especially useful in crossing over racially segregated and racially polarized constituencies. However, it may be unrealistic to assume that such a system will be adopted at the federal level in the United States, where the simpler single-seat, winner-take-all format is firmly entrenched. A principled compromise might well recommend the use of racially designed districts in empowering minorities, with the hope that the identity politics encouraged by that system might eventually effect interracial dialogue.

The design of formal and quasi-formal institutions can also influence the quality of deliberation between citizens and elected government officials. Term limits can free representatives from the lure of campaign bribes and also encourage them to criticize—and not merely inform—their constituents. Conversely, public governmental hearings that provide for the involvement of NGOs and other public service groups can diminish the "propaganda" effect of official oratory and force-appointed technocrats to explain themselves in simple terms. Another added benefit of public hearings is that they force officials to justify their interest-driven policies in terms of more impartial aims, which can then be used against them should they continue to support policies that only benefit a few.

Before moving on to the last idea informing my book—the idea of group identity—let me close by responding to three objections that have been raised against deliberative democracy. First, the principle of justification invoked by defenders of deliberative democracy—that no norm is legitimate unless justified as the outcome of democratic procedure—seems to lack an independent justification. If democratic deliberation is the only method for justifying norms, it is at least conceivable that it might not be justified according to its own criterion of legitimacy; that is, it might not be democratically preferred. Second, deliberative democracy seems to presume that procedural considerations are the only basis for assessing the legitimacy of a democratic decision. This, in turn, seems to imply that a law's institutionalizing of racial discrimination would be legitimate so long as it was processed according to democratic procedure. Finally, it is argued that theories of deliberative democracy specifically refrain from proposing principles of substantive justice by which existing democratic societies can be criticized.

My response to the first objection is that there is no justification for deliberative democracy that isn't circular. One might try, as Habermas does, to anchor the principle of deliberative democracy in certain pragmatic expectations implicit in the idea of rational discourse. But these expectations do not directly imply the principle of democracy. In any case, Habermas concedes that they themselves are partly shaped by the historical evolution of modern liberal democracies. Despite Habermas's objections to the contrary, his thinking about the deep justification of democracy is not significantly different from John Rawls's thinking about the deep justification of principles of justice. The justification is circular in both cases because we test our intuitions about justice (or legitimacy) in light of our "considered judgments" (rationally worked up theories) and vice versa until we reach "reflective equilibrium" between the two. A similar circularity obtains between the regulative ideas underlying democratic procedures (such as freedom and equality) and the positive interpretation of these very ideas in the form of statutes defining parliamentary and courtroom proceedings, illicit hate speech, and so forth.

My response to the second objection—that deliberative democracy makes the assessment of outcomes contingent only on fidelity to procedures—is that it gets deliberative democracy wrong. The reasons that legitimate or delegitimate democratic decisions refer to substantive considerations pertaining to utility, custom, human rights, and the like. It is only the rationally persuasive force of these reasons that depends on fidelity to democratic procedure; in other words, an argument is more convincing to the extent that it holds up against the widest and most compelling presentation of counterarguments. Granting that, it is important to note that some substantive decisions—such as laws that deny certain people the right to vote—are ipso facto illegitimate on procedural grounds alone. Last but not least, given the fact that democratic procedures shape outcomes, it follows that the legitimacy of procedures is itself partly a function of the legitimacy of the outcomes they tend to produce. To return to an earlier example, if single-seat, winner-take-all districts consistently produce electoral outcomes in a given jurisdiction (with Party X's winning 80 percent of all seats) that were widely disproportionate to aggregate vote tallies (with Party X's never winning more than 51 percent of the votes cast), such districts would clearly be counterdemocratic and thus illegitimate.

The last objection focuses on the vacuity of deliberative democracy as a normative and critical theory. The objection concedes that the theory has some critical force, for example, that it rules out laws that deny racial minorities the right to vote; however, the objection then insists that the theory doesn't go far enough. My response to this objection is twofold. First, democratic theorists should not pretend to be philosopher kings. It is citizens, after all, who must choose the democratic rules under which they deliberate in light of their own peculiar needs. Stronger hate-speech statutes than those found in the United States may be necessary in the German context, given its tragic history. Second, it is entirely appropriate for democratic theorists to propose concrete reforms in their capacity as engaged citizens who interpret the requirements of theory from their own partial standpoints.

GROUPS AND IDENTITY POLITICS

My reference to interpretative standpoints returns us to the problem of identity politics and the centrality of groups in political life generally. Theorists of deliberative democracy, such as Habermas and Arendt, tend to adopt models of face-to-face communication that privilege individuals as the principal political agents. However, once we factor in the strategic organization and mobilization of individuals around shared interests—bearing in mind that these interests are further aggregated, represented, and balanced in formal democratic settings—it becomes clear that the principal political agents are groups, not individuals taken in isolation from one another. Habermas's own recognition of the way in which social movements expand the scope of deliberative democracy to include more people attests to this very fact.

For a better appreciation of what is at stake here, it might be useful to distinguish between different types of groups, their political dynamics, and the factors that render them more or less legitimate. I begin by distinguishing between *aggregate* groups and *affinal* groups. Aggregate groups are groups whose membership is constituted entirely by third persons deploying voluntarily selected criteria of membership. Examples include all persons who fall below the official poverty line or all persons who happened to vote for a certain candidate. These groups are of little interest to me. Affinal groups—the main focus of this study—are groups whose members actively identify with one another.

Affinal groups with voluntary memberships may be based exclusively on shared interests or ideologies. The political parties, public-interest associations, unions, chambers of commerce, businesses, and so forth, that comprise this category have been the traditional concern of pluralist political theory. They are not, however, the main concern of theorists of identity politics or, for that matter, theorists of group rights—although this concept is not entirely inapplicable to corporate entities or to the guaranteed representation of regions and parties in legislative chambers. *Structural* groups—including politically aware economic classes, religious groups, gender- or sexual orientation–based groups, ethnic and racial groups, and groups representing the disabled, by contrast, represent associations whose members often share something more or something other than voluntarily chosen ideological sympathies and interests. This "something other" consists of bonds of solidarity rooted in common conditions that they have either inherited or that have been inculcated in or imposed upon them at birth. Obviously, the extent to which these latter identifications are voluntarily chosen is largely a function of the degree to which the members of these organizations have critically interpreted them and appropriated them for themselves, both individually and collectively.

According to postmodern "social constructionists," no identities are predetermined at birth, not even ones that appear to be based upon physiological and biological differences. I generally accept this view, although the extent to which sexual and gender (and perhaps sexual orientation) identities are biologically conditioned remains a matter of some uncertainty for me (sex-change operations on intersex children attest to the strong pull of chromosomes, sex hormones, and possibly genes in influencing sexual orientation). However, conceding the "socially constructed" nature of identities does not contradict the notion that such identities are largely imposed upon one by one's family, community, economic class, and culture. Hence, "socially constructed" does not mean "voluntarily chosen," although it does entail a susceptibility to being voluntarily interpreted, appropriated, and resisted. The strand of critical theory descending from Foucault, in particular, emphasizes the degree to which identities that have been inculcated and imposed (literally incorporated into one's bodily habitus) are complex and open-ended in ways that invite critical interventions ("performative stylizations" and "aesthetic reinsciptions," as Judith Butler puts it).

These distinctions between types of group and group identity are important because they suggest that what is often at stake in group identifications is not "identity"—which properly applies only to individual persons with relatively continuous and bounded histories—but "social position" with respect to economic class, political power, and social status. Be that as it may, I will reserve the term "identity politics" to refer to a broad range of struggles in which identity is at least partly at stake. These struggles gravitate around injustices between groups and between groups and individuals, on one hand, and unhappy and alienated processes of socialization effecting both groups and individuals, on the other. Injustice between groups takes the form of oppression (harm caused by the unequal distribution of resources, capacities, and opportunities) or domination (harm caused by lack of self-determination). Again, the source of injustice may be impersonal and systemic—a function, say, of the market lottery, which discriminates against those with little capital—or the source may be personal and identity based. Typically, oppression and domination both accompany each other and reinforce each other. The same applies to the sources of oppression and domination. Racial- and gender-based domination in the United States, for example, is rooted in economic necessity and prejudice. The mutual reinforcement and co-originality of economic necessity and prejudice means that racial- and gender-based privilege and discrimination can also become impersonal and systemic, as when market institutions, principles of seniority promotion and retention, word-of-mouth hiring, and lending practices perpetuate and exacerbate the effects of past prejudice.

The rectification of identity-based injustice can take many forms, and not all of them involve extending special rights to aggrieved groups. For instance, group-blind electoral and parliamentary rules can be formulated that guarantee justice between groups without explicitly requiring the assignment of group-specific entitlements. Under certain conditions, open-seat legislative districts with vote-transfer mechanisms might enhance the capacity of geographically dispersed minorities to elect enough representatives of their choice to get their voices heard and their interests factored into policies. Guaranteeing minorities or women a certain number of legislative seats through quotas (or group-specific rights) is not always the best remedy for combating minority underrepresentation. However, under some circumstances it might be.

Will Kymlicka (1991, 1995) has recently put forth a theory of group rights that is intended to guide policy makers in deciding when and what kind of group-specific rights are appropriate for which groups. He distinguishes between subnational, quasi-sovereign groups, immigrant groups, and racial and ethnic minorities that have traditionally suffered discrimination from a dominant majority. Immigrants, he argues, voluntarily exit their native land and intend to assimilate into their adopted country. No special group rights ought to be accorded them as immigrants, except perhaps polyethnic rights that "accommodate" their particular needs. These rights include rights to bilingual education, understood as a remedial mechanism for promoting full assimilation in the long run, and special exemptions and protections for religious minorities who have special holidays, dietary and clothing codes, and restrictions with respect to military service. For racial and ethnic minorities who have suffered discrimination, rights to political representation may also be required, in addition to polyethnic rights such as affirmative action in employment and education. Only national groups that constitute a distinctive territorial "societal culture," such as indigenous tribal reservations and subnationalities like the Quebecois, merit rights to sovereignty.

Kymlicka refers to sovereignty, representation, and polyethnic (accommodation) rights as rights that govern the external relations between groups; and he distinguishes them from the group rights that groups claim to exercise over their own members. These internal group rights, he notes, are illegitimate from the standpoint of liberal democracy as soon as they conflict with the constitutionally entrenched civil liberties guaranteed to individuals. Although the conflict between groups and individuals may be so addressed—as a matter of justice—it is important to note that they can also be addressed as a matter of happiness and self-realization. How much power should identity groups have in policing the beliefs, actions, and identities of their constituent members? On one hand, because the happiness and self-realization of individual persons are partly a function of the self-realization and happiness of the groups to which they belong—and because group happiness, in turn, depends upon the degree to which beliefs and practices are shared—groups (or the majority of their memberships) should have a democratic right to determine the conditions of their own association. On the other hand, if group identity is something that is and ought to be critically appropriated by individuals within the group for the sake of their individual happiness and self-realization, then some deviation and dissent must be allowed within the group.

Of course, just how much is a matter of some dispute. If we are looking for a threshold of legal toleration, we might say that the individual's civil liberties must never be violated by any group; but what constitutes a violation is often unclear. Do Amish parents violate the legal right of their children to a decent education when they remove them from high school? If the aim of education is to establish a minimal threshold of moral autonomy and responsibility, as well as a basic competence to be gainfully employed, does the Amish method of education (or perhaps alternative methods of homeschooling) realize this threshold and competence? Aside from the legal question there is the ethical one: how much of my identity is my own, as distinct from my parents', my community's, or my group's?

These questions suggest difficulties or gaps in Kymlicka's theory, which I intend to address in this book. Kymlicka's discussion of the legitimacy (or illegitimacy) of group rights does not address this latter ethical question. As for the legal question, he assumes that the standard individual right to associate (or disassociate) can solve most problems of group tyranny, except when legal intervention is absolutely required. His discussion of the famous case involving the ostracism of certain evangelical members of the New Mexico Pueblos shows the limitations of this response. Kymlicka concurs with the court's decision to intervene on behalf of the dissidents, but he never addresses the fact that, from the standpoint of the group, these internal dissidents were regarded as agents of an external group who threatened the majority's right to associate freely on its own terms. To complicate matters further, the majority may well have regarded the civil rights that the court invoked in intervening on behalf of the dissidents as external—in substance if not form—to their collectivist esprit de corps.

As I argue (Ingram 2000a), there may be no satisfactory solution to conflicts like this—short of compromise, negotiation, and a willingness on all parties to accept some alteration in their respective identities. The failure to address the internal dynamics of identity politics points to a more general weakness in Kymlicka's theory: his tendency to downplay the internal complexity of societal cultures and group identities. If one takes seriously—as I do—the overlapping complexity and dynamic fluidity of identity groups, then it is unclear whether there exist any identity groups that possess the kind of well-integrated, self-contained identity of interest, belief, and practice that warrants special group rights. Related to this challenge is the tendency of groups to straddle his simple distinction. For instance, militant practitioners of deaf culture do not want to assimilate to hearing culture; but their demands for justice call for a wide range of remedies, including rights to accommodation (the provision of more signers, as well as radios, televisions, and telephones with closed captioning), greater representation (on school boards and planning boards), and even greater sovereignty (over their own schools and communities). Aboriginal tribes likewise demand a range of rights remedies, as do African Americans (whose more militant members support sovereign control over African American communities as well as greater political representation).

Kymlicka discusses the legitimacy of external group rights and the illegitimacy of internal group rights directed against dissident members, but he does not really address the legitimacy (or lack thereof) of groups as such. This is a serious failing, I believe, because not all groups are worthy of equal protection. In this volume I argue that the legitimacy of an identity group is a function of several factors: the degree to which it is generated internally, rather than imposed from without; the degree to which it allows individuals within the group to critically elaborate their meaning and significance; and the degree to which it tolerates and respects other equally tolerant identity groups. In some cases, identity groups that have an illegitimate origin—such as racial groups in the United States—may achieve a degree of legitimacy to the extent that they are freely embraced and reinterpreted by their members so as to resist the very thing that gave rise to them—in this case, racism. Affirming a positive, antiracist black identity in our present circumstances is thus legitimate, although whether it would be so in an ideal, nonracist society is less certain. By contrast, affirming a positive white identity is not legitimate, for no such identity can be enlisted to serve antiracist ends. Thus, the demand for a separate homeland (or, lacking that, racially segregated enclaves) made by some Afrikaners in South Africa is illegitimate because it uses multiculturalism as a facade for racist discrimination.

Despite attempts by Stuart Hall and Henry Giroux to translate whiteness into the register of ethnicity and culture, the fact remains that whiteness is neither. Saying this, of course, raises sensitive issues regarding the distinction between racial and ethnic categories. My objections against segregated Afrikaner communities reflect my reluctance to collapse multicultural and antiracist agendas. Broadly speaking, multiculturalism encourages us to recognize and respect the equal worth of all cultural identities, which can sometimes require that we allow the groups that have these identities to cultivate them in relative isolation from the rest of us. Antiracism, by contrast, encourages us to see how certain cultural identities—namely, those that have been correlated with white European and (more recently) white Asian identity—have been privileged over and against nonwhite cultural identities. In fighting against this hierarchy, antiracism fights for inclusion and integration, if not assimilation. If antiracism ought to have priority over multiculturalism, as I think it should, then segregation—even in the name of black empowerment and black cultural preservation—is never legitimate. Indeed, it is less legitimate than assimilation, which may or may not be the natural outcome of increased interracial and interethnic coupling. In the final analysis, increased global migration will probably alter the nature of multicultural recognition. Instead of preserving societal cultures, or indeed any cultures, in statu, recognizing them will mean accepting their fluidity, complexity, and individuality.

SYNOPSIS OF THE ARGUMENT

Chapter 1 illustrates the problem of reaching consensus on rights in the era of identity politics by examining Jean-François Lyotard's penetrating critique of democratic legitimation. Lyotard argues that the classical rights manifestos of the late eighteenth century inevitably conflate the impartial but vacuous rationalism of natural law doctrine with the concretely political but partisan discourse of nations and, more specifically, of privileged groups within nations. Coupled with this observation is Lyotard's belief that the impartial rule of law underlying legitimate government is endangered by the very procedure that is supposed to legitimate it, namely, popular democracy.

Democratic governance is compromised by partisanship (including identity politics) and procedural gaps in the democratic process that enable appointed technicians and administrators to interpret vague policy recommendations according to their own whims. In essence, popular moral deliberations about distributive justice and happiness get "trumped" by expert technical deliberations about efficient administration. Utopian visions of reform get sidetracked and retranslated into the register of instrumental policies for maintaining economic growth, government services, and a balanced budget.

Discord between groups and deliberative processes has the effect of injecting indeterminacy into the very meaning of rights. This, in turn, increases the potential for tyranny—either by political groups or by various levels of government. Lyotard is particularly interested in exposing one kind of injustice—what he calls a differend—that he believes is common to both forms of tyranny. A differend occurs whenever the lingua franca of common deliberation effectively silences one of the parties. For example, a differend occurs between government leaders and average citizens whenever the former retranslates the latter's moral concerns about economic injustice and alienation into the amoral language of technical administration. Given the monopoly that government officials have over technical expertise and classified information, average citizens are at an extreme disadvantage whenever they try to question government officials and hold them morally accountable for the justice and goodness of their policies. Conversely, government officials end up construing their deliberations with constituents in terms of disseminating and gathering information, rather than in terms of mutual criticism.

Another kind of differend reflects the dynamics of class society. Not only do workers and owners view labor and capital differently, but this difference has given rise to competing legal paradigms—liberal, welfare, and participatory—for interpreting contract, property, and tort law. Finally, differends arise in the course of identity politics when the dominant discourse of political life is construed in ways that suppress certain modes of argument (such as mass demonstrations) and understanding. Differends occur whenever the uncivil complaints of demonstrating workers are not heard. They occur, too, whenever aboriginal peoples are forced to defend their tribal land claims—their spiritual "assets," as it were—in the alien language of Anglo-American property law.

Lyotard's distinction between two types of identity politics are especially pertinent to my argument. The *separatist–preservative* (SP) type endorses the kind of political liberalism associated with Rawls's recent discussion of "overlapping consensus" and "public reason." It provides for the extensive toleration and protection of minority groups who are assumed to possess well-defined identities. Political civility between groups requires that groups refrain from holding one another accountable for the nonshareable (incommensurable) features of their respective worldviews. It also requires that they bracket the nonshareable features of their respective worldviews when deliberating with one another. In some cases, political civility requires extending special protective rights to groups that respect their right to be different. By contrast, the *syncretist–transformative* (ST) type of identity politics endorses a kind of discourse ethics of the sort associated with Habermas's notion of complete and mutual accountability. This kind of identity politics recognizes the need to generate a political language that is equitable across distinct cultures and positions. At the same time, it calls for each group to become accountable to all others in ways that threaten the stability of their respective identities, thereby also putting into doubt the saliency of protective group rights.

Problems of rights, identity politics, and deliberative democracy discussed in chapter 1 receive further articulation in subsequent chapters. Chapters 2 and 3 focus chiefly on the concept of group identity and identity politics. Taking race and disability as my test cases, I argue that the concept of identity is socially constructed rather than physiologically determined. Social constructions of race and disability, however, typically favor either the SP or the ST model of identity politics to the exclusion of the other. I argue, however, that neither of these models taken alone satisfactorily explains the kind of dynamic at play in political struggles centering on racial redistricting or disability rights. Although the ST model may appear to be preferable as an ideal, it might undermine group rights that protect racial minorities and the disabled.

As the recent conflict between "pure blood" and "black" Seminoles in Oklahoma shows, oppressed racial groups continue to be victimized by bogus conceptions of their identity that were illegitimately imposed upon them by whites. This example also illustrates the problematic relationship between race and ethnicity. In my opinion, interpreting race through the lens of ethnicity—as Henry Giroux does in defending a positive, antiracist white identity for white American youth—is seriously mistaken. "Whiteness"—even when touted under the seemingly innocent cultural banner of "European ethnicity"—is inextricably linked to privilege. However, I argue that an ST model of identity politics places all identities—as social constructs—in a precarious situation. Although patterns of residential separation that preserve distinctive cultural and racial group identities might be sustained for legitimate reasons—and so might serve as a basis for protective race-based redistricting—the pressure toward integration, motivated by increased multicultural migrations, will likely weaken strong racial identifications in the long run. Attempts to preserve these identities by legal fiat are questionable—for example, claiming an enforceable right to preserve the exclusive cultural and racial identity of a group—as the case of Afrikaner identity politics in South Africa well illustrates. Nevertheless, the homogenizing and disintegrating impact that global capitalism has on culture might justify an SP model of identity politics and, along with it, some protective cultural rights, either on religious grounds (as in the case of aboriginals) or on political grounds (as in the case of Quebec's language laws).

These insights, I believe, can be extended to identity politics involving disability. Once we accept an ST model of identity politics, deaf culture loses much of its distinctiveness and legitimacy and so appears to be a poor candidate for protection. But adopting this model of identity politics might have even more far-reaching implications for how we view disability. I argue that instituting a democratic paradigm might lead all citizens to think of themselves as disabled by environmental degradation, alienated labor, and socially induced passivity.

Chapters 4 and 5 focus on the concept of deliberative democracy. Chapter 4 examines the relationship between formal and quasi-formal political institutions and informal politics, by highlighting dilemmas associated with racial redistricting in the United States. I argue that alternative methods of election and representation comport better with aggregative and deliberative ideals underlying ST identity politics and, furthermore, that they are generally preferable. However, I note that current systems of racial redistricting using single-seat, winner-take-all districts that reinforce SP identity politics might be more practical and can be reformed in such a way as to encourage ST identity politics.

Presidential election 2000 presented itself as a veritable laboratory for testing this hypothesis. The disenfranchisement of large numbers of urban blacks—especially young black male felons serving time for drug charges and parole violations—reflects the vigor of an underground economy that has filled the void vacated by capitalism as much as it testifies to that system's uncanny ability to control its surfeit of unskilled and disposable workers by whatever means necessary. Chapter 4 reexamines the disenfranchisement of African Americans in light of American democracy's winner-take-all system—a system that illustrates the curious geographical identity politics at play in the electoral college, which guaranteed President Bush's own "election."

The chapter begins with a brief look at John Stuart Mill's classical defense of deliberative democracy and proportional representation. Using insights drawn from his theory, I examine the intersection of geography and racial identity politics by considering Lani Guinier's seminal critique of racial redistricting policies within the United States. I argue that Guinier's defense of a distinctly ST model of identity politics, and her corresponding defense of an open-seat method of electing representatives combined with cumulative voting, is theoretically more sound than the dominant SP model of identity politics underlying current racial redistricting policies. Nonetheless, I argue that her proposal fails to distinguish two kinds of representation that are crucial to deliberative democracy—interest representation and descriptive representation. Furthermore, I conclude that the ideal advantages of an open-seat method of electing representatives must be weighed against the real disadvantages of potential community disempowerment

Chapter 5 examines deliberative democracy from the standpoint of economic class. My discussion of this topic focuses on both formal and informal processes. On the formal side, I argue that, with the advent of the welfare state, the contradictions of capitalism are displaced onto law. The resulting conflict between liberal, welfare, and participatory legal paradigms perpetually threatens to infect legislation and adjudication with indeterminacy. Legislative indeterminacy in turn encourages judges and administrators to interpret laws as they see fit, usually in ways that favor a highly technical approach that privileges stability over justice and well-being. On the informal side, I argue that the emergence of a participatory democratic paradigm partly offsets this "instrumentalization" of law. Among other things, the increasing corporatism of society encourages the democratization of all aspects of civil society—including workplaces.

In my opinion, the subsequent suppression of workplace democracy and the corresponding transformation of labor law into a highly technical instrument of economic management exemplify the kind of injustice captured by Lyotard's discussion of differends. On one hand, democratic deliberation about justice and well-being is trumped by authoritarian decision making regarding economic management. On the other hand, the voices of workers seeking to realize their laboring capacities as self-determining agents are silenced by the voices of owners and managers seeking to realize their profits. Unless these injustices are rectified, deliberative ideals of freedom, equality, and reciprocity between government officials and average citizens will be thwarted, and critical capacities necessary for effective democratic participation will remain unrealized.

My defense of this claim centers on two traditions of legal thought: the pragmatist school, familiarly known as American legal realism; and the Frankfurt school, here chiefly represented by Habermas and his predecessors Otto Kirchheimer and Franz Neumann. Both of these traditions argue that formalism, with its emphasis on individual contractual rights, is moribund with the passing of classical liberalism (associated with laissez-faire capitalism) and the rise of corporate liberalism (associated with welfare capitalism). American legal realists reacted to this fact in often opposed ways: while some argued that the intervention of the corporate state into economic and civil life inevitably politicized the rule of law so that rights had no meaning apart from welfare-maximizing policies, others interpreted this fact differently. Like John Dewey, they saw this as an opportunity to democratize all areas of private and public life—courts of law as well as workplaces. Yet others saw the need to compromise popular control with adherence to just principle and procedure (or relatively entrenched rights). In my opinion, critical theorists like Habermas provide a more adequate theory for articulating the need for greater public participation in judicial and administrative hearings. However, they fail to urge the democratization of the workplace and other areas of life—a fatal shortcoming given Habermas's recognition that a legitimate system of rights must be complemented by a democratized lifeworld that meets it "halfway."

In the final analysis, neither realists nor critical theorists resolve what I take to be the central problem facing any rights regime: Under capitalism, there can be no coherent legal system and therefore no real integrity in the judicial interpretation of rights. I conclude that no matter how hard judges stick to fair procedures and try to give equal weight to all perspectives, the procedures as well as the outcomes will be compromised by competing paradigms that reflect tensions internal to capitalist society. However, as I noted earlier, even if these tensions were eliminated, others would remain. Deliberation on rights cannot entirely escape the vicissitudes of identity politics; therefore, citizens, legislators, and administrators must try to mitigate the tragic nature of democratic politics by pursuing principled compromises whenever possible and by seeking to distribute gains and losses fairly across all groups.

Chapter 3 illustrates how the dilemmas of identity politics and class conflict intersect in recent litigation over the proper interpretation of the Americans with Disabilities Act (ADA; 1990). What has prevented the ADA from adequately protecting the rights of disabled persons, I argue, is its own ambiguous status as both an antidiscrimination statute and an affirmative action policy. The ambiguity stems, in part, from the act's underlying rationale. Comparing disability with racial discrimination, the ADA demands that businesses do two things at once: not discriminate against disabled persons in hiring and promoting; and accommodate persons with special needs in an affirmative way. Deploying a medical or biological conception of group identity that resonates with an SP model of identity politics, the affirmative action paradigm suggests that the ADA applies only to a discrete class of protected persons, namely, just those persons who have a medically provable impairment that affects a major life function. The antidiscrimination paradigm, by contrast, deploys a social constructionist conception of group identity that resonates with an ST model of identity politics. Under this model there is no reason why the ADA could not apply to anyone who experiences discrimination based on perceived physical and mental differences.

The ADA thus collapses under the weight of two competing legal paradigms—liberal and welfare—and two competing models of identity politics. In my opinion, neither paradigm addresses the needs of all of the disabled. The antidiscrimination model dissolves disability into a mass of unrelated individual harms; the affirmative action model fixes disability in a way that generates a politics of resentment, pitting the protected against the unprotected. Only the democratic paradigm encourages us to transcend this politics by generalizing the condition of disability differentially throughout the population. Feminist critics, in particular, have suggested one way to do this, namely, by appreciating the extent to which all human relations are principally marked by asymmetrical dependency, vulnerability, and caring.

Chapters 6 and 7 draw upon the preceding discussions of deliberative democracy and identity politics in developing a discourse on ethical interpretation of human rights. Chapter 6 shows how the very concept of right has become a battleground for different legal paradigms. "Will theories" that conceive of rights in terms of individual rights-bearers' claims reflect the dominance of a liberal paradigm. "Interest theories" that conceive such rights in terms of persons' vital interests reflect the dominance of a welfare paradigm. The liberal paradigm tends to narrow the scope of rights to the protection of a negative freedom from interference. The welfare paradigm expands the scope of rights to include positive entitlements to resources, necessary cultivating capacities, and opportunities necessary for free action. However, it also tends to predefine the nature of basic human interests, goods, and capacities. According to the participatory democratic paradigm I defend, these interests would be defined—and redefined—by communities and groups relative to their own peculiar circumstances. Thus, standards of subsistence and (dis)ability would vary from society to society and would ideally reflect the outcome of democratic deliberations involving all affected subgroups. Although I defend the essential complementarity of security, subsistence, liberty, political self-determination, and cultural identity as basic interests meriting human rights protection, I argue that priority rankings of subsidiary rights within each category of human rights must also be established by communities and groups. This applies to group rights as well, which I understand as special remedies designed to ensure that individuals who belong to vulnerable groups enjoy equal protection under the law.

Rights, Democracy, and Fulfillment in the Era of Identity Politics argues that rights, human fulfillment, and democracy are linked. This claim is important for several reasons: Not only does it warrant the establishment—somewhere short of a constitutional global state—of legislative, judicial, and executive institutions at the international level for the enforcement of universal human rights, but it also urges the expansion of participatory democracy worldwide.

Global democracy faces many challenges. For example, many currents of Islam look askance at the separation of religious and secular authority. Their emphasis on doctrinal unity and hierarchical authority does not sit well with robust liberal notions of pluralism, freedom, and democratic equality. However, the communitarian ethos of Islam is capable of evolving its own—possibly superior—form of democracy. This ethos imposes stronger obligations with respect to aiding the poor and vulnerable than does the libertarian ethos of Christian culture. It thus promotes—in principle, if not in practice—a more comprehensive and perfectionist conception of the good than that permitted in liberal democracies dominated by capitalist markets.

In chapter 7, I examine several responses to this cultural clash. One response—famously put forward by John Rawls—views the clash through the lens of SP identity politics. Originating in the religious wars of the sixteenth century, this response is pessimistic about the capacity of persons to agree on comprehensive conceptions of the good; however, it is optimistic about their capacity to agree on basic formal rights. This formal liberal (or contractarian) notion of agreement can be extended to the international arena, where it promotes the toleration of cultural traditions that are antagonistic toward liberal democratic ideals, so long as they respect basic human rights. Rawls accordingly submits that cross-cultural agreement on basic rights is possible only if the parties to the social contract transcend the politics of identity and define rights in ways that do not privilege liberal democratic interpretations.

In my opinion, Rawls's pragmatic response to cultural schism marks the beginning—not the end—of a progressive process that aims at increasingly more substantive agreement on human rights. Such agreement is necessary for realizing human rights as legally enforceable provisions and for fostering mutual respect among peoples. Initial stages of agreement may transpire within an SP type of identity politics involving respect for differences, but full toleration cannot emerge unless the peoples of the world trust one another. That will happen only when they reason together in substantively defining the scope of human rights—that is, only when they are confident that the reasons why other people endorse human rights are good moral reasons, even if they are not reasons that can be shared by everyone.

ST identity politics will be most appropriate for this interchange. The hope here is that dialogue will produce a mutual and genuine understanding of differences. This stage—articulated by Hans-Georg Gadamer—might eventually lead to transformative discourse of the sort envisioned by Habermas, in which interlocutors criticize their own culture from the standpoint of other cultures. Because dialogue encourages the interpenetration of multiple horizons of understanding, its effect is intrinsically liberating and democratizing.

Furthermore, multicultural dialogue might lead the affluent democracies of the First World to value global community in all its diverse forms. In my opinion, such dialogue might encourage wealthy nations to acknowledge welfare rights for all the world's citizens. It might also encourage them to counteract the global side effects of market economies—uneven development, disempowerment, and ecological devastation—through multilateral collaboration with international regulation agencies. In the final analysis, women, immigrants, and subnationalities must be adequately represented in global institutions of governance, but democracy and respect for rights must evolve through dialogue, not unilateral imposition.

Chapter One

Human Rights and Differends: The Fragmentation of Reason and Identity in the (Post)modern Age

Rights, Democracy, and Fulfillment in the Era of Identity Politics is committed to the view that human rights have a basis in political reason and that political reason resides in a collective process of democratic deliberation. What justifies rights is agreement achieved through reasoned disputation involving many people, not deductive inference from certain intuitions held by persons in isolation. Although the full defense of this claim will be made in chapter 6—that, contrary to Jefferson, rights are not self-evident—we can at least understand why self-evident intuition (what philosophers call a priori reason) cannot be a sufficient ground for human rights.

The postmodern view I am proposing to defend here plays on the fact that what we can agree on, thanks to self-evident intuition, is too devoid of substantive meaning to provide much in the way of normative guidance. Perhaps personal soul-searching without the aid of communication might lead us to conclude that people should have basic rights to life, liberty, and the pursuit of happiness—disregarding for a moment that the very language of rights is a relatively modern convention by standards of social evolution. But what do these rights really mean?

What they really mean is determined by people in democratic deliberation. For instance, "we" come to agree that the right to life means not being harmed in one's personal property or that it means being entitled to receive one's basic subsistence. A lot, then, depends on what we can agree on. Obviously, the greater our cultural and social differences, the harder it is to agree.

This takes us to the central theme of this chapter: the fragmentation of our political landscape into seemingly incommensurable ways of reasoning. Two sorts of incommensurability stand out. On one hand, there appears to be an incommensurability between levels and types of reasoning. Deliberation about rights passes through many stages—popular understanding, legislation, adjudication, and administration. Each stage seems to embody several forms of reasoning—normative, prescriptive, descriptive, pragmatic, and so forth—that do not logically follow from one another. How do we know that the reasons "we the people" have agreed on in support of rights will be faithfully reflected in the technical statutes and decrees of lawmakers, judges, and administrators? On the other hand, there appears to be an incommensurability among standpoints of reasoning that prevent "we the people" from even reaching that preliminary level of agreement on the rational meaning and justification of rights.

This latter incommensurability is obviously related to the problem of identity politics. What makes "identity politics" so dangerous is its implicit threat to any rational consensus on basic rights and impartial procedures. If nations (groups, persons, etc.) disagree about these fundamentals, how can they be expected to live together in peace, let alone cooperate in solving common problems?

In this chapter I examine two models of identity politics and their respective potentials for dealing with incommensurable standpoints. The separatist–preservative (SP) model begins with the inescapable reasonableness of plural group identities and standpoints. The peculiar injustice threatened by this kind of identity politics is political exclusion. A dominant political group comes to define the meaning and scope of human rights in ways that privilege just those people who are assumed to share its standpoint. Thus, white European men of property came to define human rights in ways that privileged their position while discriminating against women, non-Europeans, and members of the laboring classes. The syncretist–transformative (ST) model of identity politics, by contrast, begins with the inescapable reasonableness of group convergence and identity fusion through efforts of mutual criticism and mutual transformation. The peculiar injustice threatened by this kind of identity politics is political assimilation. Basic moral differences that prevent total agreement on the meaning and rationale of rights are not tolerated. Thus, in an effort to eliminate indeterminacy in the interpretation of human rights, dominant powers like the United States might insist that all peoples accept just one interpretation as the only correct interpretation.

It is important to note that the problem of incommensurable standpoints (identity politics) outlined here is closely related to the problem of incommensurable levels of reasoning. Because no determinate and prescriptive rights can be logically inferred from the normative idea of rights (to say life, liberty, and happiness), the politics of defining prescriptive rights succumbs to the politics of exclusion or the politics of assimilation. The failure of identity politics to chart a course between these tyrannical extremes creates a legitimation crisis and opens up a void in the determination of our rights that is filled by administrative fiat. But administrative deliberation and decision are no more guided by impartial reason than popular democracy. They, too, succumb to a kind of identity crisis: Should rights be understood in accordance with a classical liberal paradigm, as formal permissions maximizing individuals' freedom from outside interference (negative freedom)? Or should they be understood in accordance with a social welfare paradigm, as substantive entitlements to primary goods (opportunities, capacities, resources) that enable people to act (positive freedom)? These paradigms both presume that standards of permissible freedom and ability are rationally discernable prior to democratic discussion. But that view, as we have seen, cannot be sustained.

Even administrators must interpret rights from the standpoint of a democratic paradigm that in some sense subsumes liberal and welfare paradigms among the different standpoints for understanding rights. But that returns us to the problem of identity politics and the injustices of exclusion and assimilation. As we shall see, there are obvious remedies to these injustices. Within the framework of an SP model of identity politics, one can propose the toleration and equal (neutral) treatment of different groups. Political reason here involves postulating a neutral framework of rights that abstracts from (or stands free of) the different comprehensive moral, metaphysical, and epistemological standpoints of different groups. Following Rawls, we might imagine different groups accepting this framework for different and perhaps non-shareable reasons, what he calls an overlapping consensus. The model of democratic civility conducive to this concept of reason would require that persons publicly (and perhaps privately) refrain from reasoning about rights in ways that could not be shared by all other reasonable persons. This would require them to "bracket" reasons that are deeply embedded in their peculiar comprehensive backgrounds. Conversely, persons would not be held publicly accountable for beliefs, behaviors, and attitudes that directly stem from these backgrounds. Indeed, they might even be afforded special group rights that help preserve these beliefs, behaviors, and attitudes from external threats of assimilation.

The toleration exemplified by SP political reason comes at a price, however. The level of rational agreement on rights possible under its regime is quite abstract—to the point of its being virtually empty. By contrast, within the framework of an ST model of identity politics, a remedy against a politics of assimilation presents itself that mediates abstract levels of reasoning with more concrete ones. This remedy construes political reason as something that arises in the course of political debate itself, rather than being postulated in advance of debate. Political reason does not abstract from differing comprehensive standpoints but arises out of their "fusion." Fusion, in turn, is made possible by the expansion, the opening up, and the transformation of comprehensive standpoints in critical dialogue.

The model of democratic civility conducive to this concept does not necessarily require that persons be publicly accountable for all beliefs, behaviors, and attitudes stemming from their backgrounds, for that would violate a right to privacy and freedom of conscience. But it does require that a line be drawn within public discourse that separates what is subject to public accountability from what is not. And, one implication of this might be a more invasive public that undermines the stability and integrity of beliefs, behaviors, and attitudes associated with identity groups in ways that render the very concept of group rights suspect.

Habermas's discourse ethics provides one model for conceptualizing an ST model of public reason. However, his insistence that all interlocutors reason and use language in the same way is unrealistic and homogenizing. For that reason, I propose that we supplement discourse ethics with the model of dialogue put forward by Hans-Georg Gadamer. According to this model, a "fusion" of horizons is not an assimilation of one into the other but a transformative expansion and an opening up of both in which their point of convergence allows for the retention of differences. Although there must be some preliminary agreement on terms and norms for civil conversation to happen, complete agreement would spell the end of dialogue, which by definition involves the mediation of differences through multiple voices.

The discursive paradigm of political reason suggested here also provides—as noted—a remedy for the kind of incommensurability that exists between levels of rational deliberation. The problem of incommensurability is largely motivated by a deductive, or inferential, model of argumentative reasoning. This model encourages us to view public opinion as argumentative "input" that logically determines or dictates legislative, judicial, and administrative outcomes. That it doesn't suggests that democratic deliberation is inherently flawed by a legitimation crisis. However, I submit that the proper model for thinking about rational deliberation is dialogical mediation: each level continues a process of democratic dialogue that has been initiated at other levels. The democratic mediation of levels and paradigms of legal reasoning, however, depends on the integrity of a democratic way of life, which, as I noted in the introduction, can be severely compromised by the class dynamics of market economies.

RATIONALES, PARADIGMS, AND IDENTITIES

A sampling of the cases that will be discussed in this book can help us appreciate the distinctness and interconnectedness of the conflicts between rights mentioned here.

Example 1: In an era noted for its rapacious capitalism, those who urge global democracy in resolving the world's most pressing economic and environmental problems can only be disheartened by continuing disagreements over what constitutes human rights. While all sides agree on the general normative ideals underlying human rights, they disagree on the concrete prescriptive force that attaches to these ideals. Although the U.S. State Department continues to insist that classical liberal civil, property, and political rights are the privileged conceptual paradigm for interpreting human rights, signatories to the Bangkok Declaration (1993) and many other developing countries disagree. They argue that the human rights to life and happiness are best captured by subsistence and cultural rights. And, while the State Department proudly trumpets the superiority of American-styled democracy, with its multiparty, money-driven competition for power (the essence of "free speech," so we are told), the leadership of single-party socialist regimes extols the virtues of democratic centrism with a nod toward worker- and community-managed cooperatives.

Example 2: The disagreement about human rights at the international level is reflected in domestic disagreements about property, contract, and labor rights. The emergence of corporate capitalism and collective bargaining leads to conflicting paradigms for interpreting these rights: liberal, welfare, and democratic. Are labor rights best secured through unregulated contracts in which individuals are free to reject or accept whatever terms of employment are offered them, or are they best secured through collective-bargaining provisions that equalize bargaining leverage between labor and capital? Should such provisions allow workers greater opportunities for ownership and democratic control of the enterprises in which they work?

Example 3: In what has since become a textbook case regarding the limits of federalism, French Canadian nationalists insisted that Francophone Quebecois were at a cultural, economic, and political disadvantage with respect to English-speaking Canadians. Hence the federal government was persuaded to allow Quebec to require French in business and educational settings (the latter provisions mainly affecting immigrants). Their critics pointed out that this requirement violates the universal right, guaranteed by the Canadian charter, that business owners and parents have over their businesses and children's education.

Example 4: In other cases involving federal power sharing, indigenous people living on tribal reservations in the United States and Canada demand, as a matter of treaty right, special exemptions—from civil suits, gambling prohibitions, environmental regulations, common-law strictures regulating property, liberal notions of democratic governance, and even drug laws. Their critics charge that such exemptions clash with the idea of universal citizenship, which implies an equal sharing of legal burdens regardless of differences. Also at issue in these cases are criteria governing tribal membership. In a much-debated case, "mixed blood" Seminoles of African slave descent are contesting their right to benefits granted to the Oklahoma Seminole tribe as a part of a reparations settlement. The question of what constitutes tribal identity has also resurfaced in numerous other cases, from repatriating the remains of apparently European- descended humans to the exclusion from tribal membership of children born to women who marry outside the tribe.

Example 5: In yet another case involving identity, Dutch Afrikaners living in Orania, South Africa, have petitioned the government requesting that their community be declared a separate, "cultural" (or tribal) homeland that is politically distinct from the surrounding "black" communities, thereby again raising the problematic relationship between "cultural" ethnicity and "biological" race.

Example 6: In a controversial attempt to urge the U.S. Department of Justice to embark on a policy of proportional group representation, African Americans, Latinos, and other ethnic minorities sought the creation of legislative districts wherein they would be empowered as majorities. This policy, which enabled minorities to elect substantial numbers of representatives of their choice for the first time since Reconstruction, was curtailed by the conservative majority on the Supreme Court beginning in 1993 on the grounds that it mirrors a similar policy, adopted by Southern whites during the sixties, that empowered *them* as majorities. In both instances, the Court argued, race-conscious redrawing of legislative districts has had the effect of privileging (or protecting) groups at the expense of discriminating against individuals.

Example 7: Recent litigation over the Americans with Disabilities Act shows remarkable similarities to litigation over the Civil Rights Act. In both cases there is a disagreement about the appropriate legal paradigm for interpreting these statutes. The classical liberal paradigm views these as antidiscrimination statutes guaranteeing all individuals permissive rights; the social welfare paradigm views them as affirmative action statutes guaranteeing only members of protected classes entitlements to special accommodation and consideration.

Recalling the typology between types of conflict noted at the outset of this chapter, it is obvious that examples 4 and 5 revolve around "identity politics." By contrast, examples 1 and 3 seem also to involve issues of federalism, both national and international. Here, the problem involves mediating legal norms that claim some kind of general validity—human rights that apply to all nations; or the Canadian Charter of Rights and Freedoms, which applies to all

Canadians—with prescriptive rights and statutes that are interpreted from the standpoint of the particular needs of particular nations and subgroups. Finally, examples 2, 6, and 7 illustrate conflicts between distinct paradigms of rights.

Notwithstanding apparent differences, these cases reveal interesting overlaps. Problems associated with federalism highlight tensions between abstract and concrete levels of legal reasoning that allow free play for conflicting legal paradigms and identities. The inability to deductively infer concrete prescriptive rights from abstract principles of right creates an "interpretation" gap. The same abstract principles can be interpreted from the standpoint of different paradigms. For instance, the Americans with Disabilities Act, the Civil Rights Act, the Voting Rights Act, and the Wagner Act (which established collective-bargaining rights) ostensibly "apply" and "interpret" the Fourteenth Amendment's equal protection clause, which asserts that no state can discriminate against individual citizens on account of their race, religion, or creed. Citizens must be treated equally. But does this mean giving them the same formal permission to act without hindrance, as the liberal paradigm requires; or does it mean acting affirmatively to remove or compensate for disadvantages that befall them as members of protected classes? If it also means empowering them as equals in decision making, does it do so in their capacity as individuals or as members of groups?

Tensions between formal (abstract) and substantive (concrete) levels of reasoning make possible other kinds of conflicts as well. For example, a formal liberal rights paradigm has traditionally been understood as entailing minimal government interference in civil life and so accords well with purely formal methods of "consistency" reasoning. By contrast, a social welfare paradigm empowers the state to administer—that is, efficiently manage and fairly distribute—a complex set of goods and entitlements. The weighing and balancing of competing goods and values under conditions of scarcity and complexity entail more substantive modes of reasoning. Again, by contrast, a democratic rights paradigm interprets rights not as goods or entitlements to be technically administered in top-down fashion but as social relationships that need to be reinterpreted and revitalized through shared and inclusive communication. The kind of reasoning informing this process is neither formal-deductive nor substantive-calculative, but substantive-dialogical.

Tensions between abstract and concrete levels of reasoning thus provide fertile soil for conflicts between types of reasoning. They also nurture conflicts between so-called identity groups. This is especially true of the kind of substantive-dialogical reasoning characteristic of the democratic interpretation of rights. The formal rational reasoning associated with the liberal paradigm abstracts from individual differences so that the only identities it recognizes are either abstract and universal (humanity) or utterly individual. Here, there is no logical space for recognizing group identities or identity politics. The substantive-calculative reasoning associated with the welfare paradigm, by contrast, constitutes a logical space for identifying different group identities, but it does so in a top-down, administrative manner in which identities are fixed and defined. The formal liberal paradigm defines individuals as sole legal subjects and protects them from group-based discrimination. The welfare paradigm defines groups (or individuals classified as members of groups) as sole legal subjects and accordingly discriminates among them, depending on their peculiar needs and handicaps.

It is the substantive-dialogical form of reasoning that is especially susceptible to identity politics. Here, the principle of rational justification—dialogical consensus—itself becomes a medium of reflection in which groups' identities are continually redefined and reconstituted subjectively and socially. Within this medium disability and race exist as objective social relationships that are nonetheless subject to individual and collective reinterpretation. Disability, for instance, is a function of many factors: societal discrimination, physical handicap, and subjectively felt unfulfillment owing to a sense of disempowerment. Race, too, is a function of many social factors whose legal and practical significance must be worked out in antiracist struggle.

INCOMMENSURABLE LEVELS OF REASON: THE DIALECTIC OF UNIVERSAL AND PARTICULAR

Let us begin by examining the tension between abstract and concrete levels of legal reasoning, since it is this tension that opens up the logical space for other conflicts. Drawing on the work of Jean-François Lyotard, I would like to characterize this as a tension between incommensurable language games that privilege different speaking authorities and different types of reasoning. According to Lyotard, spoken utterances (phrases) not only convey meanings and refer to persons, things, and events, but they also authorize some persons (addressees) as listeners and other persons as speakers (addressers). For instance, in mythic narratives the narrator (addresser) purports to be telling a story that was first recounted by the hero (reference) of his story, which will be repeated endlessly in the same way by each person (addressee) who hears it. Citing Andre Marcel d'Ans's studies of the myths of one traditional ethnic group, the Cashinahua, Lyotard adds that these narratives simultaneously perform both legislative and executive functions, thereby effecting a kind of authoritarian regimentation of social roles and privileges with respect to age, gender, and kinship. Because each person's name is identical to the name of some mythic hero, his or her specific power to execute commands is directly transmitted from the primordial normative source to which it is nominally identified.[1] Nazi myths effect the same kind of circular (cyclical) repetition and closure of authorization by collapsing the descent of each authentic German (established by surname) into the great saga of the Nordic peoples, whose sovereign destiny is then linked to the particular will of a single leader (Lyotard 1993, 43–47).

The seamless, circular identification of addresser, addressee, and referent characteristic of mythic narrative finds no logical equivalent in modern narratives of legitimation. A quick glance at the American Declaration of Independence (1776) and the French Declaration of the Rights of Man (1789) confirms that these documents of the Enlightenment unsuccessfully try to identify the particular commands of a single person or a select group of persons (for instance, Thomas Jefferson and the signatories to the American declaration) who claim to represent a particular subset of people (European-descended American patriots) with a more abstract, universally and naturally sanctified law that applies to all of humanity.

For example, article 16 of the French declaration asserts that "the representatives of the French People, organized in National Assembly . . . have resolved to set forth in solemn declaration the natural, inalienable rights of man." This assertion, Lyotard maintains, is patently question begging because it conflates a finite group of individuals ("representatives of the French People, organized in National Assembly") with the divine power that legislates for all of humanity. Its tacit conflation of addresser (delegates to the National Assembly), addressee (the French people) and referent (God, nature, reason, or humanity) suggests not only a logic of identification similar to that found in myth but one that is expressly forbidden by modern reason's own disjunction between universal normative foundation and particular political act. From within the logic of rational metanarrative, the determinate, historically specific prescriptions of right and wrong conduct legislated by the politician (addresser) do not necessarily follow from the indeterminate, universal norms of freedom commanded by nature or God.

The danger of equating a particular nation's determinate institutionalization of freedom with what is universally right for all of humanity is obvious: the nation in question—be it the United States in the year 2004 or France in 1789—will be strongly tempted to impose its will and identity on the rest of the world:

> The splitting of the addressee of the *Declaration* into two entities, French nation and human being, corresponds to the *equivocation* of the declarative phrase: it presents a philosophical universe and copresents a historical-political universe. The revolution in politics that is the French Revolution comes from this *impossible* passage from one universe to another. Thereafter it will no longer be known whether the law thereby declared is French or human, whether the violence exerted under

the title of freedom is repressive or pedagogical (progressive), whether those nations which are not French ought to be French or become human by endowing themselves with Constitutions that conform to the *Declaration*, be they anti-French. (Lyotard 1983, 147, emphasis added)

Thanks to its equivocation, the Declaration of the Rights of Man set in motion a world revolution whose effects are still being felt two hundred years later. Were the revolutionary wars that continued through the Napoleonic era wars of liberation (attempts to extend the blessings of divinely sanctioned freedom to all of humanity), or were they wars of imperial expansion (attempts to extend the dominion of the French government over its neighbors)? The same question applies to the colonization of Asia and Africa by Europe, the domination of Latin America and the Middle East by the United States, the hegemony of NATO in Europe, and the current influence of the World Trade Organization and the World Bank on the economies and polities of countless developing countries. Do we not have a form of economic and cultural imperialism that masks itself under the guise of human progress and freedom?

The problem of linking abstract and concrete levels of thinking is hardly mitigated by "acting in the name and by the authority of the good people of these colonies," as the signers of the Declaration of Independence put it. This attempt to link an arbitrary political declaration to a preexisting source of normative legitimacy seems viciously circular (Lyotard 1993, 41). The one who authorizes (addresser) and the one who is authorized (addressee) cannot be identical; otherwise, the constraints imposed by the former on the latter would no longer be constraints. Self-authorizing power is unlimited despotic power, not limited legitimate power (Lyotard 1983, 206). That explains why so many slaves, Native Americans, and loyalists regarded the revolutionaries as usurpers whose brand of democracy portended more, not less, oppression for them.

Lyotard's linguistic analysis of the founding human-rights documents illustrates well how the incommensurability between abstract and concrete levels of political reasoning opens up a space for identity politics based on excluding those who do not possess the right (European) form of rational identity. This possibility can also be explained in terms of logical disjunctions between types of reasoning: transcendental, normative, and prescriptive. For our purposes what is most important in this analysis is his theory of phrasal *regimes*. According to this theory, utterances can be classified into different sorts of language games (regimes) that are governed by different rules. For example, "The door is closed" is a descriptive phrase whose meaning and pragmatic acceptability are largely governed by the criterion of truth. By contrast, "Close the door!" is a prescription, or command, whose meaning and pragmatic acceptability is governed by the criterion of normative rightness, or justice (Lyotard 1993, 42).

The important thing to note is that utterances that belong to different regimes occur together in more-complex language games, such as legitimating narratives. These genres of discourse "set rules for the linking of phrases to ensure that the discourse proceeds towards its generically assigned end: to convince, to persuade, to inspire laughter or tears, and so forth" (43). As we have seen, mythic narrative conflates a number of ends. Something's being assigned a name automatically bestows on it descriptive truth, normative regularity, and prescriptive power simultaneously. Hence, descriptions, normative injunctions, and prescriptive commands follow one another seamlessly through a singular logic of identification. The same, however, does not hold true for modern forms of rational legitimation. Their Enlightenment pedigrees tacitly commit them to rational distinctions between types of phrases that resist logical connection. Normative injunctions that assert that something general ought to be done (such as respecting each individual's inalienable freedom) cannot be deductively inferred from descriptions that assert that something is a necessary fact of nature or of reason. Likewise, particular executive commands and prescriptions that permit or enjoin specific forms of behavior by specific persons do not necessarily follow from universal normative injunctions addressed to what humanity at large ought to be permitted or prohibited from doing.

Notwithstanding logical prohibitions against inferences of this sort, modern foundational narratives succeed in convincing their addressees only by eliding the logical gaps in their narrative. Nothing normatively follows from a description of fact, so the narrator is free to declare that any norm whatsoever is compatible with the facts. Nothing having particular prescriptive force follows from a general principle of right, so here too the narrator is free to command virtually anything as compatible with the idea of right. For the legitimating narrative to do its work, however, the narrator must convince the addressee that what he or she has asserted as being compatible with fact and norm is in fact necessitated by fact and norm so that no other interpretations of fact and norm are in fact compatible with them. That the American and French declarations encourage such slights of hand in turn encourages the sorts of exclusions and assimilations mentioned earlier.

But Lyotard has in mind a target that is more central to our concerns: political deliberation and decision. Deliberation and decision involve complex chains of reasoning incorporating different regimes and genres of discourse, on one side, and different agents who are authorized to speak and listen, on the other, thereby presenting multiple possibilities for injustices. These injustices (or differends, to use Lyotard's word) typically involve linkages between phrases in which one type of discourse is trumped or suppressed by—or annexed to—another. For instance, the normative questions guiding democratic deliberation ("What ought we to be?") cannot be answered without reference to descriptive assertions about human nature and, more generally, about what is within the range of human possibility (for, as Kant famously asserted, "ought" implies "can"). Suppose we answer that human nature consists of being able to act freely and responsibly so that all adults should therefore be guaranteed certain rights to go about their business unhindered by others. As we know, this normative conclusion does not logically follow from any metaphysical description of human nature, but leaving that problem aside, it doesn't get us very far in deciding the precise nature and extent of our freedom. Compounded by the fact that we do not all agree on the precise meaning of human nature and its normative implications, it is clear that we need a decision procedure—call it democracy—to settle the precise prescriptive meaning and force of our abstract right in the form of enforceable commands, or laws. Since our deliberation must be conclusive (if even only temporarily), we allow a particular group of persons (legislators, judges, administrators, etc.) to decide the matter for us. In deciding the question in a particular way, they ostensibly try to balance and compromise our competing comprehensive moral and metaphysical viewpoints, although in the end some viewpoints get privileged over others. More important, they also reduce the normative question about what universal reason demands in the way of ideal justice to the technical-calculative question about what the existing system, as viewed by one group (say, the business class), demands for its efficient management.

On one hand, justice is interpreted in accordance with a liberal paradigm that defines the right to liberty, life, and property as a permissive right. On the other hand, the side effects of an unregulated market economy create economic cycles, environmental degradation, and uneven development (poverty, unemployment, and underemployment) that require government intervention in the form of income redistribution, as well as health and welfare policies. Distributing entitlements to liberty, life, and property justly, however, requires substantive-calculative reasoning that eschews the moral language of abstract justice in favor of the instrumental language of cost-benefit compromises. Congress and the president set fiscal policy, distributing tax burdens and benefits so as to balance budgets and stimulate economic growth. The chairman of the Federal Reserve sets monetary policy, raising and lowering interest rates conducive to maintaining a healthy investment climate. Given the impossibility of achieving full employment, zero inflation, and profitable growth simultaneously, the chairman must make hard choices that constrain investment and determine the distribution of jobs and incomes.

In this way popular democratic deliberation about morality and ethics, which transpires in substantive-dialogical reasoning about normative ideals pertaining to justice and rights, gets subsumed under and replaced by technical administrative decision making about economics, which transpires in substantive-calculative reasoning about technical strategies for modeling efficiency and stability. This "hijacking" of one kind of reasoning by another is facilitated by the fact that "normative" discussions about justice and rights are thought to be too abstract and indeterminate—in short, too subjective and unscientific—to be factored in as a basis for governance. This "injustice" is abetted by the very fact that technology and science have replaced religion as a new source of authority and legitimation. Because average citizens accept their own technical incompetence in matters of governance, they voluntarily acquiesce in their own disempowerment. Communication between them and their leaders thus increasingly assumes the truncated form of "information exchange" and "fact finding," rather than mutual critique.

DIFFERENDS AND IDENTITY POLITICS

The indeterminacy of meaning attached to rights is created by gaps in political reasoning. Given the fragmentation of the political landscape, legitimation by way of democratic consensus is also not to be expected. Attempts to impose consensus are totalitarian. But simply allowing government officials to reduce politics to interest group bargaining (threats), market mechanisms for distributing government largesse based on effective demand (political bribes), or procedures for aggregating utilities (top-down administrative choices based on vote tabulations) are equally illegitimate.

The forms of injustice hitherto cataloged are characterized by what Lyotard calls a differend. A differend occurs "whenever a plaintiff is deprived of the means of arguing and by this fact becomes a victim." This happens, for instance, where the settling of a conflict between two parties "is made in the idiom of one of them in which the wrong suffered by the other signifies nothing" (Lyotard 1983, 24–25). Lyotard illustrates this kind of injustice with examples drawn from identity politics as well as from incommensurabilities implicit within political reasoning and democratic deliberation. Among the examples drawn from identity politics mentioned by him are workers who are forced to define their laboring power in the contractual language of a liberal paradigm (as remunerable exchange value) instead of the political language of a democratic paradigm. Defining labor as a commodity exchangeable in a private transaction implies no political right to participate as an equal in the democratic management of the workplace, but defining labor as social contribution (source of value) does.

Other examples mentioned at the outset of this chapter also illustrate differends. When developing socialist countries are ostracized and sanctioned for refusing to adopt Western-styled economic and political institutions (whose democracy is but a guise for oligarchy), they suffer an injustice. Conversely, when dissidents in these countries are suppressed for lobbying on behalf of more extensive, more diverse, and freer forms of democratic participation, they too suffer an injustice. When Quebecois are constrained by the English-speaking majority to conduct business transactions in English instead of French, this puts them at a certain economic disadvantage (and they suffer an injustice). When Native Americans are forced to defend their territorial claims in the alien language of property and contract bequeathed to them from English common law, they are prevented from convincing others that their land designates a spiritual locus of communal identity (and they suffer an injustice). When African Americans are forced to defend redistricting proposals that empower them to elect representatives of their choice in the "color-blind" language of formal voting rights, they are prevented from fully articulating the sense in which democracy depends on empowering disadvantaged groups as much as guaranteeing individuals the right to vote (and they suffer an injustice). And when the disabled are forced to treat themselves as inherently deficient and deviant rather than as able-bodied and capable of inclusion—but for societal discrimination against difference—they suffer an injustice.

Differends also occur whenever speakers are forced to speak the same language and mean the same thing by the words they use. According to Habermas's model of rational communication (the ideal speech situation), speakers must satisfy the formal logical requirement of semantic consistency. This requirement can have the effect of submerging and assimilating a subaltern minority voice into a hegemonic one, thereby suppressing (excluding) it. Another example: What fails to rate as acceptable "reason giving," by academic standards of conversational civility and rationality, are noisy street demonstrations, personal narratives, rhetorical bombast, and simple silence. These uses of argument are thus suppressed or dismissed. In general, superior command of academic English enables the better educated to conduct conversations toward outcomes they desire. This happens regardless of whether each interlocutor has been formally vested with an equal opportunity to speak because power is exercised indirectly and anonymously, through the exclusions, entitlements, and rhetorical strategies made available through the dominant discourse.

TWO KINDS OF IDENTITY POLITICS

Lyotard presents us two competing postmodern models of "identity politics." The separatist–preservative model, which he discusses under the rubric of a "justice of multiplicities," closely follows the theory of language propounded here. That theory assumes that there are sharp logical distinctions between types of speech acts, genres of discourse, and language games, which prevent them from being deductively linked together or translated into one another. Once we suppose that languages—or ways of conceptualizing and categorizing the world—form the cultural backgrounds in which we understand things, it is easy to see incommensurable (nontranslatable) languages as forming the incommensurable horizons of our cultural identities. This notion of incommensurable linguistic identity also resonates well with the notion of incommensurable personal identity; and in fact the theory of identity presumes that the identities of groups are analogous to the identities of individual persons in being distinct, well defined, and self-contained.

On this view (of incommensurable linguistic identities), politics is poorly conceived as a dialogical process of reaching agreement. Indeed, the attempt to engage in consensus-oriented political deliberation can seem threatening to the preservation of one's identity. SP identity politics thus takes the form of a struggle in which each group seeks to have its differences from other groups recognized. The demand for multicultural recognition takes this form. Because liberalism holds that a person's individuality is as worthy of recognition as his or her universal humanity, and because a person's individuality is constituted by his or her identifications with particular groups, liberalism too is committed to holding that a person's group identifications merit recognition (Taylor 1992). But recognizing the intrinsic worthiness of these groups and their right to exist separately signals a departure from the individual-centered, difference-blind approach definitive of the formal liberal paradigm.

The second, synchretist-transformative model of identity politics, which Lyotard discusses under the rubric of a "legitimation by paralogy," also presumes a theory of language but one that emphasizes both the "heterogeneity" of language games—their permeability with respect to one another—and their reflexivity. By "reflexivity" I mean the capacity of speakers to use language reflexively in talking about language. Used in this way, language can reflect on and surpass its own limits. It can be modified and extended to say new things—to designate and mean what it was once incapable of designating and meaning. Corresponding to this reflexive conception of language we find a reflexive conception of identity. According to this view, persons' identities are reflected through—and in some sense constituted by—other persons. As in the multicultural model discussed earlier, one's personal identity is shaped (stabilized and constituted) by the values and frames of linguistic-cultural meaning that have been inculcated in one by one's peers. The medium in which this transpires is communication. The capacity to reflect on oneself—and come to "discover" that there is a self—is itself an internalization of a capacity to split oneself into a self that is reflecting and a self that is reflected on, a capacity that is first learned in communication whereby one learns to view oneself through the eyes of another. The internalization of reflection as a dialogical process of mutual questioning and mutual identification through another leads the self to continually question its own boundaries, its own core values and frames of reference. The end result is an identity that is continually fluid and open-ended, an identity whose reflexive "preservation" is equally an act of self-constitution and self-transformation. Consequently, the politics that corresponds with this notion does not aim to recognize and preserve identities in their insular distinctness but aims to continually expand them so as to incorporate ever-wider horizons of experience. This politics thus tends toward humanistic and cosmopolitan fusion, rather than multiculturalism.

THE DANGERS AND REMEDIES OF IDENTITY POLITICS: TWO CONCEPTS OF CONVERSATIONAL CIVILITY

The distinct conceptions of identity informing the two models of identity politics discussed here are not equally sound, in my opinion. The conception of identity's informing SP identity politics wrongly presupposes that group identities are analogous to personal identities, which do in fact possess a higher degree of integrity and self-containedness. However, it also exaggerates the extent to which personal identities are themselves self-contained, rather than dialogically mediated by other identities. Furthermore, the assumption that the different languages and worldviews that frame the ways different groups understand their reality are incommensurable—or incapable of being translated into one another—is itself incoherent. As Donald Davidson has argued, it would be impossible to know whether expressions in one language were untranslatable into another language without first having successfully translated both languages into a third language, thereby rendering them commensurable (Davidson 1984).

That said, we can nonetheless adopt a sliding scale in which it makes sense to talk about languages and identities being more or less open (closed) and more or less susceptible to agreement and understanding. This takes us to the models of dialogical civility that render each form of identity politics legitimate within its proper limits. Let's begin with the SP model of identity politics. Classical liberal doctrines of toleration presume that persons are entitled to their nonshareable comprehensive doctrines and identities without having to render public account for them, so long as they exercise due tolerance of opposing doctrines and identities. Inclusion here means tolerance, and tolerance means legal protection, which can sometimes involve the use of group-specific rights. For example, guaranteeing freedom of religion for the Amish in Wisconsin may require exempting them from having to send their children to high schools; guaranteeing Native Americans freedom to define their tribal lands collectively and spiritually may require exempting them from civil actions and a host of other regulations; and so on.

What makes SP politics "inclusive," according to Rawls and others, is that each group can agree on a more general constitutional framework of mutual tolerance and cooperation by appealing to its own particular values and its own particular identity, rather than to some transcendent citizenship identity. Constitutional consensus is "overlapping" rather than dialogical or based on reasons that all can share. Civil dialogue between groups that have incommensurable doctrines and identities is still possible, but only so long as each group is willing to exercise "conversational restraint" by refraining from appealing to those aspects of its identity that are peculiar to it. A look ahead to chapter 7: When applied to the field of international law, this notion of tolerance and civility—what Rawls calls "political liberalism"—will be seen to require respecting nondemocratic, illiberal "peoples," at least so long as they incorporate what Rawls calls a procedure for "reasonable hierarchical consultation" and exercise toleration with respect to minorities.

The second model of conversational civility, by contrast, appeals to an ideal of rational autonomy that privileges the freedom of the individuals to question their own and others' identities over the right of groups to protect their identities by insulating them from the demands of public accountability. In comparison to the first model (political liberalism), this public accountability model seems less tolerant of deviations from liberal democracy and less sympathetic to group-specific rights than the first. Accordingly, we find Habermas differing with Rawls on international law and rejecting Charles Taylor's multiculturalist defense of Quebec's language laws. Habermas's belief that individuals rather than peoples (or states) ought to be the proper subjects and beneficiaries of international law resonates with his claim that Quebec's language laws inhibit individual freedom of speech.

> Even if such group rights could be granted in a constitutional democracy, they would be not only unnecessary but questionable from a normative point of view. For in the last analysis, the protection of forms of life and traditions in which identities are formed is supposed to foster the recognition of their members; it does not represent a kind of preservation of species by administrative means . . . . The constitutional state can make this hermeneutical achievement of the cultural reproduction of worlds possible, but it cannot guarantee it. For to *guarantee* survival would necessarily rob the members of the freedom to say yes or no, which nowadays is crucial if they are to remain able to appropriate and preserve their cultural heritage. When a culture has become reflexive, the only traditions and forms of life that can sustain themselves are those that *bind* their members, while at the same time allowing members to subject the traditions to critical examination and leaving later generations the *option* of learning from other traditions or converting and setting for other shores. (Habermas 1998a, 222; original emphases)

According to Habermas, rights that protect groups from cultural contamination by inhibiting freedom of speech also inhibit the free, undistorted formation of identities in cross-cultural dialogue. Applied to the context of tribal and religious autonomy, it means that traditional ways of life and their corresponding "mythic" legitimations ought not to be shielded from the partially disintegrative effects of modern ideas. Even Will Kymlicka, who defends group-specific rights for aboriginals, concedes that traditional groups should abandon their ethnocentrism and transform their collectivist identities to accommodate modern ideas of individual freedom and equality. As we shall see in the next section, racial groups, too, would eventually have to cease thinking of themselves as "self-contained" communities of interest that merit preservation.

POLITICAL LIBERALISM VERSUS PUBLIC ACCOUNTABILITY

It should be apparent by now that the two forms of conversational civility corresponding respectively to SP and ST identity politics—political liberalism and public accountability—have advantages and disadvantages. The disadvantage of public accountability appears to be its lack of tolerance, or its failure to respect the right of groups to be insular and separate and thereby shielded from the demands of public accountability. This danger may be summarized accordingly: Public accountability designates a peculiar—liberal democratic—conception of identity formation and political life that is not now, nor is it ever, likely to be universally accepted by all persons. Numerous philosophers have rejected it as entailing a metaphysical—indeed Promethean—conception of human autonomy that appears to denigrate the importance of cultural tradition and experience as an "unquestioned" background of habits and tacit understandings, against which we foreground particular traditional assumptions and experiences. They maintain that the boundaries of our identity cannot be radically questioned "all at once" without undermining the very framework of core values and meanings that lend our life purpose and direction.

A related danger implicit in the model of public accountability is that it will result in assimilating all cultural frameworks to the same identical framework. Some of Habermas's claims about the need for all interlocutors to come to an agreement on the terms of their discourse sound good in theory but not so good in practice. In some of his youthful comments directed against Gadamer's hermeneutic philosophy, he once characterized the "ideal speech situation" as one in which the speakers had achieved total transparent insight into all the background conditions underlying their thinking. If this impossible task were to be achieved, it might well yield a perfectly transparent agreement—but at what cost?

Demanding public accountability has its limits. The demand that we account publicly for all of our assumptions runs contrary to the sanctity of privacy at the heart of Habermas's own liberalism. True, the line separating private and public is not inscribed in certain intuition. It must be drawn in the shifting sands of public discourse itself. That it must be drawn somewhere, however, is not in dispute.

More important, rational dialogue need not—nor should not—issue in a static convergence of standpoints without remainder of difference. Despite our orientation to reaching mutual understanding, dialogue is as likely to preserve or magnify our differences as diminish them. Pluralism, as Rawls is fond of pointing out, is itself reasonable. But just as rational dialogue need not encourage the assimilation of cultural horizons, so need it not encourage their fragmentation and dissolution. Indeed, it is a shibboleth of hermeneutic philosophy from Gadamer to MacIntyre that cultural traditions only survive as vital ways of life by being handed down in new and different ways. Cultural preservation thus presupposes cultural reinterpretation and change, which in turn presupposes rational criticism of what is culturally anachronistic. As MacIntyre (1988) notes, traditions designate substantive lines of argument and problem solving that sometimes need the infusion of other traditions to resolve their crisis. But reaching out to and learning from other cultural traditions need not entail assimilation—the hegemonic swallowing up of one tradition by another or the effacement of both in some new hybrid tradition—it can issue in a kind of fusion or interpenetration of cultural horizons in which cultural traditions are preserved in their distinctness.

And the model of political liberalism? Like the model of public accountability, its disadvantages are one with its advantages. The price it pays for its tolerance of "incommensurable" comprehensive doctrines, identities, and ways of life is a frank agnosticism with respect to its own deeper and more comprehensive philosophical truth. There is nothing philosophically deep and convincing about supporting multicultural toleration other than the fact that it is—for whatever reason—widely accepted. But wide acceptance is purchased at a steep price. As we have seen, the level at which incommensurable doctrines, identities, and ways of life overlap in support of this principle is quite general and abstract—so much so that the principle agreed on is too indeterminate to provide much in the way of prescriptive guidance. And if we support toleration for radically different (and incommensurable) reasons, how can we trust that the others believe as we do in the same toleration—concretely interpreted and applied? Would it not therefore be advisable for us to hold one another publicly accountable with respect to such an important principle? Consensus generated by dialogue does not consist of overlapping positions that remain in a state of contentious isolation; it is rather forged out of shared reasons that have emerged in the course of each group's willingness to change in light of its exposure to other points of view. Because these reasons are not held in abstraction from any group's determinate system of beliefs and values, the resulting consensus is likewise determinate.

No political example testifies better to the possibilities of transformative identity politics than alliance building. While alliances can take many forms, ranging from a modus vivendi based on strategic compromise and temporary convenience to an overlapping consensus based on moral principles, the most stable and enduring forms occur whenever the partners in alliance alter their identities to incorporate each other's differing perspectives. Just thirty years ago a labor–environmental alliance in the United States would have been unheard of. But recent demonstrations against the World Trade Organization, in cities throughout the world, showed that such an alliance is indeed possible. Both sides realize that the important issue revolves around neither losing jobs (to environmental protection) nor sacrificing ecological integrity (to job growth) but of losing both to unregulated global trade. Both sides agree that global capitalism creates uneven and wasteful development, which in turn results in the environmental degradation and impoverishment of the most vulnerable sectors of the labor force. Finally, both sides conclude that more democratic forms of technological development and industrial organization are the key to combatting underemployment as well as environmental degradation.

CONCLUSION AND PREVIEW

I submit that the decision as to which form of identity politics ought to be adopted is a matter for contesting parties to decide among themselves, although an ST model is philosophically sounder and more congenial to the ideal of deliberative democracy. As the example of aboriginal cultures demonstrates, there are times when SP identity politics is an appropriate strategy for pursuing the aim of cultural preservation. As I noted earlier, preservation need not—nor probably cannot—take the form of freezing a culture in some pristine form, uncontaminated by outside influences. Nor can a separatist strategy be defended in the form of legal segregation and exclusion. Voluntary separation, however, has its rightful place as a strategy for self-determination.

Perhaps one should view identity politics along a continuum. In situations where groups are positioned against one another, SP politics that are oriented toward mutual respect for differences might be the best place to begin—although, as we shall see in the next chapter, not all differences are worthy of equal respect. However, for deliberative democracy to succeed and flourish, toleration and respect for differences must eventually give way to a deeper understanding of differences that can evolve, over time, into something resembling ST identity politics.

Looking ahead, I hope to show that a democratic paradigm of legal reasoning can help mitigate differends between levels and between types of reasoning as well. The appearance of an unavoidable injustice partly stems from our habitual acceptance of formal deductive and inductive modes of reasoning. We want our democratic decisions well founded in democratic deliberations so that there is no room for uncertainties in meaning that require higher-level acts of interpretation. Accusations of legislative, judicial, and administrative tyranny sometimes reflect just this desire for a mechanical programming of government deliberation and decision. But in a rational and complex democracy, deliberation and decision by government officers cannot and should not simply mirror public opinion. They should instead take up public opinion and reflectively rearticulate it to ensure a fair hearing and balancing of all interest positions. It is a question, then, of continuing a popular course of substantive-dialogical reasoning at a different level in which formal and substantive-calculative reasoning plays an added if subordinate role.

Democratic deliberation and decision thus designate a rational process—of reflection rather than of inference. Like all processes of reflection and interpretation, deliberation and decision are circular processes. The legislative and judicial acts that define constitutional procedure are in turn authorized and limited by it. This is not a vicious circle of legitimation, as Lyotard sometimes suggests. For the agents and powers specified by the procedures for amending the procedures will not be identical—for example, those responsible for drawing up a constitution are not those empowered to amend it. The separation of powers renders the circuitous process of deliberation more deliberate—and more rational—by interrupting it with checks and balances.

Not everyone will participate equally or in the same way. The danger of injustice is a permanent reality. Government officials will be tempted to hijack popular democracy and transcribe its moral and ethical deliberations about justice into the register of administrative rationality. Capitalism by its very nature encourages this tendency, as its contradictions get displaced onto the state. To conceal the fact that the welfare state both sustains and supplants market functions by redistributing tax revenues and controlling investment in ways that benefit wealthy investors—and partly compensate the victims of structural unemployment and underemployment—government must perpetuate the fraud that its decisions have no bearing on distributive justice, that they are just technical decisions designed to maintain a growing economy that ostensibly benefits everyone equally.

Short of radically reforming the economy, the best citizens can hope for is the opening up of government to public accountability and the democratizing of all layers of decision making. As we shall see in chapter 5, inclusive deliberation should be encouraged in public fora, and it should be responsible for generating the opinions that guide legislators in setting policy agendas. Less inclusive but fully accountable deliberation should obtain in parliaments, courts, and government bureaucracies, where specialized expertise is required. Citizens must come to understand how the effects of power and domination insinuate themselves into technical expertise and cybernetic technology.² It may well be, as Foucault ceaselessly reminded us, that no language is free from these effects, none neutral or impartial in articulating all possible interests. The struggle to create a language more adequate to the expression of diverse experiences (cultural, racial, class, etc.) is never ending. That is why alliances between heterogeneous groups are so difficult to forge and maintain. But without embracing the risk of radical self-transformation presented by broad participatory democracy, we stand to lose more than just our freedom; we stand to lose the world.

NOTES

1. Lyotard (1984) argues that myths and perhaps other "small narratives" *(petit recits)* that circulate in everyday life are distinguished from scientific and Enlightenment "metanarratives" in being prediscursive. Unlike metanarratives, the utterances that make up myth cannot be formulated as abstract propositions—descriptions, prescriptions, and so forth—that can be logically identified, analyzed, grounded (argumentatively deduced), and criticized (65). Instead of conveying propositional meaning and knowledge, the utterances that form oral recitations convey a kind of pragmatic know-how. Their status is more like that of rituals that get legitimated through repetition and imitation or, as Lyotard puts it, "by the simple fact that they do what they do" (18–23).

2. Lyotard (1984) recognizes the ambiguous impact of computer technology on encouraging or hindering the development of "virtual" democratic spaces. On one hand, such technology can "aid groups discussing metaprescriptives by supplying them with the information they usually lack for making knowledgeable decisions" (67). Recent use of computer technology by college students to protest sweatshops and globalization exemplifies this potential. On the other hand, computer technology can be used to undermine face-to-face interaction and (in a more sinister scenario) concentrate information in the hands of powerful elites. Lyotard's call to "give the public free access to the memory and data banks" is powerfully defended by Andrew Feenberg (1999, 105–6, 136–43). Feenberg's optimism about the use of computer democracy in organizing global labor and environmental struggles, however, is not shared by everyone.

Part One

IDENTITY

Chapter Two

White Man's Burden? Ethnicity and Race in the Era of Identity Politics

I have argued that identity politics is an unavoidable feature of liberal democracy. As such, it has an impact on the way fundamental rights are justified and interpreted. This is not unique to it. Plural interest group politics has the same impact. But while few theorists have challenged the legitimacy of voluntary interest group associations, many have denied the legitimacy of nonvoluntary structural groups, based on inherited social status and identity. It's okay for oil companies, environmental groups, and unions to lobby the government because those who belong to these associations do so mainly by choice. By contrast, when groups representing women or racial minorities lobby the government, the question arises: Who gives these groups the right to speak for all women or all members of a racial minority?

Pluralist theory assumes that legitimate political groups aggregate individual interests through voluntary memberships in representative organizations. Women and members of racial groups do not constitute their interests voluntarily—at least not in the same way that members of plural interest groups do; and they do not possess common interests that distinguish them in the same way that plural interest groups are distinguished. The legitimacy of identity politics is also questioned by those on the Left, who continue to defend the legitimacy of economic class as a locus of common interest but not race, culture, or gender.

In my opinion, gender, ethnicity, and race can define one's core interests, values, and identity just as much as economic class. To be sure, pluralist objections also apply to economic class, with some critics insisting that "universal" pension programs and stock owning have rendered the very concept of "class" outmoded. Whether the complexities of postliberal capitalism have rendered class distinctions moot is perhaps questionable. But pluralist critics are right on one point: whatever constitutes the legitimate core of a structural group identity cannot be a sharing of interests that might be easily translated into unified support for some distinctive set of policies, such as price supports. As we shall see in chapter 4, something less definite—such as a "common" perspective (or, lacking that, overlapping perspectives)—seems a more promising way to capture what it is the women and racial minorities might share.

In this chapter I propose to examine the legitimacy of structural group identity by examining the complex intersection of race and ethnicity, an intersection whose conceptual ambiguity and historical complexity has arguably played the most profound role in legitimating white privilege and working-class exploitation in North America and beyond; in addition, it now promises (in a curious reversal) to become a new site for contesting capitalism and its effects, which range from the "inner colonization" of the American black urban ghetto to the hegemonic imposition of a "global monoculture" of mass production and consumption.

From the standpoint of biology, "race" and "ethnicity" are illegitimate categories. While persons classified as belonging to racial and ethnic groups may inherit certain physical and cultural characteristics from their parents, in some degree of probability, the basis for the classification depends on social conventions. Social conventions, in turn, are subject to relationships of domination and struggle. In short, racial categories—and the racial segregation that perpetuates their prima facie legitimacy—are created by dominant groups and imposed on subordinate groups to perpetuate economic exploitation. Such, at any rate, is the origin of the dominant global racial system, which divides people into different groups based on their deviation from the European norm.

External imposition of a racial identity on a subaltern group by a dominant group renders it prima facie illegitimate. However, the internal policing of racial identity by members of a group is also illegitimate, to the extent that it denies individual members the right to constitute their own identities freely. Thus both forms of imposition—external and internal—can be understood as injustices of the sort that I have hitherto characterized as differends (cf. chapter 1). In both instances, groups or individuals are forced to define themselves in terms of categories that are imposed on them, categories that effectively silence them. It is precisely this coerciveness—inherent in the policing of identity—that leads to the familiar charge that identity politics is illegitimate at its very core: unjust as well as ungrounded. Genuine politics—so the argument goes—is a game played by individual actors who voluntarily organize themselves into discrete plural interest organizations.

I intend to rebut this charge. To do so, I argue against two standard assumptions. The first assumption is that identity politics entails rules of fairness that apply to all groups in the same way. If it's wrong for white people to affirm their interests as white people, then (following this assumption) it's wrong for blacks to affirm their interests as blacks; conversely, if it's okay for blacks to affirm their interests as blacks, it's okay for whites to do the same. The second assumption is that identity politics necessarily involves the kind of SP identity politics discussed in chapter 1. This assumption states that SP identity politics aims to preserve only the closed identity of structural groups. But it is precisely this conception of identity that involves coercive stereotyping and identity policing.

Contrary to the first assumption, I argue that there is no reason why groups positioned differently with respect to relationships of domination should have the same opportunities to affirm their interests. Affirming "black pride" is not equivalent to affirming "white pride," since the former—unlike the latter—is a defensive strategy aimed at rectifying a negative stereotype. In general, racial categories that have an illegitimate origin can come to serve legitimate political purposes when affirmed in a positive way by subaltern groups. The same does not apply when racial categories are affirmed by dominant racial groups, for affirmations of white pride—however thinly cloaked as affirmations of ethnic pride—serve to mask and perpetuate white privilege.

Be that as it may, progressive educators such as Henry Giroux have argued that white youth need to have a positive white identity to engage in antiracist struggle without feeling guilty about who they are. Following Stuart Hall's recommendation, he proposes to interpret such an identity as a postmodern ethnic identity that is congenial to a syncretic–transformative (ST) kind of identity politics. I argue here that this attempt fails, for conceptual and empirical reasons. Whiteness designates a structure of privilege, and the only recognizable cultures and identities that correspond to it are racist. Furthermore, I contend that having a progressive white identity is less necessary for engaging in antiracist struggle than is understanding the psychosocial dynamics underlying social stereotyping and in-group/out-group interactions.

My response to the second objection is more complicated. To begin with, if we accept the ST model of identity politics advocated by Hall, then the problem of preserving the integrity of "closed" racial and ethnic identities never arises. As I argue in chapter 1, this—not SP identity politics—is the preferred paradigm toward which all forms of identity politics ought to aspire. Be that as it may, SP identity politics need not presume that the identities seeking protection are closed and uniformly inculcated throughout all members of an identity group. Multicultural struggles on behalf of defending aboriginal ways of life, for instance, can be defended in terms of freedom of association and democratic self-determination, which allows for considerable individual freedom of self-definition.

Unfortunately, SP identity politics strongly inclines toward oppressive boundary policing and social divisiveness. One reason for this, I argue, is that race and ethnicity are often confused. Part of this confusion is understandable. From a purely conceptual point of view, race and ethnicity are indistinguishable: both designate the probable inheritance of physical and cultural characteristics associated with relatively insular populations. Hence, it is easy to assimilate racist separatism to the multicultural struggle for recognition, as some Afrikaners have done. Conversely, when applied to antiracist struggle, separatism in the name of ethnic (cultural) self-determination—the view espoused by many in the black power movement—replaces "assimilation" in the name of ethnic integration.

Although separatism may serve a legitimate function when the stark alternatives are either segregation or assimilation—which are both forms of racial–ethnic domination—it cannot (I maintain) be a long-term strategy for full self-determination. That goal will only be achieved within the ambit of an inclusive ST form of identity politics. The qualified defense of SP identity politics in furthering a multicultural respect for "differences" should not substitute for a qualified defense of ST identity politics furthering antiracist and interracial community.

In the United States, ethnicity and race historically designated different groups: immigrants on one side and blacks and whites on the other. The historical "racializing" of ethnicity and the more recent "ethnicizing" of race should not mislead us into conflating the vastly different historical trajectory of these groups. Today, with the waning of ethnic racialization, African and African-descended immigrants encounter a different set of opportunities and handicaps than those encountered by African American descendants of slaves. But as the following example illustrates, different trajectories sometimes merge and so likewise do race and ethnicity.

The Case of the Black Seminoles

As early as the seventeenth century, escaped and freed slaves mingled with the Florida Seminoles. Some of them were kept as slaves or sharecroppers; some served as warriors and leaders in the wars against the whites; some married into the tribe. By 1860 most of the Seminoles were exiled to Oklahoma. In 1866, the Seminole leaders signed a treaty with the government that made black Seminoles a part of the Seminole Nation, and by the turn of the century the government began distributing tribal allotments among all Seminoles. Although it is unclear how many black Seminoles participated in tribal life, they coexisted peacefully with other members of the tribe until 1976, when a court ordered the U.S. government to "compensate" the Seminole Nation for the land taken from them in Florida. A government study concluded that the $52 million in clothing, housing, and medical benefits that was to be awarded the Seminoles—many of whom lived in dire poverty—be targeted only to descendants of the Indians who originally held title to the land. After the black

Seminoles—who form about one-tenth of the Oklahoma Seminoles—sued for a share of the settlement in 1996, they were voted out of the tribe by their "blood" compatriots. Five years later a judge threw out the vote and reinstated the black Seminoles in keeping with the Department of the Interior's wishes, and today efforts are under way to release the remaining $30 million, either in the form of cash or provisions, pending readmission of the black Seminoles as full voting members of the tribe.

This classic illustration of SP identity politics raises profound questions about the relationship between race and ethnicity. Lewis Johnson, a member of the tribal council, denies that the vote to expel the black Seminoles was about race, but he adds that Indian tribal identity is related to a blood-based conception of nationhood: "If someone is not an Indian by blood, you can't make him that way." Reminded that the black Seminoles also claim to be related by blood, Johnson falls back on the idea of democracy and majority rule: "But the tribe does have an inherent right to determine who are its members."

As I noted in the introduction, in a case involving the ostracization of Evangelical Indians inhabiting the New Mexico Pueblan reservations (Ingram 2000a, 116ff), the right to exclude persons from an association is contingent on many factors. It is justifiable only when (a) those being excluded are viewed by the association as external threats to the association and its cultural identity and (b) viable exit options are available to those being excluded. In the Pueblan case, condition (a) was partly met, insofar as some of the Evangelicals divided the tribal community and disrupted its traditional theocratic way of life. Condition (b) was not, however; for many of these Evangelicals still had close ties to the land of their ancestors and could not survive without the threshing machines that were being denied them. By contrast, Catholics who are excommunicated from the Church for openly challenging its ban against ordaining women priests have viable exit options, regardless of the threat they pose to the identity of the Church; for instance, "exiting" the Church, say, by founding alternative Catholic congregations, does not involve relinquishing material benefits.

Expulsion from the tribe denies black Seminoles needed provisions, thereby depriving them of a viable exit opportunity. More important, expulsion seems morally unjustifiable, since the black Seminoles pose no threat to the identity of the community—unless, of course, one defines that identity in racial rather than in cultural terms. Lewis Johnson's specious appeal to "blood quantum" forgets that this racial concept was imposed on Native American tribes against their wishes by the U.S. government to limit land title claims as much as possible (only "pure bloods" were entitled to full allotments under the General Allotment Act of 1887). Racial ideas of tribal membership were, in fact, alien to tribes prior to contact with whites. Adopting women, children, and occasionally men—white or nonwhite—into the tribe as full-fledged members was normal.

RACIAL CLASSIFICATIONS

The example of the Oklahoma Seminoles raises profound questions regarding the legitimacy of structural group identities and identity politics. Race theorists have conclusively demonstrated that racial categories linking the physical, mental, and behavioral traits of selected individuals to a hidden nature putatively shared by them as a group are without scientific basis.[1] However, among those who find the continued use of racial classifications in science, medicine, and law problematic and illegitimate, there are some who find racial self-ascriptions acceptable as a way of referencing a shared experience of oppression.[2] Pride in being black, for example, is typically expressed as a way of combatting racism rather than asserting reverse racism.[3] By parity of reasoning, some have argued that a positive white self-identification can also be legitimate when purged of its racist connotations.

I disagree. In my opinion, the fundamental asymmetry between whites and racial minorities with respect to positions of privilege and domination renders any attempt to recover a positive white identity suspect. Most important, the attempt—recently undertaken by Henry Giroux (1997)—to reconstruct white identity as a kind of ethnic identity fails to convince. For, as I argue here, if ethnic identity is purged of illegitimate racial connotations, it ceases to function as anything more than a set of cultural markers. But whiteness does not designate any such set, except as an ideology and practice of racism. Properly conceived, whiteness designates a structure of privilege that conditions the acculturation of both whites and nonwhites, albeit in strikingly different ways. I conclude that, although white persons need not feel guilty about who they are, they should not aspire to a positive racial identification in the way that blacks and other oppressed racial minorities might.

Whiteness: Some Preliminary Observations

What, or who, do white people want to be? This question, raised by David Wellman (1997) in a penetrating analysis of whiteness and affirmative action, seems to defy a response. Indeed, the question would never have arisen forty years ago. In those days, white people took their identity for granted.[4] Their whiteness, if one can call it that, was all but invisible to them. Their place in the world—as self-ascribed bearers of Western civilization, the Protestant work ethic, and decency—was unquestioned and secure. But all that has changed now. As younger whites increasingly confront the challenges of affirmative action, multiculturalism, and identity politics, they also confront the question of their own shifting identity.

Today, white people—above all, white men—have been put on the defensive. What they have taken for granted as the fruits of hard work and virtue is now decried by others as the undeserved advantages of privilege born of racism and the correlative evils of sexism and class domination. Seeing their economic and political dominance challenged by forces over which they have no control—loss of jobs to foreign competition; depreciation of marketable skills and qualifications; and decline in wages, salaries, and benefits due to downsizing, the opening up of competitive labor markets, and so on—they feel more insecure than ever about their place in the world.

Having been placed on the defensive, whites become defensive. White supremacism is one manifestation of this reaction. A less overtly racist (and sometimes nonracist) reaction is "principled" opposition to policies, such as immigration and affirmative action, that supposedly violate the rights of American workers in general and, more specifically, the rights of white men. Here the construction of white man as victim is premised—curiously enough—on denying the "wages of whiteness," as David Roediger (1991) refers to it.

We need only recall the important role that racism played in the pivotal rise of industrial capitalism to confirm the truth of this statement. Longitudinal studies of white male identity within the American context—by Roediger (1991), Horsman (1981), Allen (1994), Ware (1992), Saxton (1990), Wellman ([1977] 1993), and Ignatiev (1995)—show that whiteness is inextricably connected to notions of class and nation. During the colonial period (and especially that part of it pertaining to Southern plantation life), whiteness denoted a distinctly aristocratic kind of breeding whose superior distinction resided in freedom from physical labor, intellectual detachment from bodily desire, and moral control over one's destiny. This sensibility was later appropriated by the white middle class and, during the nineteenth century, by skilled wage laborers. Key to this development was the suppression of any identification between black and white laborers, a process that first began in the late seventeenth century, with the passage of laws preventing the mixing of slaves and indentured servants, whose contracts could be leased or sold (Allen 1994, 97ff.). However unskilled and poor, white workers were encouraged to distinguish themselves as free wage earners—thereby undermining any alliance between themselves and slaves. As Roediger shows, the anxiety of male white workers facing the conditions of exploitation and dehumanization typically conferred on blacks (and later immigrants) led them to embrace racist myths and stereotypes, which assured them of their own sense of self-worth (hence the popularity of minstrel shows, which depicted blacks as lazy, hedonistic, and childlike).

Corresponding to this gradual "blue-collarization" of whiteness was the emergence of a settler ideology that equated Anglo-Saxon lineage with the pioneering spirit. The republican vision of a nation of independent farmers (the Jeffersonian dream) fueled expansion into the wilderness, thereby calling forth a new ideology mandating the "civilizing" subjugation of those "mongrel races" of indigenous and Spanish descent who did not live by the precepts of the Norman Yoke Doctrine, which equated full humanity with enclosure (privatization) and tillage of the land. The doctrine of "manifest destiny" thus expressed a more consolidated—indeed global—view of white sensibility.

This sensibility has persisted despite globalization and increased immigration. Phil Cohen (1997, 253–56) talks about a new, postmodern form of white supremacism that has emerged alongside a new "post-Fordist" mode of global capitalism. Whereas older forms of white identity still embraced the remnants of an aristocratic privileging of the mental over the physical, the new, postmodern forms reverse this sensibility. Targeting immigrants and racial minorities that have gained access to better-paying (if unstable) high-tech jobs in the computer and service industries (where performance rather than appearance counts), blue-collar white supremacists have reinvested, with a new sense of masculinity and individualism, jobs in mining, steel, and construction that were once regarded as dirty, dangerous, dehumanizing, and generally the proper labor of nonwhites and minorities. The "uniform" adopted by London's East End skinheads—shaved head, Doc Martens boots, T-shirt, jeans, and suspenders—and their attachment to local and national soccer teams thus articulate a new territorial and masculine version of proletarian whiteness.

In sum, however much working-class white men suffered from racial divisions that facilitated the depression of their wages (by enabling their replacement with lower-paid blacks), they also benefited from the "public and psychological wage" of white privilege (Du Bois [1935] 1977, 700). Whiteness eventually became their salvation, the very bond of racially exclusive trade unions that promoted higher wages at the expense of blacks who could have been embraced as oppressed brothers rather than shunned as competitors. Because whites disingenuously deny or remain insensitive to this history—the actual extent of present discrimination, the institutional effect of past discrimination, and the cumulative assets that have disproportionately accrued to generations of whites through wage discrimination—what is intended as an affirmative action aimed at "leveling the playing field" appears to them as nothing more than reverse discrimination. Maintaining this deception, however, requires entering into bad faith and, even worse, caricaturing minority beneficiaries as "unqualified" on the face of it, thereby fabricating a new kind of minstrel show replete with comic stereotypes (Roediger 1991; Saxton 1990; Wellman 1997).

But these defensive and reactionary reconstructions of victimization do not exhaust all the possible answers to the question about what it means to be white. When junior high and high school students form European American social clubs in response to the emergence of ethnic clubs composed mainly of persons of Asian, African, and Latino ancestry, they ostensibly do so not to proclaim their victimization but to celebrate their European culture and identity. Likewise, when practitioners of "diversity awareness" seek to train educators, workers, and managers to become conscious of how "white" culture should be privileged no more than any other, they seem to be offering their mainly white clients the prospect of reconstructing their white identity critically and positively.[5] Finally, and perhaps most ironically, the decline of what K. Anthony Appiah has referred to as *extrinsic racism*, or the idea that different races correspond to different levels of moral, cognitive, and aesthetic achievement and worth, has been accompanied by an increase in *intrinsic racism*, the idea that racial difference alone carries moral weight (Appiah 1990, 5–6). As Naomi Zack argues, the fear that many white families entertain regarding the painful lives that children designated as racially black endure still constrains them to deny or exclude any racial mixing—especially with blacks—among their members (Zack 1993, 31).

The above examples reflect a continuing obsession with racial purity, if not a white backlash, moderately disguised as a multicultural makeover of a distinctly racist form of understanding and practice. Despite this fact, educator and eminent race theorist Henry Giroux speculates that a positive, antiracist construction of white identity as a kind of ethnicity represents a viable alternative to defensive or self-abnegating constructions. His stance marks an important alternative to the view espoused by Ignatiev and Garvey (1996), bell hooks (1997), and Roediger (1991, 1994) (just to name a few), who urge whites to reject any positive identification with their whiteness. Viewed as a distorted understanding of social reality and as an objective structure of privilege and exclusion, whiteness is perceived by these critics as something to be betrayed, deconstructed, and abolished. Renouncing one's whiteness or asserting one's racial complexity by identifying with subaltern minorities, as do "wiggers" (white youth who adopt the black youth culture of hip-hop),[6] seems to these critics to be a more constructive way of dealing with their whiteness than simply withdrawing into a self-destructive paralysis of white guilt. But Giroux questions whether whites can voluntarily renounce their whiteness, if doing so involves the impossible: erasing a ubiquitous system of privilege or completely undoing a process of socialization.

A similar dilemma plagues progressive men who wish to voluntarily renounce aspects of their masculinity that are implicated in patriarchal domination: How can they reconstruct a positive "feminist" identity for themselves without in some sense renouncing their masculinity? Giroux seems to be suggesting that our racially coded identities are as much a part of our sense of who we are as are our gender-coded identities. If we allow that men must be able to reconstruct a positive antipatriarchal masculine identity (despite the complicity of that identity in patriarchy), then why not allow the same for whites in relation to their white identity?

Of course, the force of this argument partly hinges on the notion that whites must have a racial identity in the same way that men must have a gender identity. But it might be argued that in an ideal world, without domination, gender identities would disappear along with racial identities. Furthermore, transsexual and other gender-bending "performances" of sex and gender (Butler 1990) show that men "need" masculine identities as little as women "need" feminine identities. Even if it should turn out that gender and sex identities at least partially express genetically programmed hormonal differences, this is manifestly not the case with racial identities.

It is sociological—not biological—determinism that holds the key for Giroux's belief in the permanency of racial differences. Accepting without question the idea that "race will neither disappear, be wished out of existence, or become somehow irrelevant in the United States," Giroux urges "whites . . . to learn to live with their Whiteness by rearticulating it in terms that help them to formulate what it means to develop viable political coalitions and social movements." They must learn, in other words, "to engage in a critical pedagogy of self-formation that allows them to cross racial lines not in order to become Black, but to begin to forge multicultural coalitions based on a critical engagement rather than a denial of 'Whiteness.'" Ultimately, "by rearticulating Whiteness as more than a form of domination, White students can construct narratives of Whiteness that both challenge and, hopefully, provide a basis for transforming the dominant relationships between racial identity and citizenship, a relationship formed by an oppositional politics" (Giroux 1997, 299–300).

Giroux concedes that there are obvious obstacles to this project. Reconstructing whiteness within the register of multicultural "identity politics" threatens to reify both ethnicity and race in ways that perpetuate racism. As I noted earlier, SP identity politics itself has sometimes been construed—even by some of its staunchest defenders—as a way in which supposedly insular, biologically determined ethnic groups fight to preserve the rightful recognition of their respective cultural identities as pure and unique. But if ethnicity is conceived this way, as racially determined, no antiracist advantage can come from reconstructing whiteness as ethnicity.

Furthermore, reconstructing whiteness as ethnicity conceals fundamental historical differences in the way in which racial groups and ethnic immigrant groups have been treated.[7] Thanks to the "one-drop rule," persons in the United states were generally classified as either white or black.[8] Although ethnic immigrant groups were often regarded by Americans of Anglo-Saxon and Nordic descent as racially and culturally different and inferior, it was but a distinction of degree. Being not black—and therefore somewhat white—they did not suffer the extreme and qualitatively unique forms of legal oppression and discrimination suffered by blacks. Not only did ethnic immigrants distinguish themselves from blacks, but they even aspired to whiteness and, in due time and for the most part, were accepted this way by whites themselves.[9]

This fact has important implications for Giroux's attempt to use ethnicity as a way to reconstruct whiteness. Although some whites might appeal to their ethnic identities by sympathetically identifying with oppressed racial groups, they must avoid reconstructing their own ethnic group's past history of racial suffering in a way that blurs the distinction between this suffering and the suffering of today's racial minorities (especially that experienced by blacks and Native Americans). Conflating blacks with ethnic immigrants makes it easy to blame the former for not having succeeded like the latter. More important for our purposes, it obscures the way in which ethnic self-identification was and still continues to be a way of expressing white separatism and supremacy. Giroux himself notes this very danger, yet he seems less vigilant in guarding against another danger: whiteness qua ethnicity again renders whiteness qua racial privilege invisible.

Within the ambit of SP identity politics, it might seem that whiteness would assume its rightful place as a culture deserving as much respect as any other. But this is not the sort of multicultural politics Giroux has in mind. What he seeks is a way of framing "attachments and identifications" (including those associated with whiteness) that suspends blanket judgments regarding their goodness or badness, racial innocence or racist complicity (299). With a nod toward Foucauldian genealogy and postmodern deconstruction, he wants to affirm both sides of this dichotomy. To state his position more precisely: "While it is imperative that a critical analysis of Whiteness address its historical legacy and existing complicity with racist exclusion and oppression, it is equally crucial that such a work distinguish between Whiteness as a racial identity that is non-racist or anti-racist and those aspects of Whiteness that are racist" (300).

What would it mean to talk about whiteness as a racial identity that is non-racist or antiracist? Giroux answers this question by appealing to Stuart Hall's conception of "new ethnicities":

> The term ethnicity acknowledges the place of history, language, and culture in the construction of subjectivity and identity, as well as the fact that all discourse is placed, positioned, situated and all knowledge is contextual . . . . What is involved is the splitting of the notion of ethnicity between, on the one hand the dominant notion which connects it to nation and 'race' and on the other hand what I think is the beginning of a positive conception of the ethnicity of the margins, of the periphery. That is, a recognition that we all speak from a particular place, out of a particular history, out of a particular experience, a particular culture, without being contained by that position. . . . We are all, in that sense ethnically located and our ethnic identities are crucial to our subjective sense of who we are. But this is also a recognition that this is not an ethnicity which is

doomed to survive, as Englishness was, only by marginalizing, dispossesing, displacing, and forgetting other ethnicities. This precisely is the politics of ethnicity predicated on difference and diversity. (Hall 1996, 446–47)

In opposition to dominant constructions of ethnicity, nationality, and race, which appeal to "essentialist" and biological determinations, Hall urges that we view such categories simply as social constructions that serve to position any subject vis-a-vis multiple cultures and shared experiences. Because these new "identities" are contextually specific—appropriated by individuals out of their own experience—as well as open-ended, overlapping, and shifting, they cannot serve to exclude, marginalize, and dispossess specific individuals and groups. But this contextuality and open-endedness also renders them questionable as a basis for SP identity politics. Stated bluntly, multicultural and antiracist politics can no longer take the form of simply affirming essential differences that were once negatively and stereotypically distorted by the dominant racial and cultural groups. Therefore, if anything legitimate still resides within the compass of identity politics, it can only be that of individual members of groups (self-chosen or otherwise) collectively fighting against these destructive stereotypes. This politics, needless to say, is far removed from positively affirming anything remotely like a definitive identity.[10]

If Hall's defense of new ethnicity inadvertently deconstructs the very notion of insular group identity, reducing the latter to the status of a loose alliance of overlapping subject positions, it is hard to see how it can be of any use to Giroux's project of retrieving "whiteness" as an identity. Indeed, as I hope to show, the concept of a white identity is, if anything, less legitimate than that of ethnic identity. At best, the latter, when appropriately deconstructed, might be defended as a temporary locus of overlapping solidarities for individual members of oppressed and marginalized groups. Indeed, when appropriately deconstructed, ethnicity dissolves into a plurality of cultural or experiential identifications that is utterly unlike anything approximating whiteness. In the final analysis, unless we have in mind racist identifications or white supremacist ideologies, whiteness is best conceived not as a culture or experience that can be positively affirmed and subjectively identified with but as an objective system of socially constructed exclusions that constrains culture and experience covertly and subconsciously.

THE PERMANENCE OF RACE

Giroux's argument in support of a nonracist conception of whiteness rests on a number of questionable premises, including the following:

a. Racial identities are permanent (naturalist thesis).

b. If it is legitimate for oppressed racial and ethnic minorities to affirm their respective racial and ethnic identities, then it must be legitimate for whites to do so as well (symmetry thesis).
c. A legitimately affirmed racial identity must be affirmed as socially constructed, contextually positioned, fluid, heterogeneous, open-ended, and nonexclusionary (postmodern thesis).
d. A legitimately affirmed racial identity has the same status as a legitimately affirmed ethnic identity; it refers principally to a nexus of overlapping cultural and experiential aspects (reductionist thesis).

In my opinion, (a), (b), and (d) are highly questionable, if not false; (c) is true—it contradicts the naturalism of (a)—but is nonetheless misleading, since postmodern characterizations of subject positions render talk of "identities" highly suspect.

Regarding (a), Giroux offers no defense of the permanence of racial identifications in the United States. Indeed, because he acknowledges their historical specificity, it is surprising to find his affirming their permanence. To assess this claim, we must first distinguish the question of permanency from that of desirability. Given their dubious ontological and moral pedigree, it would be difficult showing the desirability of racial constructions. Only if racial constructions could be reconstructed as ethnic constructions, and only if these in turn could be reconstructed as new ethnicities, might it be argued that racial constructions are desirable. Even then, the plausibility of the argument would depend on other questionable assumptions, for instance, that ethnic pluralism is necessary for cultural pluralism and that cultural pluralism is necessary for human flourishing (which is intrinsically desirable).

I return to the question of ethnicity and cultural diversity at the conclusion of this chapter. Since the desirability of racial reconstructions hinges on the plausibility of (d), I limit my discussion here to the permanence of race. Now, there are two possible ways to interpret the permanence of race. First, it might mean that racial reconstructions are so deeply embedded in the social fabric of current American society that they are not likely to disappear soon, although they might do so eventually. Second and more strongly, it might mean that racial constructions are in some sense natural, either "hard-wired" into the brain (perhaps as the result of natural selection) or at least based on essentialist modes of cognition that are virtually universal to all human society. The former view, defended by Pierre van den Berghe (1981) and Lucius Outlaw (1995), holds that group solidarities based on physical and cultural differences have an evolutionary ("anthropological") basis (Outlaw, 179). Although both insist that biologically based constructions of race are historically specific, they argue that identification with specific groups secure bonds of trust necessary for cooperation and survival. Furthermore, Outlaw notes that individuals like to see their own physical and cultural likeness duplicated in their offspring—a possibility whose likelihood is increased to the degree that their mates resemble them in the relevant respects (192).

The evidence supporting Outlaw's argument for the permanence of group solidarities constructed on the basis of physical and cultural similarities is weak. Even if it were true that cultural and physical similarities functioned as principal loci for group solidarities in the past, it is not necessary that they will continue to do so in the future. Indeed, the insularity of racial and ethnic groups seems to be declining, thanks in part to the loosening of traditional prejudices and forms of insular bonding. In the United States, this factor has combined with multiracial and multiethnic immigration to increase the overall percentage of interracial and interethnic couplings—itself a significant counterindication of the sort of psychological identification alluded to by Outlaw.[11]

The second view, defended by Lawrence Hirschfeld, accommodates the fact of interracial mixing better, partly because it makes no sociobiological claim about a person's "natural" predispositions to bond with people like themselves (Hirschfeld 1996, 80–81). Hirschfeld's claim is more modest, namely, that the propensity toward categorizing people into racial groups, although not innate or natural, builds on naturalizing ways of understanding human groups that quite possibly are innate, given their universal ubiquity in virtually all human societies:[12]

> Race, I have repeated several times, is not a "natural" category of the mind. Human kinds are natural categories of the mind, in the sense that the mind is prepared to find them with little or no external encouragement. Moreover, I have proposed that human kinds predicated on intrinsicality are a category of the mind which human beings are prepared to hold. The notion of race is the outcome, the consequence, of this preparedness as it makes contact with contexts in which complex relations of power and authority are played out on the group level. An appreciation of this complex and contingent relationship between mind architecture and power politics follows from appreciation of the singular and recurrent ways racial cognitions develop across time and across cultural contexts. (Hirschfeld 1996, 189)

According to Hirschfeld, folk psychological tendencies to form naturalistic group stereotypes are propelled by a kind of cognitive economy, or unconscious simplification of expectations regarding persons. The average person in any society typically operates with relatively fixed expectations regarding gender, age, class, status, and so on. When raised in an environment in which social relations are structured by racial caste, children no older than three years of age will quite readily learn to classify persons in accordance with racial essences whose immutability, distinctness, and heritability do not correspond to perceived reality.[13]

Important for our purposes is Hirschfeld's conclusion that racial thinking is a culturally conditioned, opportunistic instantiation of—and therefore not equivalent to—a quasi-natural cognitive predisposition. Furthermore, however universal the cognitive predisposition underlying naturalizing folk psychology might be, it is a disposition that can be exposed, criticized, and resisted on philosophical and scientific grounds. Essentialist racial and ethnic identifications continue to thrive in contexts marked by racial–ethnic mixing. For instance, in the United States, most offspring of mixed white–black parentage continue to identify themselves as black, while in countries where mixing has become generalized and commonplace throughout the population, such as in Brazil, offspring racially identify themselves in more complex ways. Yet, however much they do so, they might not in the future.

In sum, neither of the two ways in which the permanence of race is formulated supports the view that racial identities are a permanent feature of the human landscape. Moreover, there is no evidence supporting the view that people are compelled by nature to group themselves into racial and ethnic solidarities based on physical and cultural similarities. Most important of all, research in cognitive psychology shows that a young child's disposition to categorize people racially, while strikingly adult in its understanding of the underlying race concept,[14] does not issue in a correlative disposition to interact differently with persons classified as racially different. The latter disposition, associated with adult racial attitudes, is entirely the result of a distinctly racist form of acculturation.

RACIAL ASYMMETRIES

The second premise in Giroux's argument, (b), bears more directly on his conclusion, which in some respects actually contradicts the naturalism of (a). Giroux argues that, if progressive whites are to be allowed to identify themselves with a white identity, then it must be an identity that is nonracist and nonessentialist. Excluded from this thesis is the possibility (evoked by hooks [1997], Ignatiev [1995]) that whites can reject or betray their whiteness in favor of identifying themselves as black, brown, or simply nonwhite.

In one sense, Giroux's exclusion of these options is partly correct. If racial systems are part of a publicly recognizable institutional fact, then it is not entirely up to me to determine how I am classified and identified. But then, racial systems are never so well formed as to be fully determinate for all persons (cf. note 2). To the degree that such systems invoke conflicting criteria of racial identification, and to the degree that these criteria are ambiguous in meaning and vague in application, they become less determinate in particular cases. Perhaps not so long ago the infamous one-drop rule functioned in the

United States to determine one's racial identity in terms of a relatively simple binary scheme (black or white). But today that rule has weakened somewhat,[15] and others based on some loose combination of factors (physical appearance, cultural habits, ancestry, etc.) have gained increasing hold. The weakening of determining criteria has not only complicated the old binary scheme by introducing new multiracial identifications, but these in turn have encouraged those whose racial identity is complex to view it as something that is less objectively ascribed than subjectively chosen.

What Giroux means by racial identity is not to be confused with a classification imposed on persons—often against their will—by an objective racial system. What he means by racial identity is rather the way in which one subjectively—and increasingly, deliberately—identifies oneself. Taken in this latter sense, racial identity is not institutionally preordained; it is perfectly possible and reasonable for white individuals to reject the classificatory scheme that determines their racial identity in public and institutional settings by expressly identifying themselves as black, brown, nonwhite, and so on. Furthermore, even if racial identity is difficult to sustain in ways that contradict socially recognized schemes of racial identification, persons who feel that they fall through the cracks of America's biracial system will feel that they have greater freedom to reject a simple racial designation in favor of identifying themselves as racially complex, or mixed (Zack 1993, 143).

Giroux himself seems to concede that "whiteness" is not the only "racial" identity available to white individuals. His point, however, is that it *should* be available to them, perhaps in addition to the other options proposed by hooks, Ignatiev, and others. Why? Partly because he thinks that renouncing their whiteness by identifying themselves as black, brown, or nonwhite imposes grave psychological risks to their sense of self-worth that could feed into a white racist backlash. The risks are especially grave for those whites who wonder where they fit in with respect to today's identity politics. To the extent that racial and ethnic minorities continue to engage in an exclusionist SP identity politics that positions whites as oppressors and outsiders, whites will find it difficult to identify with such minorities. Finding it difficult to identify with them, they will either retreat into a state of self-loathing and guilt—renouncing their whiteness without the comfort of optional identifications—or they will react against their positioning as oppressors by reasserting their whiteness in a racially insensitive (if not blatantly racist) manner.

Giroux's symmetry thesis thus boils down to the idea that if it is acceptable for minorities to engage in identity politics, and thus if it is acceptable for them to affirm their racial and ethnic identities in the cause of antiracism, then the same opportunity should not be denied to antiracist whites. Significantly, Giroux understands this thesis as a counterresponse to the kind of symmetry thesis often advanced by liberals who attack identity politics. The liberal version of the symmetry thesis states that, because racial identifications are immoral (and would not exist in an ideal world composed of individuals who recognize one another as free and equal), it is just as wrong for minorities to appeal to them as it is for whites. Thus, according to this thesis, affirmative action preferences are nothing more than "reverse discrimination."

The liberal symmetry thesis insists that the color- and difference-blind treatment of individuals that would obtain in an ideally just society be instituted now, in total disregard for the way in which the current system of white, male privilege continues to discriminate against women and nonwhites. Insisting that people be treated exactly the same way who are in fact positioned differently with respect to racial discrimination, however, is a recipe for unjust—and unequal—treatment. Giroux himself concedes as much. Hence, his symmetry thesis does not insist on sameness of treatment for whites and nonwhites across the board but only with respect to the possibility of having a positive, antiracist racial identity.

It seems to me that Giroux fails to appreciate how deeply asymmetries in racial positioning render even his own symmetry thesis problematic. Regardless of what one thinks about the legitimacy (or lack thereof) of subjective racial identifications in an ideal world, they are (at least arguably) legitimate for nonwhites struggling to combat the current regime of white privilege. Racial identification on the part of African Americans and other oppressed racial minorities is an important means for counteracting self-defeating racial stereotypes. It is all the more so when the racial identification in question is purged of any essentialist and deterministic connotations, as no less a defender of racial identity as Du Bois himself noted.[16]

Even when the racial identification in question is not so enlightened, it might still reflect a legitimate response to negative racial stereotypes. Indeed, I would go so far as to say that the reverse racism advanced by some black nationalists is—however deplorable—partly excusable as a nonaggressive, purely defensive reaction to white racism. The white supremacists' claim that their racism is just as defensive and excusable neglects, once again, the basic asymmetry between whites and nonwhites. White racism more often elicits aggressive behavior on the part of its adherents than does black racism; and even when it does not, the "defensive" mode in which it is expressed carries the weight of a backlash threat that is far greater than any danger posed to whites by black racism, given the overwhelming economic, social, and political domination whites currently exercise over blacks.

In short, systemic racial asymmetries provide oppressed racial minorities with more compelling reasons (moral as well as psychological) for embracing a positive racial identity. There simply exists no equivalent motivation for whites, misplaced feelings of victimization notwithstanding. But perhaps there is a different but no less legitimate motivation. Let us leave aside the questionable view that whites are psychologically compelled to identify racially on pain of denying some natural impulse. One might argue, following Giroux, that the emergence of a narrow kind of SP identity politics has made it imperative that sympathetic whites refashion their racial identity in some positive way. Without such an identity, Giroux fears, sympathetic whites will simply position themselves as the enemy, and, helpless to alter the fact of their privilege, they will withdraw into feelings of guilt and self-abnegation. Aside from the moral dubiousness of such feelings, which stem entirely from a social positioning that is beyond one's control, Giroux raises the discomfiting thought of sympathetic white spectators looking at the struggle against racism from the outside, as it were, without a positive identity that might enable them to politically engage their minority brothers and sisters in antiracist struggle.

Why does Giroux think that sympathetic whites will be incapable of connecting with their minority brothers and sisters unless they do so on the basis of a positive white identity? Far from explaining why, his own pronouncements on the matter suggest other alternatives. If we assume that the kind of identity politics that Giroux finds acceptable is carried on under the banner of inclusive and open, rather than exclusive and closed, ethnic identities—in other words, if we assume that it models ST identity politics—then there is no problem with whites' identifying with minorities rather than with their own whiteness (as hooks and Ignatiev urge). Or—to take a different tack—perhaps all that is necessary for whites to engage in sympathetic antiracist struggle is a deep understanding of the psychosocial dynamics of stereotyping, in-group/out-group interaction, and their own racial positioning, including an understanding of the complex genealogy of the racial system in which that positioning occurs. In that case, whites can understand that the system positions them as white without identifying with whiteness as such.

As for addressing the problem of white guilt, educators need to point out to their white students that they are not responsible for creating the system of white racial privilege. Of course, feelings of guilt should accompany racist acts and other moral boundary violations; and feelings of personal shame should accompany our failure to interrupt racist acts and perhaps also our failure to resist racial privilege by not actively supporting affirmative action and other similar policies. Beyond that, we as Americans should all feel collective shame for the enormous gap that exists between our nation's professed ideals of equal respect for all and our current laws, practices, and institutions.

I have argued that antiracist pedagogy need not (and should not) play on white students' guilt about being white. Indeed, in struggling against racism there are many positive nonracial identities whites can embrace—religious, secular-humanist, and civic patriotic. However, before leaving the topic of racial symmetry, it would behoove us to look at another example of how some whites have sought to develop a positive racial identity, namely, through the formation of European American clubs on junior high and high school campuses. Although I suspect that the formation of many, if not most, European American clubs reflects a white backlash against the formation of Asian American, Latin American, and African American ethnic clubs,[17] I concede their legitimacy as a possible venue for exploring European languages and cultures. Be that as it may, there remains an important difference between these clubs and their Asian American, Latin American, and African American counterparts that relates to my earlier discussion regarding the asymmetry between whites and nonwhites.

It is tempting to think of European American clubs as symmetrical with these other ethnic clubs. After all, if cultural immersion alone is what these clubs are about, and if all cultures are worthy of equal respect, then what goes for one club should go for all of them. Things look more complicated, however, once we understand that the members of Asian American, Latin American, and African American ethnic clubs are typically members of ethnic groups that have also experienced—and more important, continue to experience—racial discrimination.

If my analysis of the asymmetry between racial identities is correct, then it follows that what might go for Asian American, Latin American, and African American clubs might not go for European American clubs. To begin with, members of ethnic minorities that face continued racial discrimination might be expected to have a heightened sense of their racial identity. Hence, their legitimate concerns will include issues pertaining to this identity that go well beyond issues of culture. By contrast, a similar racial awareness is inappropriate for members of European American clubs. For while all exclusive identities are misleading fictions and, for that very reason, morally questionable, they are less questionable when held by those who have suffered discrimination because of them.

It is thus understandable that members of oppressed ethnic or racial minorities might exclude others (especially members of the oppressor group) from their club, if doing so facilitates the unconstrained formation of that club's political consciousness (the same rationale is available to women who exclude men from participating in rape-awareness events, spousal abuse counseling, and other consciousness-raising group activities). No comparable exclusion—and no comparable SP identity politics—should attend the membership policies of European American clubs. Of course, not so long ago many ethnic Europeans faced systematic racial discrimination, but today these same groups are positioned as "white" vis-a-vis many Asian Americans, Latin Americans, and African Americans (cf. notes 11, 17). Because they lack a compelling nonracist reason for engaging in identity politics, European American clubs should function simply as cultural clubs and nothing more.

RACIAL ETHNICITY/ETHNIC RACE

As I noted earlier, Giroux's belief that progressive whites should be given the opportunity to refashion a positive white identity mainly stems from his concern that, without such an identity, whites will be excluded from engaging in antiracist identity politics. However, his postmodern thesis, (c), renders this concern null and void, to the degree that it undermines the exclusiveness of ethnic and racial identities. Once this thesis is embraced, SP identity politics evolves into ST identity politics; and the conflict between mutually self-contained and opposed identities becomes a dialogue between multipositioned individuals.

More radically, however, the thesis renders any concept of racial and ethnic identity problematic. To avoid any misunderstanding on this point, let me begin by noting that members of groups need not expressly identify themselves as sharing a distinct racial or ethnic identity. They may simply identify themselves as persons who happen to live together, do roughly the same things, or are treated by others in a certain way. Only when groups are confronted with other groups whom they view as significantly different from themselves do they create racial or ethnic in-group/out-group distinctions. More precisely, only when groups feel threatened by other groups (or set themselves over and against them) do they feel the need to justify their way of life to themselves. From this moment on, members of groups so challenged might begin to construct—consciously if not deliberately—one ethnic/racial/national identity for themselves and another for the other.[18]

There is nothing inherent in the notion of a group identity that requires its transmissibility or heritability. Members of voluntary associations share an identity that is transmissible only through voluntary consent (between them and between prospective members). Nonetheless, members of ethnic and racial groups typically hold that their respective racial and ethnic identities are not a matter of choice but are determined entirely by biological descent. More precisely, the commonly accepted view is that one might lose one's ethnic identity by ceasing to consciously identify with one's inherited ethnicity, but one could never acquire an ethnic identity of any sort save the one that corresponded to one's inherited ethnicity. To be sure, this deterministic view of ethnic identity is relaxed in some cases, depending on the group in question. As I noted in my discussion of the black Seminoles, many aboriginal peoples did not regard biological descent as integral to their identity (with adoption of outsiders into the tribe being rather common). Orthodox Jews, by contrast, are generally loath to recognize non-Orthodox Jews as fully Jewish and are hesitant to recognize adopted non-Jews into the fold. Despite this variability, members of most ethnic groups probably believe that their birth parents' possession of the corresponding identity is a necessary condition for their possession of it as well. For example, an Irish American who decided to acculturate himself into Polish culture in a way that rendered him virtually indistinguishable from one who had been brought up in that culture would not normally be characterized as ethnically Polish. And yet there are more problematic cases that render this presumption premature. If our Irish American had been adopted at birth by Polish immigrants and acquired his Polish acculturation that way, it would seem odd to describe him as Irish American. This oddness suggests that neither the biological nor the geographical origin of one's birth parents is essential to determining one's ethnic classification. If our Irish American eventually became aware of his birth parents, he might wish to claim an Irish American identity, and that in turn might influence how others chose to classify him. But if he claimed a Polish American identity, others would likely accede to that claim as well.

I don't wish to overgeneralize this case of ethnic classification and identification. If our Irish American had African ancestry, the peculiarities of the one-drop rule might incline some to classify him as black (or African American) regardless of his own preferences to the contrary, although given the peculiar politics of identity surrounding race relations in this country, he might also come to consciously embrace that identity as an expression of solidarity with blacks.[19] The interesting question is how far one's own preferences can determine how one is classified by others. In the above example, it might seem that being raised by Polish American parents determines the Polish American identity of the adopted child, which in turn constrains others to classify him accordingly. But what difference should being raised Polish by ethnic Poles have to do with one's ethnic identity? What is decisive about ethnic identity is conscious identification with a particular cultural group and its language; the manner of acquiring the identification seems utterly irrelevant.[20]

I raise this point because conceptual distinctions between ethnicity and race—in contrast to American distinctions between ethnic and racial groups—are at best relative.[21] Ethnicity, like race, is traditionally understood by folk psychology in a racial way, as consisting partly of physical traits that are passed down from birth parent to child (hence the racial depiction of Jews, Italians, the Irish, and others, in American folk ethnography); conversely, race is traditionally understood ethnically, as consisting partly of cultural folkways. Indeed, as we have seen, what is common to both ethnicity and race in American folk ethnography is the idea of a relatively permanent nature that is generally inherited.[22] Now, if the distinction between ethnicity and race is relative, the above counterexamples to descent-based notions of ethnicity should also apply to race—being that they are examples that show how ethnic classification can just as easily be a function of ethnic self-identification (ethnic identity). Because ethnic identity (and ethnicity) is capable of being acquired rather than inherited, so is racial identity (and race). Anglo-American youth's voluntarily identifying with African American ethnic culture and voluntarily identifying themselves as black confirms this.

If most Americans resist the idea that Anglo-Americans could be black, it is because they are beholden to the dominant "racialist" understanding of race and ethnicity, which presumes that both are ultimately about heritable destiny rather than voluntary acculturation. On this view, children born of Irish American parents who are adopted by Polish immigrants and acculturated into Polish culture remain Irish American, regardless of their identity. But this view is self-defeating. For by defining race and ethnicity in terms of origin, we end up with the result—given the common descent of the species out of Africa—that there is ultimately only one race. Attempts to avoid the implications of monodescent by referring race and ethnicity to something other than endogenous origins—for instance, by defining them in terms of a more recent geographical locus of descent—end up denying these concepts the very intrinsicality that folk psychology imputes to them.[23]

The postmodern condition, however, raises a deeper question about the very meaning of ethnic and racial identity when all that remains are multiple and individually elective points of identification. To appreciate the force of this point consider, once again, the way in which ethnicity is traditionally conceived in racial terms. For instance, consider the way in which white supremacists have caught on to the allure of identity politics and have begun to defend racial segregation on multicultural grounds. Despite their attempt to link whiteness to Anglo-American, European, or some other "ethnicity," it is clear that whiteness for them is essentially not a cultural phenomenon. Of course, Afrikaners living in Orania appeal to Dutch Afrikaner culture, rather than race, as grounds for demanding that their exclusive white community (including the contiguous strip of land that continues west along the Orange River) be declared a separate tribal homeland, on par with other tribal homelands that have been granted special cultural rights under the South African constitution. However, their resistance to a new political redistricting plan that amalgamates Orania with Hopetown and the nearby black community of Strydenburg shows that their appeal to cultural difference is disingenuous at several levels. First, many if not most of the black and colored inhabitants who live in these outlying regions speak Afrikaans and share the Afrikaner's Protestant work ethic, as summarized in their new credo that "Our own labor makes us free." Yet these inhabitants continue to be harassed whenever they try to enter Orania. Second, the appeal to cultural difference is itself a racial appeal insofar as it is made on behalf of some essential, heritable identity that demarcates a rigid boundary separating in-groups from out-groups.

Interestingly, many persons who oppose the Oranians' white racism come dangerously close to buying into their logic of identity. Writing in *Race Trai-*

tor, Christine Sleeter maintains that whiteness has come to mean "ravenous materialism, competitive individualism, and a way of living characterized by putting acquisition of possessions ahead of humanity." Although she herself concedes that "one need not be of European descent to participate in such a way of living," she still insists that "Black South Africans have difficulty learning white culture" because "it is a way of living that people of European descent constructed and sell, and one that we are persistently socialized to identify with and support."[24]

Sleeter might be right that black South Africans have difficulty learning English and Dutch culture. Some black South Africans probably do resist this culture as a colonial remnant. Others who want to learn it have difficulty doing so because of the residual racism of the Dutch and English. Finally, many—like most of us—simply have difficulty learning any new culture. In any case, if they are resisting it because they think that culture is not a part of their inherited identity, they might be in more agreement with the Oranians and their racial concept of culture than they would perhaps like to think. Also—ironically—in agreement with them might be Sleeter herself, who, despite her proper rejection of racial thinking, needs to explain how her own apparent equation of competitive individualism and materialism with white European culture implies that it would be wrong for black South Africans to betray their cultural identity by adopting the alien ways of the West. To cite Zack (1993, 153), "What is so important about the past as a source of identity[?] . . . How can one have a debt or answerability to people and to situations that no longer exist?"

We've come full circle. Perhaps the only way to erase all vestiges of racial thinking is to abandon the notion that cultures rest on some ethnic identity or memory that gets passed down intact in some pure, uncontaminated form from generation to generation. For those who insist that they share an identity with others, we remind them that this identity can be nothing more than a loose overlapping of experiences, perspectives, beliefs, practices, and understandings. For those who insist that their identity is discovered rather than chosen, we remind them that acculturation is not something passively suffered but something remembered, and, as such, it requires a continuous and active effort of inventive appropriation and interpretation. Whatever debt we owe to past generations is not a debt that can be repaid in slavish conformity to an inherited identity; it can only be repaid in keeping alive the memory of suffering and sacrifice, and that means renarrating and reinventing our histories. For those who insist otherwise, we remind them that determination by the other—be it for the sake of preserving the group or for the sake of policing society's boundaries—is domination when not undertaken voluntarily and mutually with the other, and, like all domination, it must be actively resisted.

CULTURE AS RACIAL IDENTITY

So far I have argued that any attempt to resurrect a legitimate conception of ethnic identity must reject what is typically thought to be a necessary condition of having such an identity, namely, (a) descent from one who already has the identity and (b) acculturation into a well-defined set of practices and beliefs that are impervious to individual variation. Ethnic identity, so construed, is simply shorthand for diverse, shifting subject positions, or individually tailored, contextually situated ways of appropriating from a relatively inexhaustible stock of beliefs, practices, and other modes of cultural understanding.

In his fourth thesis, (d), Giroux proposes to reduce whiteness, understood as a kind of ethnic identity, to a similar stock of beliefs, practices, and modes of understanding. I argue to the contrary that it is misleading to think of whiteness in this way. Whiteness is not a culture, and thinking it is misleads us into imagining that it might be worthy of equal respect alongside other ethnic cultures. If whiteness can be said to designate anything remotely like a culture (belief system, practice, or mode of understanding), it is one so intermeshed with a structure of domination as to be unworthy of respect and positive identification.

The concept of culture is doubtless vague. For simplicity's sake, I regard the term as consisting in any of the following: beliefs, practices, artifacts, languages, and modes of understanding. When Giroux speaks of whiteness as a new ethnic identity, we must understand him to mean an identity that revolves around one or more of these cultural constituents.

In what sense can whiteness be said to designate a set of beliefs? Persons classified as white do not, as a whole, share any beliefs that define them as a group. This condition, however, applies as well to persons classified as belonging to other ethnic and racial groups. Even ethnic groups that are closely identified with a religious affiliation (Jews, for instance) are not characterized by uniform adherence to any defining beliefs (witness, for example, the case of Jewish atheists and Jewish born-again Christians). By contrast, peer groups often require that their members swear allegiance to specific creeds. Here, we find a sense in which whiteness does designate a group belief or attitude, namely, the belief in white superiority (or white victimization) that solidifies defensive, reactionary whites.

Perhaps Giroux might have better luck locating a nonracist concept of white culture in practices. Here again, the same difficulty that attended the equation of ethnicity with beliefs attends the equation of ethnicity and practices. Unless one defines practices very broadly to include linguistic practices, the equation fails. The capacity to speak a certain language can hardly be considered a necessary condition for identifying with an ethnic culture.

Children born of Mexican immigrants and raised in English-speaking environments may speak only a little Spanish (much less than someone born of non-Spanish-speaking parents), and yet they may identify strongly with other aspects of Mexican culture. Engaging in shared practices and rituals, however, is sometimes a necessary (and perhaps sufficient) condition for membership in certain peer groups. For instance, shunning minorities, uttering racist epithets, and acting on negative racial stereotypes is de rigueur among white racists.

Although it might be appropriate to speak of whiteness as designating the set of racist beliefs and practices held by white racists, such a limited conception of "white culture" seems far removed from what Giroux intends by whiteness, understood as an ethnic category ascribable to whites as a whole, including nonracist whites. In speaking of whiteness as an ethnic category, Giroux seems to have in mind a more elusive conception of culture: that of a mode of understanding. A mode of understanding encapsulates many things: a subconscious yet omnipresent way of perceiving and interpreting the world; a set of taken-for-granted norms that often insinuates itself in the form of habits and reflexes rather than explicitly acknowledged rules; a tacit "know-how" and practical familiarity with things. Philosophers from Heidegger and Wittgenstein to Bourdieu and Foucault have typically conceived such a mode of understanding as a necessary condition for having any kind of experience at all. It constitutes the background set of assumptions, the framework of possible relationships, and the prior mapping of coordinates, in terms of which all our particular experiences and expectations of people and things are highlighted, foregrounded, and situated in a space of potential meaningfulness.

Ethnic cultures are often said to embody distinctive modes of understanding, typically characterized as ways of life or ways of being. Of course, once these ways of life are transposed to the postmodern register, they cease to designate perfectly uniform assumptions. As Hans-Georg Gadamer (1975) has so forcefully argued, our "horizons" of understanding are constantly open to new experiences and to fresh encounters with different horizons of understanding, whether we will it so or not. Moreover, because my horizon of experience is uniquely situated with respect to my immediate situation, my understanding of things will always be different from anyone else's. That said, however, the fact that the situation and position I occupy has much in common with (or overlaps) others who have suffered the same experiences as I have means that my horizon of understanding will have much in common with theirs as well—so much so that we might, with appropriate qualification, talk about our sharing a common perspective or mode of understanding. In this respect, it is not stretching things to say that African Americans who grow up in a white supremacist society such as the United States share a common experience and perspective born of discrimination and oppression. As W. E. B. Du Bois remarked a century ago in *The Souls of Black Folk* (1903), who among black folk have not acquired a "double consciousness" of experiencing themselves and their world through the double lens of the oppressor and the oppressed (Du Bois [1903] 1997, 45)?

If it makes sense to talk about a distinctive black perspective (suitably individualized and contextualized), then why not talk about a distinctive white perspective? If we are hesitant to do so, is it because whites as a group seem infinitely more diverse in their experience and acculturation than blacks? It might be argued that the existence of de jure and de facto segregation throughout the history of the black diaspora in North America has led to the emergence of distinctive African American ethnic styles that have no obvious parallel in the case of whites; but this would be mistaken. Each European American ethnic group generated its own racial perspectives based on its own racial experiences. These perspectives have gradually ceased to reflect differences in education and socioeconomic attainment between them; as European Americans assimilated, their former racial–ethnic consciousness receded. In its place, and motivated in part by an antiblack backlash, a new European American identity (and subidentities) has emerged that centers on the myth that all "ethnic" groups face the same discrimination (cf. note 17). Although this "identity" hardly designates a culture shared by all European Americans, it does designate a reactionary mode of understanding shared by many of them, as recent studies by Kinder and Sanders (1996) fully attest.

Because this new ethnic identity is not generally accepted by all European Americans, it cannot function as a locus of shared identity among them. Is there a mode of understanding that can? Perhaps. Complementary to the "double consciousness" that informs blacks' self-understanding is the mode of understanding of persons who do not have to worry about being discriminated against because of their skin color, who can view the world around them as a sea of open opportunity, and who, because of their privileged position, can universalize this "color-blind" experience as normative for all social relations. If whiteness designates a generalized understanding, it is nothing more, nor nothing less, than the obliviousness of whites to their own privilege (indeed, obliviousness to race is part of the privilege).

Whites can become aware of their privilege. Becoming so, however, eliminates neither the privilege nor the obliviousness of it—at least not entirely. Like most ingrained parts of one's being, whiteness functions subconsciously unless explicitly challenged—contra Memmi (2000, 56), it need not be consciously intended. For most whites, unless they interact with nonwhites on a routine basis, the assumption of privilege is not challenged. While whites are interacting with other whites, the privilege remains largely invisible to them.

Giroux's problem, however, concerns the peculiar dilemma faced by whites who have become aware of their privilege as an identity-shaping force. What would it mean for progressive whites to identify with their whiteness? When blacks identify with their blackness, celebrating its beauty and power, they are engaging in a political act: the dispelling of negative stereotypes. Nothing comparable to this happens when whites identify with their whiteness, for whites live in a world in which their beauty and power is the norm. Again, when blacks talk about their identity as an oppressed group that has been forced to internalize the depreciatory gaze of the other, there remains the potential for positive identification. Out of the experience of oppression and divided consciousness is born (as Hegel taught) a critical self-awareness and with it, an emancipatory consciousness that aspires to mutual concern and compassion with one's fellow human beings in a world without taint of privilege. When progressive whites talk about their way of life as members of an oppressor group that has been acculturated into privilege and obliviousness, there remains nothing for them to identify positively with. At best, they can (and should) trace the genealogy of their whiteness from the standpoint of their own subject position, suitably situated with respect to class, gender, and nationality. This is an exercise that calls for cold analysis and explanation, not warm, empathetic identification. As Ruth Frankenberg astutely notes (1997) the "slipperiness" of whiteness with respect to those who have considered themselves or have been considered by others as "borderline white"—from "white trash" poor to European immigrants (especially from Southern and Eastern Europe)—suggests that whiteness is at bottom not a cultural self-designation at all. More precisely, "although ostensibly marked by the clearly distinguishable behaviors or characteristics of self-designated selves, and of others named as such by those self-designators just mentioned, whiteness turns out on closer inspection to be more about the power to include and exclude groups and individuals more than about the actual practices of those who are to be let in or kept out" (13).

If Frankenberg is right that whiteness is ultimately about the power to include and exclude potentially anyone from privilege for whatever reason, then maybe we should reconsider our minimalist conception of whiteness as a mode of understanding. Heeding Foucault's advice against cultural idealism in this particular instance would mean regarding whiteness as an objective yet infinitely malleable structure of exclusions embedded in language, practice, and "technologies of the self." As a system of power relations, whiteness would still function like a mode of understanding, but it would not as such be consciously reflected in our self-understanding so much as structure it unconsciously from the outside. So construed, whiteness would cease to designate anything that one could possibly identify with, except in the reactionary senses mentioned here.

INTEGRATION, SEGREGATION, AND SEPARATION: THE DILEMMAS OF SP IDENTITY POLITICS

I would like to conclude my discussion of whiteness by touching on the moral perils that attend conceiving whiteness as an ethnicity, ethnic identity, or culture. The greatest peril is that in today's multicultural politics of identity and recognition whiteness will be seen as meriting the same respect accorded to other ethnic cultures. (As I noted earlier, this danger manifests itself even when it is done under the banner of celebrating European ethnic pride, which is often just a euphemism for white pride.) This, of course, would entirely conceal the sinister aspects of whiteness that differentiate it from otherwise respectable ethnic cultures.

Unfortunately, as we have seen, the virtual indistinguishability of race and ethnicity poses dangers of an altogether different sort. The defense of multiculturalism and the promotion of SP identity politics can be prosecuted under the guise of racial (biological) thinking. And it can be done in ways that initially seem quite plausible. For instance, it might be argued that culture—an acknowledged good—only thrives in the form of diversity. It can then be argued that diverse cultures thrive only when cultivated in their integrity, that is, only when maintained by specific groups that reproduce themselves in their integrity. From that premise it follows that ethnic groups should try to maintain their biological purity by not encouraging interethnic marriage for fear that it will result in their dissolution.

Numbers count. As we have seen in the case of Native American and other aboriginal microcultures, when tribal populations are depleted, displaced, or simply assimilated, their respective cultures often die out. Sad as this may be—it represents a loss of cultural knowledge and, along with it, potentials for future learning and adaptation—I would strenuously argue against those who would save these tribes by urging eugenic solutions. To begin with, cultures, like life forms, come into existence and pass away for reasons that have nothing to do with environmental carelessness and (in the case of Native Americans) willful genocide. In and of themselves, such natural and cultural events need pose no palpable threat to the good of species or the world.

I do not wish to be understood as saying that defending cultural groups against cultural imperialism is unwarranted, but I hardly think that biological policing is an acceptable method for doing so. In any case, the greater concern is not over any isolated instance of cultural imperialism but over the emergence of a global monoculture, fueled perhaps by the exigencies of mass consumption and mass production inherent in a global capitalist economy.

I will leave it to those wiser than me to argue over whether today's global economy encourages uniformity or diversity. The point is that most everyone thinks that cultural diversity is a good thing. Assuming that cultural diversity is a good thing, would it not likely be compromised with the disintegration of ethnic groups through interethnic coupling? For example, in a fully integrated United States much that is associated with the ethnic culture of segregated African American urban communities might not survive—for instance, the culture of spiritual overcoming that is cultivated in African American churches. If it did survive, it would most certainly be transfigured. Forged in the crucible of slavery and segregation, African American spirituality might continue to flourish as a universal tradition to which all peoples might identify. To some extent, its expression of suffering, resistance, and spiritual redemption—so movingly conveyed in Negro spirituals—has already achieved this status, along with jazz and the civil rights movement. Thus, cultural remnants are not necessarily drained of vitality by being detached from their ancestral carriers and mixed with "new blood." Indeed, cultural traditions are as likely to grow as diminish in validity and authority through such mixing, as can be seen in the case of the great world religions.

In sum, there is no evidence to show that a culture once associated with a particular ethnic group cannot survive the passing away of that group. In a fully just and emancipated world, people might still be attracted to people who are like themselves, although evidence that they will—based on past history—is notably unreliable, given the role that racism, ethnocentrism, and religious intolerance have played in mate selection. Integration—understood as the elimination of intergenerational communities with distinctive racial and cultural identities—might not be ideal, or at least it might not be the only ideal. Besides integration and legal segregation, there is voluntary separatism based on positive attraction of those who think, act, talk, and (yes) look alike. Such "identity separatism" is benign, so long as it is based on attraction to those who are like oneself, rather than on hatred of those who are different from oneself. The boundaries of distinctive communities of identity should not be policed; otherwise, association and disassociation cease to be voluntary. However, all of these reflections about benign intergenerational communities of identity will be rendered moot if current patterns of migration keep pace with global economic dislocations. For in that case we can expect that persons will be marrying people who are very unlike themselves. If so, ethnorace and SP identity politics might become a thing of the past.

NOTES

I am grateful to my colleague and partner, Jennifer Parks, for her useful suggestions in revising this chapter. I am also grateful to Naomi Zack and Kory Schaff for providing extensive criticism of an earlier draft of it. The chapter reflects a revision of the view I defended in *Group Rights* (2000a), which, while properly taking note of the distinction between ethnic and racial groups in the United States, failed to stress the conceptual equivalence of race and ethnicity. Consequently, I now feel less compelled to defend the existence of ethnic groups as necessary conditions for cultural diversity in an ideal (in my opinion, raceless) society.

NOTES

1. That biological descent is integral to the idea of the race concept is disputable. Biological conceptions of race are of relatively recent vintage, with some accounts dating their emergence as late as the nineteenth century. The extremely deterministic conception associated with the one-drop rule that emerged in the United States as late as the mid-nineteenth century today mainly survives in the biologically attenuated form of hypodescent, in which offspring of racially mixed couples are assigned the racial status of the parent bearing the most socially subordinate racial status. Thus, when the census bureau counts offspring of mixed "black" and "white" parentage as black, no presumption of biological determinism is at play, because the motivation for the classification is political or customary, rather than ontological. Moreover, even when biological conceptions of race are invoked, the degree of determinism implicated may vary considerably (for instance, Nazi race criteria allowed persons of Jewish ancestry to become officially non-Jewish if their ancestors had dropped their Jewish surnames for four generations). Yet, however obvious it may be for us to think of race as designating a biological essence, the tendency among some societies—both modern and premodern—to form nonbiologically designated racial stereotypes grounded in geographical, cultural, or economic–occupational causes points to a more primitive psychological dynamic. Combined with evidence showing that children learn to categorize people into races independently of forming biological conceptions of race, these facts strongly suggest that biological racial categorization is a subset of racial categorization and that racial categorization is a culture-specific subset of naturalizing (or essentializing) social differentiation that is common to all societies (Hirschfeld 1996, 197–98). Not only do broader conceptions of race better enable us to explain the genesis of distinctly modern, biological senses of race from premodern, nonbiological antecedents, but they help us to understand the psychological durability of racial categories even in the decline of biologically informed racism. Admittedly, conceiving of them in this broad way renders them less distinct from other social categories. Perhaps what distinguishes racial categories from other social categories that are commonly conceived essentialistically, such as gender, is that the former refer to groups that are able to reproduce by themselves, as independent populations (Hirschfeld 1996, 197–98). For arguments defending a broader definition of race, see Memmi (2000, 78, 97); for arguments defending a narrow, biological conception of race, see Appiah (2000, viii).

2. It scarcely needs mentioning that systems of racial classification are historically specific and diverse. Some are explicitly racist in their functioning, and some, such as those found in modern anthropology, are not. Racial systems can be more or less complete, well-formed, and uniform. Ideally, a racial system would contain uniformly ap-

plied, clear-cut rules for assigning every individual an unambiguous racial identity. But this is a condition that no racial system—scientific or otherwise—has ever fully satisfied. Any given racial system typically appeals to multiple and conflicting criteria of classification, ranging from somatic appearance and birth descent to cultural attribution and self-identification (Zack 1993). Even the one-drop rule used to classify blacks in the United States, which comes as close as any criterion for specifying a clear-cut basis for distinguishing blacks from whites, contradicts the common (African) origin of the human species and the subsequent spreading out and remixing of racial groups.

To complicate our taxonomy, one should also distinguish between objective and subjective senses of race (Mills 1998). Objectivism conceives race as existing independently of personal beliefs and decisions. One kind of objectivism holds that race designates a hidden essence (typically biological) that is necessarily transmitted from parent to child in the form of distinct physical (and perhaps moral-cognitive) attributes. The other kind of objectivism (also known as social constructivism) denies that race refers to any biological reality, holding instead that race designates an intersubjectively recognized, publicly institutionalized system of social norms. More precisely, objectivism of this sort holds that race designates a culturally selected way of constructing physical (and perhaps cultural) characteristics into racial types. Using evidence from modern genetics, race theorists view racial characteristics as nothing more than arbitrarily chosen sets of physical traits that statistically predominate among relatively closed breeding populations. Barely 0.012 percent of any person's genetic endowment accounts for racially identified physical traits—a percentage that is far less than the percentage of genetic endowment that distinguishes any two persons who happen to share the same racial traits (Dubinin 1965, 61–67). Given the fact that each of us is the product of a mixed genealogy dating back to the origin of the species and beyond, and given the fact that the genes that determine physical characteristics are both isolable and recombinable, racial characteristics never occur together in any pure sense and are never passed down whole and intact from one generation to the next. Consequently, the only reality to which race might refer is an artificial system of social classifications that, like any social norm, can be criticized, resisted, reinterpreted, and overturned by active, self-aware subjects. To the degree that such resistance becomes trenchant and general, racial identification loses its objectivity and becomes subjective, that is, subject to conscious choice.

3. I agree with Memmi (2000, 50, 83) that such expressions of pride can be motivated by illegitimate racial (and racist) stereotypes designating a reverse hyperbolic evaluation. However deplorable they might be, such illegitimate evaluations on the part of oppressed people are a natural reaction to negative stereotyping on the part of the oppressors and may be morally excused to the extent that they enhance the solidarity of the oppressed and thereby indirectly promote the end of racial stereotyping in the long run.

4. There exists a vast literature on the topic of whiteness. The concept has been used to designate a variety of phenomena, from white supremacist ideologies and movements to unconscious structures of privilege and power. In every instance, what is designated by the concept is something that is dynamic and historically variable.

Frankenberg (1993) has taken this analysis a step further by exploring the gendered tropes that have underwritten the historical construction of a distinctly American white sensibility:

> White Woman is frail, vulnerable, delicate, sexually pure. . . . White Man is strong, dominant arbiter of truth, and self-designated protector of white womankind, defender of nation/territory. . . . Man of Color . . . is sexually rapacious, sometimes seductive, usually predatory, especially toward White Woman . . . and Woman of Color is also sexually eager, seductress, willing and able consort, especially for the White Man of this tropological family, personally unhygienic, overly fertile, but also usable for breeding, when this is beneficial to White Man, and for tending white children and adults, again when beneficial to White Man or White Woman. (11–12)

5. Ruth Frankenberg (1997, 18) cites the following passage, contained in a handout distributed by the Center for the Study of White American Culture (245 West Fourth Avenue, Roselle, NJ 07203), as exemplifying the difficulty of generating an "anti-racist practice of whiteness" that doesn't implicitly collude in a white backlash: "Some of our issues [as white Americans] are unique. While minority cultures have struggled to obtain power, white Americans must struggle to share the power we have. While minority cultures have struggled to retain their autonomy, white Americans must struggle to make our culture exist without dominating other cultures. We need to develop a public discussion of issues that apply uniquely to us as white Americans in a multicultural America."

6. Lott (1996, 109n51) cites the example of the white rap group Young Black Teenagers, "who explain their appropriation of this title (along with such tunes as 'Proud to be Black' and 'Daddy Kalled Me Niga Cause I Likeded to Rhyme') as an expression of their having grown up in a predominantly black youth culture in New York City.

7. Although there is no conceptual difference between ethnicity and race when viewed scientifically, there are considerable differences between ethnic groups and racial groups within the American context. Historically, the concept of ethnicity first emerged in the writings of American sociologists during the thirties to describe the different populations that immigrated from Eastern and Southern Europe to the United States around the turn of the century—populations that we commonly associate with such expressions as Italian American, Polish American, and so on. The concept was later used by historians to describe the European nationalist movements of the nineteenth and twentieth centuries. Accordingly, this use of the concept was extended to include irredentist groups—such as the German-speaking communities living in France, Poland, Czechoslovakia, and Yugoslavia, whose presence threatened the European balance of power during the thirties—and to other oppressed and disaffected subcultures and subnationalities, including today's Tamals (Indonesia); Kurds (Turkey, Iran, and Iraq); Chechens (Russia); Hutus and Tutsis (Rwanda and Burundi); and Croats, Albanians, and Bosnian Muslims (former Yugoslavia).

Only in the last forty years or so has "ethnicity" been widely used in a more generic sense to refer to cultural groups in general, including African Americans and Native Americans, whose histories are vastly different from American immigrant and national groups. As racial minorities who suffered unique forms of dehumanization, African Americans and Native Americans were only belatedly encouraged to assimilate into mainstream white society. Indeed, while European immigrant groups often lived in separate communities, their skin pigmentation made it easier for them to cross over to the "white" side of the color line; unburdened by the legacy of slavery and possessing full-fledged European ancestry, they eventually escaped the harshest effects of the American race system. By the end of World War II, Jews and Asian Americans had also managed to cross the race barrier, despite the fact that they continued to be stereotyped in quasi-racial ways (cf. Marable 2000).

8. The one-drop rule continues to function in the 2000 census proposal, for counting minorities recently entered into the federal register before President Clinton left office. The 2000 census forms, and other documents requesting information about racial membership, indiscriminately list cultural and geographical categories, such as Asian Indian, Chinese, and Native Hawaiian, alongside racial categories such as African American/Black/Negro and White. The new Census 2000 forms seem to jettison older, essentialist conceptions of race and ethnic identity—for instance, persons will now be permitted to identify themselves in accordance with more than one racial category (up to six) and either Hispanic or non-Hispanic, thereby generating 126 combinations; however, the very fact that those who identify themselves as both "white" and "nonwhite" in accordance with one or more minority categories will still be counted as "minorities" shows that the old one-drop rule has not been jettisoned. Interestingly, the NAACP and other major civil rights organizations advocated retaining separate racial and ethnic categories using this rule—against the inclusion of a "multiracial" or "mixed race" category. Persons declaring themselves multiracial, they feared, would not have been counted as minorities, and this, in turn, would have led to a reduction in funding for civil rights enforcement and social benefits targeting minorities, as well as a reduction of minority-designated legislative districts. Although a preliminary study conducted by the Census Bureau showed that very few respondents select more than one racial category once Latinos are *not* identified as a distinct racial group, the fact that children of interracial families have grown from fewer than one-half million in 1970 to about two million in 1990 (not counting mixed couplings involving Latinos) suggests that persons' preferences for some kind of multiracial self-identification will increase. Disregarding the treatment of hispanics as a separate ethnic group rather than as a racial group (a policy first implemented in 1972), the method of counting proposed by the Clinton administration and favored by the NAACP will continue to reinforce the old racial (and racist) asymmetry that views being "white" as a privileged—pure, undiluted, and untainted—racial identification in comparison to other racial identifications. Besides potentially inflating the number of minority totals beyond the number of people who actually exist—people might be counted more than once for each race they select—the new census form is sure to generate competition between different minorities seeking to claim higher numbers for themselves.

9. Despite the many refinements introduced into the global system of race classification, which was strikingly dichotomous (European/non-European; white/black), different subcategories of European descent did not escape stigmatization as

"black"—at least not entirely. Not only the Irish but Slavs, Mediterraneans, and Jews were viewed as darker than racially superior Anglo-Saxons and Nordics (Ignatiev 1995). Interestingly, blacks today are more likely than whites to view darker-skinned ethnic Europeans (whom they sometimes refer to as "munglos") as black (Zack 1993, 37).

10. Defending a "politics of difference" against charges of promoting an insular, self-interested "identity politics," Iris Young argues that the very concept of group identity is philosophically bankrupt. What members of groups share in common, if anything, is a social positioning that is defined in relation to the social positioning of other groups. Although individuals fashion personal identities for themselves on the basis of social positions that are not of their own making, such identities do not conform to the logic of substantial or intrinsic essence but to that of dynamic and multivalent relationship. Although very little of what goes under the politics of difference involves struggles for mutual recognition and cultural identity pure and simple, Young notes that combatting negative stereotypes and modes of cultural discrimination constitutes a legitimate form of politics that is only poorly captured by the expression "identity politics" (Young 2000b, 99–107).

11. It is estimated that 70 to 80 percent of American blacks have some white ancestry. While the U.S. census data for 1990 suggest that 2 percent of all marriages are mixed race, the same data for 2000 shows that 2.4 percent of all respondents (about 6.8 million of the nation's 281.4 million people) claimed more than one racial descent. This response underrepresents the true extent of racial mixing, since only 4.8 percent of blacks and only 2.5 percent of whites claimed more than one race. This is further confirmed by the fact that, although 48 percent of Hispanics listed themselves as white, only 1.2 percent listed themselves as American Indian and only 2 percent listed themselves as black (42.2 percent designated that they were of "some other race," with many writing in "Hispanic" as a race). These statistics were reported in the *Chicago Tribune*'s main cover story for Tuesday, March 13, 2001.

12. As Hirschfeld notes (1996, 192), "Learning to use kinship terms (by learning who is and who is not a member of one's family), culturally appropriate forms of politesse (in knowing one's own and others' status-group membership), and even mastery of language itself (in which awareness of human collectivities based on gender, relative age, or degree of familiarity between speakers is necessary to selecting the appropriate syntactic or lexical form), all rest on an ability to distinguish and label human groups."

13. Hirschfeld's experiments with children strongly suggest that, far from producing an inductive basis for category generalization, children's perceptions of racial difference are created out of a prior quasi-theoretical understanding of race, conceived in terms of an abstract, nonperceptible principle of immutability, heritability, and intrinsicality. If so, children's conceptual awareness of group differences precedes their visual discrimination of group attributes; thus, young children often express uncertainty about what physical attributes—hair color, skin color, and so forth—determine their racial categorizations (Hirschfield 1996, 138). Only with regard to their relative incapacity to integrate racial concept and physical percept—and not with regard to their implicit understanding of folk principles of racial classification—do young chil-

dren differ from adults. The fact that young children seem to distinguish skin color as being more intrinsic to identity than other heritable features, such as hair color and body build, shows that race is "theorized" by them in ways that are not reducible to simple reasoning about biology or observed similarities and dissimilarities between individuals. This is the case even if they are unable to articulate this distinction as part of their theory; in fact, children who seem to be guided in their identifications by skin color will sometimes cite hair color or some other attribute in making their judgment. Indeed, as Hirschfeld argues, racial categories follow a logic that is highly "domain specific" and quite distinctive from the cognitive logic by which the categories of animal and plant species are generated (the latter reflects a folk logic that is still much more closely tied to environmental and perceptual cues than racial thinking, despite its unscientific oversimplification and "essentializing" of natural kinds; Hirschfeld 1996, 183–85).

14. It is a large question how much children's understanding of race directly reflects adult understanding. In a society like the United States, where ambiguities in racial identification are not tolerated (a direct outcome of the one-drop rule that proved so indispensable to nineteenth-century slaveholders in reproducing their slave holdings), children learn that race is not mixable and that offspring of interracial couples are unequivocally assigned race in accordance with the principle of hypodescent (Hirschfeld 1996, 195). However, children's understanding of race differs from adult's understanding in being less aware of the importance of distinctive physical attributes (cf. note 13); very young children are more likely to view occupational status as no less intrinsic to identity than race: in one of Hirschfeld's experiments involving three-year-olds, occupation was chosen 40 percent of the time in comparison to 45 percent for race in transitive orderings factoring in body build as a third dimension of comparison—although here we see, once again, the role of culture affecting children's expectations, since it is men, not women, whose occupational status children regard as essential (Hirschfeld 1996, 106). In yet another experiment, cultural environment is shown to have an additional impact on the capacity of older children to cognize persons of mixed racial blend; whereas 75 percent of fifth- and sixth-graders attending a largely all-white school in a largely all-white community held a version of the one-drop rule, about an equal percentage of children attending an integrated school in an integrated community rejected it (Hirschfeld 1996, 168–69, 178–79).

15. But traces of the one-drop rule continue to influence the way children of mixed white–black parentage identify themselves and the way in which census data are counted (cf. note 8). As recently as 1986, the Supreme Court let stand a ruling forcing a Louisiana woman who was one-thirty-second African American to be declared legally black (cited in Teresa Wiltz, "Who Defines Race?" in the *Chicago Tribune,* Feb. 26, 1996, sec. 4, 1.)

16. Nowhere is Du Bois's nonessentialism more apparent than in his later assertion that

> the actual ties of heritage between the individuals of [American blacks] vary with the ancestors that they have in common with many others: Europeans and Semites, perhaps Mongolians, certainly Marican Indians. But the physical bond is least and the badge of

color relatively unimportant save as a badge; the real essence of this kinship is its social heritage of slavery; the discrimination and insult; and this heritage binds together not simply the children of Africa, but extends through yellow Asia and into the South seas. (Du Bois [1940] 1975)

For a good discussion of the debate surrounding Du Bois's views regarding the conservation of race, see Lott (1996).

17. Richard Alba (1990) notes that we are now witnessing the emergence of a new ethnic group: "one based on ancestry from anywhere on the European continent" (3). Reviewing census data, Alba shows that by 1950 European ethnicity ceased to have a significant bearing on educational attainment and socioeconomic status. The meaning of ethnicity for persons of European descent has thus been transformed into something purely symbolic: an optional identity in which one can choose to participate; a genealogical concern; or an aesthetic experience shared across ethnic lines (eating ethnic foods, attending ethnic festivals, etc.). Significantly, Alba sharply distinguishes European ethnic groups from their Asian, Latin American, and African American counterparts. European Americans intermarry freely but marry non-Europeans much less often; and (most important), they define their own symbolic ethnic identity in reaction to what they perceive to be the inability of Asians, Hispanics, and African Americans to detach their ethnic identities from educational and socioeconomic deprivation. The new ethnic mythology invented by them—which obscures significant differences among the experiences of various European immigrant groups—is summarized by Alba accordingly: "Our groups too faced prejudice and discrimination; we haven't made it to the top of American society, either, as is shown by our sparse representation at elite levels; and it is not fair to change the rules in midstream" (317).

In short, the new mythology that constitutes the core of an emergent symbolic European ethnic identity overgeneralizes one ethnic paradigm to the point where the peculiar evils of America's racial system, especially as it bears on the fates of African Americans, Native Americans, and Hispanics, is simply ignored. Thus, although race and ethnicity are indistinguishable from a purely scientific point of view, in the United States these categories refer to distinct (if overlapping) paradigms of social order.

18. Among the many who have written at length on the socially constructed nature of national, ethnic, and racial identities, Etienne Balibar and Immanuel Wallerstein have insisted on the crucial function these categories play in sustaining neoliberal global capitalism. In their opinion, racial classifications map onto the axial division of labor in the world economy, the core–periphery antinomy; the system of nations designates the political structure wherein governments compete at the interstate level on behalf of their own people; and ethnic groups specify subgroups and minorities whose occupational differences from one another—often a source of ethnic pride—can be used to legitimate social inequalities generated by the system (1993, 71–85). For a good discussion regarding the construction of ethnic identities in America, see Alba (1990), whose work I discuss in note 17; and Mendieta (1999a; 1999b), who points out that the label "Hispanic" corresponds to no national–ethnic identity. As they note, "Hispanic" ("Latino(a)") first becomes a possible locus for group identification—as distinct from an oppressive stereotype—to the extent that Latin American immigrants

who possess very different national identities begin to experience overlapping forms of discrimination (linguistic, racial, or religious) and thus come to see themselves as having common political interests. The same, of course, applies to persons classified (or self-identified) as Asian American (cf. Lowe 1996) and African American.

19. Why this self-identification shouldn't become criterial for social classification escapes me. However, one reason for resisting such a subjective approach—at least when filling out census forms—is that it undermines progressive policies. For example, allowing whites to classify themselves as black and blacks to classify themselves as white would endanger affirmative action, racial redistricting, and other group-based policies that benefit blacks (although if a significant number of whites began to identify themselves as black on census forms, more resources might be targeted to blacks).

20. Studies conducted by Twine (1997) involving young girls of black–white parentage growing up in predominantly affluent, white suburbs confirms that racial identity shifts in ways that are neither entirely voluntary nor externally imposed. Prior to puberty these girls were treated no differently than their peers and were encouraged by their parents and others to identify themselves as white—or rather, as racially neutral in a homogeneous culture of middle-class consumption and group-detached individualism. Only with the onset of puberty and the experience of discriminatory dating and mating rituals did these girls begin to experience their racial difference as not fully white. For many, this experience was heightened once they began to attend colleges with sizable black-student populations. There, peer pressure, combined with growing awareness of racial identity politics, led many of them to self-consciously identify themselves as black for the first time in their lives.

21. The convergence of race and ethnicity is already implied in the derivation of *race* from the Latin *ratio*, which means, among other things, "chronological order," or *radix*, which refers to lines of descent. Originally applied to animal breeds, the term *race* was not used to designate human types until the beginning of the seventeenth century. Hence, although race is a fairly modern concept, its ancient roots converge with notions of cultural difference, economic caste, and familial descent. The nobleman's concern about guaranteeing the "purity" and legitimacy of his bloodline later resonated in the fears of the nineteenth-century bourgeois about intermingling with members of the working class (British prime minister Disraeli once characterized the middle and lower classes as "two nations" that were "bred by a different breeding") and in Jim Crow antimiscegenation laws designed to maintain racial caste. Likewise, older, hierarchical distinctions between cultural in-groups and out-groups (e.g., between those classified as "true believers" and those classified as "heathens") supported the unequal treatment of "inferior" Indians and Africans by their Christian European "superiors."

Because the Indian and African could always convert, the peculiar economic exploitation to which they were subjected—which was similar to other caste systems in its rigid occupational hierarchies and restrictions on class mobility—needed a new, distinctly racial justification that, in effect, grafted older cultural hierarchies (of moral worth and intellectual capacity) and newer class hierarchies onto hierarchies of descent. In turn, these hierarchies were conveniently correlated with a fourth system of physical types that could be visibly distinguished for easy monitoring. By the nineteenth century, this racial scheme—which distinguished European from non-European—was superimposed on different European subnationalities, thereby generating new ideologies of national superiority. For further discussion of the genealogy of race and racism, see Memmi (2000), Zack (1993), Pagden (1995), Flandrin (1979), Stoler (1989), and Hannaford (1996).

22. However, if one were to designate a feature of race and ethnicity that is common to all folk ethnographies, it would be intrinsicality rather than heritability. Seventeenth-century French speculations about interracial contamination caused by breast-feeding; eighteenth-century worries about the racial degeneration of Europeans transplanted to the savage environment of North America (later repeated in Conrad's *Heart of Darkness*); and the conversion of Jews and heathens via a miraculous (divinely mediated) transformation of their intrinsic nature all testify to the idea that naturalness of race and ethnicity is conceived in many ways, not all of which are biological (Hirschfeld 1996, 48–50).

23. Significantly, the pairing of distinctive DNA signature traits with particular geographically delineated groups refutes, rather than supports, the idea that racial and ethnic groups have distinctive endogenous attributes. Dr. Daniel G. Bradley and colleagues at Trinity College in Dublin have developed evidence showing that the Irish men in Connaught are almost all descended from an ancestral population of hunter-gatherers that inhabited Ireland before the advent of agricultural peoples. The key evidence consists in an almost perfect correspondence between their ancient Irish surnames and a DNA signature that is carried on the Y chromosome, which is bequeathed unchanged from father to son. The first carriers of the ancestral DNA signature are estimated to have lived in Europe thirty thousand years ago, principally congregating in Spain and then migrating northward, through Brittany, Ireland, and the west of Scotland as the glaciers retreated. Not surprisingly, the DNA signature displays a pronounced gradient across Europe, reflecting the degree of mixing between farming peoples migrating from the Near East beginning about ninety-five hundred years ago and Europe's ancestral hunter-gatherer population. Thus, while 98 percent of the Connaught men carry the signature and 89 percent of the men in the Basque country of Northern Spain carry it, only 2 percent of Turkish men carry it. This latter fact is telling because the DNA signature in question dominates in groups whose ethnic identities are regarded as otherwise quite unrelated. *Chicago Tribune,* March 23, 2000, sec. 1, 7.

24. This citation appears on page 22 of a version of Sleeter's article that was reprinted in *Lip* (August–September 1997): 18–22. For an incisive critique of all implicit conceptions of cultural identity—from cultural memory to cultural reinvention, rediscovery, and reappropriation—see Walter Benn Michaels, "Race into Culture: A Critical Genealogy of Cultural Identity," in *Identities,* ed. K. Anthony Appiah and Henrey Louis Gates Jr. (Chicago: University of Chicago Press, 1995), 32–62.

Chapter Three

Identity Politics and the Law: Reflections on Disability

In the previous chapter I argue that the conflation of race and ethnicity has two unfortunate consequences. First, it encourages us to view antiracist struggle as a struggle for multicultural recognition. Multiculturalism often takes the form of separatist–preservative (SP) identity politics oriented toward preserving cultures in their distinctness, so viewing antiracist struggle as an instance of it totally obscures what that struggle is about, which is the achievement of interracial community. Interracial community, in turn, comes to fruition through the opening up and altering of self-enclosed cultural and racial groups in syncretist–transformative (ST) identity politics. Even if ST identity politics allows cultural and racial differences to exist—and in this respect it differs from a politics of assimilation—its promotion of transformative dialogue is not conducive to the preservation of fixed cultural and racial identities, and it may even lead to the kind of integration in which these boundaries become blurred and all but nonexistent.

The second unfortunate consequence of collapsing the distinction between ethnicity and race is that it perpetuates white privilege. On one hand, when "blackness" is interpreted as an ethnic phenomenon, blacks are blamed for not having achieved the same kind of upward mobility achieved by ethnic European and ethnic Asian immigrants. On the other hand, when "whiteness" is interpreted as an ethnic phenomenon, whites are seen to be deserving of equal treatment vis-a-vis blacks and other minorities. All of this, however, obscures the fact that "whiteness" is primarily a structure of domination and only secondarily a culture—of racial supremacy. Together, this structure and culture have shaped white male working-class consciousness since the early nineteenth century, thereby dividing the working class along racial lines.

In this chapter we will examine how the racializing of ethnicity and the concomitant privileging of SP identity politics has affected a very different area of concern: the conceptualization of disability as a locus of legal entitlement. The reasons for examining disability are obvious in that disability has been compared to both culture and race by identity theorists, but they are also less obvious, insofar as the concept of disability indirectly impinges on the other two themes that are central to this book: human rights and deliberative democracy. First, the obvious reasons. There has been growing recognition that disability and capability are not medically definable concepts. What constitutes disability is a complex mix of physical impairments and societal norms and constraints. Once we factor in the element of social norm and constraint, those who have been labeled "disabled" can appropriate that identity differently. For instance, they can question the societal norms that judge them to be intrinsically deficient, and they can positively affirm their disabled status. The fascinating case of Deaf World shows to what lengths the disabled can defend their new identity, and it is precisely here where we see the value of race and culture in illuminating disability identity politics.

As for the less obvious reasons in taking up disability, it seems that any discussion of human rights and deliberative democracy can benefit enormously from examining the concept of disability as a principle of distributive justice. As I noted in chapter 1, human rights designate basic human capacities—or abilities—that have been earmarked for special protection. In this sense human rights can be understood as protecting against and compensating for disabling conditions. As we shall see, the kinds of principled compromises that are called for in securing justice for the disabled— compromises that call for a combination of integrating and prioritizing needs—are indispensable to fully realizing any system of rights. Also, by focusing on disability, we see that rights have a eudaimonistic dimension that critical theorists have long sought to bring to the fore, along with the justice dimension. In short, the aim of human rights is to secure a minimally decent life for everyone as well as promote the maximal flourishing of human capacities.

Finally, the politics of disability provides a textbook case for examining the centrality of deliberative democracy for resolving issues of distributive justice. Deliberative democracy assumes a just distribution of opportunities to participate in the life of the community. But modern liberal societies are torn between competing interpretations of distributive justice: formal liberal, substantive welfare, and participatory democratic. In examining how this differend affects disability rights, we will gain a better appreciation of the advantages and disadvantages of each paradigm. Most important, we will see why a participatory democratic paradigm that allows room for prioritizing principles provides the best chance for achieving principled compromises in other difficult areas of policy.

DISABILITY AND IDENTITY POLITICS: THE CASE OF DEAF WORLD

Before we address the relationship among disability, rights, and democracy, we must first see how disability has migrated from the private confines of the medical clinic to the public space of identity politics. The following case serves as an excellent entree to our discussion.

People were shocked when they heard that Sharon Duchesneau and Candy McCullough, a deaf lesbian couple, had sought a sperm donor from a deaf friend whose family had a history of congenital deafness, to guarantee that their child would be born deaf. Baby Gauvin McCullough, now ten months old, has a slight amount of hearing. The donor is also the biological father of their five-year-old daughter, Joanne, who is also deaf. Critics such as Peter Garrett, research director of LIFE (the leading pro-life group in the United Kingdom), decried the couple's decision, arguing that "to deprive a baby of a natural faculty is unethical behavior." McCullough, however, sees deafness as no more intrinsically disabling than being born black: "Black people have harder lives. Why shouldn't black people be able to go ahead and pick a black donor if that's what they want?"[1]

For the parents of Gauvin and Joanne, deafness is not a "medical condition" requiring treatment but a heritable identity—no different from race and ethnicity. In their opinion, whatever "disability" attaches to it is caused by societal discrimination and lack of accommodation. After all, why not genetically engineer your child to be deaf if it's just society's problem? Harlan Lane and Michael Grodin go even further, arguing that parents like Duchesneau and McCullough have an obligation to perpetuate deafness. More precisely, they argue that implanting cochlear hearing aids in deaf children is morally wrong because it disrupts their learning of American Sign Language (ASL), thereby contributing to the destruction of a distinctive culture: Deaf World.

Like Duchesneau and McCullough's reasoning, the arguments proffered by Lane and Grodin directly link back to our earlier discussion of race—but with the express intention of affirming an SP identity politics aimed at preserving racial and cultural differences. In short, Grodin and Lane argue that it is not only unethical but also illegal to undermine Deaf World, since doing so violates international conventions against cultural genocide (Lane and Grodin 1997, 237–38). However, it is their conflation of cultural ethnicity and race—a fallacy we dissected in the previous chapter—that is especially striking. According to these experts, just as white parents should think twice about adopting black children for fear of undermining the black community, so too should hearing parents of deaf children think twice about the potential harm caused to the deaf community when considering implantation for their children.

Now Grodin and Lane make two assumptions, namely, that deafness should be chiefly defined as a culture, not as a disability, and that every culture has an absolute right to exist. Let's examine the second assumption first. Grodin and Lane apparently assume that if cultural diversity is an inherent good, then every culture has a right to exist. But one can be a multiculturalist and still deny that every culture has a right to exist. As I argue in the introduction, a group's right to exist is partly a function of its legitimacy. Cultural groups that survive by denying their members any opportunity for exit violate their members' rights to free association and so are less legitimate than others. The kind of SP identity politics advocated by Grodin and Lane on behalf of preserving Deaf World has as its aim the transformation of Deaf World into such an illegitimate community. There is considerable evidence to show that children who are denied cochlear implants at an early age will not develop communication skills enabling them to function well as full-fledged members of nondeaf culture (Ingram 2000a, ch. 4). Therefore, denying them implants effectively forces them to remain within deaf culture. Contrary to Lane and Grodin, the potential harm perpetrated on deaf children by denying them implants is not compensated by the good produced from preserving deaf culture. Indeed, allowing cultural preservation to trump freedom of choice is antithetical to a liberal rights regime.

But is deafness even a culture? ASL is a culture that legitimately meets the needs of the deaf. But because deafness is an externally—indeed, biologically imposed—status, so is ASL. Unlike racial and ethnic identities, which are mainly passed down from parent to child (90 percent of deaf children are born to hearing parents), deaf identity arises almost entirely from peer-group socialization. Whereas socialization into racial and ethnic identities can be undone through subsequent efforts at voluntary resocialization, socialization into deaf identity is virtually unalterable.

One might respond to this objection by noting that all ethnoracial and cultural identities are externally imposed on children in ways that leave little room for choice. To make the argument against deaf culture's legitimacy, one would have to show further that the condition for participating in this culture robustly—deafness—is itself intrinsically disabling. But Lane and Grodin have a ready response to this objection. Comparing deafness to being black, they argue that all the disabling effects that attend deafness stem from social discrimination.

Grodin and Lane are right on that score. But conceding the disabling effects of discrimination is compatible with believing that deafness is also intrinsically disabling in a way that being black is not. If we bracket racial prejudice, dark skin pigmentation is not disabling under any circumstances. By contrast, only in a world populated mainly by deaf people would deafness not be disabling. More precisely, unlike the disability associated with deafness, the disability associated with being black was deliberately created by society as a way of oppressing blacks. In comparison to accommodating deaf people, remedying societal discrimination against blacks is not only more obligatory (our obligation to repair harms we have caused or benefited from is higher than other obligations), but it is more cost-efficient. The cost of trying to accommodate deafness—rather than eliminate it altogether—might be prohibitively high in comparison to the few persons who are benefited and might detract from other worthwhile expenditures, such as eliminating institutional racial discrimination (Wendell 1996, 82).

Does this mean that advocates of deaf culture have no legitimate basis for wanting to preserve their culture? As a cultural community diminishes in numbers, it becomes more vulnerable politically. Viewing deafness as a medical disability increases this vulnerability by stigmatizing deafness as a sign of inferiority.[2] Although I am sympathetic to this argument, I remain unconvinced that preserving Deaf World is morally warranted and cost-efficient. To recall the closing arguments of chapter 2, no culture is worth preserving to the extent that it requires excessive identity policing of the sort advocated by Grodin and Lane.

HUMAN ABILITIES AND DISABILITIES: UNIVERSAL RIGHTS VERSUS PARTICULAR CONTEXTS

Our examination of deafness suggests that most disabilities have social as well as natural causes. This fact alone injects an element of moral relativity into our assessments of disability. To the extent that disability ceases to be defined in terms of the "universal" language of biological dysfunction, it ceases to designate a standard against which disabilities can be cross-culturally identified and remedied. Since human rights protect against and compensate for disabling discrimination, the absence of any universal standard of human (dis)ability renders such rights meaningless.

Clearly, advocates of human rights need both universal and context-sensitive standards of disability (both socially and culturally). The United Nations' definition of disability tries to capture both kinds of standards in its distinction between impairments, disabilities, and handicaps:

> *Impairment*: Any loss or abnormality of psychological, physiological, or anatomical structure or function. *Disability*: Any restriction or lack (resulting from an impairment) of ability to perform an activity in the manner or within the range considered normal for a human being. *Handicap*: A disadvantage for a given individual, resulting from an impairment or disability, that limits or prevents the fulfillment of a role that is normal, depending on age, sex, social and cultural factors, for that individual . . . . Handicap is therefore a function of the

relationship between disabled persons and their environment. It occurs when they encounter cultural, physical, or social barriers which prevent their access to the various systems of society that are available to other citizens.³

The UN defines *impairment* and *disability* in terms of cross-cultural standards of "normal" human structure, function, and ability. By contrast, it defines *handicap* as a disadvantage—resulting from the encounter between impairment and disability on one side and the social environment on the other—that limits the fulfillment of a socially defined role. The reference to *universal* standards of normal function, structure, and ability obviously favors a medical definition of disability. The advantage of such a definition is that it provides a universal standard for critically evaluating any society's treatment of the disabled. It provides a baseline of normal human ability requisite for determining the human rights of the able-bodied as well as the disabled (Wendell 1996, 15).⁴ Conversely, the reference to culture and society-specific roles and barriers acknowledges that "disability" is relative to social roles and is caused in part by social barriers.

Despite accommodating our intuitions that disability has both organic and societal components, these UN definitions are very problematic. By defining *handicap* in terms of an incapacity to fulfill a given society's (or culture's) roles, we assume that fulfilling these roles is entirely free of handicap and disability. This is simply not true. Some societies impose gender roles on women that require them to become physically handicapped—genital mutilation and foot binding being but extreme cases—or mentally handicapped, through domestic confinement and lack of education (Young 1990b, 153). Indeed, societies can stultify the capabilities of virtually all their members. Marx's indictment of alienated labor still rings true today, even where the brutality of laissez-faire industrial capitalism has been superceded by postindustrial welfare capitalism: "[Labor] produces beauty, but mutilation for the worker. It displaces labor through machines, but it throws some workers back into barbarous labor and turns others into machines. It produces intelligence, but for the worker it produces imbecility and cretinism" (Marx [1844] 1994, 61).

The concept that whole societies and planetary systems of production can be "disabling" is crucial to the utopian, or eudaimonistic, strand of critical theory. However, before developing this theme further, I would like to examine its key premise, namely, that all human beings share a common essence—or common set of capacities and potentials—that "strive" for fulfillment. In the words of Herbert Marcuse, the individual's "best possible existence is measured against the 'essence of man' in such a way that the highest potentialities open to man in his historical situation take precedence in development and gratification over all others in which man is not free but rather dependent on what is external" (Marcuse [1938] 1991, 162).

The question we now need to ponder is whether there is a human nature—a common set of capacities—in terms of which socially imposed disability can be seen. As I noted earlier, Marx himself eventually came to reject abstractions such as the "essence of man," arguing that they falsely "naturalize" what are in fact historically contingent potentials. Defining standards of structure, function, and ability in terms of medically determinable, universal standards of normal human functioning prevents us from seeing how these standards themselves often reflect cultural biases. In fact, what "normal" and "healthy" human functioning *does* depend on is social context. A person who is illiterate or slow functioning in a literate, computational society will be disabled in a way that she or he would not be if living in a simple agrarian society.

Ultimately, we need both cross-cultural and culturally sensitive standards of impairment, disability, and handicap. The question is, How do we arrive at them? The accepted practice has been to allow medical experts to determine standards of disability. But the medical establishment is hardly unbiased. Indeed, the very standards of scientific rationality that inform medical practice seem complicit in maintaining an authoritarian and undemocratic—and therefore disabling—way of life.

REALIZING HUMAN ABILITIES: CAPITALISM AS INHERENTLY DISABLING

First-generation critical theorists such as Adorno, Horkheimer, and Marcuse did not focus their attention directly on medical theory and practice. However, they did so indirectly by addressing the scientific and technological rationality that informs it—and all of modern life. Using capitalism as a textbook illustration, they argued that a society structured in accordance with a certain kind of scientific and technological rationality is inherently disabling.

A convenient place to assess this extraordinary claim is by examining the way in which scientific and technological rationality informs capitalism itself. Maintaining competitiveness (and increasing profitability) through cost-cutting competition encourages the design of technologies that replace costly skilled workers with less-costly unskilled workers. The "de-skilling" of labor through automation typically separates what were once integral functions and processes into atomized tasks. In this way, the detailed division of labor inherent in the Taylor model of production exacerbates the division between mental and physical labor, thereby promoting an ever-greater division between those who "manage" and those who "work." In short, the process of "dumbing down" the workforce through automation disempowers workers—alienates them from the production process and its controlling powers—and cements the managerial authority of technological elites, who are charged with integrating the disparate tasks of production "from above" (Marcuse [1941] 1982).

The modern regime of specialized expertise prevalent in capitalist science and technology thus reinforces top-down domination and control by laying off otherwise irreplaceable skilled workers whose power over the work process gives them bargaining leverage. As David Noble's study of the post–World War II aircraft industry conclusively shows (1984), the introduction of automated machining devices did not increase accuracy or productivity immediately, but it did succeed in solidifying the power of the capitalist class and its technological–scientific elites over the production process. Because the technologically "disabled" worker no longer has either the opportunity or the ability to run a highly technical, highly integrated work process, he or she must be made to accept the wisdom of taking orders from above (just as Plato once admonished the artisans and guardians in his ideal Republic to obey the authority of technically trained philosophers).

Modern medicine is not immune from this type of technological domination. As Michel Foucault persuasively argued in his genealogy of the medical clinic (Foucault 1973), the human sciences that emerged during the Enlightenment greatly enhanced the power of governing authorities. Modern prisons and hospitals would have been unthinkable without extending the classificatory paradigm of knowledge to human populations. Statistical methods, archives, and other tracking devices helped the state divide its population in ways that conduced to greater economic productivity (Foucault 1979). Here, for the first time, we find the mass confinement of entire "subrational" and "nonproductive" populations: the mad, the infirm, the homeless, the criminal (Foucault 1965). Removing these populations from the general workforce served as an ominous warning to those who resisted the new discipline of labor, even as it eased saturated labor markets. For the first time ever, "medical expertise" was now called on to pass judgment on whether those who were deemed "deviant" were capable of being reformed in the mold of productive citizens.

Forty years ago when Foucault was writing his genealogies on clinical medicine and psychology, the confinement of the mentally disabled was much more commonplace than it is today. The pseudoscientific moral judgments of psychoanalysis have been replaced with nonjudgmental treatments involving the use of psychotropic drugs. Meanwhile, the segregation of the disabled from the able-bodied has also disappeared—albeit with ambiguous results (Lupton 1997). The mass expulsion of the mentally disabled from institutional confinement in the United States, begun in the eighties under the ambiguous banner of "emancipation" and "cost-cutting," has been accompanied by a meteoric rise in mental disability among the general population, with a substantial portion of children and adults taking some form of psychotropic medication. In addition to this mass sedation and control of the population, the earlier question raised by Foucault regarding the medicalization of life reappears with renewed vigor: Does the "integration" of the mentally disabled into society affirm their dignity and autonomy, or does it force them to assume responsibility for their new found destitution and homelessness? Does the general disabling of a stressed population ensure a growth in the "pastoral power" of the therapeutic welfare state; or does it portend the beginning of a breakdown in the system?

I digress. The question that is before us is whether modern medicine is capable of defining a universal standard of disability that is not itself disabling. Perhaps the place to begin answering this question is experimental science, which treats persons as passive subjects whose feelings of disability are discounted as "objectively" unfounded. It wasn't until the twentieth century that modern medicine had succeeded in fully discounting patients' first-person descriptions of their experience of sickness and disability in favor of information provided by more "accurate" diagnostic tools. (Women especially have found their experience of malaise dismissed as mere hypochondria and hysteria.) Thus, it should come as no surprise that, until scientific studies confirmed that multiple sclerosis (MS) could cause pain, patients reporting pain were simply told that they were wrong.[5] In sum, the patient–doctor relationship has been gradually transformed from a dialogical relationship to an instrumental one, in which the patient is increasingly reduced to a passive object of clinical observation and control (Wendell 1996, 122).

Medicine may control the disabled, but it is capital that controls medicine. Driven by the profit motive, medicine has every reason to maintain a monopoly over medical knowledge and medical power. To cite Wendell: "It is clearly in the direct financial interests of insurers of all types to recognize as few medical problems as they can while still making a convincing case to consumers that they offer valuable coverage. It is in the financial interest of government bureaucracies that provide various forms of relief and support to people with disabilities to recognize as few disabling conditions as they can" (Wendell, 132). Ultimately, the monopoly exercised by the medical establishment over medical knowledge and medical treatment enables it to be the final arbiter in determinations of criminal competency and disability—a role that by its very nature tends to conspire with business and government in discounting popular experiences of injustice, suffering, and unfreedom. For this reason the definition of disability should not be left to medical experts.

LEGAL DIFFERENDS MEET THE
POLITICS OF IDENTITY: THE CASE OF THE ADA

The eudaimonistic strand of critical theory examines the pathological and disabling effects of class societies that render citizens unrealized and unfulfilled. This strand appeals to a normative conception of human nature and human capacities that must be locally applied and interpreted within the ambit of ST identity politics. The deontological strand of critical theory, by contrast, examines shortfalls in the distributive justice of class societies that render some citizens more vulnerable than others to oppression and domination—more disabled in terms of opportunities for fulfillment and active political participation.

Here we encounter differends, those injustices discussed in chapter 1 that concern the silencing of voices and the suppression of one language of rights by another. To see how this is so, I propose that we turn to the committee reports that urged Congressional ratification of the Americans with Disabilities Act (ADA). Comparing disability to race, these reports urged the extension of civil rights protection to the disabled. However, the mandate to extend an abstract and indeterminate principle of racial equality to the disabled can be interpreted in terms of two civil rights models: antidiscrimination and affirmative action. While the antidiscrimination model focuses on discrimination based on socially perceived disability, the affirmative action model focuses on lack of equal opportunity (accommodation) based on medically proved disability.

The tension between these two civil rights paradigms is reflected principally in the definition of the ADA's beneficiaries, and it is precisely here that we begin to see the connection between legal and identity-based differends. From the standpoint of the antidiscrimination model, anyone who has been victimized by social prejudice because of appearing to be unattractive, unhealthy, or simply abnormal could claim damages. By contrast, from the standpoint of the affirmative action model, only those who can medically demonstrate a natural physical or mental handicap can demand special accommodation.

The courts have generally adopted what appears to be an affirmative action model in interpreting the ADA. Subsequently, they have construed the intended beneficiaries of the ADA quite narrowly, partly to protect employers and service providers from frivolous law suits. However, it is my contention that in doing so, the courts have also unquestioningly accepted the medical definition of disability. Rejecting this definition in favor of a "social constructivist" definition that views disability as partly or even mainly a function of societal impediments shifts disability policy away from compensating for lack of public access (through better medical treatment and greater welfare benefits) to providing it (through vocational training, workplace renovation, job redesign, and job placement).

However, to appreciate the full extent of the differend underlying disability policy, we need to recall that the antidiscrimination and affirmative action rationales underlying the ADA descend from conflicting legal paradigms—formal liberal and substantive welfare. As I argued in chapter 1, only one of these paradigms is compatible with identity politics. The formal legal paradigm is individual centered, and it aims at protecting the individual qua individual in abstraction from his or her "disability." The substantive welfare paradigm, by contrast, is group centered, and it aims at protecting the individual insofar as he or she is medically predefined as disabled.

In my opinion, applying either of these paradigms in isolation from a democratic paradigm commits a differend. The formal liberal paradigm suppresses the voice of those groups of persons who press to have special compensation and accommodation as a matter of right. The substantive welfare paradigm, by contrast, suppresses the voice of persons whose peculiar disabilities are not preselected for group-based protection and who therefore feel victimized by what they perceive to be selective or "reverse" discrimination. The democratic paradigm deals with these problems in the following way. By expanding public dialogue about the disabling effects of the social environment on all people—children, elderly, the unemployed, and the employed—we will hopefully come to regard disability as a general condition that effects everyone at some point in life. Perhaps we can also come to distinguish those aspects of generalized disability that are intrinsic to the human condition from those that are caused (partly or entirely) by social institutions. Maybe then we will see that it is not in our interests to engage in a divisive SP identity politics premised on a politics of resentment in which those who are defined as disabled are regarded as forming a uniquely "deviant" and "privileged" group."[6] If this change in thinking about disability were to take hold of the public at large, the public might then take it on itself to shift the burden of providing reasonable accommodation to society and state, perhaps—who knows—even to the point of revolutionizing society itself.

A Closer Look at the ADA

The ADA was enacted in 1990 to consolidate and extend the gains of two earlier acts: the Rehabilitation Act of 1973 and the Civil Rights Act of 1964. The different aims underlying these acts has led the courts to interpret the ADA much more narrowly than its authors intended. What the extension of the Rehabilitation Act effectively provides when it includes accommodation is special consideration for a relatively discrete class of persons who possess medical impairments, in much the same way that affirmative action provides special consideration for disadvantaged women and racial minorities. By contrast, the extension of the Civil Rights Act to include protection against discrimination based on real or perceived differences in functioning provides universal (or nonspecific) protection to a class whose membership is indefinite.

Since its passage, the courts have narrowed the act's beneficiaries to conform to the spirit of the Rehabilitation Act; they have defined its beneficiaries as just those persons who possess one or more medically proven physical and mental impairments. At the same time, the courts have narrowed the meaning of "accommodation" in conformity with the limited, nondiscrimination provisions of the Civil Rights Act. Persons suing under the ADA therefore find themselves in a curious catch-22. If they succeed in convincing the courts that they are medically disabled in a major life function, they inadvertently show that their impairment cannot be reasonably accommodated by businesses and public services. If, however, they succeed in convincing the courts that their disability can be reasonably accommodated, then they show that it is not one that substantially limits a major life function.

In the final analysis, those who succeed in circumventing this dilemma—men with lower-back injuries, for instance—are those whose disabilities are most easily accommodated. Thus, the ADA excludes from the pool of potential beneficiaries many of those for whom it was originally targeted—persons suffering from serious impairments and stigma-based discrimination—while at the same time decreasing the level of protection afforded to them.

I believe that the problems with the ADA originate in its guiding model, which sees disability through the paradigm of race. Unlike race, disability designates a much less-definite principle of classification—one that encompasses all of us at some point in our lives but in very different ways. Disability policy must reflect this indeterminacy by being articulated in different ways as well. For instance, disability policy could be subdivided into two separate policies: one outlawing discrimination based on socially perceived disability; the other providing affirmative accommodation based on actually existing disability, as defined by the public in consultation among themselves and with members of the health profession. This division has the advantage of clearly demarcating two distinct types of harms and corresponding remedies. Unlike racial and gender discrimination, discrimination based on perceived disability is sometimes (if not often) very specific—targeting the individual as such apart from his or her membership in a given class. Lack of accommodation, by contrast, need not reflect any discriminatory intent, yet it almost always affects individuals as members of disabled classes.

However disability policy is articulated, it must be done so democratically, in ways that fully acknowledge the dynamic and heterogeneous nature of disability as it is experienced by average persons. Articulating disability policy through the lens of a democratic paradigm will likely complicate litigation. Although the paradigm does not expressly favor a social constructivist understanding of disability, it nonetheless encourages us to view disability—whether medically or socially constructed—as something to be defined by the public and, more specifically, by those who are most affected by it. Accommodating a broader and more fluid class of disabilities will most certainly complicate disability litigation and result in greater social costs.

The most problematic provisions of the ADA are Titles I, II, and III, which address (respectively) employment, government services, and public services and accommodations provided by private entities. Title I prohibits private employers, state and local governments, employment agencies and labor unions (with fifteen or more employees as of 1994) from discriminating against people with disabilities in hiring, firing, advancement, compensation, job training, and so forth. Employers are further required to make "reasonable accommodations" to allow persons with disabilities to participate in the workplace.

Recent studies by Susan Mezey (Mezey 2002, 52) show that between 80 and 90 percent of plaintiffs suing under Title I lose. One reason for this dismal record, as mentioned earlier, is that the ADA inconsistently defines those who are entitled to use it. The ADA's legislative record mentions a discrete class of beneficiaries (forty-three million Americans) who fall under its definition. This reference corresponds to one definition stipulated by the ADA: a person with a disability is one who "has a physical or mental impairment which substantially limits one or more of such a person's life activities." However, what the ADA also defines as disabled is anyone who "has a record of such impairment, or is regarded as having such an impairment."[7] The inconsistency in the ADA's definition of disability has allowed the court's to interpret the act as narrowly as possible. In effect, they disregard the second definition almost entirely and interpret the first definition as narrowly as possible. Not only do they require strict medical proof of an existing disability, but they now rule out "correctable" medical impairments, such as myopia and high blood pressure.[8] Most recently, in January 2002, the Supreme Court unanimously accepted Justice Sandra Day O'Connor's view that an actionable disability must limit a person in the performance of an activity central to most people's daily lives, not simply in the performance of specific jobs.[9] The focus on who counts as disabled stands in marked contrast to the kind of legal questions that were central to litigation under the Rehabilitation Act, which was entirely taken up with matters of reasonable accommodation.

In addition to being strapped by a narrow definition of disability, the ADA has also had to contend with the "new federalism" propounded by a conservative court.[10] The court increasingly appeals to the Tenth and Eleventh Amendments in arguing that government employers are exempt from Title I discrimination suits.[11] Because disability is not thought to be a "suspect classification" that has been used mainly to single out the disabled for invidious discrimination in the same way that racial classifications have traditionally discriminated against blacks and other minorities, the courts do not require state and local governments to show that their unequal treatment of the disabled is necessary for satisfying a compelling state interest. Held to a less-strict threshold of scrutiny, state and local governments are required to show only that their discrimination is rationally related to fulfilling a legitimate government interest. Such an interest is not difficult to establish because the ADA's "reasonable accommodation" requirement is a federally "unfunded mandate" that imposes financial burdens on state and local governments that they will legitimately seek to avoid.

Furthermore, the ADA is not recognized by the court as having the full force of a constitutional requirement, even though it ostensibly implements the commerce clause of the Constitution as well as the Fourteenth Amendment's equal protection clause. Because "disability" is not defined as a "suspect classification" meriting the highest antidiscrimination protection, state and local governmental discrimination against the disabled has not been construed as a violation of these constitutional provisions. Indeed, the courts have come close to declaring the ADA itself in violation of the Tenth and Eleventh Amendments, which grant certain powers and immunities to the states not expressly denied by the Constitution, including immunity from lawsuits by private parties in federal courts without the state's consent.

This constitutional challenge is most acute when we turn to Title II of the ADA. Already one federal circuit court has ruled that Title II may violate these "states' rights" amendments.[12] Currently, plaintiffs suing under Title II have had greater success (54 percent) than their counterparts suing under Title I (Mezey 2002, 53). Among other victories for the disabled, the court's have ruled that prisons must provide "public services" to disabled inmates and that states must place disabled persons in institutions that are the least segregating, least restricting, and most conforming to a disabled person's desires (*Olmstead v. L.C.* [1999]). However, because these services are federally unfunded mandates, the level of service that is required is entirely relative to what the state believes is rational to fund, given its legitimate security and financial interests. If the courts rule that Title II suits infringe on state's rights, then states will be entirely free to ignore the needs of the disabled.

Title III cases are rare, but one case in particular (*PGA Tour, Inc. v. Martin*) stands out for its notoriety. On May 29, 2001, the Supreme Court ruled by a seven–two margin that professional golfer Casey Martin must be allowed to use a golf cart to participate in the PGA tour. Martin suffers from a degenerative circulatory disorder that prevents him from walking golf courses. He sued the PGA under a provision of Title III requiring that an entity operating "public accommodations" make "reasonable modifications" in its policies when necessary to afford such "accommodations to individuals with disabilities, unless the entity can demonstrate that making such modifications would fundamentally alter the nature of such . . . accommodations." Noting that the walking rule does not apply to the PGA's Senior Tour, the court decided in favor of Martin, holding that "shot making," not "walking," was the essence of golf. Important as this victory was to the disabled, its wording was so narrowly crafted as to establish no clear precedent for subsequent cases.

Cross-cultural studies are useful in assessing the strengths and weaknesses of the ADA. If the ADA has any strong point, it must surely be its recognition, however halting, that disability has a social dimension and that society has an obligation to "accommodate" the physical and mental impairments of its citizens within reason. Its weak point, however, is that it takes race and civil rights law as its primary model. In contrast to the Canadian Charter of Rights and Freedoms, it does not satisfactorily address the importance of resource distribution for both the disabled and their caretakers as a necessary condition for equal inclusion and democratic empowerment. As Jerome Bickenbach observes (Bickenbach 2000), taking civil rights legislation as a model led the authors of the ADA to define disability in conflicting ways. In the final analysis, the class of disabled persons is not nearly as homogeneous as the act presumes. Some seriously disabled persons suffer little or no discrimination; meanwhile, persons who suffer from statistical abnormalities (shortness, obesity, "ugliness," etc.) suffer tremendous discrimination despite being unimpaired; indeed, from the standpoint of discrimination, those whose shortness is nonpathological suffer the same disadvantage as those whose shortness is caused by hormonal deficiency. Again, the main beneficiaries of the act are middle-class white men who have sustained late-onset physical injuries (mainly back)—hardly representative of the class of disabled persons taken as a whole (Bickenbach 2000, 346).

Obviously, there are many ways in which the ADA could be revised. The least radical revision would minimally require that persons discriminated on the basis of appearing abnormal or dysfunctional be included among the beneficiaries of antidiscrimination law (Wasserman 2000). A more radical revision would ensure that affirmative action provisions for the disabled be incorporated under the equal protection clause of the Fourteenth Amendment. This will prevent states from shirking their federally mandated responsibilities to the disabled and their caregivers. Finally, antidiscrimination and affirmative action provisions of the ADA should be statutorily distinguished. Having a separate statute that focuses on perceived disability discrimination would offer protection to anyone unfairly discriminated against on the basis of physical or mental abnormality. This statute would be costless (except for litigation) and would not require special accommodation. It would be potentially universal in scope, protecting those who are discriminated against because of age, infirmity, or any other perceived difference. Indeed, as Mark Kelman argues (2000), if the aim of antidiscrimination law is to prevent employers from discriminating on the basis of nonmarket considerations, then there is no reason why such a law should focus on protecting groups as distinct from individuals, except perhaps for the fact of administrative convenience—that is, the convenience of being able to appeal to the statistical probability that members of certain groups are more likely to suffer discrimination than members of other groups. Because of its universal scope, it would circumvent the politics of resentment that accompanies an identity politics in which discrete groups are perceived as seeking special privileges.

A separate "prioritizing" affirmative action statute targeting those with special medical needs should be defined more narrowly so as to ensure that whatever costs are born by society in accommodating them are fairly and efficiently distributed. However, defining disability should not be left in the hands of doctors and legal experts. It is ultimately up to the public and its elected representatives to set these standards "democratically," in a way that will minimize judicial and executive discretion as much as possible.

DISABILITY RIGHTS AND JUSTICE

Reforming disability policy will be costly, and hard decisions regarding distributive justice will have to be made. The question thus arises: Which legal paradigms—formal liberal, substantive welfare, or participatory democratic—offer the most principled way of compromising competing values, interests, and perspectives?

Let's begin with the substantive welfare paradigm. This paradigm is most often interpreted along utilitarian lines and applies cost-benefit analyses in determining which distribution of resources efficiently maximizes overall societal well-being. Assuming that additional units of utility beyond a baseline threshold of minimal utility yield increasingly diminished increments of satisfaction (the principle of marginal utility), this approach has strong egalitarian implications that would likely justify compensating the abnormal unhappiness (lower quality-of-life opportunities) of the disabled with above-average benefits in education, health, and welfare.

Critics have adopted a formal legal (social contractarian) approach as a result of familiar problems associated with utilitarianism—namely, that it (a) potentially sacrifices the good of the individual for overall social well-being; (b) falsely assumes a harmonious and rationally calculable ordering of societal preferences analogous to a rational choice by a single individual; and (c) accepts all preferences as equally legitimate. Adopted by Kantians such as Rawls (Rawls 1971), this approach holds that the proper way to reason about justice and rights is to do so from the idealized standpoint of purely reasonable and rational individuals who are seeking mutually advantageous terms of cooperation. To ensure that the parties to this "hypothetical" social contract are reasoning justly, or impartially, we imagine them to be ignorant of any and all facts that might bias them in any way, including facts about disability (the veil of ignorance). Because the parties know that any one of them might be disabled, they will ensure that the disabled have the same basic rights as everyone else. Furthermore, assuming that rational persons who calculate probabilities under conditions of uncertainty are risk aversive, any principle of distributive justice they adopt would likely mandate that social and economic institutions work to the advantage of the least well-off, which would likely include many people who are classified as disabled.

The participatory democratic paradigm does not reject formal liberal and substantive welfare paradigms, but it does incorporate them within ST identity politics. In other words, it holds that questions of distributive justice and definitions of disability must be sensitive to different group-based standpoints. In the literature on disability, advocates of this approach are frequently associated with feminist standpoint ethics (Mahowald 1998). Feminists make the obvious point that the dominant position of those who are under the care of others—the profoundly disabled, the elderly infirm, and children—is one of dependency. They then go on to argue that dependency also embraces the caregivers, who are almost all women. The dominant fact of mutual dependency combined with the dominant denial of care work as remunerable labor has led some of these critics, such as Eva Kittay (1999) and Jennifer Parks (2003), to demand greater state support for social policies that will enable caregivers not only to become active participants in all walks of life but also, above all, to shape decisions that affect them directly.

Let me begin my discussion by examining the social contractarian approach as adopted by Rawls and his followers. This is appropriate given the fact that Rawls himself allows for utilitarian cost-benefit analyses in the application (if not choice) of his principles of justice. Hence, instead of addressing utilitarianism as a separate approach, I will be discussing two different applications of Rawls: one that is predominantly rights centered, oriented toward nondiscrimination policies; and another that is predominantly welfare centered, oriented toward affirmative action and redistribution. The feminist critique of Rawlsian social contract theory will be addressed at the conclusion of this chapter.

The two principles of justice defended by Rawls (1971) reflect these two different applications. The first principle (liberty) states that each person is to have an equal right to the most extensive liberty, compatible with a similar liberty for others. It views injustice as the denial of equal treatment, or as wrongful discrimination. The second principle (difference) states that social and economic inequalities are to be arranged so that they are both (1) reasonably expected to be to everyone's advantage and (2) attached to offices open to all. It views injustice in terms of unchosen inequalities of birth and social circumstance that render some worse off than others vis-a-vis opportunities for human flourishing and societal inclusion (Rawls 1971, sec. 11).

Before proceeding any further, it is important to note that there are at least two ways to apply the second principle to the question of disability (Pogge 2000, 34). According to the weak interpretation, it might be that current institutions—including, say, a capitalist market that discriminates against the disabled in terms of employment and other benefits—contingently make the disabled better off than they would be in a more egalitarian society. For instance, it might be argued that productivity is heightened by discriminating against the disabled in employment. Or, it might be argued that a more egalitarian system that taxes business heavily to compensate for the disabled lowers work and profit-making incentives, thereby drastically decreasing tax revenues that can be used for ameliorative purposes. According to the stronger interpretation, by contrast, a society must focus all of its resources on bringing each and every person who is a member of a worst-off class to a normal level of average functioning.

To complicate matters somewhat, there are gradients in the application of the strong version of the difference principle. On the weaker side, Gregory Kavka (2000) has defended affirmative action hiring of the disabled on the grounds that (a) everyone has a right to self-respect (a Rawlsian primary good); (b) self-respect in most societies is closely linked to socially productive work; and (c) aside from work, the disabled have fewer opportunities than the nondisabled for gaining self-respect. Regardless of whether Kavka is right about the disabled's receiving a special boost in their esteem from affirmative action (which might be stigmatizing), his defense of affirmative action has been criticized for being weak in leaving open what kind of "work" that they are entitled to (Daniels 2000, 260).

Norman Daniels (2000), Thomas Pogge (2000), David Wasserman (1998), and Richard Arneson (2000) have gone further than Kavka in addressing the cost-benefit side of applying the difference principle. Among these Rawlsians, Daniels has remained closest to the stringent demands of a strong difference principle. First, he argues that because health is so central to the enjoyment of all other primary goods, society has an obligation to ensure its equitable distribution above all else (1990). Second, he insists that society is unjust if it does not try to raise everyone to the level of "normal" (or "species-typical") function as defined "by nature." Clearly, the costs involved in trying to achieve that noble end might well be prohibitive. Should society spend vast sums of money discovering cures for extremely rare "orphan diseases," even if this means sacrificing the needs of the less-desperately needy?

Daniels's contention that satisfying persons medical needs should take precedence over satisfying other needs is right in principle: we do need to prioritize needs to resolve cost-benefit compromises in a principled way. However, it seems arbitrary to privilege medical needs over other needs that bear on basic abilities. Given legitimate skepticism about the medical establishment's capacity to define our native abilities, we need to turn to a more democratic paradigm to resolve problems of prioritization.

Doing so might mean adopting a more modest cost-beneficial approach. Pogge's counterproposal points in this direction. Pogge argues that the goal of the difference principle should not be to compensate for natural inequalities but to mitigate their aggravation by society (1989, 44). We are not obligated to mitigate all impairments medically, but we are obligated to mitigate the lack of resources that render such impairments disabling to the point where the impaired have no access to basic opportunities enjoyed by everyone else. Thus, all persons with impaired motility would have access to wheelchairs and ramps, regardless of cost. Ultimately, the precise nature of what constitutes basic quality-of-life opportunities would be decided democratically (182).

Appealing to a democratic paradigm in resolving problems of priority is a step forward—but only if the quality of democratic deliberation is not distorted by irrational prejudice. A quick glance at the Oregon Health Plan bears this out. Designed in 1990 to provide Medicaid coverage to all Oregonians living in poverty, the plan ranks medical diagnoses and treatments and denies coverage to low-priority services. Public opinion polls regarding the quality of life that patients would expect after having undergone specified treatments (the list eventually contained 709) showed disturbing results. Orthodontic treatment for thumb sucking ranked high on the list; transplantation ranked low. Treatments that saved lives with a likelihood of lifelong impairment were also ranked low. Yet studies show that disabled people with lifelong impairments report living a high quality of life, thereby suggesting that the public's discrimination against disability is based on prejudice (Brock 2000, 225).

Pogge does mention one principled constraint on the public's right to decide on the kind of coverage it wants included in its universal health-insurance scheme. He notes that health-related problems due to societal causes—such as pollution, poverty, and so on—ought to be given much higher priority than those caused by "nature" or bad luck, since the former are social injustices for which society itself is responsible. This difference—between naturally and socially caused health risks—leads him to argue that society's obligation to remedy socially caused disability is relatively absolute (1989, 109ff).

Arneson has made this sort of prioritarian interpretation of the difference principle the centerpiece of his theory of distributive justice for the disabled. Like Pogge, Arneson argues against a "maximin" approach that requires spending as much as it will take to make the lives of the worst-off as good as the average:

> What society owes me by way of distributive justice is responsive both to the extent of my bad luck and the extent to which I can benefit from compensation. the issue is: (1) how badly off I am, by comparison with the well-being expectation levels of others who might be helped or might be called on to assist me; and (2) how much I can benefit from measures that might be taken to aid me, by comparison with the extent to which others can benefit if the compensatory measures are instead directed toward the improvement of their quality of life. Justice requires calculations of costs and benefits and trade-off rules to determine the moral value of the policies we might choose. (2000, 26)

Arneson qualifies his prioritarian theory further by noting that, all things being equal, persons who have acquired their disability through reckless choice are less morally deserving than those who have acquired it through bad luck. He also argues—much less persuasively, in my opinion—that there is no sharp conceptual moral boundary separating the extreme neediness of disabled persons from the extreme neediness of persons with expensive tastes. That being so, we once again find ourselves facing the classical utilitarian dilemma of having to compare and rank subjective needs. This latter conclusion, however, only follows if—like Arneson—we narrowly equate welfare with psychological states of well-being rather than with more objective criteria of measurement, such as the possession of basic capabilities (Sen 1982) or basic resources (Dworkin 2000).

As I have noted approaches that narrowly equate welfare with psychological well-being encounter greater difficulty in setting distributive priorities with regard to disability, since disabled people can lack mental and physical abilities and still lead fulfilling lives. Although I find Arneson's principle of prioritization appealing, it would be difficult to implement as a policy regulating public discussion about disability. A person's "voluntary" decision to act recklessly in a way that results in impairment very often has social and (in the case of drug addiction) natural causes. But in that case, there is nothing that fundamentally distinguishes the "injustices" suffered by the disabled from those suffered by the poor, the unemployed, and countless other "at risk" and "needy" groups. Hence, Wasserman (1998) proposes that health care needs to be treated as having no more priority than other welfare needs. In his opinion, the costs and benefits of any medical treatment will have to be democratically measured against the costs and benefits of other "utilities," with priority rankings being assessed on a case-by-case basis.

The unavoidable complexity of such priority rankings is further complicated by the fact that disabled people can lack both mental and physical abilities and yet lead fulfilling lives. Policies that target quality of life are often made in an unavoidably politicized way, within the ambit of a polarizing SP identity politics, which has led critics to reject substantive welfare approaches in favor of formal liberal ones. Most outstanding among them is Anita Silvers (1998). Silvers criticizes the welfare paradigm on the grounds that it (a) is too costly; (b) unjustly penalizes the able-bodied by making them pay for remedying disabilities for which they are not responsible; (c) invariably defines disability in terms of a fixed, medical definition; and (d) ends up stigmatizing the disabled as inferior. In her opinion, the only harms that require legal rectification are those that involve a violation of "negative" freedom, such as hiring policies that discriminate against the disabled simply because they are disabled. Once we reject the medical model of disability and see that disability is caused by lack of social accommodation, then it becomes apparent (so she argues) that failure to provide adequate accommodation amounts to real discrimination.

Silvers's concerns about the undemocratic and stigmatizing way in which the welfare paradigm treats disability has some merit. But her claim that it is too expensive and penalizes the able-bodied seems unwarranted. This is apparent once we examine Silvers's method of justifying her view that most disabilities are caused by societal discrimination—or unequal infringements of liberty—rather than societal failure to compensate for natural impairments. Silvers invokes a curious variation of Rawls's thought experiment to make her point. Instead of imagining that we are party to a hypothetical contract in which we are ignorant of all facts that might bias our judgment (the veil of ignorance), she advocates "historical counterfactualizing" (1998, 129). We imagine a society in which, say, the normal level of functioning of the majority was characterized by sightlessness, deafness, or lack of lower-body mobility. The sorts of accommodations that would be established by people living in that society would also be the ones that our society should establish not to discriminate. Thus, to avoid discriminating against the deaf, society would have to ensure that signers and closed-captioning devices were made available in all public and private (commercial) settings (32, 74).

Silvers's "thought experiment" is certainly useful in getting us to see how standard institutional designs work to limit disabled persons' access to jobs and public places. To that extent, it is useful in revealing how much of what we call "disability" is really caused by societal indifference rather than physical or mental impairment. However, on closer inspection it might not tell us very much in this regard. As Pogge notes, there's no way to perform historical counterfactualizing without begging important questions (2000, 38ff.). Which disabilities are we to counterfactually imagine as prevalent? Suppose we imagine a society composed mainly of deaf people. Is it certain that some institutional designs would have evolved and not others? Is it certain that members of this society would have preferred to remain deaf (as Silvers seems to think) rather than enhance their hearing through cochlear implants (much as humans enhance their mobility through automobiles, bicycles, planes, and tennis shoes)?

For the sake of argument, let's suppose that a predominantly deaf society would have made signing and closed captioning part of its institutional design. Does this really tell us anything about how much of the disabling effects suffered by the deaf in our society is caused (a) by lack of signers and closed captions and (b) by wrongful discrimination? Suppose that it tells us that the disabling effects are caused by a lack of signers and closed captions. That needn't reflect any deliberate discrimination—or indeed any injustice. Non-English-speaking immigrants from Vietnam are also "disabled" with respect to employment and public access, but in a society in which they constitute the majority (Vietnam), their lack of English is not disabling. Must we therefore conclude that they suffer unjust discrimination in the United States owing to a lack of Vietnamese-speaking translators and Vietnamese-language captions? But in fact the absence of translators and linguistic cues for speakers of minority languages (even native American languages such as ASL) tells us nothing about whether the disabilities speakers of these languages experience are mainly society's fault, their own fault, or nobody's fault (Pogge 2000, 42).

Historical counterfactualizing has its limits. We cannot imagine a self-reproducing society of profoundly paralyzed people or profoundly mentally handicapped people. Accommodating these people will therefore require welfare entitlements, not formal liberties. But Silvers's discussion of disability has the virtue—unintended to be sure—of showing why formal liberties require welfare entitlements for their implementation. By Silvers's own account, society discriminates against persons who care for the profoundly disabled when it does not compensate them for the amount of time, energy, and resources they spend on caregiving—expenditures that deprive them of the liberty to pursue other interests. Moreover, as our study of the ADA shows, accommodation is more analogous to affirmative action, vocational training, rehabilitation, and a whole host of resource entitlements than it is to nondiscriminatory treatment (Illingworth and Parmet 2000).

FEMINISM AND DEMOCRACY: TOWARD A NEW PARADIGM OF DISABILITY AND CAREGIVING

Our discussion of distributive justice has led us to appreciate the unique injustices that befall caregivers. Caregiving activity is not recognized as socially productive work under current law, and so those who care for family members—almost all of whom are women—do not receive extended social welfare benefits that would compensate them for their labor or free them from it. As even its staunchest supporters (Gilligan 1982; Noddings 1986) must concede, the once highly vaunted feminist ethic of care has a serious downside. Those women who practice it virtuously can lose their independent identities. To recognize this injustice, we need to adopt a democratic paradigm of justice that goes beyond formal liberal and substantive welfare paradigms.

Formal liberal approaches depart from the standpoint of independent self-interested persons who are seeking terms of fair cooperation under conditions of scarcity that will be mutually acceptable to everyone. As Eva Kittay rightly notes (1999), this way of formulating the "circumstances of justice" falsely presumes that we are free, independent, and mutually and fully cooperating over an entire lifetime. The failure to consider dependency and disability as a normal fact about life is reflected in the view that acting justly does not imply caring for others. For example, while arguing that persons in the original position would want to set aside some provisions for sickness and other deviations from normal health (a primary good), Rawls nowhere mentions that dependency befalls all of us in the normal course of a lifetime (1993, 272n.10).

If one begins from the fact of mutual but asymmetrical vulnerability and dependency over a lifetime, then the proper model of reciprocity is intergenerational and "nested." One must care for one's own caregivers—past, future, known, or unknown. Kittay acknowledges this moral imperative in her extension of the Greek concept of *doulia*. Justice demands more than caring for caregivers; it demands that caregivers be relieved of care work in ways that affirm their own autonomy and self-realization. It demands that men do their fair share of caregiving. And it demands government support for paid care providers, with the proviso that these providers, who are often recruited from among the most vulnerable sectors in society, are in turn provided for with decent wages, benefits, and care. To cite Jennifer Parks (2003):

> Home care should be democratized by ensuring that even the "lowliest" of home care workers have some control over their working conditions. This democratization can be achieved through a variety of means, including unionizing and developing worker owned and operated agencies, where aids have meaningful input into their work. (140)

Unfortunately, the passage of welfare "reform" in 1996 and the Family and Medical Leave Act of 1993 (FMLA) couldn't be further from the spirit of Kittay's and Parks's proposals, since it makes work in general—and not just remunerated care work—a burden for caregivers. As many commentators have pointed out, welfare has always been regarded differently than social entitlements based on paid labor. Typically, those who receive welfare—who are overwhelmingly single-women caregivers—are stigmatized as lazy and sexually promiscuous. These stereotypes emerged in full force during the debates leading up to the welfare "reform" bill passed by Congress in 1996, when federally funded welfare, or Aid to Families with Dependent Children (AFDC) as it was then known in the United States, was abolished and replaced by a program of block grants that could be used in discretionary ways by individual states. This new program, Temporary Assistance to Needy Families (TANF), was explicitly punitive. Most notoriously, it rewarded states for slashing their welfare rolls and reducing the size of "illegitimate" births (without the aid of government-funded abortion). Assistance was capped at five years; states were encouraged to withhold increases in stipends to recipients who had additional children; and many women were forced to work as a condition for receiving any benefits at all—in many cases, without adequate child-care support.

No wonder welfare reformers were accused of hypocrisy. While declaring the family to be the bedrock of social virtue and societal well-being—and women to be the bedrock of the family—the reform effectively undermined the integrity of the family by withdrawing support and separating women caregivers from their children (incredibly, mothers were forced to work outside the home while also being required to spend most of their earnings on day care). On one hand, welfare reform imposed a contractual relationship on the family—demanding that single parents be independent wage earners, even if this meant abandoning care work for wage work. On the other hand, it did so in the name of fostering caring relationships. But the relationships that were fostered were often very far from caring. Even when families managed to escape cycles of neglect violence caused by workfare and reduced supports, states did not; they continued to impose their punitive form of "welfare" care work on recipients presumed to be pathological and in need of paternalistic discipline.

Social conservatives, of course, would prefer that the family assume a stable nuclear form, with women as caretakers at home and men as wage earners out in civil society. Leaving aside the inherent repressiveness and injustice of this gendered division of labor, the decline in wages over the past forty years has made that model of the family virtually impossible, save for a few families. The need for dual wage-earning capacity has forced women into simultaneous roles—as family caregivers and as wage earners. Women caregivers, their families, and society at large pay a huge price for this unprincipled compromise. The only way to eliminate this palpable injustice and thereby lower psychological stress[13] is to raise wages, abolish the gendered division of labor, and increase governmental support for caregivers.

Policies such as the FMLA do not go nearly far enough in this direction. Unlike similar family-leave policies in most other advanced industrial democracies, the FMLA does not provide for paid leaves; it exempts businesses with less than fifty employees (thereby leaving most of the workforce unprotected); and it applies only to traditional familial relationships involving parents (or parental surrogates) and spouses. Perhaps the central problem with the FMLA and current welfare policy is the political system in which they were enacted.

As we have seen, this system adopts a dual legal paradigm that divides people into autonomous, formal legal rights bearers and wage earners on one side (traditionally men) and dependent welfare recipients on the other (typically women). While the former paradigm holds individuals responsible for their own fate and so leaves them without assurance of care, the latter ensures care—but reservedly and only in the form of paternalistic dependency that robs recipients of dignity and autonomy (Fraser 1989). Hence, these paradigms need to be subsumed under a democratic paradigm in which questions of role identity—independent versus dependent, able-bodied versus disabled, masculine versus feminine—are themselves critically questioned in inclusive discussions involving everyone (Habermas 1996).

NOTES

1. See "Couple 'Choose' to Have a Deaf Baby," *BBC News Online,* April 8, 2002, 10:11.
2. Mahowald (1998, 234) makes this point, adding that any decision to abort a fetus simply because it is disabled is prejudicial to members of the disabled community. However, she notes that aborting a fetus for other reasons, such as hardship of caring for an exceptionally needy child, may be morally justifiable (237).
3. United Nations. *World Programme of Action Concerning Disabled Persons* (New York: United Nations, 1983), section I.c, 6–7.
4. Christopher Boorse suggests that disability can be defined "objectively" as a statistical deviation from the norm. Ronald Amundson notes, however, that deviation from normalcy is itself normal for any evolutionary theory that accepts the individuality and contextuality of biodiversity. Norman Daniels (2000) and Dan Brock (2000) are among those who have sought to define disability subjectively as well as objectively. Subjectively, disability is supposedly experienced as a diminution of "quality of life opportunities." However, Amundson rightly notes (2000) that people with good wheelchair mobility, for example, often experience high levels of functioning and high-quality opportunities. Amundson thus concludes that categories of disability are no less arbitrary than categories of race.
5. Janet James, *One Particular Harbor* (Chicago: University of Chicago Press, 1993), 241.
6. For an excellent discussion of how the politics of difference as deviance (Minow 1990) enters into ADA litigation, see Iris Marion Young (2000a).
7. American with Disabilities Act, sections 3.2.B., 3.2.C.
8. In *Sutton v. United Airlines* (1999) the courts ruled against twin sisters who wanted to be pilots for United Airlines but were denied this opportunity by United

because they were judged to be too myopic, despite the fact that their vision was entirely correctable using appropriate eye wear. In *Murphy v. UPS* (1999) the courts ruled against a driver for UPS who lost his job because he suffered from high blood pressure, a condition for which he had been taking medication.

9. The case, *Toyota v. Williams* (2002), involved a woman who was transferred by Toyota from one job, which she performed perfectly well, to another one, which she performed poorly because of carpal tunnel syndrome.

10. I am indebted to Russell Powell, S. J., for explaining the ramifications of this jurisprudence.

11. See *Board of Trustees of the University of Alabama v. Garrett* (2001), which involved a nurse at the university hospital who was forced out of her supervisory role after contracting breast cancer and forced to take a job that paid $13,000 less. Writing for the majority in a five–four split, Chief Justice Rehnquist said that states "could quite hard-headedly—and perhaps hardheartedly—hold to job qualification requirements which do not make allowance for the disabled" so long as "their actions toward such individuals are rational."

12. *U.S. v. Morrison*, 120 S. Ct 1740, 1743 (2000).

13. Recent estimates show that stress stemming from life-changing events such as divorce, having children, and losing a job has increased by 45 percent over the last thirty years. Such stress disproportionately affects women and children, and it does so in ways that can elevate behavior- and learning-altering hormones and even affect brain cell development. Numerous studies have shown direct links between elevated levels of stress hormones (such as cortisol) in pregnant women and higher rates of premature birth (one in nine children in the United States is born prematurely—the highest rate of any industrialized country and a rate that has climbed by 17 percent since the early 1980s). Premature children are disproportionately represented among those who fail in school, have behavioral problems, suffer from depression, and exhibit aggressive and criminal tendencies. Long periods of elevated stress hormones can disturb neural functioning and can even kill brain cells. MRI brain scans of forty-three girls who had suffered sexual abuse showed that their brains were significantly smaller than average, and all had lower IQs. In general, children who receive less emotional support in the form of love, talk, time, or touch exhibit higher levels of stress hormones. In general, economic factors that force parents to split up, spend less time (and less quality time) with their children (today, almost all fathers and almost half of all mothers work outside the home) and exhibit stressful behavior in front of their children all contribute to temporarily, if not permanently, "disabling" the children. See Ronald Kotulak, "Kid's Health Suffering as Family Stress Trickles Down," *Chicago Tribune,* September 24, 2000.

Part Two

DELIBERATIVE DEMOCRACY

Chapter Four

Democracy and Racial Identity: Reconsidering Representation

Our foray into identity politics has enabled us to appreciate the advantages and disadvantages of two ways of engaging one's group identity politically. Separatist–preservative (SP) identity politics promotes group solidarity. This purpose can be legitimate, especially when one's group is numerically weak and otherwise threatened by a dominant majority, as in the case of aboriginal peoples who are struggling to preserve their cultural identities. Syncretist–transformative (ST) identity politics, by contrast, promotes intergroup solidarity. Breaking down cultural and racial barriers, it seeks to foster an open and integrated community in which one's identity is complex and chosen. The advantages of SP and ST identity politics mirror their disadvantages: whereas the former inclines toward racial (biological) and deterministic modes of self-identification that are illegitimate—or too constrained—the latter inclines toward individualistic (atomistic) and voluntaristic modes of self-identification that are ideological—or too unconstrained.

The examples of race and disability discussed in chapters 2 and 3 highlight these advantages and disadvantages. In both cases, I have argued that SP identity politics may be a legitimate tool for organizing vulnerable groups and increasing their political leverage vis-a-vis other groups; however, as a long-term strategy, it conflicts with the ideal of deliberative democracy. This ideal asks that citizens enter into dialogue in which the values, interests, interpretations, and narrative identifications intrinsic to their identities are placed at risk. Our discussion of disability, in particular, has shown how this kind of dialogue—which is the heart and soul of ST identity politics—can destabilize what otherwise appear to be self-evident identities. However, in addition to expanding our concept of disability to include all of us in one sense or another, this discussion led us to appreciate the way in which democratic deliberation itself is enabling, just as undemocratic dictatorship—as instituted in capitalist organization—is disabling.

The maintenance of class domination depends on dividing the masses—and using SP identity politics in which discrete racial groups are pitted against one another facilitates this. In this chapter, I examine whether one kind of SP identity politics might instead empower racial minorities. More precisely, I focus on the quasi-formal mechanisms integral to democracy—voting procedures and systems of electoral representation—to compare racial redistricting with alternative systems of representation that model ST identity politics.

A MULTIVECTOR MODEL FOR EVALUATING DEMOCRATIC PROCESSES

Before doing so, let me briefly review the functions and values integral to voting procedures and electoral systems and explain how these affect other levels of democracy. First, democracy embraces at least three levels of political action: formal governmental institutions of representation and decision, such as legislatures, courts, and executive offices; informal public spheres conducive to generating public opinion; and quasi-formal systems for electing officials and determining methods of representation.[1] Although formal systems are intrinsically oriented to decision making, and informal institutions are intrinsically oriented to inconclusive deliberation, the fact is that deliberation and decision are integral to both systems. Government officials deliberate among themselves and with their constituents; and citizens act on their political decisions. Quasi-formal systems—which are often thought to be the heart and soul of political democracy—provide methods of election and recall by which citizens influence government officials and hold them accountable for their decisions. Ideally, the political agendas of government officials should be shaped by an informed public; but the interaction between citizens and government officers should be one of mutual dialogue, in which both sides inform and critically respond to one another.

Second, interest aggregation and critical dialogue are complementary functions operating at all three levels of democratic politics. Interests, values, and perspectives—the basic input of all strategic negotiations—become legitimate items of political consideration to the extent that they have been tested in rational dialogue; conversely, dialogue becomes a rational medium for raising and resolving problems to the extent that it is widely informed by the fullest range of alternative inputs. Most important, dialogue as such may be necessary for interest aggregation. Using ordinal voting for ranking three or more alternatives may result in the kinds of voting cycles first diagnosed by Marquis de Condorcet, in the eighteenth century, and more recently by

Kenneth Arrow and other decision theorists (Ingram 1995, 34). These paradoxes, and the profusion of conflicting interests that render aggregation so challenging, might be diminished under a system of democracy that encourages citizens to talk about the social costs of pursuing their interests—costs that might constrain them to agree on less-costly interests (229).

Finally, it follows that the rationality and fairness of aggregation and dialogue can be assessed along three dimensions: equality, autonomy, and reciprocity. Formal institutions embody aggregative equality to the degree that they permit the inclusion and equal weighing of all reasonable interests, values, and perspectives; institutionally speaking, such equality is exemplified by the separation and federal delegation of governmental powers. They embody aggregative autonomy to the extent that they provide an expansive range of choice, covering many policy options; institutionally speaking, this value can also take the form of an independent judiciary that factors in additional constitutional and moral considerations. Finally, formal institutions embody aggregative reciprocity to the degree that they promote good-faith bargaining and strategic compromise among competing parties; institutionally speaking, this function is exemplified by the system of checks and balances. Formal institutions embody dialogical equality to the extent that all parties involved in deliberation have equal opportunities to speak out and be heard; they embody dialogical autonomy to the extent that said parties are free from external and internal (ideological) constraints that might otherwise prevent them from being open to opposing viewpoints; and they embody dialogical reciprocity to the extent that they are predisposed to reaching agreements that are fair to all concerned.

Informal institutions embody the six values of aggregation and dialogue somewhat differently. Leaving aside the constitutional separation and delegation of powers and their mutual checks and balances, formal institutions tend to sacrifice dialogical autonomy for the sake of furthering equality and reciprocity. For instance, courts are constrained to tailor their decisions narrowly to legal precedent, thereby drastically limiting the range of alternative outcomes and rationales that might be deployed; and almost all government officials are under a heavier burden than average citizens when it comes to justifying their decisions in terms of reasons that might be acceptable to everyone. Informal institutions, by contrast, are less attentive to dialogical equality and reciprocity—rules of parliamentary debate and decorum seldom obtain in the hurly-burly of everyday political debate—but permit the expression of a much wider range of opinion.

Now our present concern is not formal and informal democratic processes but quasi-formal systems of voting and election. However, narrowing our focus to what is traditionally regarded as an "aggregative" feature of democracy that covers "quantitative" concerns—such as the determination of voters, the assignment of votes, the relative impact (numerical weight) attached to votes, the number of candidates over which votes can be cast, and the size of electoral districts—need not require shifting our focus from the qualitative, or dialogical, features integral to deliberation; for the way in which voting, election, and representation are formally structured has a direct bearing on campaigns—among the most important venues for generating public opinion—and the rationality and fairness of parliamentary debates.

Quasi-formal systems of this sort can also be evaluated in terms of the three values of aggregation and dialogue mentioned here. Such systems can enhance aggregative freedom by providing voters with a wider range of parties and candidates for whom they can vote. They can enhance aggregative equality by extending equal numbers of votes to all electors, by ensuring the equal value of such votes, by providing for the proportional representation of subgroups, or by instituting bicameral systems that equalize political power across regions and groups. They can enhance aggregative reciprocity by encouraging coalition building between different parties. Finally, they can enhance dialogic freedom, equality, and reciprocity by encouraging candidates and parties to engage a broad spectrum of citizens in rational discussion. At their best, they can promote ST identity politics conducive to building interracial community.

As I argue in the following, how we deliberate—as individuals or as members of groups—will surely affect how we vote, how well we are protected, and how well our interests are satisfied. By stressing the deliberative function of democracy, the participatory democratic paradigm views rights and policies as the outcome of a concerted reflection on identities that transforms differences in the direction of fair and mutual accommodation. Instead of deducing formal rights from innate prepolitical reason, it views them as agreements designed to protect and foster our most basic capacities, as we have collectively interpreted them. Instead of distributing resources on the basis of prior calculations about what human nature in the abstract demands, it distributes them only after the distinctive needs and identifications of those affected are taken into account, which is to say, only after they themselves have deliberated on them.

PRELIMINARY REFLECTIONS: JOHN STUART MILL ON DEMOCRATIC REPRESENTATION

John Stuart Mill was certainly one of the first thinkers to defend the kind of participatory democratic paradigm I am here proposing, and a brief overview of his ideas on representation will prove useful in illuminating the functions and values of democracy as I have hitherto presented them. In the spirit of

Alexis de Tocqueville and James Madison, Mill expressed ambivalent feelings about the new mass democracy that had taken shape in the United States and in England. Like them, he was drawn to its potential for energizing the masses and checking governmental abuses. But he also shared their worries about the potential for majoritarian tyranny and the degeneration of political life: "People will give dishonest or mean votes from lucre, from malice, from pique, from personal rivalry, even from the interests or prejudices of class or sect." (Mill [1861] 1975, 311).

The problem of majoritarian tyranny is especially troublesome given Mill's own utilitarian point of departure, which eschews social contractarian and natural law conceptions of human rights. His predecessor, Jeremy Bentham, had argued that utilitarian-inspired democracy was far more preferable to these conceptions, which he regarded as "nonsense on stilts." As a strong defender of aggregative equality (each person's preferences or votes count no more than another's), Bentham thought that democracy would serve to both maximize aggregate utility and define and protect the rights of citizens against tyrannical rulers. For Mill, however, aggregative equality without deliberative autonomy makes for bad legislation, since taking the masses' unreflected preferences as the supreme standard for public right and good leaves no check on majoritarian tyranny.

Mill's most important treatises on political thought, *On Liberty* (1859) and *Representative Government* (1861), place aggregative and deliberative autonomy at the center of democratic reform. Adopting an "indirect" mode of utilitarianism, Mill argues that the public welfare is best encouraged by furthering the self-realization of each individual's humanity and individuality, which in turn is furthered by respecting their rights to pursue their conception of the good unimpaired by government paternalism. Even if individuals are not always the best judges of their own good, government attempts to impose a conception of social welfare based on perfectionist ideals or utility aggregations will infringe on the individual's freedom of choice and action, which is itself the chief condition for a person's full development and happiness. More important, Mill stressed the importance of deliberative autonomy, noting that freedom of choice and action is enhanced or stunted to the extent that people critically reflect on their preferences and core identities in critical dialogue.

According to Mill, dialogue and diversity go together: without the diverse opinions and lifestyles that make possible aggregative freedom, nothing would be left to discuss or reflect on; without dialogic reciprocity, diversity would degenerate into divisiveness and anarchy. It is in this context that an assessment has to be made of Mill's defense of deliberative democracy as a model of ST identity politics and as an exemplar of aggregative and dialogic autonomy. Despite his insistence on the power of critical dialogue to transform differences of opinion into converging opinion, Mill nonetheless believed that robust deliberation requires that individual as well as group differences be respected and protected against assimilation and uniformity (cultural and class hegemony as well as tendencies toward consumer conformism; Mill [1859] 1975, 90).

In sum, a participatory democratic paradigm that esteems individual freedom and reasonable plurality combines and elevates the advantages of formal liberal protection and social welfare aggregation. The protection of individual and group rights proves useful in funneling diverse opinions and lifestyles toward collective problem solving, with the latter in turn fostering the moral, intellectual, and imaginative capacities that make genuine autonomy and reasonable pluralism desirable ends in themselves. To cite Mill:

> the most important point of excellence which any form of government can possess is to promote the virtue and intelligence of the people themselves . . . . The first point is that the rights and interests of every or any person are only secure from being disregarded, when the person interested is himself able, and habitually disposed, to stand up for them. The second point is, that the general prosperity attains a greater height, and is more widely diffused, in proportion to the amount and variety of the personal energies enlisted to support it . . . . Still more salutary is the moral part of the instruction afforded by the participation of the private citizen, if even rarely, in public functions. He is called on, while so engaged, to weigh interests not his own; to be guided, in case of conflicting claims, by another rule than his private partialities; to apply, at every turn, principles and maxims which have for their reason of existence the common good. ([1861] 1975, 167, 186–87, 197)

This passage attests to the importance of broadly inclusive participatory democracy as a mechanism for protecting rights, generating rational opinion regarding interests, and furthering the moral development of individuals as autonomous and self-determining agents. But Mill's focus is on representative government, not direct participatory democracy, so we need to understand how representative institutions enhance grassroots participation.

Critics of representative democracy such as Rousseau have long argued that representation is either redundant—we could just as easily find out what the masses want by allowing them to vote directly on legislative referenda—or illegitimate; for if the outcome of votes in representative legislative bodies were different from the outcome achieved by popular referendum, this would violate the democratic principle of popular rule. This criticism, however, assumes a false model of representation. It assumes that "representing" is akin to "mirroring," or "repeating." Such a conception of representation would only make sense if we understood "popular rule" to descend from "the *united* will of the people." However, as our earlier discussion of the indeterminacy of delegated and represented decision making clearly attests, not even a single will would be capable of being represented in its integrity, without alteration. This would obtain regardless of whether the will in question was internally divided or not. For the idea that democracy could represent any will presumes that the essence of democracy consists in willing—choosing and acting. But democracy, we know, is not exclusively a process of choice—and certainly not a process of choice analogous to the volition of a single ideally rational agent. As we have seen, it is a process involving deliberation at many different levels—instrumental, evaluative, normative, prescriptive, and executive. These levels of deliberation are not determinately linked—there are gaps that create possibilities for differends. The judicious balancing of a diverse public opinion by legislative, judicial, and executive bodies necessarily involves reinterpreting and qualifying that same opinion.

Once we concede that it is a public conversation embracing plural voices that is represented and not (pace Rousseau) a general will, representation ceases to be a process of mirroring. Properly understood, representatives extend the ongoing process of dialogical reflection occurring in public debate by contributing their own particular voices, which reflect their own autonomous standpoints. Representatives are neither trustees nor delegates, but something in between. Like delegates, they are guided by the concerns of their constituents, but like trustees they are empowered to act on behalf—and independently—of their constituents in reformulating and compromising these concerns in light of the concerns expressed by other representatives.

Given that elected officials must act independently, their membership in the identity group whose interests, values, and perspectives they are advocating—what is sometimes referred to as descriptive representation—becomes especially crucial in guaranteeing their trustworthiness and accountability and therewith the legitimacy of their decisions in the eyes of their constituents.

Mill's impassioned defense of extending the franchise to women and, above all, to the working class reflects this line of thinking—a line of thinking that also supports greater descriptive representation of racial and ethnic minorities. The virtual representation of the interests of these groups by middle- and upper-class white males does not ensure its legitimacy in the minds of those whose interests are so represented; and it does nothing to promote their own empowerment as full-fledged political actors. In principle, a paternalistic government might succeed better in protecting their rights and aggregating their interests, but it would not promote their moral and intellectual development.

Mill proposed to enfranchise the working class in conjunction with a formula for proportional representation. Although he proposed this last principle and other provisions (such as plural voting indexed to education) chiefly as a check on the dangers of working-class "tyranny," his principled defense of proportional representation contains a valuable lesson for progressive identity politics:

> In a representative body actually deliberating, the minority must of course be overruled.... But does it follow that the minority should have no representation at all? Because the majority ought to prevail over the minority, must the majority have all the votes, the minority none? Is it necessary that the minority should not even be heard?... In a really equal democracy, every or any section would be represented, not disproportionately, but proportionately. (Mill [1861] 1975, 248)

This argument for proportional representation appeals to the values of aggregative equality and autonomy and, most important, dialogical equality. The single-seat districts (SSDs) used to elect members to the House of Commons during Mill's time and ours—and currently used in the United States to elect representatives to the House and Senate—only award representation to those who voted for the winning candidate—thereby "wasting" the votes of those who voted otherwise. This system also discourages minority groups from posting candidates who are unlikely to win against candidates posted by the majority, thereby constraining aggregative freedom. Finally, the unequal acknowledgment of winners and losers is duplicated in legislative chambers, in which the losers are denied an equal voice.

To remedy this injustice, Mill proposed implementing the voting method set forth by Thomas Hare, which combines proportional representation with an ordinal-voting scheme. Discarding the principle of geographical representation, Hare's system would require that voters rank all candidates running for Congress. First choices are tabulated first. If a voter's first choice garners a minimum number of votes to be elected (with the percentage being one-nth of all votes cast, where n is the number of seats up for election), then his or her second choice is counted, and so on down the line.

Following Hare's recommendation, minority groups in the United States—especially those who were geographically dispersed—would have an easier time electing representatives who would give voice to their concerns. Whether it is the best and most practical remedy to the injustices inherent in SSDs is a matter I will leave for later. Presently, it is important to remember that the inequities in the American electoral system go well beyond the defects of SSDs and include racial biases embedded in the Constitution itself—as a reprise of the events in Florida on the eve of presidential election 2000 amply testify.

RACIAL POLITICS IN PRESIDENTIAL ELECTION 2000

"It felt like Birmingham last night." That's the way Mari Castellanos, a civil rights activist, described a rally of fourteen thousand people at the New Birth

Baptist Church, a primarily African American congregation, who were protesting the obscene number of black voters who were turned away from polling booths in Dade County, Florida, during presidential election 2000. So much attention was focused on faulty voting machines—more ballots were invalidated than were cast for third-party candidate Ralph Nader—that people ignored the racial dimensions of the election. To begin with, more than four hundred thousand ex-felons were denied the right to vote in Florida according to state law—about half of them black; in fact, many who were not ex-felons were also stricken from voter-registration lists by mistake. Next, consider the electoral college. Without this venerable institution, Al Gore wins the presidency by a comfortable margin. Overlooked by the pundits counting chads, however, was the fact that the electoral college is also a relic of racial politics. It was designed to give Southern states an edge in presidential elections. "Virginia slave owners," Lani Guinier reminds us, "controlled the presidency for thirty-two of our first thirty-six years" (2000). By awarding states electoral votes equal to their number of representatives and senators, the Constitution gives voters living in less-populated states, such as Wyoming, proportionally greater clout than voters living in populated ones. Guinier notes, for instance, that in Wyoming one vote in the electoral college represents 71,000 voters while in Florida one vote represents 238,000 voters. Under the original method of apportioning House districts, Southern states were also allowed to count slaves as three-fifths of a person, thereby boosting their number of representatives—and electoral votes—even more. Today, African Americans and other minorities who tend to be concentrated in the more-populated states, such as California, suffer from a new racial politics. In the Senate, their votes are likely to be worth about one-fortieth of the vote cast by white residents of Wyoming. Worse still, under the winner-take-all system of electing members of Congress, minority votes simply don't count—period (Lazare 1996). Finally, African American communities in Florida and elsewhere have typically been subdivided by electoral districts designed mainly by white legislators to dilute their power to elect representatives of their choice.

Focusing our attention on this last problem reveals something about the prevalence of SP identity politics in America's troubled race relations, which often assume the form of zero-sum contests in which blacks invariably lose (Hochschild 1989). It also reveals something about democracy that was veiled from public view in the aftermath of presidential election 2000. As Mill rightly noted, democracy is not simply a matter of aggregating votes into preference rankings or interest sums. It is also a matter of getting one's voice heard—by electing representatives of one's choice—and having the education and economic wherewithal to organize politically, something that many of Florida's blacks lacked.

Extrapolating from the functional analysis of democracy proposed at the outset of this chapter, we are now in a position to identify three purposes of democracy that were short-circuited during the Florida election. One is to protect citizens from hostile officials by giving them the power of recall—a function not available to outnumbered blacks, who were unable to recall the white Republican bureaucracy responsible for diluting their votes. To this function—surely one of the most venerable according to the formal liberal paradigm of rights—must be added the balancing and aggregation of interests, the function highlighted by the welfare paradigm. This function was also unavailable to blacks, who were neither as free nor as equal as whites in exercising their franchise and who were not treated with full reciprocity as strategic members of the Democratic Party. Finally, there is the deliberative function heralded by civic republicans, which encourages citizens to realize their moral and intellectual capacities through active, civic-minded participation in the affairs of their community. By getting citizens to think about themselves and their various identities as part of an ongoing, transformative dialogue, the deliberative function fosters a reassessment of preferences in terms of their social costs, thereby furthering an orientation toward a nonoppressive common good. Again, Florida's blacks were less capable of exercising political choice (thanks to Florida's segregated public schools, a significant percentage were illiterate and could not understand the balloting instructions); they were denied equal access to mass media to voice their opinions; and they were not treated with full dignity and respect by the white power structure—Democratic or Republican.

THE CASE OF RACIAL REDISTRICTING

The Florida election highlights a history of black disenfranchisement that was supposedly rectified by passage of the Voting Rights Act of 1965. This act and subsequent judicial decisions progressively enhanced the aggregative equality of Southern blacks by eliminating onerous voting qualifications (poll taxes, literacy tests, etc.) and vote dilution caused by the racial gerrymandering of electoral districts (Ingram 2000a, ch. 9). The latter involved redrawing the boundaries of SSD districts in which blacks formerly formed a majority, or, as in the case of state and municipal districts, it involved replacing them with larger, multimember districts (MMDs) in which whites were the majority.

By the mideighties the Department of Justice was endorsing a more radical solution to the problem of minority vote dilution: racial redistricting, or the creation of SSDs with a majority or substantial plurality of minority voters. Since the early nineties, racial redistricting has been attacked on grounds that it predefines the identity and options of voters and promotes racial divisiveness. In the remainder of this chapter, I propose to assess these charges, examining the potential of this system for empowering blacks and other minorities. My standard is the values pertinent to aggregation and dialogue. Because dialogical autonomy and equality are relatively independent of voting procedure and electoral design, I mainly focus on aggregative values and how they affect dialogical reciprocity, within campaigns as well as within legislatures and public-opinion formation.

The question I am addressing is this: Does racial redistricting tend to promote dialogical reciprocity conducive to ST identity politics, and, if not, are there other voting procedures and electoral schemes that do? One alternative scheme, which has been defended by Lani Guinier, is MMDs with cumulative voting (CV). This scheme, I argue, might well promote ST identity politics better than racially redistricted SSDs because under certain circumstances, it would encourage white and black candidates to appeal to voters outside their primary racial constituencies. However, other schemes, such as the ordinal-voting scheme proposed by Mill, might prove even more efficacious in this respect—at least in theory. In the final analysis, the tendency for any scheme to promote interracial dialogue and ST identity politics depends on local and national circumstances. I conclude that no system can effectively maximize all six aggregative and deliberative values so that principled compromises will have to be made—especially with respect to values of freedom and equality.

MINORITY–MAJORITY SINGLE-SEAT DISTRICTS (M-MSSDS)

A good place to begin our assessment of racial redistricting is by examining its efficacy as a remedy against minority vote dilution. The record is mixed. While M-MSSDs have increased black and minority-descriptive representation, they have not done so in numbers proportionate to black and minority populations. For example, during the heyday of racial redistricting (from 1990 to 1994) the number of black members in the House of Representatives grew from 26 to 39—out of a total of 435 representatives. Not only did the increased percentage of black representatives (8.9 percent) still inadequately reflect the potential voting strength of blacks (who compose 12.5 percent of the population), but thirty-five of the thirty-nine districts that elected black representatives did so by margins exceeding 65 percent of the vote—a sure sign that surplus black votes were being wasted (Hacker 1995, 220).

M-MSSDs also score low on another index of aggregative equality: they likely decreased the representation and bargaining leverage of black interests overall by reducing the total number of seats held by white Democrats (whom the Leadership Council on Civil Rights rates higher than their Republican counterparts in supporting civil rights measures and redistributive policies targeted toward ameliorating the condition of minorities). To complicate our assessment of M-MSSDs aggregative equality, the racial and ethnic complexity of such districts often dilutes the voting power of "double minorities" (minorities within minorities). For example, M-MSSDs in New York have empowered African American majorities at the expense of Caribbean black minorities.

Here we arrive at the second shortcoming of M-MSSDs: their diminution of the aggregative autonomy of constituent voters. Critics of race-conscious redistricting frequently charge that it reinforces old racial stereotypes, thereby encouraging a divisive SP identity politics in which one group tries to impose its identity and interests on other groups. As Justice Sandra Day O'Connor puts it, "A racial gerrymander may exacerbate the very patterns of bloc voting that majority-minority districting is sometimes said to counteract," thereby leading representatives to believe that their primary obligation is to represent only members of the racial group that elected them "rather than their constituency as a whole."[2]

Grouping minorities together according to racial categories, whether for purposes of affirmative action or for racial redistricting, encourages "us" to view "them" not as individuals with unique identities and interests but as faceless caricatures based on racist stereotypes. In O'Connor's words:

> A reapportionment plan that includes in one district individuals who belong to the same race, but who are otherwise widely separated by geographical and political boundaries, and who may have little in common with one another but the color of their skin, bears an uncomfortable resemblance to political apartheid. It reinforces the perception that members of the same racial group -regardless of their age, education, economic status, or the community in which they live think alike, share the same political interests, and will prefer the same candidates at the polls. We have rejected such perceptions elsewhere as impermissible racial stereotypes.[3]

These objections are not entirely ill founded. As I note in chapter 2, legitimate, nonstereotypical references to group identity must accord with two important facts. First, an individual's identification with any group is increasingly a matter of voluntary choice, and this applies as well to racial groups, the constituent members of which might not all consciously identify themselves as racially marked in any particular way. Second, an individual's identification with a group is seldom if ever exclusive; he or she typically identifies with many groups and their sometimes incompatible interests. These sentiments are echoed as well by those who, like Lani Guinier, defend the concept of racial identity.[4]

However defined and redefined, contextualized and complicated, the almost irrefutable existence of something like a racial minority group identity suggests that a vital political system must accommodate those who *choose* that identity. To make room, however, does not mean to evict other identities. To this end, a racial minority group identity should be represented to the extent that its members in fact act collectively. Mere assumptions about alleged uniformity should be insufficient to justify measures to ensure group representation. This approach acknowledges that one's racial group is not the only club to which one belongs. Collective group preferences might be measured by using innovative electoral schemes like cumulative voting and proportional representation. In this view, unity is defined as collaboration rather than as sameness. (Guinier 1994, 131–32)

Guinier undercuts the standard conservative objection against group representation by arguing that a properly conceived notion of group identity—compatible with both individual choice and mixed identity—is "incompatible with the sort of monolithic sameness that evokes the impression of false stereotyping." As she points out, an authentic concept of group identity is premised on the fact that no identity exists in a state of self-contained passivity, as racist advocates of sociobiological determinism would like us to believe. Although an identity may be imposed on a group or individual—as it is in the case of racial identities—the act of imposition not infrequently calls forth a counterresponse on the part of those who have been imposed on. For instance, many African Americans have come to identify consciously with being black, despite the fact that their being so identified by whites was not of their choosing. Hence, the mere fact that racial classifications (and their corresponding identities) originated in illegitimate acts of domination and false ideologies of sociobiological determinism need not diminish the legitimacy of racial identifications among those minorities who now consciously embrace them. Indeed, because minorities who have suffered racial segregation and oppression understandably organize themselves into distinctive political communities on the basis of race, their demand for group representation seems even more legitimate than similar demands made by members of other groups.

If we leave aside the intriguing possibility that racially designated communities form political interest groups that are more stable and enduring than those designated by partisan vote tabulations (which the Court accepts as a legitimate basis for redistricting; Rush 1993), we are left with Guinier's idea that minority identity need not stereotype racial minorities's interests. If the legitimacy of a racial group identity is proportionate to the degree to which those who share it do so actively (as a matter of rationally informed choice), and if the preeminent medium of rationally informed choice is the critical exchange of opinions that occurs only collectively in democratic debate, then the legitimacy of a racial group identity—and therewith the stability of its interest base—is scarcely conceivable apart from its being affected, as it were, by other group identifications. Hence, an individual's rational identification with a given group and its set of interests will seldom (if ever) be so exclusive as to rule out identification with other groups and their interests.

In the passage cited earlier, Guinier suggests that her nonmonolithic conception of group identification has important implications for electoral redistricting. As I remarked in my discussion of Mill, a deliberative democracy that encourages free and impartial debate about the core interests, values, experiences, and perspectives informing one's identity will complicate individuals' group loyalties. Regardless of whether they are considered separately or in conjunction with one another, the usual indicators of political interest and identity—be they defined by race, ethnicity, class, ideology, or place of residence—will be insufficient to identify the dominant interests of any particular group of persons. Although black persons will share an interest in combating racism, and although persons living in the same political subdivision will share an interest in having effective utility service, neither antiracism nor effective utility service can be presumed to be dominant interests, respectively, of black persons or persons living in the same political subdivision. For some blacks, effective utility service will be more important than antiracism, just as for some residents of a city, antiracism will be more important than effective utility service. This last point suggests that the problem of imposing a group identity is inherent in the very nature of SSDs and is not exclusive to racial redistricting.

Drawing electoral boundaries affects this kind of imposition, even when the intention is to ensure that residents of the same neighborhood, city, or county have control over (for instance) the people who run their local utilities. The only way to avoid prejudging individuals' interests would be to abolish electoral boundaries and allow voters to vote for at-large candidates, in effect allowing them to create their own subjectively chosen constituencies.

The fact that all SSDs involve imposing a preconceived group (constituency) identity on voters within a district points to the inherent one-sidedness of O'-Connor's critique of racial redistricting. One could just as easily agree with her colleague on the Court, Anthony Kennedy, in condemning redistricting proposals guided by stereotypes based [on "religious, sexual or national class"[5] for persons sharing the same ethnicity, nationality, gender, and religion will also have divergent interests. But if group classifications cease to designate a locus of common interest deserving of political representation, then not only racial redistricting but any redistricting scheme based on protecting the supposed group interest of a geographically defined community would be illegitimate, including the brazenly partisan redistricting that is currently tolerated by the Supreme Court. Defenders of race-conscious remedies rightly condemn the arbitrariness of the Court's belief that partisan voting patterns — but not racial affinities — demarcate communities of political interest meriting representation. If drawing electoral boundaries for the sake of protecting political parties and incumbents is acceptable, then why is it not acceptable to draw electoral boundaries for the sake of protecting racial minorities in their right to elect representatives of their choice?[6] The usual response — that racial characteristics as such do not permit inferences regarding interests — ignores the fact that racial group identities often do gravitate toward shared affinities, if not interests.

Conservative critics of racial reapportionment presume that the only thing that representatives represent are the concrete interests of individual constituents, which can be neatly correlated with specific policies. However, the mere fact that persons of the same race do not share the same concrete interests (or, for that matter, the same values and ideological commitments) need not doom the concept of racial group representation, because citizens want their perspectives as well as their interests represented.[7]

We must first distinguish two ways in which the black community's interests might be understood. Broadly speaking, the black community designates all black persons who have experienced racist discrimination or who know what it is like to feel diminished in the eyes of white persons (what W. E. B. Du Bois famously referred to as the "double-consciousness" of blacks). This community knits together blacks of all economic backgrounds and ideological persuasions, from progressive radicals such as the Reverend Jesse Jackson to stalwart conservatives such as Justice Clarence Thomas. Although having experienced discrimination no doubt predisposes virtually all members of this community to have an interest in promoting antiracism and antidiscrimination policies, that might be the only interest they have in common. Given their ideological and class differences, not all members of the black community broadly construed agree on antipoverty and affirmative action programs designed to combat racism and discrimination. Hence, their common interest in combatting racism and discrimination, which flows directly from their common experience of discrimination and, in turn, informs their common perspective of seeing themselves through the lens of a double consciousness, will not translate into specific interests or policies that could satisfy the interests of each and every one of them.

A narrower conception of black community, by contrast, refers expressly to a plurality of more or less geographically compact and ideologically homogeneous communities. As William Julius Wilson and other sociologists have pointed out (Wilson 1987), the most urgent problems confronting the "urban underclass" — the lack of jobs and the corresponding ills associated with unemployment, such as unstable families, high crime rates, poverty, and illness — are not those confronting the black middle class, at least not to the same degree. More important for this latter group are diminished opportunities for professional advancement and increased earnings.

The interests of blacks living in urban ghettos will overlap with the interests of blacks living in middle-class communities, especially as regards antiracism and antidiscrimination, but it is less likely that these groups' interests will overlap to the same degree regarding other issues. One of the most obvious examples is that middle-class blacks, like their middle-class white counterparts, will be concerned about the erosion of middle-class entitlements, whereas blacks living in urban ghettos will be concerned about the dismantling of welfare, job training, food stamps, public housing, and Medicaid.

My detour into the concept of a political community's interests underscores a point I made earlier with respect to Mill's support of descriptive representatives. The one thing that most members of a racial minority have in common—and the one thing that transcends their chosen preferences and value commitments—is a unique perspective on racism that stems from having grown up in a community that has been discriminated against. Thus, while it is true, as Abigail Thernstrom notes (1987) that white persons might effectively advocate the values and interests of blacks, it is at least arguable that they might not effectively advocate blacks' general perspective on society.

I am not saying that only a member of an oppressed minority can fully understand that group's perspective. This mistaken notion of having to identify personally with the perspectives of one's constituents leads to the absurd conclusion that representatives must exactly mirror what each of their constituents thinks and feels. Rather, what I am suggesting is that minorities must elect some representatives from their own group, perhaps in rough proportion to their percentage of the overall population,[8] for them to feel confident that their perspectives have been accorded due respect by the majority.

Ensuring that members of an oppressed group have a chance to elect representatives who share their perspective provides legislatures with firsthand information about what it is like to be a member of such a group, which is vital to the legislative process and difficult to obtain otherwise. Even if white representatives can obtain secondhand information about what it is like to be one of the oppressed, it is important that such information also be articulated by representatives who actually have that perspective, for this symbolically shows that the majority respects the minority as an equal and autonomous advocate for its own perspective.

To conclude, the conservative objection against racial redistricting is based on a disingenuous distinction between geographically, racially, and politically imposed constituencies as well as a fallacious understanding of what constitutes a legitimate community of interest and how best that interest might be represented. Nonetheless, it is true that SSDs limit the freedom of voters to choose their constituencies. This limitation, in turn, negatively affects the capacity of such districts to promote aggregative and dialogical reciprocity.

Guinier notes that the real benefits of single-seat black districts in mobilizing the black community and provoking critical reflection on the part of whites quickly diminish once it is understood that representatives of these districts are but tokens who wield little influence in legislatures. Divested of political influence, they end up compromising, selling out to special interests, or succumbing to the perks of patronage; as incumbents virtually assured of reelection, their interest in the community wanes (Guinier 1991, 1111). Conversely, voter mobilization in support of them ceases to be politically informed and becomes symbolic and routine.

Certainly many of Guinier's complaints against single-seat black districts reflect the inordinate power that incumbents and monied interests wield in politics generally and so apply to all electoral districts (single-seat or multi-seat, white or nonwhite). However, according to Guinier, the very fact that black representatives from majority–minority districts do not have to compete for reelection with representatives from white districts explains why the former are particularly powerless to mitigate racial polarization and effect policy reforms on behalf of their constituents. Because representatives from white districts do not have to compete with representatives from black districts, they can afford to dismiss or ignore them. This "ghettoization" of black representatives in the legislature, which Guinier calls "deliberative gerrymandering," only reinforces racial segregation and stereotyping and does nothing to advance the black community's political agenda. To ensure the equal satisfaction of interests, representatives of white districts would have to see that it was in their interests to negotiate in good faith with their minority compatriots, and that, Guinier insists, would occur only if they were forced to run for reelection in multiseat districts with a substantial minority population. Under these conditions, neither white nor black candidates could take the black community's support for granted, and so members of this community would again have the opportunity to mobilize themselves and become politically educated.

ALTERNATIVE SYSTEMS OF REPRESENTATION AND VOTING

Before moving on to discuss Guinier's proposal for MMDs using cumulative voting (CV), let us briefly examine several other systems of representation that have been proposed to protect minority vote dilution. As in the case of the SSD, these systems of representation involve various combinations among three factors: the size and character of geographic districts (single seat, multiple seat, or open); the formula for electing candidates (numerical threshold for election, by individual or party list, etc.); and the structure of balloting (single or multiple voting; categorical or ordinal voting).

One method, which has been used in New Zealand to empower Maoris; in India to empower lower castes; and in Lebanon to ensure equitable power sharing among Maronites, Shi'ites, Sunnis, and Druze; involves reserving a certain number of seats for minority groups. In closed-role, reserved-seat systems (New Zealand), only members of a protected group can vote for candidates from the group who are competing for a limited number of reserved seats. In open-role systems (India and Lebanon), members of other groups can vote for candidates from the protected group who are competing for these seats.

Generally speaking, reserved-seat systems perform poorly in promoting aggregative autonomy. Although members of protected groups are at least guaranteed a minimal level of representation—which is freedom enhancing— the fact that they are bound to a list (in New Zealand, Maoris can opt out of the list) is clearly not freedom enhancing. Such systems may improve the aggregative equality of their members to the degree that the number of reserved seats is proportional to their percentage of the population and to the extent that such groups do not contain double minorities that might be denied representation by the majority. As for improving aggregative and deliberative reciprocity between groups, such systems fare as poorly as M-MSSDs, although open-role systems perform better than closed systems (Lijphart 1994).

Another scheme, proportional representation by party list (PR), deploys MMDs, party lists from which voters can rank or select individual members, a proportional election formula applied to parties, and a categorical ballot. As one might expect, PR increases the aggregative freedom of minority groups by encouraging the formation of small parties. Aggregative freedom is also enhanced by the fact that voters choose their preferred constituency rather than have it geographically dictated by legislatures and courts. PR's potential for increasing the aggregative equality of minority groups is somewhat less certain. Fewer votes get wasted than those wasted in SSD systems, but disadvantaged double minorities still lose out. As for aggregative and deliberative reciprocity, there appears to be little incentive for candidates to appeal to voters outside their own party, given the categorical nature of voting. At best, the system encourages multipartisan coalition building within legislatures (Lijphart 1994, 150).

Systems that encourage aggregative and dialogical reciprocity—and that promote interracial ST identity politics—generally deploy ordinal or multiple balloting. Alternative voting systems (AV) allow voters to rank candidates in SSDs or MMDs. If no candidates receive the minimum threshold of votes necessary for election (50 percent is normally required), the candidate with the fewest number of first-place votes is dropped from the ballot, and the second-place votes of those who voted for her are then tabulated. In general, AV enhances aggregative autonomy by encouraging the formation of smaller parties; voters whose small-party candidates cannot get elected can still transfer their second vote to another candidate who is more likely to win. The outcome in presidential election 2000 would have been entirely different if those who had voted for Green Party candidate Ralph Nader had had their second-place votes transferred, since the majority of these would have gone to Al Gore. This outcome shows that AV also enhances aggregative equality, although this benefit decreases as the number of seats in the electoral district increases (indeed, as studies of AV in Australia show, candidates who win the most first-place votes do not always get elected; Wright 1986, 131–32).

A variation of the AV system that is used in MMDs, the single transferable vote (STV) combines the ordinal ballot with a Droop proportional representation quota, which equals the total number of votes cast (N_v), divided by the number of electoral seats (N_s) plus one, plus an additional one: $(N_v/[N_s + 1]) + 1$. For example, if one hundred votes are cast in a three-seat district, the number of votes needed for election would be twenty-six:

$(100/[3 + 1]) + 1 = 26$
$(100/4) + 1 = 26$
$25 + 1 = 26$.

If any seats remain unfilled after this formula is applied, an alternative vote transfer is implemented. Either the last-place candidate is dropped and the second preference votes of those who voted for him or her are transferred, or the second-place votes of winning candidates are distributed according to a complex formula, using a transfer quotient, which equals the number of excess votes divided by the number of votes received. Using the previous example, if a winning candidate received thirty-nine votes—or thirteen more than the necessary twenty-six—the candidate's transfer quotient would be one-third: $13/39 = 1/3$. All thirty-nine second-preference totals would then be multiplied by this quotient and distributed. For instance, if candidate P received six second-preference votes among the thirty-nine cast, P would be awarded two extra votes to his or her first-place tally: $6 \times [1/3] = 2$. Using this system ensures that those winning candidates receiving the largest number of excess votes will have the highest transfer quotients, which reflects their proportional advantage in voter preference over winning candidates with smaller numbers of excess votes.

I mention this complex system because it has been used successfully in Cincinnati's municipal elections. Its most striking feature is its diminution of vote dilution through both a proportionality and an ordinal-vote transfer formula. In practice, the latter appears to promote aggregative autonomy as well as encourage interracial dialogue and ST identity politics. For instance, blue-collar blacks in Cincinnati's MMD elections were able to use the ordinal transfer mechanism to express a primary preference for a black representative and a secondary preference for a working-class representative. Thanks to this vote-splitting strategy, their increase in aggregative autonomy was matched by an overall increase in aggregative and dialogical reciprocity (Straetz 1958, 121–42). Republican candidates, for instance, were encouraged to reach out to the black electorate, even though blacks—who constituted 11 percent of the electorate—were too outnumbered to elect their primary preference (Amy 2000, 133–34).

Cumulative Voting

Another electoral system that has been touted by Guinier as a solution to minority vote dilution and racially polarized voting involves the use of MMD and cumulative voting (CV). In an MMD containing four seats, citizens could distribute four ballots as they saw fit, thereby increasing their aggregative autonomy. For instance, an African American environmentalist could effectively express both her antiracism and her environmental preferences by casting two ballots for a candidate running on an antiracism platform and two ballots for a candidate running on an environmentalist plank.

CV would also enable minorities who are not geographically concentrated to elect representatives of their choice in numbers more proportional to their actual percentage of the population. Suppose that a racial minority that forms 25 percent of a given population is evenly distributed throughout a region. If the region is divided into four districts, and if—as in the United States—there is a strong tendency for racially polarized voting, the minority will have a difficult time electing a representative of its choice. By contrast, if the region were configured as a four-seat district that permitted cumulative voting (granting four votes per person), the minority group in question could elect the candidate of its choice simply by having each of its voting members cast all four ballots for the candidate. (By receiving 25 percent of all votes, any candidate in a four-seat race would be guaranteed election.)

Besides increasing the aggregative equality of minority voters, CV would promote aggregate and dialogic reciprocity. Candidates would be encouraged to pitch their campaigns to broader constituencies, and they would be less tempted to advocate on behalf of a narrow range of interests and groups. Given the significant incidence of segregation and racial polarization in American politics, the need for candidates to build broad electoral coalitions spanning racial divisions might move the electorate from a divisive SP identity politics to a solidarity-promoting ST identity politics.

According to Guinier, CV also satisfies the black community's interests more efficiently than racial redistricting, but this is less certain. Let us assume for the sake of argument that CV might result in the election of more officials—black and nonblack—who are sympathetic to combating racism and discrimination. Given the problems of wasted votes and "deliberative gerrymandering" cited by Guinier, this assumption is not implausible. In that case, Guinier's policy for reforming the election of officials is more likely to further the satisfaction of the black community's interests broadly construed than the current policy of racially redistricting single-seat districts. However, it is not more likely to satisfy any particular black community's interests narrowly construed. Indeed, a representative from a small single-seat district might more effectively advocate the distinct perspectives, values, and interests of that district's inhabitants than if he or she were to represent—along with others—the perspectives, values, and interests of several different communities forming a large district.

Guinier's belief that CV is more likely to promote the satisfaction of the black community's interests is plausible only if we define those interests very abstractly, as a strong preference to end racism and discrimination. However, Guinier herself feels that the promotion of antidiscrimination alone hardly satisfies the interests of middle-class blacks, who strongly desire affirmative action policies; and impoverished urban blacks, who strongly desire job creation and social support policies. Although these interests might conceivably be advanced more successfully using CV, it is equally conceivable that they will be better promoted by a race-sensitive single-seat system (a conclusion that seems especially compelling when applied to the virtually unique problems confronting urban ghettos).

Guinier's belief—that CV will better advance the black community's interests—is conceptually problematic for another reason. Guinier believes that CV encourages the kind of ST identity politics that works by destabilizing (or, in her words, disaggregating) the preference rankings of individuals and groups (Guinier 1991, 1136n.287). It does this by provoking critical reflection on the social costs of satisfying our interests, on the worthinesss of the core values that anchor them, and on the reliability of our experiences and the open-mindedness of our perspectives. By setting our identities in motion, mutual criticism destabilizes our interests as well as our group sympathies.

Given the peculiar volatility of interests under CV, Guinier would be better advised to downplay the importance of representing and satisfying the black community's interests in favor of representing its social perspective, which is perhaps less susceptible to the vicissitudes of ST identity politics. Although individual blacks also perceive their oppression and stigmatization personally and variably, there is a degree of overlap and constancy in their diverse perceptions that is wanting in their concrete interests. The stress on representing the black community's perspective, rather than satisfying its interests, in turn recalls the need for electing more black representatives, even if doing so does not obviously promote the satisfaction of any particular black community's interests. But if we want to get more blacks elected to office, why not simply push for a more efficient kind of race-conscious redistricting, involving, say, the creation of more SSDs, instead of opting for Guinier's proposal for multiseat districts?

Consideration of the destabilizing impact of multiseat districts on interest positions leads me to question the other reason why Guinier favors such districts, namely, their capacity to further genuinely transformative interracial dialogue. Using CV, black as well as white representatives will have to expand their base of support to include each other's primary constituencies. However, as experience has all too painfully shown, for impoverished black communities to compete effectively for influence with more-affluent white communities inhabiting the same multiseat district, the economic, educational, and demographic inequalities between the two communities would have to be mitigated. Unless the political dialogue in which electoral bargaining occurs is independent of social inequalities and other constraints, it cannot be an effective or legitimate medium by which individuals can freely choose their group affiliations. And, as a matter of related concern, there is no reason to think that representatives from multiseat districts will be any more immune to the corrupting influence of patronage, special interests, and compromised politics than those from single-seat ones.

Perhaps neither electoral system can ensure full minority participation in political life. Guinier mentions at least two other controversial policies that would have to be implemented for her model of transformative democracy to flourish. First, the system of proportional interest representation might have to be supplemented by supermajoritarian parliamentary procedures, including minority veto privileges and office rotation, thereby ensuring periodical minority control over governmental agendas.[9] Second, to maintain minority community solidarity against the disintegrative effects of a pluralistic competition for influence, minority communities would have to revitalize themselves as protest movements.

THEORY AND PRACTICE

Our examination of the social and economic backgrounds conditioning electoral systems suggests that the choice of a system cannot be decided in the abstract. Given the weakness of the party system in the United States, PR and reserved-seat representation are not feasible options. That leaves systems that favor individual-centered representation: CV, AV, and STV. CV is an effective device for reducing wasted minority votes when the minority's percentage of the district's population approximates the district's Droop quotient (21 percent in a four-seat district). However, marked deviations below or above that percentage will result in wasted votes. Where minorities are geographically concentrated and constitute a large plurality or majority of the district's population, no advantage over racially redistricted SSDs obtains. Indeed, from a purely theoretical point of view, CV promotes aggregative equality less efficiently than STV, since there is no efficient mechanism for transferring excess votes and no base threshold for election (theoretically, a candidate in a four-seat district could win a handful of votes and still be elected, so long as she or he placed fourth in overall vote tabulations). Finally, it is far from certain that CV will promote ST identity politics. Under the conditions mentioned here, where a minority's population approximates the Droop quotient of the district and there exists racial polarization, the minority group in question might be well advised to encourage its members to cast all their votes for their own descriptive candidate, thereby discouraging candidates favored by other groups from reaching out to them.

In terms of policy reform, replacing SSDs with CVs at the federal level in American politics will be destabilizing in its own right, and it might provoke a strong white racial backlash. Indeed, any "radical" attempt to mitigate the racial inequities of the current system—from revising the system of bicameral legislation to abolishing the electoral college—will be met with strong resistance on the part of those who stand to lose. This is not an argument against radical change, but it reminds us that less-extreme reforms—such as expanding the number of House seats—might well go far in accomplishing the same ends.

By contrast, radical changes appear more promising at the local level—and, indeed, CV, AV, and STV systems have been passed into legislation using popular referenda. Despite its somewhat more-complex structure, the STV systems formerly in use in Ohio cities and currently in use in Cambridge, Massachusetts, generally promote aggregative equality, autonomy, and reciprocity (and dialogical reciprocity) more effectively than either CV or AV.

To conclude, once we factor in social, economic, and political context, decisions for reforming electoral systems will have to make do with principled compromises. Racial redistricting may be the most practical solution to minority vote dilution at the federal level; if so, its capacity to promote aggregative equality for minorities may well be purchased at the price of limiting autonomy in choice of constituency and in perpetuating a divisive SP identity politics. Even the capacity of racial redistricting to foster closer identification between descriptive representatives and constituents is less certain than it might seem. For, as we shall see in the next chapter, the dialogical interaction between government officials and citizens favors a one-sided exchange of information in which critical deliberation is often frustrated.

NOTES

1. I borrow this vector model, as well as its application to electoral and voting systems, from Michael Rabinder James (2004) and Jack Knight and Jim Johnson (1994).
2. *Shaw v. Reno, U.S. Supreme Court Reports,* 125L Ed 2d, no. 1 (August 6, 1993), 529.
3. *Shaw v. Reno,* 529.
4. According to Lani Guinier (1994), "The goals of the Voting Rights Act can and should be defended by framing them philosophically within a theory of group representation" (113). Instead of offering "a theory of exit for minority group members who choose to emphasize their individual identity," she proposes a theory that will "empower those whose chosen identity is group-based" (123).
5. *Miller v. Johnson, U.S. Supreme Court Reports* (slip op.) 94-631(June 29, 1995), 9.
6. Although there are conceptual differences between partisan and racial redistricting, in practice the two often overlap. Redistricting proposals that are based on precinct vote tabulations aim to protect incumbents and ensure that the share of candidates put forward for election by a given party roughly approximates its share of the votes cast. Theoretically, at least, this aim can be realized by simply totaling the chosen preferences of individuals without taking into account their particular identities and interests. Because voting patterns among racial minorities have a strong partisan flavor, it is possible that in many cases partisan redistricting alone suffices to ensure black communities their right to elect representatives of their choice.
7. The distinction among interests, values, and perspectives has been developed extensively by Iris Young, in numerous contexts. Here I draw from Young's essay "Deferring Group Representation," in *NOMOS: Group Rights*, ed. W. Kymlicka and I. Shapiro (New York: New York University Press, forthcoming).
8. However, as Iris Young (1990a) indicates, "proportional representation of group members may sometimes be too little or too much to accomplish that aim" of representing group experiences, perspectives, and interests; for if it were implemented in the United States, American Indians and other small groups would still be without representation while women, who constitute more than 50 percent of the population, might be represented at the expense of other minority groups (108).
9. Guinier (1991, 1140). A consensus-building minority-veto rule was ordered as part of the remedy for structural vote dilution in the city of Mobile, Alabama; see *City of Mobile v. Bolden*, 446 U.S. 55 (1980). In Selma, Alabama, the city council agreed to appoint five whites and five blacks as voting members to the school board, with a chair rotating annually between the two groups. Guinier also cites John Calhoun's supermajoritarian proposal, which requires a concurrent majority of minority representatives (in this case, Southern legislators) in the ratification of federal legislation.

Chapter Five

Democracy and the Rule of Law: Differends and Crises in Postliberal Capitalism

Myth-making and fatherly commands must be abandoned—the Santa Claus story of complete legal certainty; the fairy tale of a pot of golden law which is already in existence and which the good lawyer can find, if only he is sufficiently diligent; the phantasy of an aesthetically satisfactory system and harmony, consistent and uniform, which will spring up when we find the magic wand of a rationalizing principle. We must stop telling stork-fibs about how law is born and cease even hinting that perhaps there is still some truth in Peter Pan legends of a happy juristic hunting ground in a land of legal absolutes.

—Jerome Frank[1]

In the preceding chapter I remark that no system of election and representation can realize all the aggregative and deliberative values underlying a rational and just democracy. Principled compromises should be struck between them depending on context. Given the peculiar institutional and racial realities of American democracy—single-seat districts and racial segregation—racial redistricting may be the most pragmatic short-term remedy to minority vote dilution. Still, whatever aggregative and deliberative equality is gained by racial redistricting purchased at a steep cost: decreases in aggregative autonomy with respect to choice of constituency and political identity, and disincentives for interracial reciprocity.

As our brief discussion of presidential election 2000 has shown, principled compromises such as this are constrained by compromised social institutions. Capitalism is one such institution. It is the crucible in which working-class white identity—and its racially polarized politics—have taken shape. In this chapter, I examine how capitalism compromises formal and informal institutions of democratic deliberation and decision in a more emphatic way. To put it bluntly, containing class conflict requires containing democracy, which means defusing volatile feelings of injustice by translating popular discontentment into the less-incendiary rhetoric of economic compromise and technical problem solving. But this, too, is an injustice—a differend, in Lyotard's lexicon, in which the voices of the masses are suppressed, silenced, and coopted by a different discourse. In this discourse, government officials cease to represent their constituents, in Mill's sense, and instead become their managers, imposing solutions on them, as well as identities (in the case of racial redistricting), and doing so from on high, through judicial and bureaucratic fiat.

Stated differently, the kind of critical dialogue between government officials and their constituents that is necessary for holding the former accountable to the latter is replaced by information pooling. Citizens learn that the issues discussed by government officials are too technical for them to understand, so they accept a diminished role in deliberation: they "inform" their elected leaders about problems they experience in their everyday lives and hope that they will be addressed, knowing full well that the manner in which they will be addressed will involve legal technicalities that far exceed their ken. Meanwhile, elected leaders seldom challenge their constituents to critically reconsider their preferences in light of their social costs to others— doing so, after all, might jeopardize their reelection—so they, too, are limited to informing them about how government is trying to satisfy their preferences.

Leaving aside the government's dissemination of "misinformation" among even its own members as well as its manipulation of the public—often with the latter's acquiescence—it is clear that deliberative autonomy, equality, and reciprocity between government representatives and their constituents are often severely compromised and especially so when sensitive issues of economic justice and class privilege are at stake. It is also clear that partial responsibility for this failure in representative democracy resides in the public's apathy and disability. The public's willingness to defer to managerial authority is symptomatic of its own lack of knowledge, critical acumen, and passivity. But this, too, has its deeper sources in the capitalist mode of production. Efficient production for profit centralizes global-planning decisions in corporate boardrooms and delegates partial-planning decisions to subcontractors and subaltern managers—often entirely bypassing rank and file input. Centralizing knowledge in this way also centralizes control over the workplace, thereby depriving once-skilled workers of any control over their work stations and therewith any bargaining leverage they might have had with respect to management. The "divide and conquer" strategy that once proved so efficacious in preventing white and black workers from banding together reappears in the intense division of labor, in which workers are isolated from one another in segmented work stations; condemned to repeat their fragmentary, routinized labors; and cut off from any larger understanding of the global aims and functions of the production process. Having ceded control over this—the active and productive—part of their lives, is it any wonder that average citizens retreat into their private familial cocoons to cultivate what vestigial dignity and autonomy remains to them—as consumers and clients?

And so we now see that the informal institutions wherein deliberative democracy is said to flourish—the public spheres where people gather to discuss issues—is itself adversely affected by the economic institutions of civil society and not only in the obvious sense that "money talks." There is certainly injustice aplenty in the manipulation of the mass media by the wealthy few. But more important for our purposes is the "other" injustice: the way in which our identities as active producers have been suppressed, as well as the vocabulary of living labor as the primary means by which we express and develop our humanity. What I am talking about here is another differend in which the means for life, freedom, dignity, and solidarity have been reduced to a mere instrumental means—labor power—that can be bought and sold, cultivated or stunted, at the whim of a privileged few.

In sum, capitalism disables democracy by encouraging two interrelated differends: it disables formal representative democracy—the dialogue between government representatives and citizens—by suppressing the popular discourse of moral outrage directed against economic injustice behind the anodyne technical discourse of maximizing stable economic growth and aggregating preferences; it disables informal popular democracy—the dialogue among citizens regarding the fullest realization of their productive powers—by expunging it from the one place where it should matter the most, the workplace, and substituting in its stead the base language of the marketplace, wherein laboring activity is just another commodity to be purchased and consumed.

The latter differend is structurally embedded in capitalism; the former—somewhat surprisingly—is not, and that is what this chapter is about. Following an idea first advanced by Georg Lukács and more recently rearticulated by Herbert Marcuse and Jürgen Habermas, I argue that the suppression of political debate about economic injustice behind the scientific and technological discourse of efficient management first emerges in the twentieth century, with the transition from laissez-faire capitalism to state-managed (corporate or postliberal) capitalism. Coinciding with this transformation in capitalism we notice a profound change in legal paradigm. The highly complex and mediated nature of corporate capitalism cannot be harmonized with the formal liberal paradigm, which assumes that fully determinate property rights can be logically deduced with absolute certainty from intuitively transparent notions of individual ownership and contractual exchange, without having to be processed through the divisive filter of partisan politics. The resulting indeterminacy and uncertainty of abstract formal law in the face of complex economic relations subsequently led legal pragmatists and others to champion the new social welfare paradigm, whose emphasis on aggregating and compromising competing values and interests seemed conducive to top-down social engineering on the part of government elites. Here we encounter a deference to administrative and judicial tyranny that is as legally unprincipled as it is undemocratic. That judges and administrators must interpret the law as they apply it to particular cases goes without saying; that they must also make law—arbitrarily choosing among competing paradigms depending on partisan ideology—is scandalous.

Now, I am sympathetic to the notion that a certain amount of indeterminacy and uncertainty affects any law when confronting "hard cases" generated by an increasingly complex and dynamic system. I therefore share the pragmatist's skepticism regarding the formal liberal paradigm. However, I believe that much indeterminacy and uncertainty reflects the compromised nature of the postliberal capitalist state, which is beholden to a contradictory imperative: maintain noninflationary economic growth while compensating the victims of such growth—and in a way that is fiscally and environmentally responsible. Invariably, the impossibility of fulfilling this imperative exacerbates economic crises—mainly in the form of government fiscal crises—which in turn spill over into other areas of life in the form of declining social services and deteriorating habitats. Such crises call forth more bureaucratic damage control and more resistance from a public that has become increasingly wary of the government's "therapeutic" intervention in their lives.

Here we detect a silver lining to what is otherwise a rather ominous-looking cloud: the repoliticization of the public and a nascent clamor for more participatory democracy. Indeed, it is my contention that the participatory democratic paradigm of law emerges alongside of—and in reaction to—the governmental regulation of social welfare. Both pragmatists and critical theorists welcome this resistance and suggest ways in which it can be institutionalized in both formal and informal democratic fora. My own recommendations for reform reflect their thinking. Following Habermas, I propose that a participatory democratic paradigm can be extended to courts and government bureaucracies, thereby making these institutions more publicly accountable and legitimate. At the same time, I argue that all such deliberation will remain badly compromised as long as capitalism and its unjust hierarchies of class hold sway. But how does one galvanize popular support for ending class domination? Unless everyday life becomes more democratic, the grassroots movements that might seek to transform capitalism as we know it will be lacking. Here I draw inspiration from Dewey, who understood that the solution requires implementing workplace democracy.

THE STRUGGLE FOR WORKPLACE DEMOCRACY IN AMERICA

The struggle for democracy in America has a richer history than most Americans realize. Even after we have gone beyond "protectionist," "market-simulating," and "welfare-maximizing" conceptions of democracy to embrace participatory models, there remains that distant, uncharted territory of "workplace" democracy. Workplace democracy brings to bear a different kind of "identity politics." As I remark in chapter 1, the struggle between labor and capital is also a struggle over control of one's most basic living conditions, on par with that other struggle—the right to privacy and the right to control one's reproductive life. This raises doubts about the logical consistency underlying our thinking about the political right to control one's life and participate as an equal in decisions that affect one equally, as Michael Walzer puts it (1983). How can renters be granted the right to control their domiciles while workers are denied the right to control their workplaces? How can women be granted the right to control their reproductive lives while both men and women are denied the right to control their productive lives?

The answer, Lyotard would say, resides in the terms of discourse. Capitalists define labor as a commodity that they have purchased and thus have the right to control. Workers define labor as an expression of their identity, their way of life, their very being. Unfortunately for workers, capitalists are the ones who chartered contract and corporate law, so it is their definition of labor that counts.

There was a time in American history when this injustice (differend) in contract law litigation was being seriously challenged and workers were asserting their right to participate as equals in the workplace. Prior to passage of the National Labor Relations Act of 1935 (also known as the Wagner Act), workers were regarded as individual subcontractors who confronted capitalists as formal equals. The fact that they were not equal in substantive bargaining power was deemed irrelevant. Not surprisingly, capitalists used their inordinate bargaining power—the right to deny workers their sole source of livelihood—to extract concessions from them. Workers were often required to sign "yellow dog" contracts, which forbid them to form unions. In effect, these contracts denied workers any opportunity to bargain as equals, since only a concerted strike threat was sufficient to counterbalance the owners' threat of replacing individual workers with cheaper—often black—labor. Writing the majority decision in the infamous case of *Coppage v. Kansas* (1915), Justice Pitney opined that yellow-dog contracts were not coercive, since workers would in principle find work elsewhere—perhaps in the dwindling frontier out West.

It took the Great Depression and the threat of class warfare to change the minds of lawmakers regarding the right to collective bargaining. The Wagner

Act was part of a sweeping revolution in constitutional jurisprudence that supplanted an older formal-legal paradigm with a newer social-welfare paradigm.[2] Supreme deference to the formal contractual model of rights that had stymied previous attempts by state legislatures to limit work hours and control working conditions (cf. *Lochner v. New York* [1905]) was overthrown in footnote 4 of *U.S. v. Carolene Products Co.* (1938), in which Justice Harlan Fiske Stone ruled that courts would henceforth give a higher level of protection to civil liberties and political rights than to property and contractual rights. As Bruce Ackerman notes (1991), the restriction on market freedom had to be compensated for by expanding civil and political freedom. The Wagner Act was also written in this spirit. Its authors expressly appealed to the promotion of industrial democracy as well as bargaining equity and freedom of choice in justifying its override of formal contractual freedom.

The victory of industrial democracy over contractualism proved to be Pyrrhic. From 1937 to 1941 the courts reinstated contractualism by allowing employers to unilaterally impose terms and conditions of employment on concluding lawful negotiations to impasse and by prohibiting workers from threatening midterm work stoppages (*NLRB v. Sands Manufacturing Co.* [1939]). However, even subsuming collective-bargaining rights under the aegis of substantive distributive justice proved deadly for industrial democracy. By viewing labor arbitration as an extension of public interest litigation, the courts instituted a corporatist solution to class conflict that removed labor disputes from public oversight and from democratic action by workers. On one hand, workers were denied the right to engage in mass picketing, secondary strikes, and sit-down strikes, which would have affirmed their right to control the means of production. On the other hand, labor agreements took the truncated form of wage-and-benefit contracts, which effectively transferred control of bargaining processes from the rank and file to union leadership (Geoghegan 1992, 52).

Since passage of the Taft-Hartley Act (1947), American workers have seen these and other rights eroded further. However, the greatest damage hasn't come from government injunctions forcing striking workers to go back on the job. It has come from bureaucratic enforcement mechanisms built into Taft-Hartley itself. Taking advantage of time-consuming delays in petitioning courts to enforce the act (it takes an average of three years for a complaint to reach the National Labor Relations Board and be processed by the U.S. Court of Appeals), companies quickly learned that it paid to break the law. The penalties imposed on companies for firing union organizers are indeed minuscule (employers can deduct from the back-pay award any other money the worker has earned since being fired from the job), and the rewards are great. Of those who win reinstatement, 80 percent are fired within the year. In fact, studies show that at least one in every twenty workers who try to organize will be fired (Weiler 1983). The Wagner Act also makes forming a union a tedious, bureaucratic process. In Canada, a union is formed when 55 percent of the workers sign to authorize it. Not surprisingly, Canadian unions have risen from 25 to 32 percent of the workforce. In the United States, after 30 percent of workers sign to authorize a union, the employer can still challenge the "appropriateness" of the bargaining unit on grounds that the workers who choose to join it represent dissimilar job categories and have dissimilar interests—a process that can drag on for years (Geoghegan 1992). Thanks to this coercive identity politics, union membership in the United States has correspondingly fallen to about 13 percent, from a high of about 35 percent in 1960.

Today, the great challenge for labor is as global as it is domestic. What is paramount is replacing the stockholding model of the corporation as a private entity whose only duty is to maximize profits for owners. Until we've instituted a stakeholding conception of the corporation that views production, labor, and capital assets as communal "stakes," workers' demands for justice will continue to be undercut by undemocratic legal paradigms that overregulate their organizing efforts, predefine their identities as productive agents, and consign their working lives to proprietary management by business and government.

THE CRISIS OF AMERICAN
CAPITALISM AND AMERICAN LEGAL REALISM

We now see that underlying the story of American labor's struggle for workplace democracy is another story, a story about the decline and rise of legal paradigms. We have already glimpsed the basic outline of this story. The older, formalist jurisprudence associated with classical liberalism could not adequately absorb the revolutionary social transformation wrought by the overthrow of laissez-faire capitalism; its futile effort to secure property, contract, and tort law on a purely rational basis—without regard to social facts—paralleled its equally futile reduction of economic freedom to individual consent. The New Deal replaced this individual-centered conception of freedom with a more community- and corporate-centered variety. Responding to this change, a new school of pragmatic jurists, legal realism,[3] came to regard economic rights as outcomes of democratic decision rather than as conclusions to be deduced from the inherent nature of law. At the same time, their concern over the absence of a stable democratic consensus supporting reform led them to entrust reform-friendly administrators and judges with extensive lawmaking powers, to the point where any connection between law and justice was all but occluded and rights were regarded as nothing more than tools of social engineering.

The story of the rise and fall of realism in American jurisprudence thus provides us with a cautionary tale about the pitfalls of progressive democratic reform that requires closer examination. The rise of realism is a story about the practical and conceptual undoing of legal formalism and the economic system that it sought to interpret and legitimate. Now, legal formalism as such is a relatively recent export to American jurisprudence that was motivated less by economic ideology than by scientistic ideology. During the latter half of the nineteenth century, Anglo-American jurists such as Christopher C. Langdell used arguments similar to those found in Kant and Hegel to make property, contract, and tort law more predictable and transparent by immunizing it against the dual uncertainties of common-law litigation and democratic politics.[4] Their aim was to transform law into a neutral, deductive science on par with natural science.

Despite its purely scientific justification, this academic form of legal formalism neatly resonated with another, less politically neutral variety. Indelibly etched into American jurisprudence by the likes of A. V. Dicey, the Vinerian Professor of Law at Oxford, this view held that "the rule of law" (an expression first coined by Dicey), depends on securing the "rational" and "impartial" justice of laissez-faire capitalism against political incursions by administrators acting in the name of democratic majorities.[5] To American jurists schooled in the Madisonian precept, expounded in *The Federalist Papers* (no. 10), that "the most common and durable source of factions has been the various and unequal distributions of property," Dicey's admonition recalled a familiar theme: the need to preserve the "natural" sanctity of private property against "tyrannical" attempts to redistribute wealth for the sake of the social good.

Theoretically, scientific and economic formalism are distinct; in practice, however, they were closely linked. Scientific formalism sought to immunize the rule of law against changes emanating from the external pressures of a dynamic social reality; its resistance to pragmatic, consequentialist forms of reasoning was of a piece with its conservatism. Formal legal reasoning relied on tight categorical distinctions between different areas of law and different legal concepts. For instance, the rules and principles of contract law were reduced to "will"; those of tort law to "negligence"; and so on. Most important, principles of private law were regarded as "natural," "rational," and "unchanging," as distinct from the fluctuating political imperatives informing public law. The net effect of categorical reasoning was to eliminate conflicts between different principles and rules of law, thereby circumventing any need for balancing "differences of degree" by appeal to consequences.

Categorical reasoning also involved distinguishing between formal procedures and substantive outcomes; processes and consequences; rights and remedies; proximate causes and remote causes; and so forth. In contract law, for example, formalism required that all agreements entered into voluntarily (as objectively evidenced by signed oaths demonstrating a "meeting of minds") be upheld as valid, regardless of any substantive impact on third parties. As I note in my brief discussion of American labor law, substantive inequalities in bargaining strength between wealthy employers and their employees were as irrelevant in determining the voluntariness of agreements as were considerations of moral unconscionability in determining their justice.

Besides categorical thinking, formal jurisprudence relied on generalization; purifying legal categories of anomalies and other extrinsic elements went hand in hand with reducing diverse technical rules to unifying general principles. Ironically, the desire to reduce different rules of law to more unitary principles exposed a fundamental contradiction within formalist reasoning: by analogically stretching the conceptual boundaries of rules and categories held to be conceptually distinct, it weakened the coherence of the system and paved the way for extralegal criticism of a pragmatic nature. For example, with the emergence of the stock market, the need to "analogically" extend "physicalist" conceptions of property to include market values and future expectations of income became increasingly urgent; however, it also led to the notion that any government regulation of a business that decreased its profitability amounted to a "taking" that required "compensation." Not only was government prevented from taxing income, it could not even regulate the very monopolies whose conduct threatened the freedom and income of smaller competitors and consumers.

Realists had little difficulty exposing the absurdities of formalist reasoning on issues such as regulation and taxation. Their general strategy, however, involved attacking formalist reasoning on philosophical grounds that anticipate the sorts of postmodernist deconstructions of universal reason that we examined in chapter 1. Arguing philosophically, they denied that uniquely determined decisions could be derived from indeterminate propositions of a general nature. In the famous words of Justice Oliver Wendell Holmes Jr., whom they frequently cited, "General propositions do not decide cases."[6] A similar philosophical objection was leveled against common-law analogical reasoning. Recall that formalist jurisprudence was constrained to extend "physicalist" conceptions of property to include such nonphysical concepts as "market value." This extension was made possible by use of analogy. Appealing to Lockean conceptions of natural law, formalists held that anything that someone had invested with value was private property; by analogy, anything that others were willing to pay for had (market) value; therefore, anything created by a private party that anyone was willing to pay for was private property. Using this analogy, formalists could argue that any government regulation that impeded the unhampered ability of businesses to increase their future market value—whether it be the imposition of occupational safety codes, minimum-wage standards, antitrust laws, or even income taxes—amounted to a kind of "taking," or divestiture of private property that required equal compensation by the government. Realists countered that such abstract analogizing was but a fallacious subterfuge for masking partisan, probusiness sentiments behind the facade of rational neutrality.[7]

Realists also objected to formalist jurisprudence on pragmatic grounds. To begin with, the complexity of new corporate capitalism generated new conceptions of corporate property and ownership that effected profound changes in contract and tort law. On the old model, stockholders were business partners who shared equal liability and equal powers of decision making; on the new model, they were investors whose liability and decision-making powers were limited. On the old model, employees were "agents" or "servants" assumed to carry out the will of their "masters"; on the new model, they were masses of factory workers, whose connection with management was often impersonal and indirect. On the old model, the terms and effects of simple, face-to-face transactions between local proprietors of small, family-owned farms and businesses were relatively transparent and determinate; on the new model, the terms and effects were anything but transparent and determinate, for they were complex impersonal transactions involving multiple parties—stockholders, managers, financiers, intermediaries, subcontractors, employees, and so forth—who operated in gigantic enterprises with offices, markets, and suppliers spanning the globe.

The growing complexity of corporate capitalism thus meant that the transparency of the terms and the determinacy of the effects of legal agreements that had been naively presupposed by classical formalists were becoming even less representative of social reality than they had once been. The emergence of trusts and monopolies threatened to constrain the freedom of consumers and business proprietors in ways that had never been imagined; large businesses had the capacity to employ at will—and for whatever wage and under whatever condition of employment—masses of desperate workers (many of them newly arrived immigrants) who threatened to constrain the freedom of workers to enter into mutually advantageous contracts. Finally, the enormous wealth generated by corporate capital created new inequalities between rich and poor, powerful and powerless, that threatened to explode the liberal democratic basis underlying the legitimacy of law generally.

What formalists denied—and what realists affirmed—was the emergence of a new legal paradigm that now competed with the old. With its individualistic, natural-law assumptions, the older, liberal paradigm was being superceded—at least in part—by a newer, corporate-welfare paradigm. The classical liberal invocation of a hard distinction between private and public law was abandoned, along with the view that private law rested on reasons that were privately intuitable or monologically deducible. Once legal reasoning was regarded like any other rational inquiry or deliberative process, it made more sense to think of it as social activity open to public, democratic participation. But public reason did not obviously favor any legal paradigm. The problem of competing rules and standards that had always challenged the formalist pretense of mechanically deducing the *one* rule that necessarily applied in any given hard case was now being exponentially magnified by the emergence of new rules and standards. Resolving which paradigm, standard, or rule best applied to a given case would thus require a capacious knowledge of economics and social science leavened with public opinion—an unstable compound that would lead critics to charge realists with being unprincipled nominalists and casuists.

Realists did not provide a systematic reconstruction of the procedural ideals underlying their theory and practice. Their hostility to Enlightenment rationalism and to overgeneralizing formalism, both of which they perceived to be an ideological mask for libertarian individualism, partly explains this neglect. Political instability surrounded the New Deal in the years leading up to and following its inception, including the very real prospect that industrial democracy might supplant the aristocracy of capital. It may be, as Bruce Ackerman remarks, that this instability made it more risky to synthesize that older tradition of liberal thought with newer regulatory and political forms of law associated with democratic and welfare paradigms than to reinterpret older common-law categories pragmatically, on a case-by-case basis—for instance, by simply extending the older doctrine of contractual consideration suitably qualified by new ideas of unconscionability and equality in bargaining power (1984, 15-18). However, absent any rational construction of a liberal social-democratic paradigm, their emphasis on impartially weighing different values, interests, and perspectives all too easily evolved into a kind of relativistic intuitionism that, somewhat paradoxically, worked to conserve a reactionary, common-law–based defense of private property.

Hostility to normative theorizing, in turn, provided a pretext for conceiving realism as a nonmoral sociology of law. Karl Llewelyn, who with Jerome Frank first coined the expression *legal realism,* accordingly conceived realist jurisprudence as a value-free "technology" divorced from political ideals of any sort. Notably, some realists—most prominently, Lon Fuller—understood that the reactionary implications of this turn to social science actually ended up letting "the Ought acquiesce in the Is" (1934, 461).

The failure to provide a systematic justification of a principled method of adjudication eventually allowed later realists to embrace a conservative social-engineering agenda. The advent of the New Deal suddenly catapulted realists from being outside critics to being inside administrators. The need to justify technical expertise and decision making in the face of a recalcitrant court obviously favored the positivistic—not the critical—brand of realism.

Here again, the positivistic assumption of value relativism combined with scientific hubris fed the appetite of uncritical interest aggregation and public-welfare maximization that would later become the hallmark of the conservative law and economics movement.[8]

The new breed of realism, exemplified in James Landis's *The Administrative Process* ([1938] 1974) sought to justify administrative social engineering by questioning the classical separation of powers doctrine. The older, "delegation" model, which assumed that administrators do not make law but simply discover the most efficient means for implementing it, still appealed to this doctrine, whose main justification had been a defense of representative democracy, or the notion that elected legislatures—the formal representation of the general will of the people (Rousseau)—were preeminent with respect to unelected administrators and judges. However, the idea that administrators and judges merely execute the will of the people rests on an increasingly problematic assumption, namely, that the will in question is unified and transparent and that the laws that give it force are equally unambiguous and transparent. The model accurately described the functioning of the Interstate Commerce Commission (1887), which had in fact been delegated very specific powers. But it did not apply to the Federal Trade Commission (1914), which was given broad power to eliminate unfair competition; and it did not apply to the Securities Exchange Commission (1933). Unlike the earlier law, which still mainly applied to a laissez-faire economy, these laws were designed to regulate the new corporate form of capitalism, the complexity of which required a new kind of regulation. The need to "balance" conflicting values—preserving market freedoms while at the same time controlling market excesses—required that the law be vague and flexible enough to permit administrators and judges broad discretion in interpreting and applying it.

Today, the chair of the Federal Reserve Board—a position filled by presidential appointment with congressional approval—exemplifies the enormous power "delegated" to administrators in interpreting the law. In effect, the power the chair exercises over monetary policy sets the course for the entire economy and all that depends on it—including most government policies. But this power does more than merely execute the ostensible will of the people in some neutral, scientific manner; it is also a quasi-legislative power that has enormous implications for distributive justice, determining rates of economic growth and employment while simultaneously protecting the viability of finance capital at the expense of other interests.

Landis's desire to mold American government along the lines of European bureaucracy presumed the general vagueness of social and regulatory mandates as well as the indeterminacy of democratic outcomes in an era of full-blown class conflict. However, in all fairness to Landis, the elevation of administrators to supreme legislators could not have succeeded had the art of administration not been portrayed as an extension of democracy rather than social engineering. For confirmation of this fact, we need look no further than President Franklin Roosevelt's own wry comment that "many [in the legal profession] prefer the stately ritual of the courts, in which lawyers play all speaking parts, to the simple procedure of administrative hearings which a client can understand and participate in."[9]

Roosevelt's remark was made on the eve of realism's decline. By the end of the Second World War, naive faith in the democratic accountability of government administration had fallen into disrepute. The same could also be said of administrative pretensions to scientific impartiality. By the sixties, claims of professional expertise to a privileged truth rang hollow, and even realists observed with dismay that the experts on regulatory commissions tended to come from or reflect the orientation of the industries being regulated.[10] Such skepticism regarding the competence of scientific expertise in all areas of law would culminate decades later in Foucault's withering critique of the arbitrary normalizing power of social scientific management over all aspects of life (Foucault 1979). This "juridification" of everyday life involves more than the "institutionalization of class conflict through collective bargaining law and labor law and . . . the juristic containment of social conflicts and political struggles" (Habermas 1987, 410–18; 1975, 63ff., 111ff; 1989, 141–42; [1968] 1991, 117–45; Neumann 1944, 10–11, 166–69, 397–98, 468–69, 522–23; Kirchheimer [1941] 1982, 49–70). It also involves a "pathological" expansion of bureaucratic regulation in areas of everyday life—education, family, health, and welfare—that had formerly been the responsibility of free citizens acting in concert with one another.[11]

THE UNFULFILLED LEGACY OF REALISM: PARTICIPATORY DEMOCRACY AND PRINCIPLED JURISPRUDENCE

The history of realism recounted here has led critics to level two distinct and seemingly contradictory charges against it. On one hand, realism is said to be overly obsessed with viewing jurisprudence as value-free social science—the undemocratic, social-engineering model defended by Llewelyn. This obsession is symptomatic of a social welfare paradigm of law that submerges popular discontentment aimed at structural economic injustices and unfulfilled democratic aspirations under the cold calculus of conflict management, interest aggregation, and scientific economic planning. On the other hand, realism is said to overpoliticize law—infusing it with too much value, too much democracy. This latter criticism is directed against two shortcomings: the failure of realists to distinguish rights from value-maximizing public policies;

and the failure of realists to ground their decision making in any principled theory of jurisprudence that might satisfy minimal demands of impartiality, predictability, and certainty. As Habermas puts it, "From the standpoint of Legal Realism . . . one can no longer clearly distinguish law and politics . . . because judges, like future-oriented politicians, make their decisions on the basis of value orientations they consider reasonable . . . [or] justified on utilitarian or welfare-economic grounds" (1996, 201).

Appearances notwithstanding, these distinct lines of criticism are intimately connected to one another. The objection that realism overpoliticizes the law is based on the assumption that democracy is bereft of any normative regulation that might incline it toward impartiality—nothing more than an unprincipled clash of preferences and values that have no deeper justification than the mere fact that they are preferred and valued. If one accepts this skepticism about the rationality of values and preferences, then one should indeed be concerned about a jurisprudence that appeals to values and preferences, or more precisely, "the judge's interest position and social background, her political attitudes and personality structures, or . . . ideological traditions, power constellations, and economic pressures inside and outside the legal system" in adjudicating fundamental rights (Habermas 1996, 201). Or (following Llewelyn) one should at least ensure that such jurisprudence is scientifically—if not normatively—impartial, aggregating and balancing competing values and preferences so as to maximize economic performance and overall satisfaction of interests.

We have seen that the twin indictments of social engineering and unprincipled appeal to preferences and values do indeed apply to one—perhaps the institutionally dominant—current of realist jurisprudence. But does it accurately reflect progressive currents of realist philosophy? Perhaps not. To begin with, realist jurisprudence did not reject general legal concepts out of hand. Some realists merely argued that general concepts needed to be qualified by social facts, the assumption being that such concepts could acquire concrete prescriptive force and functional efficacy only by being interpreted and applied contextually (Horwitz 1992, 166ff.). Of course, excessive dependence on customary practices and standards did sometimes degenerate into an unprincipled contextualism and relativism—ample testimony of which can certainly be found in realist literature. However, a cursory examination of some of that literature shows, I believe, that many realists understood the process of judicial reasoning to be principled if not totally impartial.

To begin with, progressive realists differed from contemporary neopragmatists and postmodernists in embracing relatively robust conceptions of truth, rational impartiality, and moral justice. For many, Dewey's pragmatic "logic of inquiry" provided the proper antidote to sterile, deductive conceptions of reasoning.[12] In "Logical Method and Law" ([1924] 1993), Dewey accepted Holmes's rejection of formalist reasoning but took partial exception to his view that "the life of the law has not been logic: it has been experience" (Holmes 1963, 5). In Dewey's opinion, legal deliberation possesses a pragmatic logic, or general procedure, that distinguishes it from the formal logic of legal exposition. Whereas the latter involves rationalizing conclusions already obtained, the former involves reasoning to conclusions not yet obtained, conclusions that function as responses to problems embedded in indeterminate and uncertain situations. Legal certainty and stability, Dewey notes, is indeed a legitimate aim of pragmatic inquiry. But the logic of legal inquiry, which aims at "adjusting disputed issues in behalf of the public and enduring interest," is "a logic *relative to consequences rather than antecedents*," an "intellectual survey, analysis, and insight into the factors of the situation to be dealt with" (Dewey [1924] 1993, 189, 193; original emphasis).

For Dewey, the logic of inquiry designates a general procedure of reasoning common to all areas of practical conduct. In law, its "collectivistic character" is determined by the overall guiding aim of "social justice." Thus, one could say that justice and "collective intelligence" are coeval. In Dewey's words, "Everything discovered belongs to the community of workers . . . . Every new idea and theory has to be submitted to this community for confirmation and test" (1962, 154–55). Dewey's allusion to industrial democracy also redefines instrumental reason as a communicative process ("scientific thought is experimental as well as intrinsically communicative"). Many realists were inclined to agree with him. Citing Dewey's insistence on experimentalism, Jerome Frank, one of the leading realists of his day, insisted that a fearless devotion to truth was necessary for criticizing the belief in "infallible law." At the same time, he criticized as "anarchic" the refusal to acknowledge as conditionally "fixed and settled" some "rules" (or "temporary absolutes"; Frank 1993, 207, 211).

Progressive realists were emphatic that among these absolutes was a commitment to impartiality. Arguing that "a judge . . . would err if he were to impose on a community as a rule of life his own idiosyncrasies of conduct and belief," Benjamin Cardozo noted that

> one of the most fundamental social interests is that law shall be uniform and impartial . . . . There shall be symmetrical development, consistently with history or custom when history or custom has been the motivating force, or the chief one, in giving shape to existing rules, and with logic and philosophy when the motive power has been theirs . . . . The social interest served by symmetry or certainty must then be balanced against the social interest served by equity and fairness or other elements of social welfare. (1993, 176–77)

Cardozo's opinion that the judge's impartiality in balancing social interests stems "from life itself," just as the legislator gets it, anticipates Dewey's conviction that technical decision making needs to be opened up to democratic participation. Other realists were more explicit in drawing this conclusion. Commenting on the fact that "our social experience is limited to one class of people though we must govern all classes," Herman Oliphant warned judges against relying on their own experience and knowledge. "Socialized jurisprudence," as he understood it, would require a procedure of consultation, both with science and with all those affected by a decision (1993, 200–201). Felix S. Cohen was even more explicit. Rejecting the "intuitionist" view that judges simply act on personal "hunches" in deciding hard cases, he observed that the "realistic judge"

> will frankly assess the conflicting human values that are opposed in every controversy, appraise the social importance of the precedents to which each claim appeals [and] open the courtroom to all evidence that will bring light to this delicate practical task of social adjustment . . . . It is more useful to analyze a judicial "hunch" in terms of the continued impact of a judge's study of precedents, his conversations with associates, his reading of newspapers, and his recollections of college courses, than in strictly physiological terms. (1993, 222–23)

Also reflected in the realists' functionalist taxonomy of rights was Cohen's reconstruction of realist adjudication as a principled process of reconciling or balancing different perspectives, values, and interests through open and public "conversations" with scientific experts, affected parties, and the broader community. For them, rights designated not unconditional freedoms and entitlements of an abstract nature but rather (in keeping with Wesley Hohfeld's analysis) legally actionable claims, liberties, powers, or immunities. Believing this to be the case, however, did not prevent them from sincerely upholding established rights as trumps against adventitious public policies emanating from government bureaucrats or popular majorities.

TOWARD A PROCEDURALIST DEFENSE
OF A PRINCIPLED REALIST JURISPRUDENCE

Dewey's logic of discovery probably came the closest of any realist proposal to approximating a general procedure of judicial reasoning. Given the charge that realist jurisprudence is unprincipled, what is most important about his procedure is its insertion of experimental problem solving within a democratic nexus extending throughout all spheres of society—including workplaces. Here we find a link among reason, knowledge, communication, and universal morality that would later become the centerpiece of another legal theory—the discourse ethics of Jürgen Habermas. What pragmatism taught Habermas was that knowledge is something acquired by persons in reasoning together. The lesson he drew from this reverberates throughout his subsequent philosophy: not bureaucratic hierarchy but participatory democracy is the best organization for problem solving.

My brief survey of the progressive strand of realist jurisprudence—which was greatly influenced by Dewey's logic—belies Habermas's one-sided portrayal of it as unprincipled social engineering. Dewey himself insisted that the quest for certainty—however fallible and never ending—is a principled undertaking, a fact that seems to have been largely ignored by those latter-day realists associated with the critical legal studies movement.[13] Stabilizing the world—making it predictable according to our ideal moral expectations of what conduces to conflict-free interaction and mutual fulfillment—is what law is all about: law limits action in predictable ways that enhance the rational pursuit of individual aims. But law cannot make reality predictable if law itself is unpredictable. So law's predictability must also be ensured by constitutional procedures governing its creation, interpretation, and implementation.

The question naturally arises whether these procedures can be made predictable, on the basis of certain facts about human interaction. Both Dewey and Habermas respond in the affirmative: the social—above all, communicative—nature of learning privileges a principle of deliberative democracy whose rationality depends, as we have seen, on the realization of six values. In the next section, I examine how well these values are theoretically articulated in Habermas's discourse ethical account of law.

HABERMAS'S THEORY OF JUDICIAL DECISION MAKING

Habermas discourse ethic is motivated by some of the same concerns that motivated realists, namely, the sterility of formal deductive modes of legal reasoning. Formalists thought that legal decisions could be deduced from intuitively reasonable general principles of law without appeal to social facts or consequential reasoning. The fact that such principles were far from intuitively reasonable, combined with the fact that particular prescriptive judgments do not logically follow from general principles, compels us to rethink the nature of legal reasoning.

One way to do this has been suggested by Ronald Dworkin (1986). Like Cardozo, Dworkin argues that legal decisions are legitimated by a procedure of interpretation that charitably presumes that an entire body of law—statutes, constitutional procedures, precedents, and moral principles of justice—can be made ideally coherent over time. Judicial interpretation must try to render the entire body of law in the best light possible, which can sometimes require rejecting pieces of it that violate its deeper moral principles.

Consistency—deciding like cases alike—is not enough. In addition to abiding by this procedure, judges must be guided by a sense of integrity, upholding equal concern and respect for the interests and rights of all citizens. By this standard, the Jim Crow laws that mandated segregation in the South—and the Supreme Court decisions that upheld them until 1954—violated both the fairness and integrity of law. But according to Dworkin, affirmative action—which also discriminates racially—did not, since its aim was to compensate blacks and minorities for the effects of racism.

Modeling judicial interpretation on the assumption that a body of law aspires to moral integrity marks a definite advance over formalist jurisprudence because even though particular decisions cannot be derived from general principles, they can be understood as concrete exemplifications (interpretations) of them. Conversely, even though general principles cannot themselves be logically deduced from anything more abstract and basic, they can be justified indirectly, in terms of the range of acceptable outcomes they permit and the range of unacceptable outcomes they rule out. That said, Dworkin's interpretative model of judicial reasoning unrealistically assumes that law can aspire to perfect integrity—an expectation that is belied by the fissure of legal paradigms and, most important, the dis-integrity of capitalism. Leaving aside this difficulty, the model also presumes that judges possess an infallible, Herculean knowledge of an entire body (and tradition) of law.

Finally, it is unclear whether the model endows legal decisions with the kind of certainty Dworkin thinks they must possess. Dworkin is convinced that legal decisions will be uncertain if there is more than one correct interpretation of a hard case—a possibility, he believes, that is discounted by the complete systemic closure and coherence of the legal tradition, which determines only one right decision. Overlooked is the fact that each interpretation of a hard case becomes a new addition to the body of law, thereby changing its fundamental meaning and identity. The meaning of the legal tradition is thus never closed and systematically completed. Its meaning and identity are rendered "indeterminate" relative to future interpretations—or "deferred," to use Jacques Derrida's phrase. The accretion of new meaning to the legal system as a whole does not simply preserve and continue that tradition in its integrity. Novel interpretations (extensions) of the law also break with the law and create new law.

A simple example will suffice to illustrate my meaning. Until *Griswold v. Connecticut* (1965) was decided, the constitution recognized no right to privacy and therefore no right to family planning (contraception). By creatively reinterpreting fragments of the constitutional record, *Griswold* rewrote the constitution. It was this "new" constitution—not the one that preceded it—that retrospectively legitimated *Griswold*. And it was with this new constitution—not its predecessor—that *Griswold* cohered. The revolutionary change in constitutional paradigm inaugurated by *Griswold* has since made abortion and private sexual acts between consenting adults legal, and it might well require extending to homosexuals the same rights currently granted to married heterosexuals.

To return to my assessment of Dworkin's procedure of judicial reasoning, the difficulties we encounter in using it in multicultural and conflict-ridden contexts of the sort that typify modern capitalist societies compel us to search for another procedure of judicial reasoning, a procedure, in short, that allows for multiple interpretations, revolutionary breaks in the legal tradition, and fallible and partial knowledge—all without discarding the principle of procedural predictability. That procedure is democratic deliberation. Such deliberation depends on the multiplicity of interpretations to ensure the mutual criticism and enlargement of otherwise partial and fallible perspectives. However, it produces reasonable decisions only to the extent that the deliberation itself is principled or approximately satisfies the three values of equality, autonomy, and reciprocity that, as noted earlier, inform aggregation and deliberation.

Habermas's discourse ethic explains why this is so. Conceptually speaking, there is a principled distinction between being rationally convinced and being manipulated or deceived. Rational conviction increases to the degree that we know that (a) all relevant arguments and counterarguments have been given an equal hearing by those who most fervently advocate them and (b) they have also been assessed solely with regard to their merits, free from the blinding effects of prejudice, lack of education, and self-interest. What makes such an ethic compelling, according to Habermas, is the degree to which society itself values individual responsibility. Voluntary cooperation between responsible adults—one of the signal features of any modern society—rests on the rational conviction that there are true facts and right norms on which all could be persuaded to agree.

Habermas's theory of law embodies this discourse ethical insight. The values of equality and reciprocity informing this ethic imply a principle of integrity in Dworkin's sense: law must treat everyone with equal respect and equal concern for their interests. But contrary to Dworkin's model, integrity cannot be conceived "monologically," as the outcome of decisions made by a single, omniscient, and infallible legislator/judge. It must be conceived "dialogically." In other words, the legal integrity of a system of individual rights—what Habermas calls "private autonomy"—cannot exist without democracy, or public autonomy, which makes possible mutual dialogical questioning oriented toward rational consensus (1996, 108).

Public fora, parliamentary bodies, courts, and administrative proceedings all incorporate democratic ideals in their deliberations. Such ideals assume a different form depending on legal context. In legislatures the democratic ideals of fairness and integrity imply an ideal of universalization, which states, in effect, that "just those norms are valid to which all possibly affected persons could agree as participants in rational discourse" (107). In their deliberations, citizens and lawmakers must avoid imposing "tyrannical" constraints and burdens on fellow citizens—constraints and burdens that they could not in principle reasonably accede to. The principle does not require that laws advance the universal interests of all equally—the compromising and balancing of differently weighted interests are acceptable, so long as they are done in a principled way, showing equal concern for the interests of everyone. Thus, certain segments of the population (present and future) may be required to assume heavier burdens than others, so long as they are compensated in other ways for doing so. Most important, compromises such as these are principled only if agreement on a norm that would be mutually advantageous to everyone cannot in principle be reached. Unprincipled compromises—or what Habermas calls "pseudo-compromises"—balance interests in ways that reflect the actual balance of power and numbers without questioning the reasonableness of these interests in terms of their social costs to others (Habermas 1975). A compromise that allows companies to pollute the environment so long as they continued to employ workers would probably not be principled, since other alternatives would likely be available that would employ those workers in nonpolluting industries. Or, in reference to our earlier example, a compromise that permits workers to organize for the sole purpose of defending wages and benefits but—in deference to the interests of capital—does not allow them to organize for the purpose of gaining control of their workplace would not be principled either. For, attaining the latter purpose is ultimately integral to ensuring the attainment of the former, which is, after all, a general interest.

The ideal of democracy obviously regulates judicial decision making in a more indirect way. To avoid usurping democratically authorized lawmaking powers, judges must restrict their role to applying laws. Here, the principle of universalization finds an analogue in the principle of impartial application, which requires that a single (technical) rule or (abstract) principle be applied that most completely and accurately captures the complex meaning of disputed circumstances. In rendering an interpretation of these circumstances, the judge is obligated to integrate impartially the perspectives of all the involved parties with the perspectives of uninvolved members of the community. So construed, judicial interpretation is not (pace Ronald Dworkin) merely guided by standards of coherence (fitness vis-a-vis extant law) and integrity (fitness vis-a-vis moral ideals' enjoining equal respect and concern for all) that a single person (the judge) applies independently. Rather, as Habermas notes, "interpretations of the individual case, which are formed in light of a coherent system of norms, depend on the communicative form of a discourse whose socio-ontological constitution allows the perspectives of the participants and the perspectives of uninvolved members of the *community* (represented by an *impartial* judge) to be *transformed* into one another . . . [thereby explaining] why the concept of coherence employed in constructive interpretation refers to the *pragmatic* presuppositions of the argumentative process" (1996, 229; my emphasis).

Here we see the import of Habermas's theory of adjudication for identity politics. In democracies characterized by multiple group identifications and standpoints, we cannot assume that there exists one "neutral" standpoint from which to judge. Contrary to Dworkin, a multicultural, multiracial, and multiclass society does not compose a wholly unified, homogeneous ethical community that a single judicial perspective might represent. The absence of such a community would portend a legal crisis if the kind of identity politics prevailing in society pitted fundamentally incommensurable and opposed identities. But Habermas (like Guinier) rejects this conception of identity politics. Adjudication, like legislation, must simulate inclusive participatory democracy in which identities and identifications converge, overlap, interpenetrate, and transform one another, without assimilating one another.

A simple example will suffice to explain my meaning. First Nation people living on Canadian reservations had mixed reactions when the Canadian Charter of Rights and Freedoms was ratified in 1982. On one hand, there was support (especially among aboriginal women) for a bill of rights that would protect individual freedom from tribal tyranny. On the other hand, there was little support for extending common-law conceptions of private property to tribal lands or for extending European forms of democratic governance to tribal counsels, which operate through less-divisive, more-consensual forms of deliberation. With the recent creation of the Inuit territory of Nunavut, the Canadian law was suitably extended and reinterpreted to accommodate indigenous conceptions of property and democratic governance. The failed Meech Lake amendment to the Canadian charter, which would have acknowledged the special status of French-speaking Quebec, likewise represented an attempt to mediate the peculiar language laws of that province with the federal charter of rights (Ingram 2000a, ch. 5).

The flexible capacity of legal categories to accommodate distinct but ever-shifting perspectives—and thereby avoid differends that would entail assimilating one perspective to another—seems to threaten the predictability of law. If the meaning of law is constituted by acts of judicial interpretation that ultimately extend beyond a narrow reading of the legal system (principles, rules, and precedents) to encompass a dynamic and indeterminately transformative mediation of indefinitely multiple, contextually situated perspectives, how can citizens rely on the law as a predictable sanction that has some certain and definite connection to a democratically authorized statute? How, in other words, can we avoid another kind of differend, or usurpation of authority, in which judges and administrators "rewrite" the law in a technical language of their own making?

Habermas's answer to this differend—now magnified enormously by the infusion of identity politics into judicial and administrative deliberation—is that citizens can rely on the procedures for interpreting law, whose substantive meaning, though hardly fixed, is less uncertain than the substantive meaning of statutes and cases processed in accordance with them. Instead of guaranteeing a predictable "single right decision," procedural rights "guarantee each legal person the claim to a fair procedure that in turn guarantees not certainty of outcome but a discursive clarification of the pertinent facts and legal questions . . . [in which] affected parties can be confident that . . . only relevant reasons will be decisive, and not arbitrary ones" (220).

COMPROMISED ADJUDICATION: THE CLASH OF PARADIGMS AND THE NEW UNCERTAINTY

For Habermas, then, legal certainty boils down to the expectation that conflicting partisan perspectives and legal paradigms will inform judicial decision making in keeping with the principle of integrity. As we saw, progressive realists seemed to be aiming at a similar notion in their talk about the balancing of values and interests. But they were not naive enough to think that integrity and impartiality were achievable in a complex society riven with conflict.[14] Habermas agrees. In his opinion, "This counterfactual assumption [of coherence] has a heuristic value only as long as a certain amount of 'existing reason' in the universe of existing law meets it halfway. According to this presupposition, then, reason must already be at work—in however fragmentary a manner—in the political legislation of constitutional democracies" (232). Thus, some judicial reworking of the law is unavoidable.

Given the compromised nature of political life and legal relations under postliberal capitalism, such rational coherence may not obtain. Aside from reflecting the contradictions of capitalism, law's complexity—and its subsumption under identity politics—alone supports Habermas's contention that such systems are far from coherent. Although judges are normally relieved of the burden of justifying laws—that is the legislator's responsibility—the very prevalence of "norm collisions" means that "judges cannot avoid a reconstructive assessment of the norms given as valid" (232).

The convergence of Habermas and the realists regarding the compromised nature of law in capitalist society is especially evident in their discussion of conflicting liberal and social welfare paradigms—a topic that had also been dealt with extensively by his Frankfurt school predecessors Otto Kirchheimer and Franz Neumann.[15] As Habermas remarks, liberal and welfare paradigms help reduce the indeterminacy that affects judicial decision making. With some exceptions, liberal conceptions of formal equality (sameness of treatment) find greater application in criminal law, while welfare conceptions of substantive equality (differential treatment) find greater application in social law (220, 394). Paradigms like these rank legal norms in transitive order by pairing them with generalized descriptions of specific situations to which they apply. For example, situations described in terms of free economic exchange pair well with a liberal, formal legal paradigm, which in contract law favors a principle of caveat emptor; in the law of torts, a principle of deterministic causation linked to individual liability; and so on (221). By contrast, situations described in terms of unavoidable social costs—such as market disallocations caused by rising interest rates—pair well with a welfare paradigm, which in contract law favors a principle of minimum wages and benefits; in the law of torts, indeterminate causation (or proof of negligence without causation) linked to shared liability; and so on.

Unfortunately, paradigms succeed in reducing indeterminacy only to the extent that they become ossified into closed ideologies that exclude alternative interpretations of situations and rights. Conflicts between formal legal and welfare paradigms in the same area of law, involving competing descriptions of the same situation, thus reintroduce indeterminacy at a higher level. This fact, Habermas notes, reinforces realist skepticism that "coherent case interpretations inside a *fixed* legal paradigm remain fundamentally underdetermined, for they compete with equally coherent interpretations of the same case in alternative paradigms" (221–22).

Habermas, as we have seen, is not as optimistic as Dworkin is that conflicts between paradigms can be resolved, given the contradictions, complexities, and SP identity politics informing modern capitalist society. Because advocates of competing paradigms contest the same legal terrain, the outcomes of specific court decisions in settling hard cases is still often uncertain (as critical legal studies scholars observe). As we saw in chapter 4, there is considerable disagreement among members of the Supreme Court today concerning whether the Voting Rights Act guarantees only the individual right to cast an equally weighted ballot (as formalists maintain) or a right to elect members of one's group in some rough proportion to their numbers (as nonformalists maintain).

In Habermas's opinion, the absence of coherence in the legal system does not render the execution of justice totally futile. Judges must allow a dialogue to emerge between advocates of competing paradigms, so these paradigms themselves become "reflexive," or self-critical. Reflexive paradigms incorporate elements from one another: A reflexive welfare paradigm incorporates and reinterprets the liberal paradigm of individual rights whenever it empowers clients (communities and individuals) democratically by allowing them to define their own needs as active citizens with claims to entitlement rather than as anonymous pathological cases dependent on begrudging charity. Conversely, a reflexive liberal paradigm incorporates and reinterprets the welfare paradigm of social equality whenever it empowers clients democratically by allowing them to view their freedom as socially conditioned by the satisfaction of basic needs (the "dialectic of legal and factual equality"; 391). By mediating liberal and welfare paradigms—as well as different ethnoracial perspectives, as our examples of the Canadian charter and the Voting Rights Act illustrate—judges have a better chance at applying the one principle, paradigm, or rule among the several competing alternatives that most fairly applies to the case at hand (217).

The only way to resolve contradictions between formal legal and social welfare paradigms, then, is through recourse to a more general participatory democratic legal paradigm, which Habermas variously refers to as "reflexive," or "procedural." This "metaparadigm" requires that the choice and interpretation of the other paradigms be open to democratic discussion. It means that before legislators and judges make decisions about how people should be treated similarly or differently and about what concrete rights they should have, they should first consult them (421ff). Thus, to take the example of the Voting Rights Act, any decision about the appropriateness of racial redistricting with regard to a particular jurisdiction should be made only after minorities living in a specific community have had an opportunity to (a) discuss their politically representable commonalities and differences in public fora; and (b) decide for themselves whether their interests, taken individually and collectively, will be better advanced by this method of voting, election, and representation than by any other feasible policy. Ideally, the decision regarding redistricting would summarize two transformative dialogues: a dialogue between advocates of different legal paradigms (defenders of formal individual rights and defenders of substantive group interests) as well as a dialogue between different racial groups and their individual members.

CULTIVATING DELIBERATIVE DEMOCRACY IN THE PUBLIC SPHERE: WORKPLACE DEMOCRACY RECONSIDERED

The participatory-democratic approach to administrative and judicial decision making is perhaps conceptually sounder and more appealing, ethically speaking, than formal-legal, pragmatist, or coherence approaches. Like coherence approaches, the participatory-democratic approach views judicial decision making as an interpretative process that ideally strives toward rendering the law in its best light, as a system that incorporates moral values of fairness and integrity. Like formal legal approaches, it grounds judicial interpretation in basic moral principles—in this case, revolving around fairness and integrity—that have a deeper purchase in human action. These principles are reflected in the formal values of freedom, equality, and reciprocity that underlie a discourse ethic, a regulative ideal that in turn models basic assumptions of social cooperation underwriting any modern society. Finally, like pragmatism, it acknowledges that legal systems in complex modern societies will be dynamic and multifaceted so that only general procedures of deliberation, not basic outcomes, will be relatively predictable and certain.

Habermas defends his participatory-democratic paradigm by partly conceding the truth of the charges against it: that it is merely an ideal that has no real purchase in actual processes of governmental decision making. Most important, he recognizes that decision making will be compromised so long as society is. Principled compromises between reflexive, formal liberal and substantive welfare paradigms and between different group perspectives will be harder to forge in societies premised on arbitrary and undemocratic hierarchies of power, status, and class. Ultimately, these hierarchies conspire to compromise the very rule of law by short-circuiting democratic deliberation among agents of the government, between government and citizens, and among citizens.

We have examined one such differend in our discussion of social engineering, viewed as a symptom of unrepresentative government. The translation of citizen discontentment directed against the injustice of economic policies into competing technical recipes for managing stable growth has contributed to the diminution of citizen involvement in political life. Citizens respond to this injustice with cynicism and apathy, regarding politics as the privileged and arcane domain of expert policy "wonks." At the same time, the need for ever-greater government regulation of the economy and its uneven— often destructive—side effects has called forth antigovernment reactions from the public, who resent top-down therapeutic interventions in their daily lives. The subsequent repoliticization of the public at the local level poses a serious threat to government planning, which seeks the greatest amount of unaccountable leeway in decision making commensurate with its managerial imperative. This legitimation crisis (as Habermas refers to it) reflects the inability of government to intervene in ways that will be acceptable to all interests. Accompanying it, however, is a more general "identity crisis" that is also a social disability: the erosion of our identity as responsible agents who are capable of freely and democratically regulating our own lives in concert with others. So entrenched is this identity, that citizen resistance to big government and big business is often less motivated by dissatisfaction with particular policies and decisions than by fear of being overwhelmed by forces that are beyond one's control.

Resistance to big government and big business returns us to our opening theme: the realization of deliberative democracy in the public sphere. Much has been said by Habermas and others about how deliberative democracy at this level is threatened by economic and government forces. However, little has been said about how the public sphere is adversely affected by the organizing principle of capitalism itself: the corporation.

Applied to corporate and contract law, one would expect that a participatory democratic paradigm would redefine corporations in terms of a "shareholding" model in which workers as well as members of the supporting community have some say in how the corporation is run. This makes sense because alienated labor disables critical aptitudes associated with competent participation in public affairs. Or, as Habermas puts it, the separation of management and labor contributes to a "fragmentation of consciousness" in which "the need for normatively secured or communicatively achieved agreement is decreased and the scope for merely instrumental attitudes, indifference, or cynicism is expanded" (1982, 281). Resignation and apathy are further abetted by insecurity. The safety nets provided to the unemployed under the welfare paradigm do not compensate for—in Habermas's words—the "scandalous 'natural fate' of the labor market." For that paradigm merely replaces insecurity with government dependency and paternalism. This disabling of freedom will continue so long as "the social welfare project" itself is not "pursued at a higher level of reflection," involving a massive restructuring of "the capitalist economic system" (1996, 410). Because "the relation between capitalism and democracy is fraught with tension" (501), Habermas concludes that capitalism itself must be abolished: "The informal public sphere must . . . enjoy the support of a societal basis in which equal rights of citizenship have become socially effective. Only in an egalitarian public of citizens that has emerged from the confines of class and thrown off the millennia-old shackles of social stratification and exploitation can the potential of an unleashed cultural pluralism fully develop" (308).

The logic of Habermas's reasoning thus compels him to view "constitutional democracy [as] the accelerated catalyst of a rationalization of the lifeworld beyond the political" (489). In this respect, his critique of formal legal contractualism as it applies to the individual could just as easily be applied to the modern corporation: "To the extent that we become aware of the intersubjective constitution of freedom, the possessive individualist illusion of autonomy as self-ownership disintegrates" (490). As our brief history of realist jurisprudence shows, market systems are no more self-regulating than labor contracts: both depend on social intervention for their realization. The principle of inclusive democratic participation transforms the corporate enterprise into a public sphere of stakeholders whose liberties are "staked" on their social equality. In short, there is no reason why basic activities of consumption and production on which our private freedom depends should be left in the hands of private persons, especially since other, less-basic areas of life—the governance of municipal planning and school boards—are not.

Although the logic of Habermas's reasoning compels him in the direction of workplace democracy, his actual pronouncements suggest a somewhat different conclusion. Indeed, the general tenor of his thought has been to limit popular democracy to the public sphere—or the political narrowly construed. Part of his thinking reflects his concern that workplace democracy—like socialized democratic centralism—will replace market mechanisms with collective planning. In his opinion, the "idea of workers' self-governance had to fail—and fail even if the workers' social utopia was imagined, with Marx, as a realm of freedom to be established on the basis of an on-going, systemically regulated realm of necessity" (479). This assessment reflects Habermas's justifiable skepticism regarding the efficiency of planned economies in satisfying needs. However, it might also be driven by Habermas's tendency—which he criticizes in Weber—to equate rationalized economies with capitalism tout court (505), whose conception of efficiency is inimical to workplace democracy. If so, then it is especially noteworthy that Habermas elsewhere disavows this equation, remarking that models for market socialism "pick up the correct idea of retaining a market economy's effective steering effects and impulses without at the same time accepting the negative consequences of a systemically reproduced unequal distribution of 'bads' and 'goods'" (1997, 141–42). Given this positive assessment of market socialism, Habermas's failure to develop the implications of a reflexive democratic paradigm for corporate law and the workplace are all the more striking.

THE PRAGMATIC LIMITS OF DISCOURSE ETHICS IN GROUNDING DEMOCRATIC REFORM

We are now in a better position to assess the pragmatic limits of discourse ethics in grounding democratic reform. Discourse ethics designates a formal procedure for reasoning that regulates—without determining—substantive outcomes. The formalism of discourse ethics has led critics to charge that it is too "thin" to provide a standard of social critique. Indeed, this has often been the case with other so-called procedural theories of democratic process. Political theorists, from Joseph Schumpeter to Robert Dahl, also sought to defend democracy as a system of impartial rules whose process alone bestowed legitimacy on majoritarian outcomes. But they conceded that such outcomes might not conform to substantive standards of justice and could even be subversive of the very procedure that gave rise to them (Schumpeter 1942; Dahl 1956). Most important, they noted with dismay that impartial procedures can be distorted by substantive bargaining inequalities emanating from civil society.

In the introduction, I argue that some substantive outcomes—such as Jim Crow laws' denying blacks the right to vote—are unjust simply because they violate the basic spirit of any democratic procedure. However, as realists noted, much, if not most, of the critical force implicit in democratic theory comes from incorporating substantive conceptions of justice and value-laden sociological descriptions that are largely extrinsic to whatever formal procedures might be thought to capture the general idea of deliberate democracy. Our discussion of the importance of context in choosing which among many substantive procedures of representation and election maximizes values of aggregation and deliberation illustrates this point. So, too, does Habermas's application of discourse ethics to formal and informal democratic institutions.

Discourse ethics may tell us more about Socratic philosophizing than about when and how to reform democracy. Unlike participants in Socratic dialogue, judges and jurists cannot radically question core elements of law (especially when doing so implies usurping powers of a democratically elected legislature), and paradigm shifts involving radical reinterpretation of the constitutional tradition are hardly exercises in spontaneous deep reflection, generally taking years to work themselves out. Habermas's model is even further weakened when applied to Anglo-American jurisprudence, with its heavy reliance on case law's possessing customary rather than statutory (democratic) authority. Again, the adversarial nature of legal proceeding that is especially marked in Anglo-American jurisprudence is no more exemplary of consensus-oriented dialogue than is the agonal discourse of democratic politics. Habermas believes that adversarial contests can be effective instruments for revealing the truth and achieving justice so long as judges and counsel exercise vigilance in enforcing gag rules and other procedures designed to ensure impartiality (1996, 235–37). Yet the irony in this gesture is hard to miss. In Habermas's discourse theory of adjudication, it is not Socratic dialogue or even procedure that ensures impartiality, as we might have been led to believe, but a single person (the judge), who is burdened with the lonely task of intuitively "transforming" the multiple perspectives of the various parties into an impartial legal description.

Discourse ethics is not a mere utopian ideal; it actually structures—however imperfectly—real institutional deliberation. The attempt to demonstrate this might have the unintended consequence of diluting whatever critical content that ethics possesses (recall the problems associated with legal formalism's tendency to overextend general legal categories). Habermas is on firmer ground with the realists when he observes that pragmatic considerations pertaining to social system and culture determine a particular polity's application and interpretation of discourse ethical ideals.

The progressive extension of a democratic procedural paradigm to the workplace illustrates this point as well as any. As in the case of judicial reasoning, the ideal must be suitably qualified with respect to social realities. In this case, Habermas is right to note that any modern society that seeks to implement the ideal at the level of industrial democracy will have to come to terms with one structural precondition of that society: the existence of economic markets. That impersonal market mechanisms, rather than democratic commands, must determine some features of production and distribution in any modern society may sound harsh to the ears of radical democrats, but that is a principled compromise that social reality itself dictates.

Again, the extension of democracy to the workplace is not as such compelled by discourse ethics or even a broader theory of communication action. In some sense this extension is compelled by sociocultural values, such as the notion—already operant in other areas of life—that one should have some control over whatever affects one's life deeply and importantly. Perhaps, too, it is compelled by the basic concept of having an enforceable right. For as we shall see in the next chapter, the exercise of any right whatsoever may entail the exercise of certain basic rights, including the right to security in one's life; and the condition for exercising that right with full confidence may entail having control over the very conditions that guarantee it. Finally, the extension of democracy to the workplace may be compelling in light of one's partisan identifications with the working class.

This assortment of reasons—some philosophical, some partisan—reflects what realism is all about. Realists saw their pragmatism in a complex light. Some viewed it as a form of antirationalist skepticism.[16] Others saw it as an attempt to base legislation and adjudication on one set of political values instead of another, more conservative set of values. Some held that higher moral principles or ethical values of a more parochial (national) nature ought to guide criticism; others held that social science should.

Without trying to defend an authentic version of realism, I accept Horwitz's judgment that realism's most significant and lasting contribution was its questioning "the traditional foundations of thought and structures of understanding," challenging "the claimed objectivity of deductive and analogical reasoning," and accepting "the socially constructed character of frames of reference, categories of thought, and legitimating concepts" (Horwitz 1992, 182). Assuming that Horwitz is right, the enduring contribution of realist thought would be a critical theory of jurisprudence that acknowledges the need to integrate competing legal paradigms, interpretative perspectives, and justificatory rationales in a principled manner that does justice to justice.

The absence of justice and integrity in legal systems—due in part to the increasing complexity of modern society, in part to capitalism itself—renders this jurisprudence problematic. The pragmatic solution to this problem is greater participatory democracy, leading to the eventual abolition of SP identity politics and capitalism itself—principled compromises trumping compromised principles. In the words of Horwitz,

> "result oriented" jurisprudence is regularly equated with opportunism, and principled jurisprudence with sticking to one's principles regardless of consequences. Only pragmatism, with its dynamic understanding of the unfolding of principle over time and its experimental appreciation of the complex interrelationship between law and politics and theory and practice, has stood against the static fundamentalism of traditional American conceptions of principled jurisprudence . . . . Until we are able to transcend the American fixation with sharply separating law and politics, we will continue to fluctuate between the traditional polarities of American legal discourse, as each generation continues frantically to hide behind unhistorical and abstract universalisms in order to deny, even to itself, its own political and moral choice. (Horwitz 1992, 271–72)

NOTES

1. From Frank, *Law and the Modern Mind* (1930), excerpted in Horwitz, Fisher, and Reed (1993, 206–7).

2. This change is well documented by Karl Klare, "Judicial Deradicalization of the Wagner Act and the Origins of Modern Legal Consciousness, 1937–41," in A. Hutchinson (1989, 229–55) and Bruce Ackerman (1991, 125).

3. Realism evinces a concern with the pragmatic and instrumentalist functions of law in a way that clearly distinguishes it from analytic, historical, and natural-law approaches. It is instrumental in its view that legal theory ought to (a) view laws as tools for serving practical ends; (b) explain how laws can be made useful to administrators and public officials; and (c) articulate the variety of uses to which law can be put, its legal machinery, and so forth. It is pragmatic in its reliance on a distinctly American pragmatist tradition that is epistemological and moral and that privileges empiricism, experimentalism, and values associated with democracy. For further analysis of the uniqueness of legal realism vis-a-vis natural-law, analytic, and historical approaches, see Robert Samuel Summers (1982, 19–35, 268–81).

4. Continuing through the middle of the nineteenth century, American law still relied on the system of common-law writs, or forms of action. This system appealed to remedies provided by the state and so failed to provide a rational, prepolitical basis for individual property rights of the sort prescribed by Lockean social contract theory (Horwitz 1992, 12).

5. A. V. Dicey, *Lectures Introductory to the Study of Law* (Macmillan, 1885).

6. *Lochner v. New York*, 198 U.S. 45, 76 (1905) (J. Holmes, dissenting).

7. The clash between formalist and realist views on the matter of analogical reasoning came before the Supreme Court in the case of *International News Service v. Associated Press* (1918), in which the Associated Press sought to enjoin a newly organized competitor from "stealing" news. Reasoning analogically for the majority, Justice Pitney (a proponent of classical formalism) upheld the injunction on the

grounds that news was a quasi property whose protected status preempted statutory limits. Dissenting, Justice Louis D. Brandeis argued that such analogical reasoning was both fallacious and politically obstructionist (in this case, curtailing "the free use of knowledge and ideas") when extended beyond very simple cases (*Int'l News Service v. Associated Press*, 250, 262–63, 267; Brandeis dissenting; U.S. 215 [1918]).

8. Some of the most familiar names associated with the Chicago School of Jurisprudence are Ronald Coase, Richard Posner, and Guido Calabresi. While the law and economics approach extends the model of the contract in dealing with torts and other legal problems (for instance, by hypothetically viewing a harm as the outcome of both parties' failure to negotiate the relative costs of preemptive action), the realist approach limits and undermines it.

9. Franklin D. Roosevelt, veto of Walter-Logan Bill (86 Cong. Rec. 13, 942–43 [1940]).Cited by Horwitz (1992), 231.

10. Horwitz (1992), 133–246. In a 1960 report commissioned by president-elect John F. Kennedy, no less a spokesperson for administrative lawmaking than James Landis himself noted with dismay that regulative agencies had developed a tendency toward "industry orientation . . . frequently expressed in terms that the regulatees have become the regulators" (J. Landis, *Report on Regulatory Agencies to the President-Elect* [GPO, 1960], 70). Another example of a supporter of administrative lawmaking turned critic is Louis Jaffe, who by 1954 had concluded that "expertise" had trumped the "rule of law" and that scientific "rationalism" had served as a mask for advancing the "self-interest" of private industry against democratic customs and the "fragile bonds of society." See L. Jaffe, "The Effective Limits of the Administrative Process," *Harvard Law Review* 67 (1950): 1113, 1129–30; and "The Judicial Universe of Mr. Justice Frankfurter," *Harvard Law Review* 62 (1949): 410–11.

11. J. Habermas (1987, 357; 1996, 410–18). Like Foucault, Habermas alludes to the way in which social scientific and legal discourses conspire to predefine the needs, identities, and rights of specific classes of persons, such as women. For his discussion of feminist legal theory as a test case for a discourse-ethical conception of law, see Habermas (1996, 418–27).

12. Dewey's other seminal writings on law include "Austin's Theory of Sovereignty" (*Political Science Quarterly* 9 [1894]: 31) and "My Philosophy of Law" (1941).

13. Realists frequently commented on the conflicts among legal rules and on the gaps between rules and concrete decisions. These are sources of indeterminacy that critical legal studies (CLS) scholars would later develop. But while realists were chiefly preoccupied with the referential vagueness of general statutes—a vagueness that could in principle be reduced by consulting the purposes of lawmakers—CLS scholars focus on the vagueness of more fundamental standards and principles. For example, a realist would wonder whether a statute that allows capital punishment in cases involving the killing of witnesses applies to anyone killed by a convicted murderer (since anyone killed by a convicted murderer would have been a potential witness, had he or she not been killed). By contrast, a CLS scholar would wonder whether defining "witness" broadly (to include those murdered) or narrowly (to apply only to those already scheduled to testify in court) could be done in a way that was philosophically consistent. For a good summary of the differences between realist and CLS schools of jurisprudence, see Mark Kelman (1987, 11–13, 45–49).

14. Habermas argues that, due to the "binarily coded" nature of validity claims to rightness and appropriateness in judgment—validity claims that "do not admit of degrees of validity"—judges must assume that a "single appropriate" decision exists in any given case. However, for them to assume this, they must also counterfactually assume that, as Klaus Gunther puts it, "all valid norms ultimately constitute an ideal coherent system which gives for each case exactly one right [i.e., appropriate] answer." See Gunther (1989, 163).

15. Habermas's predecessors in the Frankfurt school, Otto Kirchheimer and Franz Neumann, grappled mightily with the contradictory mishmash of older and newer legal forms that characterized the new social state. In general, they sought to counter criticisms of social democracy that had been advanced earlier by Max Weber, who feared that using law for partisan social aims would destroy its formal impartiality. Like Habermas, they insisted that social policy aims could be harmonized with the democratic rule of law without (as Carl Schmitt had argued) requiring the undivided decision of a sovereign *Führer* as proxy for the unified legislative will of the *Volk*. See Neumann ([1936] 1986) and Neumann and Kirchheimer (1987). Those seeking a comprehensive understanding of Neumann's and Kirchheimer's respective legal theories should consult Scheuerman (1994).

16. Karl Llewelyn's view of realist jurisprudence as a value-free scientific "method" exemplifies this strand of realist thought better than any other view. Such value skepticism owes much to the youthful work of Oliver Wendell Holmes Jr., whose attack on the subjectivism and moralism in natural-law approaches to tort law in *The Common Law* (1963) ushered in a new, economics- and statistics-based jurisprudence. See K. Llewelyn, "Some Realism about Realism" (1962, 55, 72).

Part Three

RIGHTS

Chapter Six

Toward a Pragmatist and Perfectionist Theory of Rights

The previous two sections of this book are devoted to explicating two notions that are fundamental to a critical theory of rights: identity politics and deliberative democracy. These notions are often thought to be inimical to rights. According to the classical liberal theory, rights are claims advanced by individuals against state and societal interference, even when that interference is undertaken for the benefit of the group and in the name of democratic majority rule. Conceived in this way, rights have a prepolitical foundation in reason itself, understood as a neutral or impartial tribune that is impervious to the partisan wrangling of class and identity politics.

The dialectic of universal norm and particular command diagnosed by postmodernists (chapter 1) and elaborated by legal realists (chapter 5) refutes this conception of rights. Indeed, recall in the introduction that this line of criticism has a long pedigree, extending back to Marx. Marx questioned both the meaning and justification of formal liberal rights. These rights, he argued, free individuals from feudal bonds in a one-sided way: they endow them with proprietary freedom to "own" and exchange property, here broadly construed as anything that could be said to belong to them, including their bodies, speech, religious convictions, votes, and so forth. This freedom is only negative in its functioning, limiting governmental and societal infringements on the pursuit and expression of personal interests. Such negatively conceived rights neglect the positive side of freedom, the development of human capacities and social opportunities necessary for action and choice. The substantive welfare paradigm of rights, by contrast, acknowledges that the provision of collective goods that enable freedom is most efficiently guaranteed in the form of a societal responsibility. However, even when conjoined with this latter paradigm of rights, the formal liberal paradigm fails to emancipate the individual fully. Ironically, by treating everyone the same way—as common citizens or as members of predefined protected classes—it ends up submerging the distinctive needs and identitities of individual persons under a general group classification.

Marx's critique of rights thus reveals a fundamental differend: The perfectability of individual freedom depends on conceiving rights positively, in terms of substantive welfare, but the legal form in which rights are realized and perfected imposes a language of uniformity that suppresses individuality. This differend is reinforced by the way in which rights are justified. The "rights of man"—be they formal liberal or substantive welfare—supposedly follow from an ahistorical conception of human nature. Such a natural-law view of rights in turn imposes common expectations on all, regardless of differences in social and cultural position.

Our examination of realism suggests a possible response to Marx's critique. First, we need to be realistic. Marx thought that legal form, which imposes uniformity as a condition for predictability, was not essential to modern society and would be unnecessary in a communist society that had overcome all class division. This view is naive: societal divisions based on identity and social position are endemic to emancipated and enlightened societies in which individuals are free to cultivate their identities in different and opposed ways. Aside from the relative permanence of identity politics and social conflict, the legal imposition of predictable, uniform expectations makes rational planning and social coordination possible. In short, law itself must be understood as a principled compromise between two utopian aspirations: for personal self-determination and social reconciliation with the other.

Second, following progressive realists, we must view rights as serving multiple functions and having multiple justifications. Rights need not take the form prescribed by the formal liberal paradigm: individual claims for negative freedom. They can also take the form of entitlements to positive welfare based on common interests, claimed or otherwise, individual or group specific. Most important, if rights are not to be regarded as imposed from above, they must—at least in principle, if not in actual fact—be agreeable to all concerned. As progressive realists have argued, such rights must be defined and legitimated in accordance with a democratic procedure that allows for the freest, fairest, and most reciprocal communication between different legal languages and group perspectives. Indeed, even human rights must encompass this plurality. Although such rights by definition protect capacities that are universal to human nature, what defines human nature are particular languages of interpretation that reflect our distinctive social, cultural, and economic standpoints. In short, rights are perfected—not vitiated—by democracy and identity politics.

Third, the fact that rights are perfected by democratic identity politics need not render them indeterminate and ineffectual. As we saw in the last chapter, a certain degree of indeterminacy necessarily infects the meaning and scope of rights, since the reasons why they are agreed to are themselves various and conflicting. Such indeterminacy enhances the legitimacy of rights by rendering them applicable to multiple and changing contexts. Conversely, too much indeterminacy undermines their prescriptive force, rendering them unenforceable. Under conditions of reflexive transformative dialogue and ST identity politics, tensions between different languages and perspectives can be mitigated, if not resolved, thereby enabling agreement on a more precise specification and ranking of rights. But postliberal capitalism magnifies the opposition between liberal, welfare, and democratic legal paradigms and encourages an SP identity politics that renders such agreement all but impossible.

In this chapter I propose to examine how a participatory democratic paradigm of rights might address some of the conceptual problems that attend opposing legal paradigms and identity politics. In the first section I argue that the meaning of rights implies both a pragmatic and perfectible signification. The most important moral rights can become fully effective only when they are legally institutionalized and enforceable. Their perfectibility thus entails a pragmatic compromise with the social realities of modern complex societies. One feature of this compromise, which we examined in the previous chapter, concerns the complementarity (or principled compromise) between formal liberal and substantive welfare paradigms of law. I therefore conclude that neither claim-based nor interest-based theories of rights are complete on their own. Following an argument developed by Henry Shue, I argue that different categories of rights—to negative and positive freedom, subsistence and security—realize one another. Finally, I argue that the principle of integrity, which requires treating each individual with equal respect and equal concern for his or her interests, also requires treating like cases similarly and unlike cases differently. This idea, which clearly informs welfare law, is applicable to identity politics as well and extends the meaning of differential rights to include group rights.

The second section further articulates the perfectibility of rights in terms of their potential for legitimacy. I argue that rights are not fully effective unless recognized as legitimate by those whose conduct they regulate. Legitimation—or the general acceptance of morally binding authority—in turn must be conceived as the outcome of participatory democracy. Such legitimation, however, must be distinguished from justification. Persons may acknowledge the legitimacy of democratic outcomes they otherwise believe are unjustified. The justification of rights—including human rights—cannot be established with intuitive or deductive certainty in a way that will convince every one of their moral validity (truth or rightness). However, persons subscribing to radically different religious, philosophical, and commonsensical beliefs will agree that rights are justified for different reasons, so long as their beliefs are reasonable or informed by the broader political culture of liberal democracy.

PRAGMATISM AND PARADIGMS OF RIGHTS

The vocabulary of rights is but one of several moral languages we deploy. It is a negative vocabulary, used not to praise virtues or benevolent acts but to condemn violations and infringements of a grievous sort—not mere vices or commonplace harms. Because there is disagreement about what sorts of acts constitute such violations and infringements, there is wide disagreement about what sorts of rights—and correlatively, what sorts of duties regarding them—people have.

Some philosophers sought to resolve this disagreement by defining rights in terms of certain natural properties that any possessor of rights must have. Here a person is said to have a right in the same way she or he has a body. Natural rights theorists such as Locke, for example, argue that our rights descend directly from our rational being. One difficulty with this view is that it commits the "naturalistic fallacy." Rights take the form of injunctions or prescriptions ("ought claims") that do not rationally derive from factual descriptions. Another difficulty is that persons (such as criminals) can be said to forfeit at least some of their basic rights without ceasing to be human (or rational). To be consistent, a natural rights advocate such as Locke must argue that a criminal who forfeits his or her rights has in fact ceased to be human, having become, in Locke's words, "a noxious Creature, like a Wolf or Lyon." Related to this final difficulty is the previously noted fact that the concept of human nature's underwriting human rights is itself open to interpretation, if not ideological distortion. White men of wealth who monopolized positions of authority were inclined to define human nature in ways that confirmed their privilege while denigrating or excluding the humanity of others.

The formal liberal paradigm of rights provides a less-problematic way of defining rights. It views rights as claims that persons have against other persons in virtue of two sorts of contracts: real and hypothetical. Real contractors agree to mutually binding terms that endow them with specific claims against one another. We can also imagine claims arising from the very terms of human society, understood as a kind of contract for mutually beneficial cooperation. Regardless of whether anyone has expressly consented to the terms of this contract—which include rights to pursue one's good, free from external interference—we can imagine that ideally rational and fair-minded persons would.

The advantage of this contractarian view of rights is its simplicity. Rights are claims to which individuals have expressly consented or to which any rational and reasonable person would consent. In the language of legal formalism, rights are "willed" by a rationally transparent "meeting of minds." Hence, there can be no disagreement about when they are violated and by whom.

Or can there? As I note in the previous chapter, it is far from clear that labor negotiations between workers and capitalists approximate this model of rights. Do workers freely and rationally consent to the capitalist's definition of their laboring power as a mere commodity to be used at will? Do they consent to limiting their claims to wage schedules and benefits rather than control over their productive lives? Or, to recall an earlier example, do the welfare rights of the mentally disabled follow by contractual agreement or consent? If so, are the terms of their agreement with their caretakers mutually transparent and freely willed?

Difficulties such as these—thoroughly dissected by postmodernists and pragmatists—have led some moral philosophers to reject the usefulness of rights language in capturing strong moral duties (Wohlgast 1987). Why, for instance, assume that our strong duty to desist from torturing animals, to nurture children, and to assist starving strangers entails a corresponding right that animals, children, and starving strangers have against us? Aren't the grievous harms that explain our duties in these cases best accounted for in terms of the avoidance of great suffering rather than in terms of the violation of some right or neglect to make good on some claim that others have with respect to us? Can we not assign social responsibility for great economic injustices despite the fact that none of us has expressly assumed such responsibility or otherwise intentionally done anything unjust?

Perhaps. But there are other ways to overcome the difficulties raised by these queries: we can either supplement the formal liberal paradigm of rights or accept a different paradigm of rights. Pragmatists have followed both paths. Some, such as Wesley Hohfeld, argued that claim rights were but a subcategory of rights, which included liberty rights, immunity rights, and power rights. Others, such as Dewey, seemed to opt for a different rights paradigm. The substantive welfare model of rights he preferred views possession of interest, rather than contractual claim, as the basis for ascribing rights. According to this model, it makes perfect sense to say that children and mentally disabled persons have rights against their caretakers, even though they might not be capable of claiming them for themselves.

This may apply to children and mentally handicapped people, but, can a mentally competent adult be said to possess a right if he or she is in no position to claim it as his or her own? Before women got the vote, it was often argued that their interests and therefore their political rights were spoken for by their husbands. This doctrine of "virtual representation" has also been extended to minorities and other groups who were thought to be incapable of defending their interests and claiming their rights. Of course, the interests of women and minorities might conceivably be represented by white men; but that misses the whole point of political representation in a democracy, which is to empower all groups as spokespersons for their own interests and as claimants for their own rights. So here we notice a salient difference between children and adults, which suggests that claim rights are, after all, the basic form all rights should aspire to—regardless of whether they arise from interests or mutual agreements (Feinberg 1980, 159–80). Only if adults have been conditioned to accept dependency and disability as so natural a part of their identity that the very idea of claiming their rights would never occur to them is it acceptable for others to claim them on their behalf.

PERFECTING RIGHTS PRAGMATICALLY

A better way to demonstrate the inadequacy of the formal liberal account of rights is to show that such rights cannot be fully realized and perfected (effectively enforced and exercised) without supplementation from substantive welfare rights. Formal liberal rights are generally thought to protect the most basic condition for procuring life: negative freedom; or freedom to think, choose, and act as one wishes, without constraint. But eliminating constraint entails positive freedom; or enabling opportunities, capabilities, and resources. To begin with, the safe and secure exercise of any right whatsoever requires the positive expenditure of law enforcement resources. Rights to safety and security, however, will be insecure unless persons also have "membership" rights (to citizenship in a state that enforces legal protection), due process rights (to fair and timely court proceedings), and participatory rights (to influence and elect government officials). But without sufficient food, clothing, shelter, medical care, education, or viable environments, people will be unable to exercise even these rights competently. So substantive welfare rights are also necessary for the full enjoyment of formal liberties.

But showing that negative freedom cannot be perfected without positive freedom and that formal liberal rights cannot be perfected without substantive welfare rights does not seal the argument for extending rights beyond formal liberal rights. There are also pragmatic considerations that have to be attended to. Libertarians argue that only formal liberal rights can be legally enforced because substantive welfare rights are by their very nature uncertain in scope and meaning and require expenditures that exceed the capacities of many (and perhaps all) governments.

Take, for instance, a familiar class of formal liberties: civil rights. Because they demand forbearing from interfering with the like liberty of others, these rights do not require any positive expenditure of wealth on the part of individuals who enjoy them; furthermore, the expenditure of state tax revenue required to enforce them, while not insignificant, seems easily within the reach of most communities. Furthermore, it is somewhat easier (at least most of the time) to determine when these rights have been violated and by whom. For very often it is the government—its agents and leaders—that are directly responsible for the violation in question.

By contrast, it seems that failure to provide substantive welfare has its primary source in the anonymous workings of the economy. It is one thing when a powerful leader confiscates famine-relief supplies targeted for malnourished people, thereby violating their right to subsistence. Here we might say that the agent of the rights violation is directly assignable. But who is to blame when the cause of starvation is more impersonal? If the causes of famine are natural, if the region beset by famine lacks any agency resembling a government, and if people are allowed to die, has anyone expressly violated their right to subsistence? Or, to take another example, when thousands of peasants lose their means of livelihood due to the combined forces of globalization (introduction of mechanized agriculture, export production, etc.) and the government's downsizing of welfare programs and when they accordingly starve for want of employment income or government relief, who is to blame? Government leaders in heavily indebted Third World countries are often forced by international banking institutions such as the International Monetary Fund (IMF) to make draconian cutbacks in government services to continue financing their onerous debt. Even if they and the people they serve were not directly responsible for accruing that debt, they must pay it off so that they will receive more foreign investment and aid. How can these leaders be held responsible for the starvation and the accompanying rights violation?

The problem with including basic welfare among the things that people are due by human right is magnified by the very fact that rights are claims that can be addressed to particular persons. Nevertheless, it may well be that the problem with conceiving subsistence rights as formal claims is less serious than it first appears. After all, it is people—many of whom inhabit affluent countries—who elect the government leaders whose policies allow market structures to operate so destructively. Perhaps in some indirect way it is they who are responsible for causing this harm to happen. Certainly this is true for those among us who know how our leaders' policies harm others yet who continue to support them. Others might be guilty of gross negligence for failing to take adequate precautions against electing them—for instance, by failing to inform themselves about the effects of their leaders' policies. The starving millions who have been displaced from their jobs by global market mechanisms might have claims against these people, who are in a position to effect a change in leadership but have chosen not to do so. Indeed, these claims are all the more grievous to the extent that we as a people are positively enriched by the market mechanisms that harm others.

The social welfare paradigm of rights provides a more transparent basis for condemning this harm because it defines rights primarily in terms of important human interests that need protection, quite apart from whether anyone has tacitly or voluntarily assumed responsibility for protecting them. But perhaps changing or regulating these mechanisms is too costly, violating other obligations we have with respect to distributive justice. Certainly, that argument has been made regarding a much less-ambitious policy: famine relief. The right to subsistence, it is argued, might well cost more money than can be afforded by some communities. But if the resources needed to satisfy a claim are lacking, the claim can't be mandated by right. In this instance, the right in question would be more like a moral desideratum whose full realization would be "utopian."

However, on the social welfare model, the duty to fulfill subsistence rights would fall mainly on affluent countries, who in fact can easily afford to do so simply by rechanneling a higher percentage of their defense spending to famine relief and development. But here we encounter the final formalist objection: There is no easy standard for determining when a substantive welfare right, such as the right to subsistence, is met. There is, after all, some elasticity to the notion of basic subsistence levels (what "basic subsistence" means for an American is not what it means for a Mayan peasant living in Guatemala). Indeed, corresponding to the ever-constant, technologically driven, elevation of baseline expectations regarding basic human welfare, we notice a palpable inflation in the number of welfare rights that are claimed as basic (article 24 of the UN Declaration even mentions "a right to rest and leisure"). Yet the elevation of expectations also applies to formal liberal rights. The enforcement of law and order and the perfection of due process can be fine-tuned according to standards of moral progress. Likewise, making environments safe and secure for the untrammeled exercise of negative freedom can be extraordinarily costly—as the American response to terrorism all too painfully shows.

Last, the recent discussion of so-called third generation rights to cultural autonomy suggests that "elasticity of welfare expectations" might not be as pragmatically deadly to the implementation of welfare rights as formalists maintain. Technologically driven standards of well-being invariably reflect the imperatives of capitalist growth. As a result, people in advanced capitalist societies increasingly come to define their welfare in such elevated terms that, were this standard and acted on throughout the world, enormous environmental costs would be incurred. One way to guard against the cultural imperialism wrought by wasteful and destructive consumer capitalism is to defend the rights of aboriginals and other peoples and to cultivate less wasteful and more environmentally sustainable standards of welfare.

As we learned from our discussion of disability (chapter 3), neither psychological nor biological definitions of basic welfare are satisfactory. Defining welfare in terms of psychosocial standards of well-being relative to felt needs puts us in the awkward position of undervaluing the neediness of those with lower standard-of-life expectations in comparison to the luxurious neediness of those with higher expectations. Defining welfare in terms of biologically defined thresholds of minimum human functioning, equivalent to a baseline provision of objectively calculable resources, avoids this problem of comparing utilities, but only by denying what is obvious, namely, that basic human capabilities are inherently susceptible to higher levels of development. Furthermore, as Sen notes (1982), the attempt to reduce capabilities to the provision of basic resources in the manner proposed by Ronald Dworkin fails for another reason. The capacity to translate resources into capabilities for persons who are otherwise equally well motivated and equally well endowed resourcewise may be unequal owing to societal discrimination and the like. For example, in the United States, a heterosexual man or woman who possesses identical motivations and resources would still possess unequal opportunities to transform said resources into higher, more complex expressions of basic capabilities—such as would be involved in combining parenting and working. Simply put, there are fewer potential male partners who will accommodate a woman's preference to develop herself in this well-rounded way than there are potential women partners who will accommodate a man's preference for the same (Williams 2002, 30).

In sum, contextually sensitive standards of basic human capability—rather than inflexible standards of basic human resources—ought to be the criterion for objectively assessing baseline thresholds of humanity meriting human rights protection. However, because of the cultural elasticity inherent in the very notion of a basic capability, developing contextually sensitive standards will require judgment, since it is in the nature of a capability to be developed beyond a basic level of functioning (with the latter also shifting meaning accordingly). Judgment, however, will require making principled compromises, since again not all capabilities can be simultaneously developed, and development itself can take many forms. Thus, in comparison to people living in advanced Western societies, people living in aboriginal societies will be judged more developed along certain axes of basic capability, less developed along others.

A simple example suffices to illustrate what I mean. Consider the right to an education (article 26 of the UN Declaration). Using Amartya Sen's capabilities method of designating minimum thresholds for this right (1982, 353–69), we note immediately that the level of education required to fully develop one's capacities within a traditional agrarian community will be different than the level required to fully develop one's capacities within a postindustrial, computerized society. And, of course, the level and kind of basic subsistence appropriate to the people living in these different communities will also vary according to need. But having said that, it is important—especially in a global economy—to ensure that different levels of functioning that typify normal levels of achievement for different societies do not become so disparate that persons in agrarian communities are subject to domination by persons in urban communities. In the final analysis, something like Sen's capabilities approach must be applied—but with extreme caution. To repeat, people's subjective experiences of achievement and satisfaction should not be the ultimate ground for judging rights violations, since custom and oppression can inure people to grossly disabling conditions. Nor should people's subjective experiences of achievement and satisfaction be the final basis for making a critical judgment about rights violations.

To conclude, a reasonable amount of uncertainty—owing to both the expansion of our moral expectations and the plurality of circumstances—must be expected in our definition of rights, be they formal liberal or substantive welfare. We must therefore reject formalist standards of certainty as both unpragmatic and reactionary.

GROUP RIGHTS AND IDENTITY POLITICS

In the preceding section I argue that pragmatic and perfectionist considerations support extending the definition of rights beyond formal liberal claims to include the protection of substantive welfare interests. Our final discussion of this matter, however, raises a problem that seems more central to identity politics than to the clash of legal paradigms, to wit, the problem of cultural relativism and the right of cultural groups to define rights in ways that are sensitive to their own moral expectations and circumstances. I say more about this problem in the next chapter. Presently, we need to see whether it makes sense to talk about group rights at all.

Let me begin my defense of group rights with a story. Recent studies by the UN and other human rights organizations rank women among the groups most vulnerable to human rights violations and other forms of oppression. Not surprisingly, women are also among the most powerless. In fact, women hold just 11.7 percent of all legislative seats worldwide (in the United States, women occupy just 13 percent of Congressional seats—tied for 41st place among 107 democracies).

Many countries have tried to increase the political representation of women through adopting partial or full election based on a system of proportional partisan representation. Among the first to adopt this strategy were the Social Democratic parties in Scandanavia, which voluntarily adopted quotas mandating a certain percentage of women candidates. According to the Center for Voting and Democracy,[1] the percentage of women elected to parliament in those countries is correspondingly high—ranging from 42 percent (Sweden) to 31 percent (Norway). Other countries have mandated more stringent measures to increase the percentage of women parliamentarians. Argentina, Belgium, Brazil, North Korea, Nepal—and most recently, France—require that all parties put up a certain percentage of women for office. As the French example shows, the results are sometimes striking. In passing the parity law in May 2000, France became the only country to require that half of any party's candidates for office be women. In the French city council elections that were held in March 2001, women subsequently increased their city council representation from 22 to 47.5 percent.

The parity law mandates political justice for a specific group of persons who are identified not by formal membership in a corporation or by voluntary affiliation with a political party but by their belonging to a status (gender) acquired by birth. Women were given a new right—a group right—that exceeded their political and civil rights as individuals entitled to vote and run for office like any other person. How is this possible? Aren't rights supposed to designate standards of equal treatment that extend to all individuals the same way, regardless of their differences? Aren't rights that apply to just some groups of persons and not others really just privileges or preferences that promote unequal treatment?

In this section I argue that it makes sense to talk about group rights not as privileges or preferences that favor some persons over others but as protections that further the equal treatment of persons as individuals. In other words, although it makes sense to ascribe rights to groups, such rights are derivative of the rights of individuals.

Historically, group rights have been asserted for nonmoral—if not immoral—reasons. One need only recall the special group rights accorded to whites in South Africa—and still sought by the Afrikaners of Orania—to appreciate this fact. In fact history is replete with more or less benign examples of groups' being awarded special exemptions or privileges in return for giving up other exemptions and privileges. The League of Nations recognized the special rights of irredentist subnationalities, which eventually provided Hitler with a convenient pretext for annexing part of Czechoslovakia in 1938. Indeed, the disrepute into which such seemingly benign rights fell following the Second World War can be attributed to abuses such as these. The racial preference enshrined in Jim Crow in the American South was another example of thinly disguised group rights that likewise fell into disfavor, just at the very moment when the United States began heralding itself as the champion of the free world.

Not surprisingly, it is during the tumultuous period of the Cold War that individual-centered human rights become paradigmatic for rights in general. They continue to be paradigmatic today—despite the fact that human rights abuses here and abroad have been systematically tolerated and even promoted by the very U.S. government that has sought to present itself as their most fervent advocate. But there are conceptual—and not just historical—objections that have been raised against the idea of group rights.

One objection holds that groups are nothing but aggregates of individuals. To cite an old formalist objection: Groups lack the element of personality—of will and intention—that we associate with individuals. But it is precisely the condition of being a person that enables one to claim a right for oneself. Therefore, only individuals have rights.

I have argued that this formal liberal account of rights is partly true; it is in the nature of a right that it can be claimed. However, I have also argued that the claimant need not be the holder of the right. What is equally essential is that the holder of the right possess some interest—asserted or ascribed—whose satisfaction is important enough to require the protection or guarantee of a corresponding right. Be that as it may, it is nonetheless true that, as far as mentally competent adults are concerned, their rights must be claimed by them.

Contrary to the formalist objection, at least some groups appear to be able to do just this. I'm thinking, of course, of formally organized groups, such as corporations that have well-defined chains of command and decision making. Corporations are groups that enter into contractual relations with other entities and are recognized by law as legal persons, possessing a will of their own. Of course, legal personality in this case is totally artificial; corporations do not exist apart from a legal framework—a charter or constitution—that designates a person, or small group of persons acting in unison, to act on behalf and in the name of the stockholders (and sometimes employees).

As we saw in the last chapter, this model of the corporation is a highly stylized ideal type. Corporations possess an organizational complexity and volitional opacity that seems incompatible with the simple "will" theory of contractual right associated with the formal legal paradigm. It may be that the "stakeholder" model of the corporation as a public interest group—the view favored by the social welfare and democratic paradigms—is a more appropriate model than the "personality" or "proprietary" model. Be that as it may, the example of the modern corporation provides a good starting point for exploring the degree of agency underlying other types of groupings.

On one extreme we find true aggregates—"serial groups," as Sartre famously put it—consisting of persons who are classified as belonging together by some third person (a bureaucrat, say) wielding some arbitrarily chosen criterion, regardless of whether they think of themselves as such. For Sartre, even corporations are serial groups, since most employees are alienated from one another and their bosses and are coordinated by external mechanisms of various kinds—the market (law of supply and demand), company rules, shop stewards, and so forth. However, Sartre gives more extreme examples of serial grouping—strangers' queuing up at a bus stop—that involve even less unity (Sartre 1991).

Persons classified as "elderly," "mentally incompetent," "poor," or "female" generally exhibit no unified "group" will, unless, of course, they organize themselves expressly for that purpose. The question thus arises whether mere aggregates can be said to have group rights. According to the will theory, they cannot; according to the interest theory, they can—and it may be the responsibility of the state (and anyone else who is entitled to press a class-action suit on their behalf) to claim it for them if they are unable to do so on their own.

In the middle range of the spectrum we find groups whose individual members consciously identify with one another in varying degrees. Women, for instance, ceased being an aggregate group when they started reflecting on their oppression and began organizing themselves as a political force. In addition to the sorts of rights that are accorded to aggregate groups, "identity" groups such as women and racial–ethnic minorities can consciously organize themselves into communities of political interest claiming power rights, such as the right to be proportionally represented in legislatures and other governing bodies. As I note in chapter 2, possession of a common group identity need not reflect any specific property that all or most members of this group possess. It suffices that most share overlapping sympathies of one kind or another based on experiences of discrimination and marginalization. However, for purposes of representing themselves as a unified bloc claiming special rights, they must also represent themselves as sharing common group interests (in support of anti-sex-discrimination policies, say).

Middle-range identity-based groups reflect widely differing degrees of collective will. Structural groups based on circumstances of birth (such as race, nationality, gender, and caste) often exhibit less uniformity in interests than groups entered into voluntarily. Religious groups often exhibit more uniformity in this regard, despite the fact that their members typically acquire their affiliation through their parents. Indeed, membership in involuntary groups is often partly voluntary or dependent on conscious, willful identification. In societies marked by interracial and interethnic marriage, the identification of people as belonging to this racial group or that ethnic group will partly depend on how they themselves choose to identify themselves. As we have seen, this is becoming increasingly so, even in the United States, where the infamous "one-drop" rule has hitherto functioned to exclude racial ambiguities between blacks and whites.

What's interesting about the distinction between voluntary associations and involuntary identity-based groups is that its implications for a theory of group rights are less obvious than one might think. Common sense suggests that persons who enter into groups voluntarily will do so for roughly the same reasons. This in turn would reflect the sort of collective will that might be in a position to claim special rights for the group as a whole. By contrast, persons who enter into groups by birth need not share any aims in common, even if they happen to identify with one another. Conservative blacks disagree with most other blacks in opposing affirmative action, reparations, and racial redistricting, yet virtually all blacks identify with one another as victims of racial discrimination and prejudice.

Common sense aside, it is not true that persons who enter groups voluntarily will share many aims in common. They may share only one aim, and that aim may not be important for how they identify themselves. The example of formal organizations illustrates this point well. Stockholders in a corporation share the aim of maximizing corporate profits. But that collective aim may be relatively unimportant to them in comparison to other aims held by them individually. Employees may collectively want their company to succeed, but in a climate of strife between labor and management, this aim may be weakened considerably. On the other hand, persons who experience severe discrimination owing to their involuntary membership in a racial group may organize themselves politically in affirming a collective will that cuts to the very core of who they are and who they want to be. Even if they disagree about the particular aims for fighting discrimination, they remain united in their resistance to it—so much so that they demand at least some minimal political representation for voicing their shared discontent.

In the above passage I refer to groups whose members identify with one another as "identity" groups, as distinct from aggregate groups. This is somewhat misleading. To begin with, it suggests that persons who belong to an identity group have melded themselves into a single person with a single will. However, as I note in chapter 2, an individual will typically identify with many different groups; and it is not infrequent that there will be divisions, antagonisms, and other subgroups within groups that considerably weaken the analogy between group identity and individual identity. Strictly speaking, only individuals possess an identity (a personal one), whereas identity groups really possess nothing more than overlapping sympathies and identifications.

A related point is that talk of identities seems to privilege one sort of identity. Again, to recall my earlier discussion of identity in chapter 2, the analogy with personal identity suggests that what holds together the members of identity groups are memories and histories of a collective, rather than individual, nature. The sorts of groups that are often thought to exemplify this kind of identity are groups of national or religious descent. Hence, it is not surprising that "identity politics" today has come to be strongly associated with "the struggle for recognition" that is played out among different ethnic and religious groups. It is as if the struggle for group rights boiled down to a struggle for just one kind of right—the right of a cultural group to preserve its distinctive identity—its history and memory—in some continuous and relatively fixed (albeit living) form.

In the opening chapters of this book, I argue that this latter kind of struggle represents only one kind of identity politics: SP identity politics. However, as we have seen, identity politics by no means exhausts the full range of group-based struggles. Many struggles between identity groups do not take the form of identity politics. They take the form of class struggle, of struggle against the domination of certain groups over others in processes of governance and decision making. And they take the form of a struggle against oppression, or the deprivation of goods requisite for human development.

These struggles are almost always intertwined. Typically, struggles against domination and struggles against oppression accompany one another (Marx's concept of class struggle captures both dimensions). Moreover, both domination and oppression typically demean and stigmatize those at the bottom. The domination of one group over another—and the oppression of one group by another—normally involves (mis)representing and (mis)recognizing the oppressed group as deserving inferior treatment. Therefore, struggles against domination and oppression will very often involve identity politics. Conversely, struggles for recognition will typically involve struggles against domination and oppression (Ingram 2000a, ch. 2).

It is crucial that this point be grasped, for failure to attend to the complex intertwining of different rights struggles can lead to grave distortions. For example, the temptation to view the struggles of African Americans and women as simply struggles for multicultural recognition ignores the extent to which these groups have been subjected to systemic forms of economic and political domination and oppression. Such groups do not mainly seek recognition of their cultural difference so much as they seek empowerment and economic inclusion (Ingram 2000a, ch. 4). Likewise, the temptation to view the struggles of the working class as if they were simply economic and political struggles ignores the role that racism and sexism have played in dividing the working class and legitimating hierarchies based on difference.

JUSTIFYING GROUP RIGHTS

The model of rights I have advanced permits the ascription of rights to groups as bearers of common interests or as claimants of common interests. Is there also a moral basis for making this ascription? Can we understand group rights as in some sense derivative of the rights of individuals?

I believe we can. First, many (perhaps most) rights attributed to individuals can only be exercised by them in tandem with others, as a group. Protecting the group in which the right is exercised—by assigning the group a right—thus becomes instrumental in protecting the individual and her or his right. Second, when an individual is harmed because of membership in a group, then other individuals in the group feel vulnerable as well. So rights are needed to protect individuals not as individuals but as members of groups.

Perfecting rights entails institutionalizing a broad spectrum of formal liberal, substantive welfare, and participatory democratic rights all together. Among the welfare rights that positively enable the exercise of rights generally is a right to culture (education). One could not exercise choice unless one had acquired language, knowledge, and other relevant cultural contents and skills. Without language, knowledge, and a sense of value, people would not be able to give any weight to the multifarious needs and desires clamoring for their attention; they would not be able to identify, classify, and clarify these inclinations; and they would not be able to modulate them in light of other persons' conflicting inclinations or even calculate the most effective means for satisfying them.

But most important of all, culture is a public good—like national security or a healthy environment—that cannot be enjoyed by one person unless it is also enjoyed by others. Indeed, culture is a good that only exists through sustained cultivation by many people. There is no such thing as a private language (as Wittgenstein famously argued); and there is no such thing as a private value or norm (as distinct from a personal preference). Such collective goods as these exist because people participate in their ongoing cultivation collectively.

Education always involves socialization into a specific culture. The formal languages of mathematics and science may be universal and cross-cultural, but the vernacular languages and value systems in which we live out our daily lives are not. Because these collective goods are sustained by particular groups, it is important that they be assured the negative freedom to do so unhindered by other groups. In some cases groups might even legitimately claim special rights to protect or sustain this cultivation, as often happens in the course of SP identity politics (Waldron 1993, 339–69; Raz 1986, chs. 7, 8; Reinbolt 2001, 71–82; Gould 2001, 43–57).

A somewhat different argument can be made for extending group rights to women and racial minorities. Here the argument begins with the fact of group-based discrimination: women and minorities are denied the equal exercise of their individual human rights because of their membership in oppressed groups. To compensate them for their relative disadvantage (inequality in real opportunity) and protect them from discrimination, they are accorded affirmative action preferences and guaranteed political representation.

Of course, whether a group is justified in claiming special rights on its behalf is a large and complex question. The attempt by white Southerners to protect their slave society by appeal to "states' rights" was not justified, since slavery itself is a gross violation of basic rights. Also, as I noted earlier, assessing a group-rights claim depends on the legitimacy of the group in question. The example of deaf culture discussed in chapter 3 illustrates this principle well. Cultural groups that limit the freedom of their members may do so only on condition that they allow dissenters to exit the group freely. However, deaf children who are denied the benefit of cochlear implants at a young age potentially occupy a situation analogous to that of the dissident who has no effective right to exist. They may later want to leave the deaf community and join the mainstream but will have been denied any real opportunity to exit. Unlike some dissidents, they would retain the formal right to exit; but formal rights are empty without opportunities for exercising them.

Of course, socialization in any culture both opens up and closes off opportunities for exercising the right to exit. For instance, allowing the Amish to withdraw their children from school at the age of thirteen or fourteen so that they can work in the home or on the farm (cf. *Wisconsin v. Yoder* [1972]) arguably deprives them of opportunities for learning about other lifestyles and points of view that they might otherwise be exposed to if they extended their education through high school. A ten-year study on old-order groups such as the Amish, Hutterites, old-order Mennonites, and strict Brethren (On the Backroad to Heaven) shows that 75 percent of Amish children and 95 percent of Hutterite children remain in their communities after adulthood. The reason for this remarkable fact is fairly simple. Amish youth must join the church before they marry; they cannot inherit land from their parents without remaining in the church, and they are shunned if they leave. Most important, however, they are denied access to television, radios, most telephones, and other opportunities for learning about other ways of life. And, like deaf children, they acquire styles of behavior, customs, and distinctive languages from which it is difficult for children to escape. In the words of one of the study's authors, Don Kraybill, "It's a real culture shock. Leaving is not only hard because they would be so isolated from their parents, friends, and family, it's also like a foreign country."[2]

Acculturation in Amish culture thus severely limits Amish children's opportunities for freely choosing different lifestyles. While it might give children just enough knowledge of the outside world to enable them to understand that they do have a choice—and so doesn't violate their formal right to freely choose—it might not give them an opportunity to develop the kind of freedom of choice associated with being their own person, bucking tradition and authority, and functioning in mainstream, multicultural, and multiracial society that public schools, promoting a liberal civic education, typically seek to foster. So this kind of limited education—which is repeated in varying lesser degrees in other forms of home schooling—might still violate the substantive welfare rights of Amish children. Values can be instilled only if the bond between parent and child is one of identification, but identification that borders on brainwashing can be permanently disabling (Anderson 2001, 267–80).

In sum, the determination of whether a group's right to perpetuate or protect itself conflicts with the individual rights of its members is itself a political determination, involving collective deliberation regarding competing standards of freedom and equal protection. Even if we could lessen the appearance of social conflict by reducing the stakes—perhaps by substituting group-neutral "equal protection" remedies that indirectly have a group-specific impact—it is hard to see how such alternative remedies could be an improvement on group rights. Policies that have a group-specific impact but are not framed in the language of group-specific rights—such as admitting the top 5 percent of each high school's graduating class in lieu of race-sensitive admissions policies (affirmative action)—might decrease the potential for resentment that accompanies SP identity politics, albeit at the risk of failing to protect vulnerable target groups.[3] But that resentment may be directed against the differential impact of the policies in question—and the zero-sum politics in which they are contested—and not their express identity-based content (recall that race-neutral welfare policies were widely resented by those who mistakenly thought they benefited blacks and Latinos).

JUSTIFYING AND LEGITIMATING RIGHTS

The preceding sections have attempted to show that the formal liberal definition of rights—as individual claims against others to respect the unencumbered possession and free exchange of personal property—is inadequate. Rights need not be claimed by those whose interests are advanced by having them; and the exercise of unencumbered freedom is generally enabled and enhanced by the positive provision of substantive welfare. The full realization (perfection) of individual formal rights will involve their mediation with substantive welfare rights and possibly group-based rights. Pragmatically speaking, welfare and group-based rights need not impose fixed standards of welfare and identity of the sort whose rigid uniformity is insensitive to context, individuality, and democratic deliberation. In short, seen in light of their pragmatic perfectibility, rights need not succumb to standard objections posed by critical theorists such as Marx and Foucault.

But these critics also object to the formal liberal justification of rights as prescribing natural freedoms and duties that can be known or deduced with rational certainty. In what follows I argue that this conception of justification is mistaken and that what is more important for the perfectibility of rights is their legitimation, or general acceptance under appropriate democratic conditions.

In this regard I recommend that we look closely at the justification of rights recently put forward by Alan Gewirth. Briefly, Gewirth notes that previous attempts to logically deduce rights from the following invariably fail: formal equality, possession of interests or needs, preexisting rights, ideal contracts, and inherent dignity. Each in its own way begs the question. As I note in chapter 1, formalism is compatible with the exclusion of slaves, women, and aboriginals from full humanity. Having needs and interests may be a necessary condition for having rights, but this fact alone does not entail any corresponding obligation to satisfy them. Preexisting rights might entail for their satisfaction more basic rights (as Henry Shue argues), but then, what justifies these preexisting rights? Real contracts have no binding authority unless they are transacted freely, equitably, and in accordance with morality, which is to say in accordance with basic rights. Therefore, they alone cannot justify such rights. Ideal contracts between perfectly rational and reasonable beings would by definition be transacted freely, fairly, and in accordance with moral reciprocity and so would be sufficient to justify rights. But such contracts only exist in the imagination, not in the real world. Finally, the need to respect the dignity of persons is not an independent justification for rights, since this notion cannot be defined apart from a prior appeal to rights.

Gewirth's justification for rights avoids the question begging that plagues these other attempts at justification by beginning with the necessary conditions of human agency: "Since the agent regards as necessary goods freedom and well being that constitute the generic features of his successful action, he logically must also hold that he has rights to these generic features and he implicitly makes a corresponding rights claim" (1982). We can paraphrase Gewirth's argument by breaking it down into the following premises: We begin with the empirical assumption that (a) persons must act in order to survive and (b) unless persons are free and healthy, they cannot act. We then add another empirical assumption: that each of us wants to survive, act, and, by implication, be free and healthy. From this second empirical assumption, each of us commands the prudential maxim "I should be free and healthy." Logical consistency then compels extending this "prudential right" into a moral right that applies to all persons equally (in much the same way that the principle of universalizability in Kant's philosophy forces us to do the same): "Everyone should be free and healthy" (i.e., should have a right to freedom and welfare).

The attractiveness of Gewirth's grounding of human rights is that, first, it acknowledges that formal liberal and substantive welfare rights perfect one another; and, second, it dispenses with contentious speculations about what persons in ideal contractual negotiations—unconstrained by egoism, prejudice, and the like—might agree on, and it instead focuses on what real persons anywhere, with all their egoism and imperfection, must individually want. The obvious problem with this deduction, however, is that it still succumbs to the dialectic of universal and particular. Justifying a generic right to freedom and welfare is virtually useless until we know what freedom and welfare mean in the concrete. In other words, nothing in the way of a specific, prescriptive right to freedom and welfare follows from this deduction; yet, until we know the precise scope of our rightful freedoms and welfare entitlements, the latter cannot be prescribed, let alone enforced. But defining the precise scope of our rights is a function of democratic deliberation. In other words, the prescriptive force of rights—their moral authority to compel us to behave dutifully toward others—is at least as much a function of their legitimation, or the fact that they have been processed through fair democratic procedure, as it is of their justification.

Gewirth's justification of rights succumbs to other difficulties reminiscent of those found in legal formalism. Despite Gewirth's attempt to base his argument on the prudential desires of real-life human beings, it is clear that these human beings and their desires are historical abstractions that really reflect the desires of human beings living in modern societies. As Alasdair MacIntyre forcefully notes (1981), just because persons anywhere must desire the freedom to procure their personal well-being doesn't mean that they will recognize this desire as entailing a right. For the language of rights only makes sense if we have in fact accepted that language as a convention, possessing, among other things, its own distinctive rules and institutions. So, for Gewirth's justification of rights to avoid begging the question, he would have to show that the language of rights is more than a mere historical convention of modern Westernized societies. In other words, he would have to show that it is implied in the very generic structure of action itself.

Karl-Otto Apel, a close associate of Habermas who collaborated with him in developing a distinctly pragmatist discourse ethics, has attempted to do just this. Unlike Gewirth, however, Apel and Habermas begin with communicative interaction, the kind of action that lies at the bedrock of all other action, insofar as it is the medium in which we are socialized into language, social roles, values, desires—in short, a sense of self, or identity. As I note in the last chapter, rational discourse (or communication oriented toward resolving disagreements through rational suasion) is a background condition of ordinary communicative action—the action whereby we coordinate our individual intentional actions, as Gewirth understands it (Marsh 1995). According to Apel, the discourse principle directly implies a "primordial principle of morality," a principle that he (following Kant) characterizes as a principle of universalizability. This principle, in turn, demands that all possible members of the argumentation community—virtually anyone affected by the outcome of the argument—have equal rights to present and rebut arguments and share equal responsibility in identifying and solving problems (Apel 2002, 20). The rights that are implicit in respecting the equal autonomy of speakers—rights that include access to material conditions, capabilities, and opportunities necessary for cultivating such autonomy—are just what we mean by human rights. Because we are morally compelled by the discourse principle to resolve all our disagreements discursively, we are also morally compelled to guarantee everyone these rights (25).

Apel acknowledges that the obligation to resolve all disagreements discursively—which commits us to the discourse principle and its morality of human rights—is a regulative ideal (part A of discourse ethics) that cannot be universally implemented. Given the historical evolution of complex social relations and systems of strategic action, people must turn to coercive laws and market constraints in coordinating much of their political and economic lives. Democracy and ethical convention here function as the mechanisms by which they determine their positive legal rights and institutionally conditioned moral rights (part B of discourse ethics). However, because democracy and ethical convention are permanently compromised by "immoral" strategic constraints that force us to resolve disputes in a partisan manner, Apel concludes that actual democratic deliberation cannot be the moral foundation of genuinely universal human rights (27).

Apel's attempt to ground basic human rights in communicative interaction seems plausible because, as he rightly notes, persons engaged in rational discourse are indeed committed to certain norms of reciprocity, autonomy, and equality—denial of which entails a performative contradiction. However, the argument succumbs to familiar weaknesses. It may be that the discursive procedure implies a rudimentary *category* of participatory or political right, such as the right to freely participate in conversations aimed at resolving disputes peaceably. But this bare category of right is not itself a prescriptive right. As Apel himself concedes, it is more like what Kant calls a regulative idea; as such, it leaves the concrete determinations of what it means to be a free and equal participant up to the participants themselves to decide—the proper domain of discourse ethics part B. This part of discourse ethics can only legitimate rights, not justify them.

I return to this important distinction later. Before doing so let me first address another difficulty with Apel's deduction of rights, which we encountered in our examination of Gewirth. Apel, like Gewirth, assumes that the ethical structure of action is the same for all times and places. Indeed, it may well be that action in any conceivable society implicitly assumes (as its anticipated telos) something like a discursive ideal of rationality with its corresponding principle of moral universalizability. For instance, it might be argued that every society distinguishes between objective truth and reality, on one side, and subjective belief and appearance, on the other. Having notions of objective truth and reality in turn involves thinking beyond one's own limited perspective to include—potentially—all other possible perspectives.

Be that as it may, the anthropological record suggests that the extension of perspective taking to encompass—with equal respect—the perspectives of all human beings is probably an idea that first explicitly arose with the emergence of cosmopolitan societies and came to fruition during the European Enlightenment. Of course, we might argue against the view that this idea is but a particular convention of European(ized) culture, by following Mead, Kohlberg, and Habermas in holding that there exists a kind of logical moral progression— from preconventional to conventional and postconventional (universalistic) ways of adopting the standpoint of the ("generalized") other. But the evidence for this progression at the level of individual moral development (Owen 2002) is still much debated—so much so as to raise fundamental questions about its relevance for societal moral development (Ingram 1995, ch. 6). At best, we can be relatively certain that the bare fact of globalization—a process that has been underway for over two millennia—has led to the dissemination of cosmopolitan ideas of universal humanity that seem favorable to the cultivation of discourse ethical ideals.

I therefore conclude from the above examination that the justification for rights cannot rest on intuitively certain, or rationally demonstrable, principles. The only thing that might be justified as relatively certain—at least for those of us who inhabit cosmopolitan Westernized societies—is the discourse ethical form by which differing justifications for rights are tested and legitimated.

The distinction I am here drawing between justification and legitimation is crucial. By justification I mean the process of rationally convincing oneself and others of the truth or rightness of a belief. By legitimation I mean the process of rationally convincing oneself and others of the duty to act in accordance with a norm, even if one should happen to believe that the norm in question is not fully justified—or even just plain wrong.

Legitimation and justification are not entirely unrelated. A belief will likely appear more justified to the extent that others agree that it is so and act accordingly. It will appear even more justified to the extent that the reasons others have in believing it converge with one's own. Conversely, the legitimacy of a norm depends on its justification. I will feel more duty bound to obey a law that has the support of the majority if I feel that there is some reason to support it. One reason to obey it might be that it has the support of the majority, but this reason alone is not a very compelling moral reason. A more morally compelling reason would be my belief that the majority has weighed all the arguments for and against it in accordance with fair democratic procedure. The most compelling reason would be if I actually concurred with the majority's reasoning. However, I might still feel duty bound to obey the law despite the fact that the majority is mistaken in its support of it simply because of its good-faith effort to consider all sides of the arguments.

Should all outcomes of a procedurally fair democratic discourse be regarded as legitimate, even if there are no other independent reasons justifying them? This is a difficult question. If there are no independent reasons justifying the outcome and if there are independent reasons that strongly speak against it—suppose, for instance, that the outcome in question violates an important right—then one might feel that the outcome is not legitimate. But how likely is such an outcome? Not likely, so long as the democratic process approximately satisfies the six values of aggregative and deliberative autonomy, equality, and reciprocity. Still, when all is said and done, believing in the legitimacy of an outcome may not be enough to compel compliance with it. A person who staunchly believes, out of deep religious conviction, that abortion is murder might feel compelled to block access to abortion clinics despite acknowledging that the right to abortion has both legitimate and reasoned backing.

In sum, justification and legitimation remain distinct processes, despite their subtle interaction. What follows from this distinction is that, while there are many ways to justify rights, there is only one way to legitimate them: democratically. But—to return to the problem of justification—doesn't democratic legitimation itself presuppose (and thus justify) certain rights? Yes and no. As noted, the idea of democratic legitimation is not directly (conceptually) embedded in communicative interaction. Following Habermas, we might say that it is the offspring of two historical developments: the emergence of the rule of law—itself a product of modern economic and administrative developments—and the emergence of discourse ethical expectations in everyday communication. Combining the rule of law—the concept of regular consistency, treating like cases alike—and discourse ethical ideas of autonomy, equality, and reciprocity yields three categories of rights: personal freedom, citizenship, and due process. These are rights that any system of rights, even benevolent dictatorial ones, must have. However, because these rights cannot be secured against malevolent dictators, cannot become fully legitimate, and cannot be concretely specified without the participation of citizens, their full realization cannot be secured without institutionalizing another—political—category of right. As we saw earlier, even this category of right cannot be fully realized absent welfare rights and other enabling conditions.

What follows from this partly conceptual deduction are not prescriptive rights but indeterminate categories of right, or legal principles of justice and integrity. The process of collectively "interpreting" these categories, of applying them to a particular situation so that they acquire a definite scope, meaning, and force, is an activity that occurs in constitutional conventions, legislatures, and courts of law. Even human rights must be realized in the form of enforceable, prescriptive legal rights. They acquire their prescriptive content and coercive backing through the auspices of democratic international bodies such as the UN and the International Criminal Court. The fact that there still remains disagreement about the precise meaning and ranking of human rights—and the fact that all agreement is constrained in ways that might be described as immoral—is no argument against democracy as a "legitimating" procedure. For democracy designates (in Habermas's words) a revolutionary project: a self-reflexive process of deliberation that progressively realizes its own normative universality by becoming increasingly more inclusive, free, and egalitarian.

If democracy is the single most-justified way to legitimate rights—a process that is essential to their full justification and realization—it is nonetheless true that many sorts of reasons can justify them. Facts about "human nature" (basic capabilities and needs) may be among the reasons that persuade some people to accept rights. Other reasons may be the advantages that rights provide in serving our narrower interests, some of which may even be downright selfish. (If social contractarian thinkers such as Rawls are right, such prudential interests may be connected to social interests in mutual cooperation and therewith to moral ideas of fairness.) Even utilitarians, who are often criticized for sacrificing human rights to aggregate well-being, have solid grounds for endorsing human rights. John Stuart Mill's "indirect" utilitarianism exemplifies the reasonable view that the greatest amount of happiness is best achieved by securing each individual his or her own happiness. According to Mill, because individuals are generally the best judges of what makes them happy and because even well-intentioned and enlightened societal paternalism minimally denies individuals the opportunity to exercise capacities of choice whose enjoyment is fundamental to happiness, global well-being is best achieved by protecting the rights of individuals to pursue their own conception of happiness as they see fit. In short, there are many good reasons that persons can draw on for supporting rights (religious, scientific, traditional, deontological, and consequentialist), and it is their convergence, or "overlapping consensus," as Rawls puts it, that best explains the general legitimacy of rights.

The defense of a pluralistic approach to justifying rights, however, raises a troubling question: If people consent to the same rights for very different reasons, then doesn't this mean that they will disagree about the precise meaning and scope of these rights? Perhaps—and here we encounter a serious problem. It is acceptable for people to agree on rights for radically different reasons—but only within limits. Different reasons for believing in rights lead to different interpretations of them, thereby undermining their legitimacy and capacity for effective enforcement. Of course, from a pragmatic perspective such disagreements are not necessarily bad and can sometimes be justified in terms of acknowledging the diverse circumstances in which rights are applied. The German government's view that banning of antisemitic literature is compatible with freedom of speech is not less reasonable—given its recent history—than the opposing view enshrined in current American law. However, as we have seen in earlier chapters, disagreement about the scope and meaning of human rights often carries over into our understanding of what counts as a basic right. When such disagreement is structurally necessitated—as it is in postliberal capitalism—the legitimation and assignment of rights is severely compromised.

One way to limit the range of acceptable disagreement is to insist on criteria of reasonableness. Although unreasonable people might not be able to agree on an enforceable schedule of rights, reasonable people should, and it is their opinion that counts. The reasons that convince us to accept a given schedule of rights should be informed by (admittedly fallible) evidence drawn from the social, natural, and human sciences. Admittedly, these "sciences" are authoritative in the limited sense that they embody principles of critical self-examination and inquiry in rigorous research standards, not in the expansive sense that their practitioners all agree on the meaning and validity of actual research. In the human and social sciences especially, practitioners will sometimes disagree about the core values guiding interpretation of otherwise indisputable data and so will sometimes disagree about the relevant facts as well. Such disagreement poses serious—but not insuperable—challenges to the legitimation of human rights.

It suffices to note that the requirement that good reasons be informed by authoritative findings in the various sciences does not mean that these reasons must themselves be directly drawn from these findings. They might instead be drawn from religious teachings and other comprehensive worldviews. Indeed, it is not out of the question that a more scientifically informed reformulation of natural-law theory might provide good reasons for persons—who have fewer logical qualms than I do about the doctrine—to accept a schedule of human rights. This assumes (following Habermas and Rawls) that religious teachings have already undergone a certain amount of secularization. In other words, it assumes that such teachings have (1) reflected on the noncognitive, faith-based nature of religious conviction; (2) foresworn any attempt at converting the unconverted through force; (3) embraced the principle of tolerance; and (4) accepted the necessity of appealing to reasons shared across a broad spectrum of belief—reasons drawn from science, among other sources—in order to defend their faith-based initiatives (Habermas 2001).

To conclude, while pragmatism councils toleration and respect for different justifications and interpretations of rights, perfectionism encourages the creation of a democratic public sphere wherein these justifications and interpretations can be discursively mediated. In the next chapter, I examine how pragmatism and perfectionism might apply to the global legitimation of human rights. But this much should be clear by now. What legitimates human rights is not that everyone could agree on them for the same reasons but that everyone could, under certain preferred conditions, agree on them for reasons that do not conflict too much, that is, to the point where they jeopardize their very function, which is to protect and develop universal capacities requisite for human flourishing. By contrast, perfectionism encourages the adoption of a universal ideal of human nature and, along with it, a universal standard of human capability and human well-being, not as a uniquely necessary and universal justification for human rights, but as a necessary and universal specification of their meaning. While perhaps not directly grounded in a priori reasons, perfectionism appeals to speculations regarding the evolution of societies and other relatively irresistible tendencies of a global nature. These latter tendencies certainly produce ambivalent economic, cultural, social, and political effects that simultaneously promote and inhibit the realization of basic capacities. Hence, perfectionism must choose which of these ambivalent processes ought to be encouraged and in what degree. As we shall see in the next chapter, extending discourse ethics globally might enable practitioners of non-Western traditions to cultivate democracy within their communal societies as a way of furthering individual freedom and equality just as it might enable practitioners of Western cultures to cultivate communal solidarity within their market-driven societies as a way of furthering economic justice, global peace, and ecological harmony.

NOTES

1. The following data is provided by the center's website: www.igc.apc.org/cvd.
2. Cited in the *Chicago Tribune*, April 20, 2001.
3. Rather than focus our attention on "group rights," we could instead focus on the less conceptually problematic notion of "group harms," understood as harms perpetrated against individuals as members of groups that render other individuals within the group vulnerable to harm. Extending universal antidiscrimination protection to threatened groups might in fact protect them better than assigning them divisive special rights. See Thomas Simon (2001, 96–114).

Chapter Seven

Human Rights and International Justice

The limits of the possible in moral matters are less narrow than we think. It is our weaknesses, our vices, our prejudices, that shrink them.

—J.-J. Rousseau, *The Social Contract* (book 2, ch. 12, para. 2)

HUMAN RIGHTS INTERSECT THE GLOBAL ECONOMY: IMMIGRATION AND THE POLITICS OF IDENTITY

The ever-worsening economic disparity between rich and poor countries poses unprecedented challenges to the continued defense of restrictive immigration policies. Cosmopolitan principles of justice urge us to counteract the arbitrary privileges and handicaps of birth that are currently sanctioned by such policies. These principles support the immigrant's universal right to self-preservation against the community's right to exclude outsiders in pursuit of its own vital interests. This support seems all the more cogent when the community's interests entail waste, pollution, and obscene affluence in a world of want. But what if the interests in question involve protecting an aboriginal way of life? The European colonization of the New World and the more recent influx of thousands of desperately poor settlers into the Amazonian basin were also undertaken in the name of self-preservation. If we feel that this cosmopolitan appeal to natural right, which admittedly is often a subterfuge for shameless exploitation, carries less weight in this case, then what about other cases—in North America, Europe, and Japan for instance—in which the appeal to collective self-preservation is also made for the sake of preserving cultural, political, and economic integrity? After all, doesn't such a communitarian appeal uphold just those caring relationships and bounded identifications that make possible any self-preservation whatsoever—individual as well as collective?

Before discussing what implications cosmopolitan and communitarian principles of justice might have for determining the rights of immigrants, it is imperative that we discuss the causes of immigration. The causes of immigration seldom originate entirely from within the immigrant's native land. They are partly structural, implicating a global capitalist economy that inevitably exacerbates inequality and uneven development between industrialized and agrarian communities; and they are partly political, reflecting the effects of civil war and political repression. While responsibility for the political causes of immigration often appear to be quite local, in reality they seldom are. Much of today's civil strife and repression in underdeveloped countries reflects the legacy—indirect or direct—of the Cold War. The superpowers in this conflict fabricated authoritarian governments and ideologically polarized armies whose remnants continue to fight amongst themselves and oppress significant numbers of people. Indeed, it is not without irony that these same people now seek asylum from their oppression by immigrating to the very countries that bear the greater responsibility for instigating it—hence, the unprecedented influx of Africans and Asians into Europe, and Central Americans into the United States.

The politics of the Cold War also increased immigration by creating the world's most heavily indebted poor countries (HIPCS), chiefly in sub-Saharan Africa and Central America. The United States and its allies sold the arms required to maintain their Third World dictators in power. The oil crisis of the seventies, followed by the astronomical rise in interest rates pegged to the U.S. dollar, inflated the cost of the loans beyond any possibility of repayment. The massive amount of money required to service the loans forced many of these countries to downsize government services in health, education, and welfare, thereby making a bad economic situation all but intolerable.

Well known are the structural inequalities inherent in a global capitalist economy that impel immigration. Faith in the power of free markets to generate prosperity for all partners in the global economy has given way to skepticism, and even the heads of global financial consortiums such as the World Bank express alarm at the growing gap between rich and poor. The United Nations Development Program's *Human Development Report* for 1999 notes that of the world's population inhabiting the richest countries, 20 percent receive 86 percent of the world's income, 82 percent of its exports, and 68 percent of foreign direct investment, while those inhabiting the poorest 20 percent barely receive 1 percent of each. The combined incomes of the richest 20 percent are almost seventy-four times greater than those of the bottom 20 percent.

As many theorists of underdevelopment have argued, such inequalities are structural features of a global capitalist economy. These features include an imbalance of trade between industrialized producers of costly technologies and refined goods and their Third World suppliers of cheap raw materials. Developing nations are "encouraged" to develop one or two export crops whose prices are entirely contingent on European and North American demand. They also include Third World financial dependency on foreign credit and, thanks to the distortions wrought by economies tailored for export production, dependency on the costly importation of basic staples. The "development" of high-tech agriculture in Third World countries displaces millions of farm workers, who then join the ranks of the urban unemployed. Desperate to work at any price, they contribute to the depression of wages even as their consumption inflates the price of scarce staples. Without these exploited workers, the high profits that fuel the capitalist juggernaut would be nonexistent. And so it happens that an economic system premised on generating exorbitant profits for a few requires the impoverishment of multitudes.

The other side of this economic imbalance is a demographic imbalance. It has become increasingly evident that industrial and postindustrial capitalism imposes severe demands on a workforce that must be highly educated, highly mobile and flexible, and highly disposed toward the consumption of luxuries and expensive technologies. With women entering the public workforce in unprecedented levels—partly in response to the decline in real wages, partly in response to labor shortages, and partly in response to liberated attitudes born of education—rates of childbirth have dramatically declined. Hence, developed nations are facing a new crisis, reflecting both a labor shortage and (subsequently) a shortage of revenue needed for maintaining national pension and healthcare systems.

By contrast, the chronic underdevelopment of Third World countries produces just the opposite demographic profile. Contrary to arguments advanced by neo-Malthusians such as Garrett Hardin (1977), evidence suggests that poverty does not act as a disincentive to population growth. It rather seems that large families are economically rational when other social safety nets are absent. So taking into account the fact that the structural dynamics of global capitalism magnify rather than diminish poverty in most undeveloped countries, we can now sum up the relationship between economics and demographics as follows: While capitalism acts to discourage population growth in developed countries, it acts to encourage such growth in undeveloped countries. In other words, global capitalism by its very nature produces and maintains a demographic imbalance that threatens to undermine its own survival. To rectify this imbalance, wealthier underpopulated countries must take in more immigrants from poorer, overpopulated countries. From 1890 until 1920, the United States followed precisely this path on its march toward industrialization, and it has increasingly returned to it since the sixties, adding about 660,477 legal immigrants and 275,000 illegal immigrants to its workforce every year. Meanwhile, with a population 36 percent larger than the United States, the fifteen nations that form the European Union have absorbed on average 857,000 immigrants a year for the past decade. Indeed, not counting eastward expansion, the European Union will have to add 47 million immigrants by 2050 just to maintain its current population of 372 million; and it will have to add another 47 million on top of that to maintain its current rate of economic growth. To put these numbers in perspective, demographers predict that over the next twenty years the workforce in Europe's industrialized countries will decline by at least 2 percent—translating into a deficit of 20 million potential workers between the ages of twenty and thirty-nine—while in sub-Saharan Africa it will increase by more than 3.5 percent, increasing the surplus of similarly aged workers by 177 million.

Increased immigration, however, raises a host of problems for both supplier and recipient nations. While losing excess population might seem to be a blessing for undeveloped nations, it entails a massive uprooting of families and communities as well, as a loss of skilled professionals—most who immigrate are not the most desperate but already have contacts and established job opportunities in the host country (Sen 1994). Recipient nations, meanwhile, may experience higher levels of unemployment and wage depression in certain sectors of their economies due to increasing competition from immigrants. More important, immigrants impose psychological demands on their adopted communities. Many opponents of immigration fear that these newcomers will not blend in to the dominant society and its cultural values. Witness, for example, the current antiimmigrant wave sweeping Europe's hitherto homogeneous societies. While fear of cultural warfare is doubtless exaggerated by racist demagogues on the Right, the potential of immigration to alter the social, cultural, and political landscape of a community raises legitimate questions about the rights of communities to preserve their ways of life.

Leaving aside the undeniable fact that problems surrounding immigration will continue to worsen as long as global capitalism remains in force, what legal paradigms should guide our thinking in these matters? Here we return to the dilemma with which I began my discussion: should the community's right to self-determination, which also includes its right to control the admission of outsiders, always take precedence over the universal rights of individuals to secure their well-being? In other words, should the principal rights holders under international law be nations or individuals? Should they be groups—like refugees and immigrants—who possess common interests that transcend national borders? Assuming that individuals possess group rights as preconditions for exercising human rights, how should these rights be conceived?

The preceding chapter shows that rights ought to be conceived robustly, as guaranteeing more than the abstract formal conditions of unimpeded volition (or negative liberty). Such a formal paradigm of rights might justify unrestricted immigration but only in the name of satisfying natural property and contractual rights. Libertarians, for example, are notorious for defending globalization under the banner of market freedom, which for them instantiates a natural right to transfer labor as well as capital without communal impediment.

A welfare paradigm focused on distributive justice, by contrast, holds that a human right to associate freely is not natural but conditional. Its exercise can be limited with respect to two superordinate duties: one cosmopolitan, the other communitarian. From a cosmopolitan perspective, contractual freedom and freedom of movement can be limited if it violates global equality between persons and peoples. Immigration typically enriches the wealthier nations that serve as "hosts" while draining vital skilled and professional labor from poorer "provider" countries. The welfare paradigm thus requires decreasing incentives to migrate by transferring wealth from richer to poorer nations. Compensatory justice also figures in this equation. Those "wealthy" nations that have profited from past slavery, colonialism, globalization, and the militarization of the Third World have a duty to restore to the Third World a fair portion of their ill-gotten plunder. However, merely transferring wealth, resources, and development capital might not decrease the incentive to emigrate. For instance, although the development of sub-Saharan Africa might diminish population growth in that region over time, its immediate impact might be to increase unemployment. This would certainly be the case if development took the form of mechanized agriculture; but it might also be the case if development took a "greener" and more labor-intensive form. Few would dispute that development in social justice and rights would require the emancipation of women; but an emancipated female population would more likely enter nondomestic vocations, thereby possibly worsening already saturated labor markets.

Those who invoke a welfare paradigm also run into difficulties in determining appropriate levels of aid. As I note in chapters 3 and 6, quality-of-life standards and other indexes of well-being and flourishing have to be configured in ways that are sensitive to cultural differences. Redistributing wealth equally throughout the globe in deference to marginal utility calculations in the manner proposed by Peter Singer (1972) would require something like the replacement of a market economy by a centrally planned one—a state of affairs whose implications are neither desirable, practical, nor realistic. Taxing wealthy or resource-rich nations (or transnational market exchanges in currency, labor, capital, and commodities) seems to be less objectionable in this regard and can be implemented regardless of whether local productive assets are privately or collectively owned—although collective ownership strikes me as preferable (Schweickart 2002). Still, the level of developmental aid and other forms of assistance drawn from tax revenues must be sensitive to the fact that resource- and capital-intense forms of production and consumption characteristic of advanced industrial societies are ecologically dangerous and destructive and that ideals of well-being and human flourishing vary from culture to culture; thus, average levels of subsistence requisite for maintaining free and flourishing aboriginal communities will be vastly different from those requisite for sustaining the same in more complexly structured urban communities (Shiva 1988; Curtin 1998).

From a communitarian perspective, the welfare paradigm appears to support a balanced immigration policy, and it is here where we begin to see how it might evolve into a participatory democratic paradigm. To begin with, cosmopolitan and communitarian approaches to justice need to complement one another in fashioning a fair but balanced immigration policy. The right to exclusive association must be qualified when the association in question impinges on the integrity of other associations. The right to national sovereignty diminishes as our global interdependencies increase. Globalization increases the pressure to realize universal ideas of justice in anticipation of the eventual establishment of a democratic federation of democracies. Such a federation must be empowered through its courts and executive agencies to define and enforce laws that are vital to the well-being of all peoples, including especially "stateless" refugees, asylum seekers, and other persons who lack the full protection of citizenship rights. As we saw in chapter 6, the basic human right to exit associations that are perceived as oppressive is meaningless unless there also exists corresponding opportunities to immigrate.

The basic human need to inhabit a community of mutual caring and solidarity requires that immigrants be admitted into a new community only on condition that they willingly integrate themselves into its basic charter of cooperation (which need not be anything as thick as an identity). In liberal multicultural democracies, integration will normally involve acceptance of a particular constitutional tradition and acquisition of a dominant language (if there is one). But not all democratic polities are marked by the same degree of multicultural association. The fact that even aboriginal ones are integrated into a globalized economy—with or without their consent—does not mean that their survival depends on a steady influx of outsiders. Leaving aside the enormously complicated question concerning the repatriation of Palestinians to the homelands and territories from which they were wrongly expelled, the singularly tragic history surrounding the birth of Israel arguably justifies certain—but by no means unproblematic—ethnic and religious qualifications in the manner by which the people of that liberal democracy constitute their multicultural and multireligious identity. The same applies to less-multicultural polities inhabited by indigenous peoples who, besides being the unfortunate recipients of foreign invasions, have a uniquely religious relationship to the land they inhabit. Here, the invasion of outsiders—no matter how desperate they might perceive themselves to be—amounts to nothing less than sacrilege, no more justifiable than, say, the infiltration of atheists into a Southern Baptist convention.

HUMAN RIGHTS AND THE PROBLEM OF INDETERMINACY

The right to immigrate engages our attention because it shows how identity politics impinges on basic questions of justice, law, and democracy. The standard communitarian arguments for limiting immigration appeal to a substantive welfare paradigm of rights that privileges a separatist–preservative (SP) identity politics. These arguments assume that nations have a distinctive, cultural identity, which they seek to preserve and foster. The standard cosmopolitan arguments for opening up immigration, by contrast, appeal to a formal liberal paradigm of rights that privileges an individual-centered politics, abstracted from identity concerns.

In my opinion, both sets of arguments proceed from false assumptions. Communitarianism presumes that national identities are self-contained, geopolitically well-defined, and transmitted without change by persons born into "closed," homogeneous populations. Cosmopolitanism adopts the same principle—that identities are self-contained and self-generated—but applies it to individuals, understood as isolated atoms whose sense of self remains fundamentally unaffected by others. The question therefore arises: What happens if we abandon the principle that renders both communitarianism and cosmopolitan individualism so unworkable?

Nothing about communitarianism prevents us from extending the notion of community to include the entire world. What prevents us from doing this is an SP model of global identity politics that encourages nationalism. Nationalism is not always bad. But even when it is good— as an expression of anti-imperialism—it is only conditionally. In an ideal world, without domination and imperialism, peoples of different nations would not relate to one another with fear and hostility. So if one were searching for a communitarian ideal on which to model international relations, it would be an identity politics that was syncretic and transformative—and receptive to cross-cultural migration.

Cosmopolitanism individualism is equally malleable. The formal liberal paradigm it embodies by no means favors open immigration policies. In its proprietary social-contractarian formulation, the paradigm celebrates exclusive private ownership of assets. Transferred to the modern corporation and the corporate state, it entitles citizens no less than stockholders to exclude others from sharing assets as a matter of sovereign right, however democratically exercised. As we saw in chapter 5, this conception of proprietary right is deeply problematic. It has become more so in light of the global interdependencies linking economies and environments. The emergence of stakeholding conceptions of ownership gives new meaning to the concept of democracy and anticipates a world in which its citizens plan their shared destinies together, beyond the destructive anarchy of unregulated capitalism.

In a world without imperialism, the economic insecurities that feed anti-immigrant racism and ethnocentric xenophobia would doubtless diminish. Too, the strategic domination of one culture by another would also subside, making possible multicultural dialogue on an expanded scale. The meeting of North and South, East and West, might eventually link respect for individual rights and respect for global community. But for this to happen, such cross-cultural dialogue will have to be formally institutionalized in global governing bodies that are delegated the difficult and delicate task of resolving cultural disagreements regarding the interpretation of human rights. In fact, not only will deliberative democracy have to be institutionalized in a more effective way at the global level (perhaps by restructuring the United Nations General Assembly), but it will have to be institutionalized at the local level, requiring the democratization of governments and peoples.

This takes me to the main topic of this chapter: the importance of global deliberative democracy for the pragmatic realization of human rights. Human rights designate the most universal, most basic, highest-order moral duties we owe to each and every individual. Unlike other moral rights, such as the right to be treated with respect and decency, human rights are legal rights. Therein lies their import: they are often the only legal rights that stateless persons, such as immigrants and refugees, can turn to for relief. At the same time, their ambiguous status as both universal and legally enforceable is deeply problematic. To be pragmatically applicable across a wide (indeed universal) range of jurisdictions, human rights must be formulated in very general language. But the more general their formulation, the more indeterminate their meaning and force. We expect moral rights to be indeterminate. But too much indeterminacy renders legal rights unenforceable.

The indeterminacy of human rights accounts for the wide disagreement surrounding their interpretation. Part of this disagreement reflects the clash of legal paradigms discussed in chapter 6; part of it reflects cultural differences rooted in SP identity politics. It is not surprising that different legal paradigms counsel different approaches in dealing with these conflicts. The formal liberal paradigm—especially the well-known contractarian model put forward by John Rawls—counsels pragmatic toleration of cultural differences in a manner conducive to limited cooperation within the ambit of SP identity politics. The participatory democratic paradigm advocated by Habermas counsels multicultural dialogue in a manner conducive to fostering more extensive cooperation within the ambit of ST identity politics.

In my opinion, only the participatory-democratic paradigm can resolve the problem of indeterminacy plaguing the enforcement of human rights, but its full institutionalization in global and local governing bodies is clearly a desideratum that requires the preliminary establishment of alternative forms of cross-cultural dialogue that do not aim—at least directly—at reaching consensus on a single preferred interpretation of human rights. Ultimately, the conflict of interpretations cannot be settled so long as global capitalism holds sway, since it exacerbates the tension between legal paradigms. Only by mitigating these deeper economic contradictions can the cultural contradictions be democratically mediated.

THE HUMAN RIGHTS DEBATE

Today there is wide disagreement among nations regarding the interpretation and ranking of human rights. The U.S. State Department urged that the United Nations Universal Declaration of Human Rights be split into two treaties: the International Covenant on Civil and Political Rights; and the International Covenant on Economic, Social, and Cultural Rights. Although it supports the former covenant (1966), the State Department has refused to endorse the latter on the grounds that the rights it lists are less genuine and binding. Meanwhile, many delegates attending the first United Nations Conference on Human Rights (1993), held in Bangkok, signed a declaration supporting the opposite set of priorities. Representing developing countries, they argued that social welfare and basic subsistence are more important than civil and political freedom.

The disagreement between the State Department and the signatories to the Bangkok Declaration reflects a disagreement over legal paradigms. The State Department broadly endorses a formal liberal interpretation of rights that takes as its primary model the social contract, which views rights in terms of proprietary ownership. Accordingly, it insists that rights are claims made by individuals to negative freedom, or action uninhibited by state regulation. Using this model of rights, the State Department has urged the expansion of free trade and economic deregulation and has lobbied the World Trade Organization to hold the European Union in violation of free-trade agreements because of the latter's opposition to the importation of genetically modified organisms (almost 80 percent of all American agricultural produce is genetically modified). This proprietary view is also applied to immigration law. Despite the fact that the United States no longer uses racial quotas in determining who enters the country, the State Department's seemingly inconsistent policy of deporting Haitian—but not Cuban—asylum seekers looks racially motivated on the surface. The Justice Department's endorsement of intense screening procedures for immigrants from the Middle East and other hotbeds of terrorist activity also involves racial profiling. Last but not least, the sordid case of Elian Gonzalez revealed another little-known fact about the immigration rights of children. During the period when the decision was being made to return Gonzalez back to his father, in Cuba, the State Department recognized no right to asylum that could be claimed by children and none that could be claimed on their behalf, except by legally recognized custodial guardians. The decision to return Elian to his father was doubtless correct, but it also raised disturbing questions: what rights do young children have to asylum from oppressive conditions when their custodial guardians are missing or dead? Can the interests of the child's well-being ground a right to asylum in the absence of a parental claim on his or her behalf?

The signatories to the Bangkok Declaration might have less difficulty in responding affirmatively to this last question, since the legal paradigm they endorse stresses substantive welfare over formal liberty. Their general contention seems indisputable: that the formal liberty of individuals to act without government constraint is meaningless when it is precisely government and community that provide the collective conditions for subsistence and cultural identity—a fact that is especially well documented in agrarian tribal societies. Yet their subordination of formal liberty to social welfare is just as one-sided as the State Department's subordination of social welfare to formal liberty and seems an unlikely pretext for legitimating what appear to be oppressive and dictatorial regimes. As we saw in the last chapter, no particular category of right can be made fully secure when enforced on its own; and—to paraphrase a famous philosopher—if it is true that formal freedom without substantive welfare is empty, it is equally true that substantive welfare without formal freedom is blind.

The complementary relationship between different categories of rights is apparent as soon as we note the arbitrariness and incoherence of the UN's division of rights. Some rights, like the right to join labor unions, straddle the distinction between civil–political and socioeconomic rights. Still, the two sides of the human rights debate are correct about one thing: some rights are more basic than others. Indeed, ranking rights is perhaps the chief way to reduce the indeterminacy that affects their enforcement. The ranking in question cannot apply to categories of mutually complementary rights. As we saw in chapter 6, there are no compelling arguments for assuming that negative freedoms are inherently easier to define, enforce, and secure agreement on. So the ranking in question must apply to rights within categories. Thus, it can be argued that the economic right to acquire land and productive capacity for profit is less basic than the economic right to bare subsistence, just as the political right to contribute money to political campaigns and parties is less basic than the right to vote.

But how do we secure agreement on ranking rights, given the existence of competing cultural interpretations and the presence of global identity politics? Given widespread disagreement on this score, is it any wonder that the Universal Declaration of Human Rights is not codified into well-defined statutes with well-defined penalties attached to their violation? One might respond that this doesn't accurately describe the facts. The International Criminal Court (ICC), which was recently convened (over objections by the U.S. State Department, I might add), has successfully ordered the arrest of Slobodan Milosevic and other leaders who perpetrated genocidal war crimes in the Yugoslavian wars of the 1990s. Trials and convictions have already taken place under the court's auspices.

Despite this success, the very fact that human rights are not as well codified as legal rights, which have well-defined scopes and traditions of interpretation, partly explains the State Department's concern that their legal enforcement by the ICC will be subject to excessive judicial discretion and potential abuse—possibly to the point of jeopardizing the security of U.S. soldiers engaged in peacekeeping and policing.

The fact that human rights have hitherto remained in a state of suspended animation, imperfectly defined and therefore subject to judicial discretion, is indeed problematic, although not for the reasons cited by the State Department. The State Department could exercise a kind of veto power over errant judicial decisions by simply lobbying for the appointment of American judges on international courts—an opportunity it turned down. Rather, the problem is with judicial discretion, which stands in conflict with the principle of democratic legitimation (Campbell 2001). However, so long as human rights legislation is filtered through the auspices of the UN's General Assembly as it currently stands, it will remain indeterminate or insufficiently legitimate. Members of the assembly and UN-sponsored human rights committees are appointed by the leaders of their respective governments—many of whom are themselves self-appointed and without popular democratic backing. The main function of these delegates is to represent the interests of those who appoint them, rather than the interests of their fellow citizens. Consequently, their devotion to reaching agreement on anything more than a vague set of human rights platitudes is noticeably lukewarm.

Reform of the General Assembly involving the separation of functions (and perhaps legislative chambers) and the popular election of delegates are thus indispensable for securing the full legitimacy of human rights legislation. Equally imperative is the dissemination of deliberative democracy at all levels of state and local governance. The global institutionalization of popular and formal democracy, however, raises a new set of problems. How do we balance our need to respect illiberal and authoritarian cultures that are otherwise decent with our imperative to encourage their liberalization and democratization?

FOUR CONDITIONS OF A THEORY OF HUMAN RIGHTS

Before answering this question, it would behoove us to review what I take to be four conditions that human rights should meet. As we saw in chapter 6, a robust system of rights encompasses claim rights as well as interest-based rights, and group rights as well as individual rights. Summarizing this discussion, we see that human rights must be legitimate (or capable of being universally accepted by all reasonable persons); fully complete and complementary; and sufficiently determinate in meaning and ranking so as to be legally enforceable. The challenges in working out such a system of rights chiefly revolve around tensions between the first and last conditions and pertain to the clash of legal paradigms and the "clash of civilizations," as Samuel Huntington puts it.

Let me be more precise. An adequate theory must articulate universal rights that any rationally self-interested and reasonably fair-minded person could accept, regardless of cultural allegiance. Universal legitimacy can refer to either present or potential agreement among reasonable people. I argue that it should encompass potential agreement, where the potentiality in question does not preclude robust agreement on specific rights. Next, an adequate theory should articulate rights that are sufficiently defined to function prescriptively. This follows from the pragmatic idea of a human right as a legally enforceable claim that entitles those to whom it applies with some degree of fair warning. Such a requirement is compatible with the progressive determination of rights in accordance with their increasingly universal acceptance. An adequate theory should also distinguish basic rights from nonbasic, where basic rights are understood as guaranteeing the conditions necessary for the exercise of nonbasic rights. I argue that the distinction between basic and nonbasic rights ought not to be interpreted as privileging one category of rights (e.g., negative rights to act without interference) over other categories of rights (such as positive rights to capacities, resources, and opportunities for action). Finally, an adequate theory should be complete, in that it includes all categories of rights that are necessary for the full exercise of any human right. I argue that completeness is achieved only when liberal democratic rights are included among the schedule of basic human rights. These rights, in turn, imply cultural, social, and economic rights.

TWO PARADIGMS OF LEGITIMATION: CONTRACTARIAN PRAGMATISM VERSUS DEMOCRATIC PERFECTIONISM

In working out the details of my position, I refer to two legal paradigms: formal legal (social contractarian) and participatory-democratic. Both of these paradigms accept principled, pragmatic compromises in the area of human rights. Both accordingly forgo any attempt at providing a single right moral justification for rights in deference to the fact of reasonable pluralism. Consequently, their main focus is on explaining the legitimacy (universal acceptability) of human rights. Finally, both depart from liberal principles that enjoin mutual toleration among free and equal individuals. However, when applied to the international arena, the formal liberal paradigm allows peoples (nations) to replace individuals as the designated parties to the social contract.

My reference point for the first kind of theory is the social contract theory of John Rawls; my reference point for the second is the discourse ethical theory of democracy defended by Jürgen Habermas. Like the paradigms from which they depart, these thinkers also have much in common. Both depart from the liberal theory of international justice set forth in Kant's famous treatise *Perpetual Peace* (1795); both agree that national sovereignty must be limited by respect for universal human rights and that differing peoples must be allowed to interpret these rights in accordance with their own particular political traditions, at least within limits. At the same time, they disagree about these limits, with Habermas's affirming and Rawls's denying the necessity of liberal democratic institutions for realizing a fully legitimate and stable system of rights. Although each of these theories has distinctive virtues, neither satisfactorily meets the four conditions of an adequate theory of rights as outlined here—although Habermas's participatory democratic paradigm does point toward a solution.

Rawls's contractarian pragmatism does an admirable job of explaining how a modest schedule of relatively basic—albeit formally conceived—rights can be the subject of an overlapping, and hence legitimate, consensus. However, this approach concedes too much reasonable disagreement in the justification of rights and therefore too much uncertainty regarding their prescriptive meaning and ranking. As such, it cannot account for a more ambitious schedule of rights of the sort that is really needed, namely, a bill of rights that is substantive, complete, and enforceable. In my opinion, Habermas's discourse ethics goes a long way toward showing how these defects might be remedied. Inclusive democratic deliberation provides a framework for negotiating cross-cultural differences over time. This theory justifies the potential for an ever-expanding agreement regarding the specific meaning and deeper rationale underlying rights. Although this deeper agreement is postulated as an ideal goal to be achieved over time—hence its practical limitations as a basis for working out a universal schedule of rights in the present—it is a reasonable desideratum once we abandon the philosophically indefensible assumption of cultural incommensurability and accept the likelihood that global modernization will incline all cultures to liberalize and democratize.

In the final analysis, discourse ethics offers a better approach to resolving problems concerning immigration. Rawls's contractarianism postulates the existence of closed, homogeneous nations in a way that artificially brackets out facts about multicultural migration and diversity. It's proprietary understanding of formal liberal rights is therefore oddly compatible with illiberal communitarianism, which often appeals to SP identity politics in defense of restrictive immigration policies. Habermas's discourse theory fares much better. It incorporates multicultural diversity into its theory of nationality and allows that group rights might be necessary for realizing individual rights, as I show in chapter 6. Furthermore, its antiproprietary stakeholding view of the global economy disposes it favorably toward less-restrictive immigration policies and more-equitable distributions of the world's wealth.

THE CONTRACTARIAN APPROACH TO LEGITIMATING HUMAN RIGHTS

Of the two legal paradigms of human rights we are using as our benchmark, it is the contractarian (or formal liberal) that seems most conducive to establishing a legitimate, universal basis for rights. Contractarianism looks to factual commonalities between different national cultures in seeking its warrant for universal rights. It is therefore committed to tolerating wide disagreement with respect to specific economic and political institutions. Especially pertinent in light of recent events is Rawls's opinion that the global social contract must accommodate Islamic theocracies that do not treat all citizens equally and do not allow a spectrum of civil and political rights that is as extensive as that present in liberal democracies. This extension of contractarian toleration, however, makes for a rather untidy—and from Rawls's perspective, undesirable—form of SP identity politics in which different regions and cultures vie with one another for the privilege of imposing their preferred interpretation of human rights on the rest of the world.

To see how a contractarian approach to legitimating human rights works, let us turn to what is indisputably the locus classicus of this genre of international law. In his essay *The Law of Peoples* (1999), Rawls proposes to base international respect for human rights, principles of war, and principles of economic assistance vis-a-vis burdened nations on a contractarian conception of mutual respect between "peoples," or societal groups unified by "common sympathies" and organized around territorial states. Rawls accepts the idea that peoples, unlike the governments that act in their name (or states, in the technical sense), can be motivated by a sense of justice in dealing with other peoples rather than by sovereign self-interest; moreover, he sees no reason why they should not be fully respected, so long as they in turn respect basic human rights,[1] refrain from expansionist policies, and institutionalize a conception of justice based on reciprocal duties and the rule of law. Significantly,

Rawls holds that even illiberal, undemocratic nations can satisfy minimum thresholds of decency sufficient for them to be recognized as worthy of equal respect by liberal peoples, even if such nations do not allow equal civil and political freedom and even if their legal institutions embody a conception of justice that privileges one particular comprehensive conception of the common good over others (what he calls a "common good conception of justice," as distinct from a liberal "political conception of justice"; 1999, 64–5). Consonant with this conception of toleration, he maintains that, within illiberal undemocratic states, human rights can be assigned to persons as members of subgroups, which can be accorded unequal freedoms as required by the common good (66). In his opinion, legitimacy—if not full justice—is maintained to the degree that minority groups are tolerated, that dissenting groups are adequately responded to, and that each group is fairly represented in a consultation hierarchy (69).[2] Seen from the vantage point of economic justice, a minimally just Rawlsian world would also tolerate decent societies that choose not to provide state-funded services or promote the kind of socioeconomic equality normally thought to be essential to maintaining a healthy democracy. Hence, it would tolerate large differences in economic well-being within and among well-ordered states.

Commentators (Buchanan 2000a; Tan 1998; Moellendorf 1996) frequently note the discontinuity between Rawls's earlier contractarian theory of justice, including its most recent version—political liberalism—and his justification of a law of peoples. The earlier theory's defense of a liberal democratic conception of justice, which takes the freedom and equality of individuals as central to its vision of a well-ordered and stable legal regime, seems to have been abandoned in the essay on international law. Indeed, Rawls himself is quite explicit on this point. Once we understand that a law of peoples must encompass illiberal undemocratic as well as liberal democratic societies, the concept of what is reasonable to expect in the way of agreement on basic human rights must be considerably weakened. In his opinion, decent and not altogether unreasonable people living in illiberal nondemocratic societies will disagree about the superiority of liberal democratic schemes of justice just as reasonable people living in liberal democratic societies will disagree about the superiority of specific interpretations of liberal democracy or the superiority of specific comprehensive religious, philosophical, and moral doctrines. Therefore, it would be unreasonable—intolerant and illiberal—for liberal democratic peoples to impose their basic institutional structures on these other societies as a prerequisite for mutually advantageous cooperation. Furthermore, the mere fact that these other societies do not extend equal political rights to all their members is no argument against respecting them as equals in a community of societies, since many illiberal hierarchical organizations, such as churches and universities, are treated as equals by more liberal egalitarian groups (Rawls 1999, 69).

Although Rawls acknowledges that his concession to nonliberal, nondemocratic nations marks a deviation from his earlier theory (1971, 1999), he insists that his conception of international law is in some respects an extension of it. The earlier, individual-centered theory attempted to reconstruct a distinctly Kantian account of justice for liberal democracies by using the representational device of an original position in which hypothetical contractors agree on principles of justice without knowing specific details about themselves or their society. The later, political liberal theory (1993), by contrast, sought to show that a more general set of liberal principles were freestanding of any comprehensive philosophical doctrine—including Kantian doctrine—and so could function as a point of convergence for reasonable citizens of liberal democracies holding conflicting comprehensive metaphysical and epistemological doctrines.

The argument in support of a law of peoples also appeals to the original position and ideas associated with political liberalism. The latter idea and its correlative notions of reasonableness and of overlapping consensus is especially crucial. For example, Rawls argues that the free exercise of reason leads to an irreducible plurality of comprehensive doctrines so that no liberal democratic regime should impose a comprehensive conception of the good on its citizens in the way that an illiberal society might reasonably do. This stricture demands great forbearance from citizens, who are under a moral obligation to support only those interpretations of basic rights that could be justified by mutually acceptable reasons. This injunction against playing identity politics, however, is difficult to sustain in practice, since it requires that citizens bracket the comprehensive doctrines and cultural perspectives that constitute the core of their very identities. So Rawls is committed to the view that each citizen will appeal to these doctrines and perspectives in justifying specific interpretations of rights to him- or herself, if not to other people.

Despite the irrepressible tendency toward unreasonable pluralism and SP identity politics, Rawls notes that the comprehensive doctrines of reasonable persons inhabiting liberal democracies will at least overlap in their support of a liberal democratic constitution for the right reasons—reasons of deep moral principle—even if they do not happen to share the same reasons. *The Law of Peoples* deploys a similar line of argument. Reasonable peoples cannot but disagree on comprehensive doctrines, and so some of them will prefer liberal democratic institutions, others not. However, all decent peoples can appeal to their specific moral philosophies in consenting to basic articles of international justice, which do not depend on any particular comprehensive doctrine and so will overlap on these strictly political points (16, 18).

Now, the extension of devices such as the original position and overlapping consensus beyond the domestic liberal democratic setting to the international arena had already been proposed by Rawls in *A Theory of Justice* (1971) but did not go much beyond considerations pertaining to principles of war. It was left to others (Barry 1989; Pogge 1989; Beitz 1979; Carens 1987) to extend these Rawlsian ideas to areas of international justice touching on economic redistribution and immigration. *The Law of Peoples* acknowledges these applications but extends the original contractarian idea in a way that is fundamentally different from them. Instead of populating his global original position with cosmopolitan contractors' seeking fair terms of cooperation for free and equal individuals (heads of households), Rawls populates it with contractors' seeking fair terms of cooperation for free and equal nations.[3] In short, the law of peoples is the outcome of three distinct social contracts: between hypothetical representatives of a single liberal democracy; between hypothetical representatives of differently situated liberal democracies; and finally, between hypothetical representatives of decent illiberal and undemocratic societies. The important thing to note is that the legitimation of human rights will be different in each case. Under a veil of ignorance, representatives of liberal democracies will accept human rights as affirming the equal dignity and autonomy of all persons, regardless of gender or cultural–religious identity. Not so for representatives of illiberal undemocratic regimes. Abstracting from gender and cultural–religious identity is a violation of their cultural background, so they will interpret human rights differently, as protecting persons possessing unequal (or different) types of dignity and autonomy (Rawls 1999, 70).

In sum, Rawls's theory of international justice follows from his desire to extend the idea of a real social contract as far as reasonably possible. The pragmatic decision to demonstrate the universal legitimacy of human rights by including in the contract such reasonable and decent but otherwise illiberal and undemocratic peoples is striking in that it effectively eliminates liberal and democratic interpretations of these rights. This follows from the proprietary interpretation of reasonable pluralism implicit in the contractarian model: Agreement among what are presumed to be culturally insular and economically self-sufficient peoples will at best be overlapping, based on reasons that will not be shared by all. Thus, any consensus on rights and economic justice will at best be rather thin, conveying unspecified support for a basic right to life, liberty, property, and formal legal equality.

MAKING LEGITIMATE CONTRACTS ENFORCEABLE: TOWARD A DISCOURSE ETHICAL APPROACH

This last fact underscores a serious weakness in the contractarian approach to legitimating human rights. The relative superficiality of a theory of rights based on an overlapping consensus deprives the theory of prescriptive force.

This defect, in turn, is closely wedded to the inability of an overlapping consensus to distinguish a stable agreement based on moral trust from an unstable modus vivendi based on strategic expediency. Thus, there is nothing in principle that distinguishes international relations based on identity politics (the separatist–preservative variety in particular) from international relations based on impartial politics.

The very concept of an overlapping consensus suggests limits to what sorts of public reasons might be appropriate in official, governmental contexts. As I note in the previous chapter, in a pluralistic world, reasonable persons will typically have different—possibly conflicting—reasons for agreeing on rights. These nonshareable reasons, which stem from particular religious, ethical, and legal traditions, will also inform concrete interpretations of such principles, as expressed in definite legal and political institutions. Hence, a decent illiberal society will interpret the specific content of basic human rights differently than a liberal one. Now, according to Rawls, leaders of liberal democracies who act reasonably and civilly will recognize that reasonable pluralism among peoples imposes limits on the kinds of reasons they can bring to bear in discussing rights and other principles of justice with leaders of illiberal societies. In reasoning with them, they will not rely mainly on the nonshareable features of their specifically liberal doctrines, even though it is precisely these doctrines that ground their belief in the deeper truth of these rights and principles in the first place. In other words, when leaders of liberal democracies discuss human rights with leaders of decent but illiberal hierarchies, they will not rely exclusively on their own society's liberal democratic interpretation of rights (1999, 125, 152, 171). Submitting themselves to this kind of "gag rule" parallels the kind of civil constraint to which government leaders—and even ordinary citizens—inhabiting liberal multicultural and pluralistic democracies ought to submit to when addressing fellow citizens on the merits or demerits of rights legislation. In justifying their interpretation of constitutional rights, they, too, will appeal to "neutral" and "impartial" reasons that have broad—and legitimate—support, above the narrow confines of divisive identity politics.

It may be that private citizens who do not officially represent their nation (and do not wield the power to sanction) are not bound as strongly by such considerations of public civility and public reason. Citizens of a liberal democracy can try to persuade private citizens of an illiberal hierarchy to change their understanding of basic rights through informal arguments of a nonofficial nature that do appeal entirely to reasons held as true in accordance with deeper philosophical principles (1999, 84). Whether these reasons succeed in persuading the citizens of an illiberal hierarchy to adopt a liberal democratic interpretation of rights will depend on the extent to which the diverse comprehensive doctrines held by interlocutors on both sides happen to agree.

Given the proprietary nature of the social contract, in which different cultures and peoples are seen to be in full and exclusive possession of their identities, we can anticipate that there are good reasons—implicit in the religious and political culture of decent authoritarian societies—that strongly incline them to reject the reasons advanced by liberals and democrats. Perhaps for this reason, Rawls insists that officials of liberal democracies should not try to persuade their illiberal, undemocratic counterparts to adopt liberal democratic rights, either by offering incentives or appealing to their deepest or most comprehensive principles (1999, 84–85).

There is another hitch to the social contract that threatens to unravel the stability and trustworthiness of human rights covenants: What guarantees that an overlapping consensus is reasonable in the contractarian sense—that is, neutral with respect to and transcendent of SP identity politics? There is no way of knowing whether the incommensurable doctrines[4] that converge toward this consensus are minimally decent, short of their being justified in an inclusive, cross-cultural dialogue (Habermas, 1998a, ch. 3). For the mere fact that I observe that other persons agree to the same principles that I endorse— and for reasons that I can, if at all, barely fathom—would not entitle me to infer that their reasons were moral reasons, let alone fully reasonable (i.e., justifiable; 62–63, 90–91). In short, unless agreement on human rights stems from shared substantive norms, moral duties, and ideals of justice, there will be no way of knowing whether the agreement in question was not entered into for irrational or strategic reasons. Let us say, for example, that you are a citizen of an illiberal Islamic theocracy and I am a citizen of a liberal democracy. Leaving aside the fact that trustworthy commitments must ultimately be cemented in deeds and are thus equally reliable and stable, I have no grounds for trusting you (nor do you for me) without knowing that the reasons why you and I agree are both deeply justifiable. For all I know, your faith in rights could be trumped by fundamentalist ardour; for all you know, my secular support of the same could be trumped by economic greed.

Of course, trust is seldom an all-or-nothing affair. Ongoing acts of nonaggression may suffice to maintain minimal levels of trust between ideologically antagonistic peoples necessary for partial cooperation on pressing matters. Even the strong antagonism between the United States and its European allies regarding the death penalty and the basic rights of children doesn't undermine robust levels of trust with respect to other rights issues. However, the general rule for securing complete trust and efficient cooperation on any pressing rights issue requires addressing, sooner or later, the clash of cultures and legal paradigms that, left unresolved, lead to SP identity politics and its always immanent suppression of minority voices (differends).

Of course, achieving true consensus on basic rights is easier said than done. Once we abandon the presumption of cultural incommensurability, different possibilities present themselves. Following Charles Taylor (1999), we can imagine different legal paradigms realizing the same abstract formal "norms of action," such as the norm of reciprocity (the Golden Rule). Initially these norms might be sustained by an overlapping consensus. But one should harbor no illusions regarding the natural propensity for this kind of consensus to evolve into SP identity politics. I have argued that such a politics is entirely justified as a defensive strategy in which dominant regions, races, and cultures seek to impose their identities and preferred legal paradigms on subaltern peoples. Let there be no confusion on this point: SP identity politics can be a powerful tool in the arsenal of antiracism and anti-imperialism. But given the fact that dominant groups can play this game as well (if not better), it cannot be the final framework for negotiating a stable consensus on human rights.

If our ultimate aim is to achieve a stable consensus on a thicker and more enforceable schedule of human rights, then the only way to reach it is through syncretic–transformative (ST) identity politics. I have argued (chapters 5 and 6) that discourse ethics provides the best framework for conceiving the rationality and fairness of such a politics. Only it explains why the six values of deliberation and aggregative informing democracy move us to transform our identities, interests, and social standpoints for the sake of mutual emancipation and fulfillment. But given its demanding expectations, which require relinquishing and transforming core portions of our identity in ways that render us extremely vulnerable to the other, it cannot be the first form of intercultural dialogue we engage in.

The kind of transitional dialogue I have in mind involves a mutual understanding of substantive differences. Hans-Georg Gadamer's (1975) notion of a "fusion of horizons"—a somewhat misleading expression—comes closest to what I have in mind. In the course of understanding the other as other, we come to enlarge our horizon of what counts as meaningful and valid. This kind of understanding is not necessarily symmetrical. Gadamer, for instance, mentions that we defer to the authority of tradition when trying to understand it. Whether he is right about this is certainly open to question (Ingram 2003), but the general point is that the burden of mutual understanding may fall more on one party than the other—and rightly so. Whites, for instance, have a greater duty to understand the standpoint of blacks, who are unjustly marginalized in American society.

As Gadamer understands it, the "fusion of horizons" that accompanies genuine understanding indicates a mutual broadening and interpenetration of standpoints, not a one-sided assimilation of one into the other or their compression into a single standpoint without remainder of difference. Despite Gadamer's own tendency to link mutual understanding of differences with an orientation toward reaching agreement on some transcendent truth (the German word *Verständigung* conveys both mutual understanding and mutual agreement), the real thrust of his meaning is the preservation and transformation of differences in a higher "synthesis" in which they are more fully perfected and realized. Gadamer uses the Hegelian expression *Aufhebung* to capture this dialectical movement. For example, reading different interpretations of the same text does not cancel their differences. Instead, it produces an expanded horizon of substantive understanding rather than an abstract, formal framework of superficial comparison or overlapping consensus—in terms of which their mutual complementarity can be seen. Merely understanding them in relation to one another, against the background of an enlarged horizon (totality), changes and deepens (realizes) their distinctive meanings. As expanded horizon thus implies more than enlargement; it implies the creation of a wholly new set of meanings and standpoints not previously encompassed by the subsidiary horizons (Bohman 1995, 270).

Several examples will suffice to illustrate my meaning. The anthropocentric individualism of Western humanism and the cosmocentric ecologism of Eastern reform Buddhism can mutually enlarge and elevate one another in supporting norms of nonviolence, individual responsibility, and democracy capable of combatting predatory globalization (Inada 1990). To take another example, it may be that consensus on equal rights for women will only come after sustained efforts of mutual understanding have transformed patriarchal cultures. Reaching such a consensus is important for global well-being; for as Amartya Sen (1994) has argued, societies that go beyond minimal decency and empower women to vote, run for political office, receive and use education, and own and manage property (such as the Indian state of Kerala) show the simplest, most effective, and most acceptable way to ease the kind of overpopulation that drive immigration.

The treatment of women under Islam is especially difficult to reconcile with human rights. Abdullahi Ahmed An-Na'im (1990a) has written eloquently of the difficulties involved in implementing equal rights for women in Islamic countries. The justification for and interpretation of human rights is framed by Shari'a, or divine law, which does not grant full equality to women and non-Muslims. Women enjoy a full and independent legal personality to own and dispose of property and to conclude contracts. They are guaranteed specific inheritance shares and other familial rights. However, whereas men are granted up to four wives and are entitled to divorce them at will, women are restricted to one husband and can seek divorce only under very limited conditions. Women receive only half of an inheritance share and less compensation for criminal bodily harm. Women are generally judged incompetent to testify in criminal proceedings, and their testimony is worth half of a man's in civil proceedings. Shari'a holds that men are guardians of women and may beat women "lightly" if they become "unruly." Meanwhile, women may not hold offices of authority over men. (Incidentally, non-Muslims are also denied full rights. While they are secured their basic property, security, and civil rights, they must pay a special tax *(jiziya)* and are forbidden to proselytize and hold public positions of authority over Muslims. Muslims who leave the faith are subject to the law of apostasy, which is punishable by death in some jurisdictions.)

Despite these challenges to cultivating equal rights for women in the context of Islamic law, it is important to note that the law can be interpreted in ways that affirm the dignity of all persons, without regard to gender, race, nationality, or religion *(Surah* 49:13). The interpretation of Shari'a based on the early Mecca teachings of Mohammad, before the flight to Medina and the establishment of a Muslim state, refers to humanity as a whole, or all "children of Adam" *(The Holy Qur'an* 17:70). The conservative, Wahhabi sect of Sunni Islam, which is dominant in Saudi Arabia, and the literalist, Hanbali school of jurisprudence associated with it invoke the interpretative doctrine of *naskh* (supercession) in arguing that the later, Medina-period writings accurately preserve the complete and final meaning of the earlier writings (An-Na'im 1990b, 21). But Shiism and branches of Sufism (Islamic mysticism) view the revelation of divine meaning as a dynamic and progressive process. The Mevlevi Order, founded in thirteenth-century Turkey, and the Republican Brotherhood (of which Abdullahi Ahmed An-Na'im is a follower), founded in twentieth-century Sudan by Mahmoud Mohamad Taha, also encourage individual appropriation of divine texts through spiritual exercise and secular education.

However, to appreciate the depth of the divide separating Islamic and Western traditions of law, one need only turn to their respective interpretations of natural law. Islamic traditions collapse natural law—or universal morality as revealed by reason—into divine law, whereas Western traditions (including Catholic Thomism) distinguish them. This difference has a deeper religious basis. Christian teaching since Saint Augustine has emphasized the divided nature of humanity: the doctrine of original sin posits an infinite and unbridgeable gap between "rational" human nature and divinity, which is reflected in theological and human divisions (Trinitarianism, the separation between ecclesiastical and secular powers, and the separation and dispersal of humanity from itself and from God). The logical trajectory of this movement was a reformation whose pessimism regarding the capacity of human beings to redeem themselves and be one with God's knowledge (divine predestination) encouraged an epistemological and theological modesty conducive to the toleration of differences as well as a skepticism regarding government amelioration of social inequality.

Islam, by contrast, does not recognize original sin and instead accepts the human capacity to achieve revelation of the unity *(tawhid),* harmony, and order of a creation that is in perfect oneness with Allah. Personalism, individualism, and pluralism—and therewith, separation of church and state—are less compatible with it. Although it allows the differential treatment of men and women, in principle it is opposed to distinctions based on race and class and enjoins the state to assist the poor (all Muslims are required to pay alms—the *zakat,* or about 2 percent of one's income). Unlike Western natural-law traditions, Islamic teaching acknowledges the basic duty of state and community to provide for the economic subsistence and welfare of everyone. In addition to its stronger commitment to economic rights, Islamic tradition acknowledges the importance of social consensus *(ijima)* and consultation *(shura)* in collectively interpreting legal principles that are not clearly defined by the Qur'an and other holy traditions. In combination with the commitment to a just community, these ideals provide a basis for popular, democratic participation in governance, however constrained by accepted religious authority.

In sum, while there are possibilities for recognizing the equal rights of women in society within some currents of Islamic legal interpretation, this is not the case for all strands of interpretation. Here we encounter trenchant differences in worldview that obstruct the full and equal realization of certain categories of human rights. Dialogue aimed at mutual understanding—between different strands of Islamic thought and between these strands and Western currents—can, however, lead to a loosening of dogmatic and literalist approaches to legal interpretation over time. Such an Islamic reform would likely favor less-authoritarian and more individual-centered appropriations of holy texts, thereby opening the way for a fuller appreciation of equal liberal and democratic rights for all. Conversely, dialogue between Western and Islamic legal traditions could lead the former to (re)acknowledge the fundamental community and interdependence of all "the children of Adam," thereby motivating it to take positive initiatives in ameliorating economic inequalities between rich and poor countries.

DISCOURSE ETHICS AND THE PERFECTIBILITY OF HUMAN RIGHTS

Discourse ethics and social contract theory appeal to a rational consensus in legitimating human rights. In the former, however, consensus is understood counterfactually, in terms of a maximally inclusive and fair conversation in which all relevant assumptions—cultural, political, economic, or social—are openly criticized. Contract theory advises against doing this. It adopts what it takes to be a pragmatic pessimism regarding the capacity of comprehensive doctrines and legal paradigms to open themselves up to rational criticism from standpoints that are opposed to them.

Discourse ethics is more agnostic—perhaps even optimistic—about the capacity for insular cultures to become open and enlightened. It may well be that the irrepressible modernization of all societies through globalization—their institutionalization of some form of market economy coupled with some form of bureaucratic administration—will likely compel them to liberalize and democratize. Because equality and autonomy are deeply embedded in the fabric of our rational communicative interaction, laws sanctioning rights cannot be bestowed on persons without violating their own dignity and responsibility as self-legislating bearers of rights (Habermas 1998a, 261). As Habermas puts it, "Popular sovereignty and human rights go hand in hand" (1996, 127). Moreover, as we saw in the last chapter, categories of rights cannot be fully institutionalized in piecemeal fashion. One cannot have a secure right to anything unless one also has secure liberty and political influence. We can debate whether institutionalizing such "universal norms of action" will take the precise form of liberal and democratic rights as intended by the U.S. State Department, namely, as proprietary rights of individuals to buy and sell property, influence, or what have you (Taylor 1997; McCarthy 1997); but we cannot debate the basic complementarity of rights as such.

The very fact that countries such as China now embrace the Universal Declaration of Human Rights, after having formerly denounced it as bourgeois ideology, might be cited as evidence for this claim. This by no means implies a proprietary individualistic interpretation of them. Roger Ames (1988) notes that the Chinese word for human rights *(ch'uan-li)* has a nonlegalistic meaning that, in Confucian ethics, resonates more with ritual customs of proper behavior. Embedded in the correlative notion of human nature *(jen hsing)*, right is what enables the individual to realize his or her proper nature as a part of—rather than in opposition to—a community. Contrary to Western natural-law tradition, Chinese custom sees rights as conventions, or ad hoc negotiated agreements that facilitate the carrying out of differential roles. Accommodating differences means that "equality" is conceived differently, often in terms of a balancing of privileges and duties over a lifetime (one's duties as a child are balanced by one's privileges as a parent). China's many constitutions reflect this conventional wisdom. Instead of seeking to settle universally valid ideals once and for all, they aim to maintain harmonious relations under ever-changing and diverse circumstances. Hence, rather than instantiating abstract principles of conflict resolution based on the notion of a social contract between self-interested persons and potential adversaries, they propose concrete substantive policies for mutual self-realization. The emphasis on local context and community means that democratic deliberation will find greater purchase at that level—in peasant and worker collectives—than at the national level.

The Chinese interpretation of human rights no doubt leaves much to be desired (by purchasing flexibility at the cost of sacrificing determinacy, it makes the meaning and enforcement of rights less certain and thereby subject to greater judicial and administrative discretion). But the standard by which to judge it should not be the formal legal proprietary paradigm associated with contractarian thinking. The standard should be set by discourse ethics, which sees the indeterminacy of rights as a problem to be resolved democratically. Again, the normative force of social contract theory is constrained by a threshold of minimal decency beyond which it dare not tread. The normative force of discourse ethics is more open-ended and utopian. The equal inclusion of all in democratic deliberation also requires the (roughly equal) distribution of resources, capabilities, and opportunities that enable such inclusion, or, as Habermas puts it, "equal opportunities to utilize . . . basic rights to the provision of living conditions that are socially, technologically, and ecologically safeguarded" (1996, 128). This does not mean that human rights are justified solely on the basis of their instrumental contribution in realizing democracy (1998c, 175–76). As we saw in chapter 6, their justification embraces multiple rationales. However, it does show that the realization of any system of human rights depends on the democratic processing of rights under the auspices of a reformed UN, whose elected representatives would be held accountable to democratic constituencies worldwide. Such a global federation of democracies, in turn, would be morally compelled to protect their weakest members against the uneven impact of a global market economy (Habermas 1998c, 80–84, 120–26).

Discourse ethics may do a better job of grounding the complementarity and perfectibility of rights than social contract theory; and it may explain how the legitimacy of human rights can be purchased without sacrificing their substantive meaning, within the context of ST identity politics. But how does it help deal with the other problem of indeterminacy—the problem of prioritizing rights?

Habermas's comments on this topic leave a great deal to be desired. His assertion that social welfare rights "only serve to guarantee the 'fair value' of; i.e., the actual conditions for the equal exercise of liberal and political rights" (1998c, 187, quoting Rawls) suggests that he agrees with Rawls—and the U.S. State Department—in privileging civil and political categories of rights over social welfare categories. This view runs contrary to the position I have defended. However, the priority of the principle of liberty with respect to the principle of welfare (the difference principle) in Rawls's own theory of justice is open to multiple interpretations. Rawls's comments only apply to liberal democratic societies that have already achieved a certain level of affluence, and their general thrust is to enjoin against trading equal liberties for higher increments of welfare. Furthermore, as Rawls's own comments about securing the "equal value" of civil and political amply demonstrate, ensuring a roughly equal distribution of resources, capabilities, and opportunities is essential to realizing civil and political rights for all. The idea that human rights to liberty, security, and subsistence are complementary is further reinforced in

The Law of Peoples, which lists subsistence as a basic right. For his part, Habermas never waivers in his conviction that different categories of rights are realized together—in a system of rights.

But this tells us nothing about ranking rights within equally valorized categories of rights.

Borrowing a page from Henry Shue (1996), I would argue that there exists a priority of basic rights over less-basic rights within each category of right. Thus, within the category of economic rights, the "subsistence" entitlement to a minimally decent share of food outweighs the "market" right to acquire and transfer property without interference. This may seem obvious to most of us, but other rankings may not be. On one hand, some priorities—such as insisting on the satisfaction of basic subsistence needs before allowing market freedoms—might be relatively uncontroversial across cultures. When human-need priorities are less obvious—as happens when economic rights are weighed against environmental rights—discourse ethics can provide a framework for negotiating a principled compromise over time. Here, the imperative to achieve universal agreement on, for instance, well-defined and enforceable global standards of clean air and water, fluorocarbon emissions, and the like will have to be negotiated with an eye toward protecting the most vulnerable economies. So we see, on the other hand, that some indeterminacy in ranking—and therefore some laxness in enforcement—will have to be accepted as the price that any context-sensitive, globally instituted human rights regime must pay. To some extent, this kind of indeterminacy will also affect global standards of basic subsistence, welfare, and capability. One can only hope that reasonable, democratically empowered people will have the collective wisdom to define the minimum—and maximum—thresholds of human decency fairly and rationally.

IMMIGRATION RIGHTS

We have compared contractarian and discourse ethical approaches to legitimating human rights and found the latter more adequate as a device for grounding a pragmatic and perfectible global human rights regime. I propose that we confirm this result by returning to the topic with which we began our discussion: the rights of immigrants.

As noted, contractarianism presumes that peoples instantiate essentially self-contained political cultures. The law of peoples is arrived at through first working out the principles of justice for domestic societies. In regarding a domestic liberal society from the standpoint of the original position, we make the simplifying assumption that it is closed. We regard it as "self-contained and as having no relations with other societies," in such a way that it "reproduces itself and its institutions and culture over generations" (Rawls 1993, 12, 18); and its members "enter only by birth and exit only by death" (Rawls 1999, 26). Rawls is fully aware that, despite the simplifying abstraction of a closed society bound together by a self-perpetuating national political culture, "historical conquests and immigration have caused the intermingling of groups with different cultures and historical memories" within the same territory. Yet he continues to defend this abstraction as if it were descriptive of historical reality, even to the extent of endorsing John Stuart Mill's deterministic definition of national identity as "common sympathies" rooted in (among other things) "race and descent" (23).

Immigrants and refugees are the classical addressees of human rights, since they are often denied the rights of citizenship. Contractarian thinking, however, does a poor job of representing those rights. Proprietary peoples, Rawls insists, have good moral reasons to protect themselves, their culture, and the territory that they inhabit by instituting restrictive immigration policies—at least so long as they coexist in a world of security risks, epidemics, multicultural conflicts, and economic scarcities. These views of immigration and economic redistribution are ones that Rawls draws—somewhat surprisingly—from one of his staunchest communitarian critics, Michael Walzer (1983). As an opponent of cosmopolitan liberalism, Walzer holds that protection of a people's property, no less than of its political culture, is sufficient to limit immigration. Although Rawls is probably right to argue that the political and economic causes that drive immigration would be greatly mitigated under his proposed law of peoples, he gives no reason why the survival needs of desperate individuals should not outweigh the culturally perfectionist expectations of affluent peoples anxious to maintain a costly political culture and way of life. Like Walzer, he thinks that a global state without borders would be a cosmopolitan dystopia of deracinated men and women, and he adds that, under its regime, global capitalism would have free rein to overwhelm local communities (1999, 39). But elsewhere he seems more sanguine about the benefits of free trade; and although he is hardly oblivious to the harsh inequalities generated by global capitalism, he fails to note that the political evils contributing to bad resource management, overpopulation, lack of investment, and other factors driving immigration are partly, if not mainly, attributable to a global system that has disproportionately benefited affluent border-conscious countries.

To be sure, contractarianism needn't be so chary in extending open doors to desperate immigrants. Joseph Carens, for instance, appeals to none other than Rawls himself in justifying a prima facie unrestricted right to immigrate, on the grounds that citizenship and place of residence are as morally arbitrary as other undeserved features affecting a person's fortunes. His hypothetical contractors, however, are cosmopolitan individuals, not culturally identified peoples. Ignorant of their citizenship or residence, cosmopolitan individuals placed in an original position would relate to one another as fully free and equal and so would incline toward a liberal democratic interpretation of basic rights. They would also probably opt for principles of justice allowing for relatively unrestricted freedom of movement across borders, since that would maximize the overall well-being of the most oppressed and most numerous among them. Assuming that Rawls is right that equal and free persons placed in a domestic (liberal democratic) original position would reject utilitarian principles in favor of strongly egalitarian ones—such as his difference principle, which allows economic inequalities only to the extent that they benefit the worst off—then it is not unreasonable to suppose that free and equal persons placed in an international original position would choose the same way, thereby necessitating massive transfers of wealth from rich individuals to poor individuals (1999, 119–20).

As Rawls himself notes, the appeal to how cosmopolitan individuals might reason in the original position has less force than Carens might think. Indeed, even Carens admits that a prima facie unrestricted right to immigrate is just that—a right that can and should be overridden in light of real-world exigencies. For Rawls, one of them is the fact that not all cultures are equally susceptible to entertaining the individualizing abstraction inherent in the original position. Members of these cultures are nationally identified. So contractarian legitimation can only function if the original position is populated with nations, not cosmopolitan individuals.

If one is to effectively challenge contractarian views on immigration, it will have to begin and end with the view espoused by Rawls. In particular, it will have to challenge the basic assumption underlying that view, namely, that peoples must be conceived as nationally identified in some strong sense. As we saw in chapter 2, the kind of quasi-racialist notion of national identity that Rawls (following Mill) presumes is patently illegitimate. Indeed, perhaps the very concept of national identity is an ideological fiction (Habermas 1998c, 37) that, having once helped pave the way for democratic political integration in Europe during the nineteenth-century, now threatens to obstruct it at the international level (1998a, 112–15). Discourse ethics rightly rejects the model of SP identity politics implicit in this view. It endorses instead an ST model of identity politics in which multinational cultural identities are maintained and generated more or less reflectively and voluntarily. The very identification of peoples with closed territorial groups needs to be rethought, especially when considering cases of overlapping peoples, as in Northern Ireland and Israel/Palestine. Partitioning and SP identity politics do not always form the best solution in these cases, since the economies and spaces being contested by the contending parties are essentially shared (Young 2000b; Castells and Borja 1997).

An understanding of global interdependence and political diversity that is more sophisticated than Rawls's might lead one to sympathize more strongly with the rights of immigrants and stateless refugees. Take, for example, Habermas's own endorsement of a relatively open immigration policy, which acknowledges the fact that the First World has benefited disproportionately from "the history of colonization and the uprooting of regional cultures by the incursion of capitalist modernization" (1998a, 230–31). But there are other reasons—intrinsic to discourse ethics itself—that support less-restrictive immigration policies than those countenanced by Rawls and Walzer. More precisely, the kind of multicultural dialogue and ST model of identity politics encouraged by discourse ethics promotes the breakdown of racially self-enclosed national identities, thereby eliminating cultural barriers to immigration. Once admitted, there is no good reason—according to discourse ethics—why immigrants should not then be allowed to participate as equals in the constitutional political culture without having to "give up the cultural form of life of their origins," even if their doing so "changes the character of the community" (229–30).

Discourse ethics thus provides a salutary corrective to contractarianism by emphasizing the inherently relational construction of cultural identities. One might therefore suspect that it is simply hostile to any kind of SP identity politics. Indeed, as we saw in chapter 1, Habermas—no less than Rawls—sometimes demands that citizens "uncouple" their national cultural identities from the universal political culture they all share as rational individuals (1998a, 227). This explains his objection to the Quebec government's language policy. That policy, you will recall, requires that immigrants send their children to schools in which classes are conducted in French. Habermas's objection, however, wasn't simply that this policy violates the fundamental human right of parents to send their kids to schools of their own choosing or that it involves discriminatory treatment against immigrants in particular. His objection aimed at the futility of trying to insulate a linguistic culture from changes that invariably affect it in the course of its appropriation by individual speakers. In his opinion, ST identity politics and cultural instability are the price that any society pays for allowing immigration.

Habermas's comments on Quebec's language laws were not his final words on the subject of identity politics. He later conceded that ST identity politics and global mass culture—or what he called "postmodern neoliberalism"—might threaten some cultures (especially aboriginal microcultures) with pathological disintegration (1998c, 115, 124, 127). Recognizing the danger of pathological assimilation posed by ST identity politics, he eventually acknowledged the legitimate use of SP identity politics, including such "difference sensitive" strategies as "group-specific rights"—along with a "federalist delegation of powers, a functionally specified transfer or decentralization of state competencies, above all guarantees of cultural autonomy . . . , compensatory policies, and other arrangements for effectively protecting minorities" (1998a, 145–46).

Applying these strategies to Quebec's language laws yields a more subtle interpretation of the impact of discourse ethics on immigration policies. Quebecois nationalism is not racial but cultural. The education law requiring immigrants to send their children to French-speaking schools was intended to include them in Quebec's public life; and the language laws that applied to work spaces and signs eliminated privileges rather than limited fundamental freedoms. The laws therefore had a thoroughly rational basis: the preservation of a public space in its linguistic integrity.

In discussing these laws, Habermas argued that legal efforts to preserve a culture inevitably run up against the freedom of expression so necessary for identity formation in liberal societies (222). In light of his later reconsideration of the disintegrating effects of unregulated communication, he could have concluded just as easily that, without such laws, the very medium of free expression itself would have been imperiled. Freedom to participate as an equal in Quebec's democracy may very well require sharing a common language with others; and since this language is threatened by the incursion of a more dominant language (English)—and since, for some French speakers, the incursion of English in the workplace functions to discriminate against them—laws that "impose" French in private and public spaces also protect individuals in the free exercise of their civil and political rights.

ECONOMIC RIGHTS

As I note in the opening pages of this chapter, no discussion of immigration rights can be complete without addressing fundamental economic realities. As we have seen, Habermas recognizes that global capitalism creates unjust relationships of mutual dependence that require rectification. He thinks that regulation of this economy is best undertaken at the level of supranational oversight rather than locally, through protectionist means. In my opinion, he underestimates the possible benefits that might flow from a two-tiered strategy combining local democratic oversight of regional economies (including the use of protective tariffs) and supranational regulation—a level of regulation, I might add, that has hitherto failed to benefit developing countries.

Unfortunately, Habermas has much less to say than Rawls about what economic justice demands at the global level. Therefore, it is Rawls, not Habermas, to whom I now turn in addressing this issue. To begin with, Rawls urges decent peoples to assist burdened nations to the extent that is necessary for them to enter into relations of peaceable mutual cooperation with them. But, he adds, many decent nations could reasonably refuse to give up wealth and resources simply for the sake of equalizing the lives of cosmopolitan individuals. Hence, he opposes global distributive principles of the sort that have been advanced by Charles Beitz and Thomas Pogge.[5]

Rawls does so because, as we've seen, he does not think that all decent peoples can agree on such principles. But, as Beitz notes (2000, 681)—and as we have confirmed—deference to factual disagreement is hardly compelling. No more compelling is Rawls's view that moral psychology dictates limited expectations regarding the capacity of persons to think of themselves from a cosmopolitan view. What confuses "questions about justification and those about institutional design," in the words of Beitz (683), is the idea that we must protect the proprietary sovereignty of peoples above respecting individuals' economic rights simply because individuals identify themselves first and foremost as fellow members of a territorially bounded scheme of mutual cooperation and responsibility. Even if territorial states happen to be the most efficient mechanism for managing resources for mutual benefit and so provide an exemplary basis for determining our primary obligations as citizens, this fact alone says nothing about our psychological capacity to identify with, and care for, strangers as human beings. If persons in large multicultural states can identify with one another for this reason, surely they can identify with outsiders for the same reason; indeed, we may depend more on and have more in common with people who live outside our nation than on and with people who live within it. In any case, Rawls is wrong to adopt the communitarian maxim that moral psychology—or feelings of solidarity with fellow members (whomever they might be)—ought to determine the extent of our moral duties; for allowing this is tantamount to caving in to ethnocentric prejudice.

Rawls's privileging of peoples over individuals as the principal subjects of international law also undermines his defense of a principle of assistance to burdened societies. Rawls insists that this principle be understood not as a requirement of international distributive justice to be implemented continuously but merely as a duty to raise all societies to a minimum level of political culture and economic sustainability commensurate with requirements of minimal decency. As such, the duty has a definite "cut-off point." Here again, Rawls offers scant justification for the duty, other than the possible global security risks that unstable societies pose to the rest of the world. Although he remarks that liberal democratic societies will be morally required to relieve absolute poverty so that people can live decent lives; to mitigate the stigma of inferiority that comes with differences in wealth; and to secure fair conditions for democratic politics, he notes that these reasons do not apply directly to the international arena, except insofar as any well-ordered decent people will have met the basic needs of all citizens so that they, as equal and autonomous members of the "Society of Well-Ordered Peoples," can decide for themselves "the significance and importance of the wealth of [their] own society" (1999, 114–15).

As I noted in the last chapter, there is some merit in what Rawls is defending here. Standards of subsistence and capability are indeed culturally relative. However, nothing in Rawls's concession to this fact displays any awareness that we live in a global community in which the wastefulness and ecological destructiveness inherent in capitalism's growth imperative affect developed and underdeveloped peoples unevenly. According to this line of thinking, if it is necessary to establish a cutoff point for assistance, then why is it not equally necessary to establish a cutoff point for affluence? And why is there no recognition of the increased risks posed by global inequalities to persons inhabiting underdeveloped countries? Unlike in the individual-centered theory of justice that he developed earlier with respect to liberal democracy, Rawls here makes no reference to the inherent unfairness of allowing arbitrary circumstances, such as one's being born in a poor, resource-starved country, to diminish one's equal chances for a free and fulfilling life. Finally, why should economic decisions that affect the entire world be decided by members of individual states according to the "significance and importance of wealth in their own society"?

Rawls's resistance to submitting global regulatory and redistributive policies to global democratic oversight no doubt resides in his questionable views about the capacity of states to be economically independent and autonomous in their distribution of resources. Rawls asserts that "there is no society anywhere in the world—except in marginal cases—with resources so scarce that it could not, were it reasonably and rationally organized and governed, become well-ordered" (1999, 108). Leaving aside the questionableness of this assertion, Rawls makes no reference to causes other than lack of resources that contribute to the impoverishment of nations, except perhaps unfair trade agreements (69). This is surprising, given his understanding of how capitalist economies in liberal democracies generate inequalities whose effects on the life chances of disadvantaged persons are both arbitrary and unjust and therefore require correction through redistributive means. Thus, to take the example of trade, there is now a voluminous literature on how inequalities in capital and other resources enable developed countries to implement free-trade agreements that condemn underdeveloped countries to perpetual neocolonial dependence; weakened health, education, and welfare services; ecological devastation; political corruption; class warfare; resource depletion; and (for most inhabitants) poverty. In sum, the national resource sufficiency and international fair trade that Rawls maintains are necessary for bringing about a global "Society of Well-Ordered Peoples" are undermined by a capitalist global structure.

Rawls gives additional reasons why a principle of global distributive justice is unfeasible—none of them convincing. He argues, for instance, that it would be unjust to demand that well-ordered nations that have managed their economies responsibly—through hard work, population control, and savings—transfer some of their wealth to poorer, well-ordered nations that have not been as industrious or thrifty. As Beitz notes (2000, 691–92), the appeal of this argument tacitly depends "on an analogy with individual morality, where we typically believe that society has no obligation to hold people harmless from the adverse consequences of their own informed, uncoerced choices." The full force of this argument becomes apparent once we acknowledge that people living in most underdeveloped nations had much less choice in determining their economic fates than individuals inhabiting developed ones (recall that it was the U.S. government and its allies that loaned their leaders money for guns instead of butter).

Perhaps it is unfair to saddle Rawls's theory of economic assistance with the burden of having to deal with "marginal" cases such as these; and perhaps his strictures about fair trade might reach all the way down to regulating, in some form, the background structures and institutions constraining trade. Granting that, it is presuming a lot to suppose that representatives of peoples in the global original position of choice who seek to advance the corporate interests of their respective peoples would settle for a weak principle of charity (the duty to assist burdened peoples) instead of a more egalitarian principle of distributive justice. Would not knowledge of the short-term (and very possibly, long-term) detrimental effects of a global market system on the most vulnerable nations lead them to view continuous economic redistribution as a matter of right, necessary for guaranteeing the equality and autonomy of all trading partners? As Thomas Pogge argues, even more egalitarian principles of distributive justice, such as the difference principle Rawls invokes for liberal democratic societies, would be preferred if the representatives in the global original position represented individuals (heads of households or caretakers of dependents) instead of peoples.

As I note earlier, welfare paradigms of distributive justice have problems of their own, not the least of which is determining appropriate culturally and ecologically sensitive levels of development and flourishing. Here Rawls's reservations about applying welfare-maximizing schemes without qualification sound eminently reasonable. Indeed, as we have seen, Rawls is aware that privileging (in the words of Samuel Scheffler) "special responsibilities to the members of our own families, communities, and societies" over "general responsibilities" might be a more effective and just way of implementing global justice democratically. An emphasis on general responsibilities—as the neoliberal defense of free markets shows—can be no less antiegalitarian than an emphasis on special responsibilities can be egalitarian—as the protectionist defense of local economies likewise shows. Rawls's appeal to the rights of peoples imposes limits on any global egalitarian redistribution, but it is not hostile to egalitarian outcomes achieved through protectionist means. However, it is a very large question whether nation-states can protect their domestic economies without banding together in larger, supranational organizations that are democratically empowered to regulate market inequalities and externalities. Here again, economic self-determination at the level of the group (or community) rather than of the nation might be the most efficacious way to protect economic rights. Regional and metropolitan self-determination, however, needs to be coupled with interregional and, ultimately, supranational regulatory bodies to rein in multinational corporations and ensure equitable development.

In the current era of globalization, liberal democracies across the board are under increasing pressure from financial institutions—and, yes, from global economic entities such as the European Union—to embrace structural adjustment policies that exact a heavy toll on social services and other security nets essential to egalitarian democracy. As Allen Buchanan observes, Rawls's protectionist understanding seems to reflect a "vanished Westphalian world" that inadequately captures the interdependence of nations.[6] Specifically, Rawls overestimates the extent to which states are "economically self-sufficient" and "distributionally autonomous"[7] while idealizing the degree to which they are "politically homogeneous," devoid of internal political–cultural divisions.

CONCLUSION

I have sought to sketch a theory of human rights that satisfies four criteria—universality, prescriptive determinacy, priority, and completeness. Contractarian approaches secure the universal legitimacy of human rights at the cost of prescriptive force. Discourse ethical approaches mitigate this defect by framing agreement in terms of an evolving consensus aimed at perfecting rights. Ultimately, an adequate account of human rights must accommodate differences in social standpoint, both within and between nations, which means that the rights of groups no less than the rights of individuals will have to be politically recognized. Only in this way can the rights of women, immigrants, and nationalities be fully protected.

That is also why an international democratic federation of liberal democracies and interest groups is really the only lasting basis on which to build peace and justice. In addition to democratizing and opening up global banking and trading institutions, such as the International Monetary Fund, the World Bank, and the World Trade Organization, the UN should be restructured, either by abolishing the veto of the permanent members of the Security Council or by opening up the permanent membership to states from the southern hemisphere. In addition to this reform, Young (2000b, 273) recommends supplementing the General Assembly of nations with a "People's Assembly," composed of persons elected directly by individuals from all over the world who would represent vulnerable subgroups, including women, indigenous people, and poor people.

Until this federation becomes a reality (and we have no reason to think that it can't), full toleration and trust between nations will remain elusive. In the meantime, those of us living in affluent democracies should pressure our leaders to promote more liberal democracy here and abroad, preferably through diplomacy and not sanctions; and, remaining ever mindful of our nation's own present and past failure to honor its principles, we should pressure them to forswear any crusades that falsely and immodestly (and hypocritically) equate liberal democracy with *our* liberal democracy. Above all, we should bear in mind the fact that tolerance means something quite different in a post-Westphalian world of partially sovereign nations. It means openness to interdependency and mutual vulnerability. In today's world, we would be deluding ourselves if we thought that unilateralism—especially when arrogantly trumpeted by the world's only superpower in brazen pursuit of its own narrow self-interest—is an effective way to deal with terrorism and other global calamities.[8] In the absence of enforceable international covenants—on such pressing issues as ecological safety, economic justice, gender discrimination, and racism—human rights abuse and other morally unconscionable suffering will continue unabated, and the world will remain a less-secure place because of it.

NOTES

1. Among the human rights mentioned by Rawls are "the right to life (to the means of subsistence and security); to liberty (to freedom from slavery, serfdom, and forced occupation, and to a sufficient measure of liberty of conscience to ensure freedom of religion and thought); to property (personal property); and to formal equality as expressed by the rules of natural justice (that is, that similar cases be treated similarly)" (1995, 65). Elsewhere Rawls notes that articles 3 to 18 of the United Nations Universal Declaration of Human Rights (1948) count as universal human rights in his sense, whereas article 1, which asserts that "all human beings are born free and equal in dignity and rights," expresses a particular liberal interpretation of human rights (80).

2. Rawls excludes from the Society of Well-Ordered Peoples (i.e., peoples who are guaranteed protection from international sanction) such unreasonable peoples as outlaw states that violate human rights and benevolent dictatorships that respect human rights but deny their citizens a meaningful role in making political decisions. Also excluded are reasonable societies burdened by unfavorable economic or cultural circumstances (4). Rawls includes decent consultation hierarchies, in which only some persons are allowed to run for and hold office. Persons choose members of their own group (occupational, religious, etc.) to represent them in an assembly of group representatives but do not directly vote as individuals for government officers. Government leaders (some of whom might be chosen by a clerical hierarchy) consult the higher assembly, fairly balancing the interests of all groups.

3. Joseph Carens (supra) conceives the global original position to apply to individuals rather than nations. This approach is expressly favored by Pogge in *Realizing*

Rawls, although in a later essay (1994, 195–224) he defends a global resource tax proposal by accepting, for the sake of argument, Rawls's assumption that the global original position contains representatives of homogenous peoples.

4. Although Rawls normally talks about a plurality of "opposing" and "irreconcilable" doctrines (1993, 3), he occasionally refers to a "plurality of conflicting and incommensurable doctrines" (135). By "irreconcilable" Rawls seems to mean "uncompromising" (138); "incommensurable," by contrast, suggests that doctrines are "uncompromising" by not being fully translatable into a common public language in which they might be rationally discussed and modified. If so, incommensurability would serve to immunize doctrines from the demands of public accountability. However, as Habermas notes (citing well-known arguments by Donald Davidson), this notion of incommensurability is incoherent.

5. Rawls (117) finds Charles Beitz's "resource redistribution principle" inconsequential because he thinks that a nation's political culture is more decisive in hindering its capacity to achieve economic independence than its level of resources. He rejects Beitz's "global distribution principle," which applies the difference principle to peoples, because it would unfairly penalize a nation that had voluntarily controlled its population or increased its rate of savings and industrial development in comparison to another nation similarly situated that had chosen not to do so. Rawls is willing to accept Thomas Pogge's global resources tax on resource use but only if it specifies as its cutoff point the elevation of the world's poorest peoples to the level where their citizens' basic needs are fulfilled and they can stand on their own (119). For criticisms of Pogge's proposal, see Roger Crisp and Dale Jamieson (2000) and Hillel Steiner (1999).

6. The Peace of Westphalia (1648) that ended decades of religious warfare between European states viewed relations among largely self-sufficient and sovereign nations in military rather than economic terms.

7. For Buchanan (2000b, 702), "States are more or less economically self-sufficient if and only if they can . . . provide adequately for the material needs of their population. . . . A state is distributionally autonomous if and only if it can determine how wealth is distributed within its borders."

8. The number of international treaties rejected by the U.S. State Department is appalling. The United States cast the sole dissenting vote during ratification sessions on the Kyoto Protocol limiting greenhouse emissions; the 1975 Biological Weapons Convention; and the Land Mine Treaty (the voting margins in favor of these treaties were, respectively, 178 to 1; 55 to 1; and 140 to 1). Along with Somalia, the United States is the only country to refuse to ratify the Convention on the Rights of Children because the treaty condemns the execution of juvenile offenders. The United States has repeatedly disregarded the Vienna Convention on Consular Rights guaranteeing that foreign citizens will be immediately informed of their right to communicate with their consulate on arrest. And, it has refused the jurisdiction of an International Criminal Court on grounds that American soldiers might be arraigned on human rights violations. The current administration's defense of this "policy of exceptionalism" appeals to the special burdens imposed on the United States as the lone superpower. However, the argument from exception has been abused by virtually every rogue state to justify human rights violations.

Concluding Remarks

Achieving Global Harmony through Transformative Dialogue

Human rights and principles of global justice designate minimum thresholds of decency as well as maximum ceilings of fulfillment. They stipulate what is pragmatically possible given existing social realities, and they anticipate utopian futures where universal freedom, happiness, and perpetual peace find perfect realization.

This is the space in which critical theory operates as well. Not satisfied with merely traversing its expanse, critical theory must also measure its limits, which can be summed up in a single idea: the necessity of tailoring utopian ends to fit the exigencies of a reality that has yet to realize its proper end—in short, the necessity of principled compromises. First, the exigencies. We begin with the fact of pluralism and scarcity. No conceivable society (world) will ever eliminate this fact, because eliminating scarcity by its nature generates new needs, new scarcities, and new social positions. Social conflict and identity politics find their raison d'etre here as does social injustice. As society's needs, scarcities, social positions (conflicts and injustices) become more complex, so do the means for regulating them. The modern state, which guarantees rights under the auspices of a democratically legitimated rule of law, accordingly splits into separate functions, each with its own specialized language for processing what it receives from the others. The resulting gaps in reasoning separating what the public says it wants (justice) and what representatives and administrators say they want (order and stability) create new conflicts, new injustices—differends, in which perfectly legitimate standpoints are suppressed or silenced. These conflicts and injustices are ramified further by conflicting legal paradigms that reflect competing demands within the system—for freedom, welfare, and control of one's life.

These social facts limit critical theory's normative scope. There is no single grand narrative that can capture all the manifold conflicts and injustices within the fixed compass of a single idea—not even the narrative of class domination, which undoubtedly captures a great deal. Indeed, the fact of reasonable pluralism shows that critical theory's normative standpoints are just as contingently justified as any other and as such can claim the allegiance of only a few of us. More important, because critical theorists are cognizant of this fact, they must be modest in their beliefs about what critical theory can provide in the way of normative guidance. Beyond urging them to organize themselves, Marx generally declined to preach to the masses. We, too, must decline. But abandoning the moralizing tone of the preacher does not mean that we cannot—from our standpoint—articulate what prevents the world from realizing its own moral principles.

Critical theorists argue that structural contradictions in capitalism radiate outward, undermining the integrity of systems of justice. I make a similar claim. However, no modern, complex legal system can eradicate all injustice. The facts mentioned here regarding the trenchancy of social conflicts, identity politics, and disjointed processes of deliberation suggest that whatever certainty obtains at the highest level of principle evaporates into indeterminacy at the lower levels of deliberation and decision. What appears as pragmatic flexibility from one angle looks like unprincipled anarchy from another.

Be that as it may, I have argued that the way we conceive this dialectic matters. It matters that identity politics be conceived in a way that doesn't preclude mutual transformation and convergence on substantive agreements. It matters that rights be conceived robustly, as the subject matter of such agreements. And it matters that the paradigm for legitimating and resolving agreements be conceived as democratically as possible.

One might object that it does not matter too much. Supposing that the discourse ethical values of autonomy, equality, and reciprocity were realized on an ever-inclusive scale, there is no guarantee that deliberative democracy would promote transformations of identity conducive to achieving substantive agreement. It might instead preserve, if not promote, reasonable pluralism—and not necessarily the kind that is amenable to achieving substantive agreements (Knight and Johnson 1994). The resulting political landscape could even be more conducive to fostering what I call separatist–preservative (SP) identity politics.

That kind of politics has its place as a defensive strategy against group-based (specifically, identity-based) oppression and domination. Whether it would continue to do so in the absence of such domination and oppression is another question. Supposing an ideally just society (world) were possible,

Achieving Global Harmony through Transformative Dialogue 241

would this kind of politics still exist? The answer to this question depends on many factors. As I remark in chapter 2, the elimination of constrained separation (what is commonly known as segregation) might issue in integration and even—just possibly—assimilation into a single dominant cultural identity, unconstrained by the homogenizing tendencies of global consumer capitalism. Such integration or assimilation is unlikely, given the ineluctable dynamics underlying reasonable pluralism. So voluntary—and fairly uncompromising separatism—might still be a reasonable political option.

However, even if syncretic–transformative (ST) identity politics were not necessarily the norm—or assuming it were the norm, that it did not always transform identities into open and fluid affinities—something positive would have been gained. Instead of simply living out our diverse lifestyles thoughtlessly, we would do so with full consciousness of their social costs. We would achieve a mutual understanding of differences that would surely increase our awareness of the complexity and vulnerability of human beings with respect to things shared and unshared. Out of mutual understanding could grow compassion—and a desire for justice.

What implications this would have for the complete fulfillment of our shared humanity and the perfection of a shared system of human rights is—I must confess—less clear than I may have implied. Discourse ethics must allow for unresolvable disagreements and principled compromises. The reasonable pluralism that indelibly marks the human condition demands nothing less than this. What it means to be human—and what capabilities are integral to its minimal and maximal cultivation—will always be a matter of philosophical contention. Agreeing on formal platitudes would be the easy part.

As I remark in the last chapter, the formal conditions that any system of rights must satisfy stand in fundamental tension with one another. The universal acceptance, or legitimacy, of any human right depends on its capacity to be interpreted in different ways, in accordance with the fact of reasonable pluralism. Yet it is precisely this easy accommodation that poses serious problems for enforcement. There is nothing more contemptible than an unenforceable legal right that supposedly claims our highest moral attention. The mere fact that most states do a reasonably good enough job in enforcing them for most of their citizens is hardly reassuring to those who happen to fall through the cracks.

There are thus costs to be paid for not institutionalizing deliberative democracy and ST identity politics at the international level. But is global deliberative democracy possible? I have alluded to some general democratic reforms that would have to be implemented in the General Assembly and other governing bodies within the United Nations. As daunting a task as this is, it is relatively easy to accomplish when compared to the most important reform that will have to be undertaken: the institutionalization of deliberative democracy in all nations and at all levels—formal, informal, and quasi formal. Until popular democracy is implemented all the way down, no amount of government lobbying on behalf of equal human rights will make them popular with the people (this, at any rate, has been the story with Egypt, Nigeria, and a host of other countries dealing with Islamic fundamentalist movements, and it is no less true with respect to the American military regime currently installed in Iraq).

As in most cases, democratic reform will have to proceed at pace with economic, social, and cultural reform. The precise nature of these reforms encompasses changes that are too complex and numerous to be detailed here. My aim in this book has been more modest: to show that cultural conflicts' setting not one political theology against another but rather dogmatic fundamentalisms of all kinds (Christian, Jewish, Islamic, neoliberal) against one another and against reasonable pluralism is not as intractable as it might first seem. Toleration of reasonable pluralism—the democratic pluralism of reason—is the natural condition of modernity. But this is a modernity that, under the sway of neoliberalism and unilateral power politics, has become too tolerant of human suffering and global hegemony.

Today global hegemony manifests itself in the form of a global economic system and neoliberal ideology that pits one half of the world against another. Samuel Huntington, the director of the Institute of Strategic Studies at Harvard University, has notoriously depicted this post–Cold War confrontation as a "clash of civilizations," or, as he otherwise puts it, the "West versus the Rest":

> The West is now at an extraordinary peak of power in relation to other civilizations . . . . Decisions made at the U.N. Security Council or the International Monetary Fund that reflect the interests of the West are presented to the world as reflecting the desires of the world community. The very phrase "the world community" has become the euphemistic collective noun (replacing "the Free World") to give global legitimacy to actions reflecting the interests of the United States and other Western powers. (1993, 39)

Huntington may be wrong about the nature of this clash, which has less to do with civilizations and cultures—less to do with the "West versus the rest"— than with an economic divide separating North and South. His view that power is the "eternal essence" of all politics (2000, 11) and his belief that too much popular democracy endangers stable government administration by and for the sake of economic elites contradict the arguments presented in this book. Yet despite his conservative politics (which reflect the standpoint of the Trilateral Commission), Huntington has got one thing right: The New World order that replaced the bipolar world of the Cold War is designed to further the interests of the powerful and wealthy at the expense of the weaker and poorer. Dominated by the United States, it reflects a "uni-multipolar" system in which, in Huntington's words, "resolution of key international issues requires action by the single superpower plus some combination of other major states in which the single superpower is able to veto action by combinations of other states" (2000, 3, 5–6).

The recent invasion of Iraq presents us with a textbook illustration of how this system works. When we clear the air of ideology, it becomes evident that this invasion—long in the planning prior to the events of September 11, 2001—is less about liberating Iraqis from a brutal dictator or protecting the world from terrorism, or even securing oil reserves for jump-starting a depressed economy, than it is about consolidating the hegemonic power of the United States. But if the aim was to make the Middle East stable for long-term economic development and democratic reform under American tutelage, the effort will surely fail.

The problem is that American hegemony is designed to further the interests of American economic elites. The democracy and development it wishes to impose on the rest of the world reflect this agenda. As we saw in chapter 5, the kind of formal liberal democracy that corresponds to a neoliberal economy is designed to perpetuate the hegemonic power of economic elites. It is therefore the very antithesis of deliberative democracy. Indeed, it is the antithesis of the kind of genuinely liberal and egalitarian democracy so desperately needed in the Middle East. Courageous Muslim defenders of human rights and liberal democracy, such as Iranian political philosopher Abdolkarim Soroush (2000), continually remind us of this fact: "In the Western world we see injustice, colonialism, and arrogance toward other countries alongside the pursuit of liberty. There is external freedom, but no one is interested in internal freedom" (104). Soroush has in mind Kant's distinction between the "external," negative freedom secured by a formal liberal paradigm and the "internal," positive freedom secured by self-determination, both at the level of individual morality and at the level of democratic polity. "Equating liberalism and democracy," he tells us, "signifies at once, great ignorance of the former and grave injustice toward the latter." According to him, "decoupling" the formal liberalism of negative freedom from democracy is "analogous to the attempts of social democrats to separate democracy from capitalism" (136–38).

Soroush calls for a genuine liberal democratic reform of Islam society in accordance with the imperatives of modernity. Reasonable pluralism is one part of this reform: "If the pluralism of secularism makes it suitable for democracy, the faithful community is a thousand times more suitable for it" (143–45). Accepting such pluralism means exchanging religious fundamentalism—the absolute dogmatic certainty of literal authoritative revelation—for "democratic method." This method, as we have seen, provides a different gradient of certainty: "Democracy may be said to have a determined method toward undetermined ends. The indeterminacy, however, refers to instances and specific cases, not the basic principles and criteria of democracy which, like fundamental precepts of jurisprudence, are determined, honored, and inviolable" (151). These principles and criteria include "harnessing the power of rulers, rationalizing their policies, protecting the rights of subjects, and attaining the public good" (148).

Is this a realistic prospect for Islam? Beginning with the Ummayads and Abbasids and continuing through the Ottomans, an Islamic empire arose that in many ways reflected the complex mix of secular and religious political authorities prevalent in medieval Christendom under the doctrine of the "two swords." A genuine Islamic revival can tap into this golden age, as well as the humanism expounded by the Prophet prior to his flight to Medina. But perhaps the bigger lesson to be drawn from the possibility of genuine revival and reform of Islam is the importance, articulated by Charles Taylor and others, of "fusing" the Western secular tradition of liberal democracy with the Eastern spiritual tradition of holistic community. Such a mutual interpenetration and transformation of cultural standpoints would point the way toward redeeming the community of all living creatures from the narrow greed and wide destruction unleashed by global capitalism. At the same time, it would preserve the single most valuable contribution that economy made to the modern world: the use of reason as a basis for individual freedom. Fusing East and West in this way would involve nothing less than fusing reason and faith—or, in Hegel's terms, articulating differences within the broader horizon of an ever-changing, ever-dissolving, and ever-expanding unity. Fred Dallmayr succinctly captures this complex sentiment in discussing the possibility of transformative dialogue between East and West, North and South:

> In our globalizing age, the correlation of faith and reason carries into the relationship between historical faith traditions and the broader conversation of humankind, a conversation that includes as participants a variety of religious and non-religious voices. In this broader context, every particular faith tradition is compelled to look at itself both from the inside and the outside, that is, to shoulder the dual task of self-affirmation and self-assessment or self-critique. For a weak or shallow faith, this task is likely to be further debilitating and perhaps destructive. A living faith, however, will welcome the challenge of re-interpretation as the gateway to continuous self-renewal and reformation. (2000, 183–84)

Bibliography

Ackerman, B. 1984. *Reconstructing American Law.* Cambridge, Mass.: Harvard University Press.
——. 1991. *We the People.* Vol. 1, *Foundations.* Cambridge, Mass.: Harvard University Press.
Alba, Richard D. 1990. *Ethnic Identity.* New Haven, Conn.: Yale University Press.
Alcoff, Linda. 1995. Mestizo Identity. In *American Mixed Race: The Culture of Microdiversity*, ed. Naomi Zack. Lanham, Md.: Rowman & Littlefield.
——. 1999. Latina/o Identity Politics. In *The Good Citizen*, ed. David Batstone and Eduardo Mendieta. New York: Routledge.
Allen, Theodore W. 1994. *The Invention of the White Race.* Vol. 1, *Racial Oppression and Social Control.* London: Verso.
Ames, R. 1988. Rights as Rites: The Confucian Alternative. In *Human Rights and the World's Religions*, ed. L. Rouner. South Bend, Ind.: University of Notre Dame Press.
Amundson, R. 2000. Biological Normality and the ADA. In *Americans with Disabilities: Exploring Implications of the Law for Individuals and Institutions*, ed. L. P. Francis and A. Silvers. New York: Routledge.
Amy, Douglas. 2000. *Beyond the Ballot Box.* Westport, Conn.: Praeger.
Anderson, E. 2001. Group Rights, Autonomy, and the Free Exercise of Religion. In *Groups and Group Rights,* ed. C. Sistare, L. May, and L. Francis. Lawrence: University Press of Kansas.
An-Na'im, A. A. 1990a. Islam, Islamic Law and the Dilemma of Cultural Legitimacy for Universal Human Rights. In *Asian Perspectives on Human Rights,* ed. C. Welsh and V. Leary. Boulder, Colo.: Westview.
——. 1990b. *Toward an Islamic Reformation: Civil Liberties, Human Rights, and International Law.* Syracuse, N.Y.: Syracuse University Press.
Apel, K.-O. 2002. Regarding the Relationship of Morality, Law, and Democracy. In *Habermas and Pragmatism*, ed. M. Aboulafia, M. Bookman, and C. Kemp. New York: Routledge.

Appiah, K. Anthony. 1990. Racisms. In *Anatomy of Racism*, ed. David Theo Goldberg. Minneapolis: University of Minnesota Press.
———. 2000. Foreword to *Racism,* by Albert Memmi. Minneapolis: University of Minnesota Press.
Arato, A., and E. Gebhardt, eds. 1982. *The Essential Frankfurt School Reader.* New York: Continuum.
Arendt, H. 1958. *The Human Condition.* Chicago: University of Chicago Press.
Arneson, R. 2000. Disability, Discrimination, and Priority. In *Americans with Disabilities: Exploring Implications of the Law for Individuals and Institutions,* ed. L. P. Francis and A. Silvers. New York: Routledge.
Balibar, Etienne, and Immanuel Wallerstein. 1993. *Race, Nation, Class: Ambiguous Identities.* London: Verso.
Barry, B. 1989. *Theories of Justice.* Berkeley: University of California Press.
Beitz, C. 1979. *Political Theory and International Relations.* Princeton, N.J.: Princeton University Press.
———. 1989. *Political Inequality: An Essay in Democratic Theory.* Princeton, N.J.: Princeton University Press.
———. 2000. Rawls's Law of Peoples. *Ethics* 110 (July): 669–96.
Best, S., and D. Kellner. 1997. *The Postmodern Turn.* New York: Guilford.
Bickenbach, J. E. 2000. The ADA v. Canadian Charter of Rights: Disability Rights and the Social Model of Disability. In *Americans with Disabilities: Exploring Implications of the Law for Individuals and Institutions,* ed. L. P. Francis and A. Silvers. New York: Routledge.
Bohman, J. 1995. Public Reason and Cultural Pluralism: Political Liberalism and the Problem of Moral Conflict. *Political Theory* 23, no. 2 (May): 253–79.
———. 1996. *Public Deliberation.* Cambridge, Mass.: MIT Press.
Brock, D. 2000. Health Care Resource Prioritization and Discrimination against Persons with Disabilities. In *Americans with Disabilities: Exploring Implications of the Law for Individuals and Institutions,* ed. L. P. Francis and A. Silvers. New York: Routledge.
Buchanan, A. 2000a. Justice, Legitimacy, and Human Rights. In *The Idea of a Political Liberalism,* ed. V. Davion and C. Wolf. Lanham, Md.: Rowman & Littlefield.
———. 2000b. Rawls's Law of Peoples: Rules for a Vanished Westphalian World. *Ethics* 110 (July): 697–721.
Butler, Judith. 1990. *Gender Trouble: Feminism and the Subversion of Identity.* London: Routledge.
Campbell, T. 2001. Democratising Human Rights. In B. Leiser & T. Campbell.
Cardozo, B. 1993. The Nature of the Judicial Process. Excerpted in *American Legal Realism,* ed. M. Horwitz, W. W. Fisher III, and T. A. Reed. Oxford: Oxford University Press.
Carens, J. 1987. Aliens and Citizens: The Case for Open Borders. *Review of Politics* 49, no. 92: 251–73.
Castells, M., and J. Borja. 1997. *Local and Global: The Management of Cities in the Information Age.* London: Earthscan.

Cohen, Phil. 1997. Laboring under Whiteness. In *Displacing Whiteness: Essays in Social and Cultural Criticism,* ed. Ruth Frankenberg. Durham, N.C.: Duke University Press.

Cohen, S. 1993. Transcendental Nonsense and the Functional Approach. Excerpted in *American Legal Realism,* ed. M. Horwitz, W. W. Fisher III, and T. A. Reed. Oxford: Oxford University Press.

Crisp, R., and D. Jamieson. 2000. Egalitarianism and a Global Resources Tax: Pogge on Rawls. In *The Idea of a Political Liberalism,* ed. V. Davion and C. Wolf, 90–101. Lanham, Md.: Rowman & Littlefield.

Curtin, D. 1998. Making Peace with the Earth: Indigenous Agriculture and the Green Revolution. In *Applied Ethics: A Multicultural Approach,* 2d. ed., ed. L. May, S. Collins-Chobanian, and K. Wong. Upper Saddle River, N.J.: Prentice Hall.

Dahl, R. 1956. *A Preface to Democratic Theory*. Chicago: University of Chicago Press.

Dallmayr, Fred. 2002. *Dialogue among Civilizations: Some Exemplary Voices*. New York: Palgrave MacMillan.

Daniels, N. 1990. Equality of What? Welfare, Resources, or Capabilities? *Philosophy and Phenomenological Research* 50, suppl.: 273–96.

———. 2000. Mental Disabilities, Equal Opportunity, and the ADA. In *Americans with Disabilities: Exploring Implications of the Law for Individuals and Institutions,* ed. L. P. Francis and A. Silvers. New York: Routledge.

Davidson, D. 1984. *Inquiries into Truth and Interpretation*. Oxford: Oxford University Press.

Davion, V., and C. Wolf, eds. 2000. *The Idea of a Political Liberalism*. Lanham, Md.: Rowman and Littlefield.

Derrida, J. 1986. Declarations of Independence. *New Political Science* 15: 7–15.

Dewey, J. [1924] 1993. Logical Method and Law. In *American Legal Realism,* ed. M. Horowitz, W. W. Fisher III, and T. A. Reed. Oxford: Oxford University Press.

———. 1941. My Philosophy of Law. In *My Philosophy of Law: Credos of Sixteen American Scholars,* ed. Julius Rosenthal Foundation. Boston: Boston Law Book Company.

———. 1962. *Individualism Old and New*. New York: Capricorn.

Dubinin, N. P. 1965. Race and Contemporary Genetics. In *Race, Science, and Society,* ed. Leo Kuper. New York: Columbia University Press.

Du Bois, W. E. B. [1903] 1997. *The Souls of Black Folk*. In *The Norton Anthology of African American Literature*. New York: W. W. Norton.

———. [1935] 1977. *Black Reconstruction in America, 1860–1880*. New York: Free Press.

———. [1940] 1975. *Dusk of Dawn: An Essay toward an Autobiography of a Race Concept*. Milwood, N.Y.: Kraus-Thomson.

Dworkin, R. 1986. *Law's Empire*. Cambridge, Mass.: Harvard University Press.

———. 2000. *Sovereign Virtue: The Theory and Practice of Equality*. Cambridge: Harvard University Press.

Feenberg, A. 1999. *Questioning Technology*. New York: Routledge.

Feinberg, J. 1980. *Rights, Justice, and the Bounds of Liberty*. Princeton, N.J.: Princeton University Press.
Flandrin, Jean-Louis. 1979. *Families in Former Times: Kinship, Household, and Sexuality in Early Modern Times*. Cambridge: Cambridge University Press.
Foucault, M. 1965. *Madness and Civilization*. New York: Random House.
———. 1970. *The Order of Things: An Archaeology of the Human Sciences*. New York: Random House.
———. 1973. *The Birth of the Clinic: An Archaeology of Medical Perception*. London: Tavistock.
———. 1979. *Discipline and Punish: The Birth of the Prison*. New York: Pantheon.
Francis, L. P., and A. Silvers, eds. 2000. *Americans with Disabilities: Exploring Implications of the Law for Individuals and Institutions*. New York: Routledge.
Frank, J. 1993. Law and the Modern Mind. Excerpted in *American Legal Realism*, ed. M. Horwitz, W. W. Fisher III, and T. A. Reed. 1993. Oxford: Oxford University Press.
Frankenberg, Ruth. 1993. *White Women: Race Matters: The Social Construction of Whiteness*. Minneapolis: University of Minnesota Press.
———, ed. 1997. *Displacing Whiteness: Essays in Social and Cultural Criticism*. Durham, N.C.: Duke University Press.
Fraser, N. 1989. *Unruly Practices: Power, Discourse, and Gender in Contemporary Social Theory*. Minneapolis: University of Minnesota Press.
Fuller, L. 1934. American Legal Realism. *University of Pennsylvania Law Review* 82: 429–61.
Gadamer, Hans-Georg. 1975. *Truth and Method*. New York: Seabury.
Geoghegan, T. 1992. *Which Side Are You On*. New York: Penguin Press.
Gewirth, A. 1982. *Human Rights*. Chicago: University of Chicago Press.
Gilligan, C. 1982. *In a Different Voice: Psychological Theory and Women's Development*. Cambridge: Harvard University Press.
Giroux, Henry. 1997. Rewriting the Discourse of Racial Identity: Towards a Pedagogy and Politics of Whiteness. *Harvard Educational Review* 67, no. 2 (Summer): 285–313.
Gould, C. 2001. Group Rights and Social Ontology. In *Groups and Group Rights*, ed. C. Sistare, L. May, and L. Francis. Lawrence: University Press of Kansas.
Guinier, L. 1991. The Triumph of Tokenism: The Voting Rights Act and the Theory of Black Electoral Success. *Michigan Law Review* 89: 1077–1154.
———. 1994. [E]racing Democracy: The Voting Rights Cases. *Harvard Law Review* 108/109: 109–37.
———. 2000. Making Every Vote Count. *The Nation*, December 4, 2000: 5–7.
Gunther, K. 1989. A Normative Conception of Coherence for a Discursive Theory of Legal Justification. *Ratio Juris* 2: 155–66.
Habermas, J. [1968] 1991. Technology and Science as Ideology. In *Critical Theory: The Essential Readings*, ed. D. Ingram and J. Simon. New York: Paragon House.
———. 1971. *Knowledge and Human Interests*. Boston: Beacon Press.
———. 1975. *Legitimation Crisis*. Boston: Beacon Press.
———. 1987. *The Theory of Communicative Action*. Vol. 2, *Lifeworld and System: A Critique of Functionalist Reason*. Boston: Beacon Press.

———. 1989. *The Structural Transformation of the Public Sphere: An Inquiry into a Category of Bourgeois Society*. Cambridge, Mass.: MIT Press.
———. 1996. *Between Facts and Norms: Contributions to a Discourse Theory of Law and Democracy*. Cambridge, Mass.: MIT Press.
———. 1997. *A Berlin Republic: Writings on Germany.* Lincoln: University of Nebraska Press.
———. 1998a. *The Inclusion of the Other: Studies in Political Theory*. Cambridge, Mass.: MIT Press.
———. 1998b. *On the Pragmatics of Communication*. Cambridge, Mass.: MIT Press.
———. 1998c. *Die Postnationale Konstellation, Politische Essays*. Frankfurt am Main: Suhrkamp.
———. 2001. Glauben, Wissen—Öffnung. *Suddeutsche Zeitung*, October 15.
Hacker, A. 1995. *Two Nations: Black and White, Separate, Hostile, Unequal.* New York: Ballantine.
Hall, Stuart. 1996. *Critical Dialogues in Cultural Studies*, ed. David Morley and Kuan-Hsing Chen. New York: Routledge.
Hannaford, Ivan. 1996. *Race: The History of an Idea in the West*. Baltimore: Johns Hopkins University Press.
Hardin, G. 1977. Living on a Lifeboat. In *Managing the Commons,* ed. G. Hardin and J. Baden. San Francisco: W. H. Freeman.
Hirschfeld, Lawrence. 1996. *Races in the Making*. Cambridge: MIT Press.
Hochschild, J. 1989. Race, Class, Power, and the American Welfare State. In *Democracy and the Welfare State*, ed. Amy Gutmann. Princeton, N.J.: Princeton University Press.
Hohfeld, W. 1919. *Fundamental Legal Conceptions Applied to Judicial Reasoning*. New Haven, Conn.: Yale University Press.
Holmes, O. W., Jr. 1963. *The Common Law*. Cambridge, Mass.: Harvard University Press.
hooks, bell. 1997. Representing Whiteness in the Black Imagination. In *Displacing Whiteness: Essays in Social and Cultural Criticism,* ed. by Ruth Frankenberg. Durham, N.C.: Duke University Press.
Horkheimer, Max. 1947. *The Eclipse of Reason.* New York; Herder & Herder.
———. 1972. *Critical Theory: Selected Essays: Max Horkheimer*. New York: Continuum.
Horsman, Reginald. 1981. *Race and Manifest Destiny: The Origins of American Racial Anglo-Saxonism.* Cambridge, Mass.: Harvard University Press.
Horwitz, M., W. W. Fisher III, and T. A. Reed, eds. 1993. *American Legal Realism.* Oxford: Oxford University Press.
Horwitz, M. 1992. *The Transformation of American Law: 1870–1960.* Oxford: Oxford University Press.
Huntington, Samuel P. 1993. The Clash of Civilizations? *Foreign Affairs* 72 (Summer): 22–49.
———. 1996. *The Clash of Civilizations and the Remaking of World Order*. New York: Simon & Schuster.

———. 2000. Culture, Power, and Democracy. In *Globalization, Power, and Democracy,* ed. Marc F. Plattner and Aleksander Smoler. Baltimore: Johns Hopkins University Press.
Hutchinson, A., ed. 1989. *Critical Legal Studies.* Totowa, N.J.: Rowman & Littlefield.
Ignatiev, Noel. 1995. *How the Irish Became White.* London: Routledge.
Ignatiev, Noel, and John Garvey, eds. 1996. *Race Traitor.* New York: Routledge.
Illingworth, P., and W. E. Parmet. 2000. Positively Disabled: The Relationship between the Definition of Disability and Rights under the ADA. In *Americans with Disabilities: Exploring Implications of the Law for Individuals and Institutions,* ed. L. P. Francis and A. Silvers. New York: Routledge.
Inada, K. 1990. A Buddhist Response to the Nature of Human Rights. In *Asian Perspectives on Human Rights,* ed. C. Welsh and V. Leary. Boulder, Colo.: Westview.
Ingram, David. 1987. *Habermas and the Dialectic of Reason.* New Haven, Conn.: Yale University Press.
———. 1988. Rights and Privileges: Marx on the Jewish Question. *Studies in Soviet Thought* 35: 125–45.
———. 1995. *Reason, History, and Politics: The Communitarian Grounds of Legitimation in the Modern Age.* Albany: State University of New York Press.
———. 2000a. *Group Rights: Reconciling Equality and Difference.* Lawrence: University Press of Kansas.
———. 2000b. Individual Freedom and Social Equality: Habermas's Democratic Revolution in the Social Contractarian Justification of Law. In *Perspectives on Habermas,* ed. L. Hahn. Carbondale, Ill.: Open Court.
———. 2003. Jürgen Habermas and Hans-Georg Gadamer. In *Blackwell Guide to Continental Philosophy,* ed. R. C. Solomon and D. Sherman. New York: Blackwell.
Ingram, D., and J. Simon, eds. 1991. *Critical Theory: The Essential Readings.* New York: Paragon House.
James, J. 1993. *One Particular Harbor.* Chicago: University of Chicago Press.
James, M. R. 2004. *Democracy and Plural Polity.* Lawrence: University Press of Kansas.
Kant, I. 1970. *Kant: Political Writings.* Cambridge: Cambridge University Press.
Kavka, G. 2000. Disability and the Right to Work. In *Americans with Disabilities: Exploring Implications of the Law for Individuals and Institutions,* ed. L. P. Francis and A. Silvers. New York: Routledge.
Kelman, M. 1987. *A Guide to Critical Legal Studies.* Cambridge, Mass.: Harvard University Press.
———. 2000. Does Disability Status Matter? In *Americans with Disabilities: Exploring Implications of the Law for Individuals and Institutions,* ed. L. P. Francis and A. Silvers. New York: Routledge.
Kinder, Donald, and Lynn Sanders. 1996. *Divided by Color: Racial Politics and Democratic Ideals.* Chicago: University of Chicago Press.
Kirchheimer, O. [1941] 1982. Changes in the Structure of Political Compromises. In *The Essential Frankfurt School Reader,* ed. A. Arato and E. Gebhardt. New York: Continuum.

Kittay, E. F. 1999. *Loves Labor: Essays on Women, Equality, and Dependency*. New York: Routledge.
Knight, J., and J. Johnson. 1994. Aggregation and Deliberation: On the Possibility of Political Legitimacy. *Political Theory* 22: 277–96.
Kymlicka, W. 1991. *Liberalism, Community, and Culture*. Oxford: Oxford University Press.
———. 1995. *Multicultural Citizenship*. Oxford: Oxford University Press.
Landis, J. M. [1938] 1974. *The Administrative Process*. Westport, Conn.: Greenwood Publishing Group.
Lane, H., and M. Grodin. 1997. Ethical Issues in Cochlear Implant Surgery: An Exploration into Disease, Disability, and the Best Interests of the Child. *Kennedy Institute of Ethics Journal* 7, no. 3: 231–51.
Lazare, D. 1996. *Frozen Republic: How the Constitution Is Paralyzing Democracy*. New York: Harcourt-Brace.
Leiser, B., and T. Campbell, eds. 2001. *Human Rights in Philosophy and Practice*. Burlington, Vt.: Ashgate.
Lijphart, A. 1986. Proportionality by Non P-R Methods. Ethnic Representation in Belgium, Cyprus, Lebanon, New Zealand, West Germany, and Zimbabwe. In *Electoral Laws and their Political Consequences,* ed. Arend Lijphart and Bernard Grofman. New York: Agathon Press.
———. 1994. *Electoral Systems and Party Systems: A Study of Twenty-Seven Democracies, 1945–1990*. Oxford: Oxford University Press.
Llewelyn, K. 1962. *Jurisprudence: Realism in Theory and Practice*. Chicago: University of Chicago Press.
Lott, Tommy. 1996. Du Bois on the Invention of Race. In *Social Justice in a Diverse Society*, ed. Rita Manning and Rene Trujillo. Mountain View, Calif.: Mayfield.
Lowe, Lisa. 1996. Imagining Los Angeles in the Production of Multiculturalism. In *Mapping Multiculturalism*, ed. Avery F. Gordon and Christopher Newfield. Minneapolis: University of Minnesota Press.
Lupton, D. 1997. Foucault and the Medicalisation Critique. In *Foucault, Health, and Medicine*, ed. A. Petersen and R. Buntun. London: Routledge.
Lyotard, J.-F. 1983. *Le Differend*. Paris: Les Editions de Minuit.
———. 1984. *The Postmodern Condition: A Report on Knowledge*. Minneapolis: University of Minnesota Press.
———. 1993. *The Postmodern Explained: Correspondence 1982–85*. Minneapolis: University of Minnesota Press.
Lyotard, J.-F., and J.-L. Thebaud. 1979. *Au Juste*. Paris: Christian Bourgeois.
MacIntyre, A. 1981. *After Virtue*. South Bend, Ind.: University of Notre Dame Press.
———. 1988. *Whose Justice? Which Rationality?* South Bend, Ind.: University of Notre Dame Press.
MacPherson, C. B. 1977. *The Life and Times of Liberal Democracy*. Oxford: Oxford University Press.
Mahowald, M. 1998. A Feminist Standpoint. In *Disability, Difference, Discrimination,* ed. A. Silvers, D. Wasserman, and M. Mahowald. Lanham, Md.: Rowman & Littlefield.

Marable, Manning. 2000. We Need a New and Critical Study of Race and Ethnicity. *The Chronicle of Higher Education* 46, no. 25 (Feb. 25): 134–37.

Marcuse, H. [1964] 1991. One Dimensional Man. Excerpted in *Critical Theory: The Essential Readings*, ed. D. Ingram and J. Simon. New York: Paragon House.

——. [1938] 1991. On Hedonism. In *Critical Theory: The Essential Readings*, ed. D. Ingram and J. Simon. New York: Paragon House.

——. [1941] 1982. Some Social Implications of Modern Technology. In *The Essential Frankfurt School Reader*, ed. A. Arato and E. Gebhardt. New York: Continuum.

Marsh, J. 1995. *Critique, Action, and Liberation*. Albany: State University of New York Press.

Marx, K. [1844] 1994. Economic-Philosophic Manuscripts. In *Selected Writings*. Indianapolis, Ind.: Hackett.

——. 1994. *Selected Writings*. Indianapolis, Ind.: Hackett.

Matustik, M. 2001. *Jürgen Habermas: A Philosophical-Political Profile*. Lanham, Md: Rowman & Littlefield.

McCarthy, T. 1999. On Reconciling National Diversity and Cosmopolitan Unity. *Public Culture* 11, no. 1: 175–208.

Memmi, Albert. 2000. *Racism*. Minneapolis: University of Minnesota Press.

Mendieta, Eduardo. 1999a. Becoming Citizens, Becoming Hispanics. In *The Good Citizen*, ed. David Batstone and Eduardo Mendieta. New York: Routledge.

——. 1999b. The Making of New Peoples: Hispanizing Race. In *The Rights of Hispanics/Latinos*, ed. Jorge Gracia and Pablo de Greiff. New York: Routledge.

Mezey, S. 2002. The Americans with Disabilities Act in Federal Court: Litigating against Public Entities. *Disability and Society* 17, no. 1: 49–64.

Michaels, Walter Benn. 1995. Race into Culture: A Critical Genealogy of Cultural Identity. In *Identities*, ed. K. Anthony Appiah and Henrey Louis Gates Jr. Chicago: University of Chicago Press.

Mill, J. S. [1859] 1975. On Liberty. In *John Stuart Mill: Three Essays*. Oxford: Oxford University Press.

——. [1861] 1975. Representative Government. In *John Stuart Mill: Three Essays*. Oxford: Oxford University Press.

Mills, Charles. 1998. *Blackness Visible: Essays on Philosophy and Race*. Ithaca, N.Y.: Cornell University Press.

Minow, M. 1990. *Making All the Difference: Inclusion, Exclusion and American Law*. Ithaca, N.Y.: Cornell University Press.

Moellendorf, D. 1996. Constructing the Law of Peoples. *Pacific Philosophical Quarterly* 77, no. 2: 135–44.

Neumann, F. [1936] 1986. *The Rule of Law: Political Theory and the Legal System in Modern Society*. Leamington Spa, England: Berg.

——. 1944. *Behemoth: The Structure and Practice of National Socialism: 1933–1944*. London: Oxford University Press.

Neumann, F., and O. Kirchheimer. 1987. *Social Democracy and the Rule of Law*, ed. K. Tribe. London: Allen and Unwin.

Noble, D. 1984. *The Forces of Production*. Oxford: Oxford University Press.

Noddings, N. 1986. *Caring: A Feminist Approach to Ethics and Moral Education.* Berkeley: University of California Press.
Oboler, Suzanne. 1995. *Ethnic Labels, Latino Lives: Identity and the Politics of (Re)presentation in the United States.* Minneapolis: University of Minnesota Press.
Oliphant, H. 1993. A Return to Stare Decisis. In *American Legal Realism,* ed. M. Horwitz, W. W. Fisher III, and T. A. Reed. Oxford: Oxford University Press.
Orend, B. 2002. *Human Rights: Concept and Context.* Peterborough, Ont.: Broadview.
Outlaw, Lucius. 1995. On Race and Philosophy. *Graduate Faculty Philosophy Journal* 18, no. 2: 175–99.
Owen, D. 2002. *Between Reason and History: Habermas and the Idea of Progress.* Albany: State University of New York Press.
Pagden, Anthony. 1995. *Lords of All the World: Ideologies of Empire in Spain, Britain, and France c. 1500–c. 1800.* New Haven, Conn.: Yale University Press.
Parks, Jennifer. 2003. *No Place like Home? Feminist Ethics and Home Health Care.* Bloomington: Indiana University Press.
Pensky, M. 2000. Cosmopolitanism and the Solidarity Problem: Habermas on National and Cultural Identities. *Constellations* 7, no. 1: 64–79.
Pogge, T. 1989. *Realizing Rawls.* Ithaca, N.Y.: Cornell University Press.
———. 1994. An Egalitarian Law of Peoples. *Philosophy and Public Affairs* 23: 195–224.
———. 2000. Justice for People with Disabilities: A Semi-Consequentialist Approach. In *Americans with Disabilities: Exploring Implications of the Law for Individuals and Institutions,* ed. L. P. Francis and A. Silvers. New York: Routledge.
Rawls, J. 1971. *A Theory of Justice.* Cambridge, Mass.: Harvard University Press.
———. 1993. *Political Liberalism.* New York: Columbia University Press.
———. 1999. *The Law of Peoples.* Cambridge, Mass.: Harvard University Press.
Raz, J. 1986. *The Morality of Freedom.* Oxford: Oxford University Press.
Reinbolt, G. 2001. What Are Group Rights? In *Groups and Group Rights,* ed. C. Sistare, L. May, and L. Francis. Lawrence: University Press of Kansas.
Roediger, David R. 1991. *The Wages of Whiteness: Race and the Making of the American Working Class.* London: Verso.
———. 1994. *Towards the Abolition of Whiteness.* London: Verso Press.
Rush, M. 1993. *Partisan Representation and Electoral Behavior.* Baltimore: Johns Hopkins Press.
Sartre, J.-P. 1991. *Critique of Dialectical Reason.* Vol. 1. London: Verso.
Saxton, Alexander. 1990. *The Rise and Fall of the White Republic: Class Politics and Mass Culture in Nineteenth Century America.* London: Verso.
Scheffler, S. 1999. The Conflict between Justice and Responsibility. In *Global Justice,* ed. I. Shapiro and L. Brilmayer. New York: New York University Press.
Scheuerman, W. F. 1994. *Between the Norm and the Exception: The Frankfurt School and the Rule of Law.* Cambridge, Mass.: MIT Press.
Schumpeter, J. 1942. *Capitalism, Socialism and Democracy.* New York: Harper.
Schweickart, D. 2002. *After Capitalism.* Lanham, Md.: Rowman & Littlefield.
Sen, A. 1982. *Choice, Welfare, and Measurement.* Cambridge: Cambridge University Press.

———. 1994. Population, Delusion, and Reality. *New York Review of Books* 41, no. 15 (Sept. 22): 62–71.
Seymour, M. 1999. On Redefining the Nation. *The Monist*, vol. 82, no. 3.
Shapiro, I., and L. Brilmayer, eds. 1999. *Global Justice. NOMOS XLI*. New York: New York University Press.
Shiva, V. 1988. *Staying Alive: Women, Ecology and Development*. London: Zed Books.
Shue, H. 1996. *Basic Rights: Subsistence, Affluence, and U.S. Foreign Policy*. 2d. ed. Princeton, N.J.: Princeton University Press.
Silvers, A. 1998. Formal Justice. In *Disability, Difference, Discrimination*, ed. A. Silvers, D. Wasserman, and M. Mahowald. Lanham, Md.: Rowman & Littlefield.
Silvers, A., D. Wasserman, and M. Mahowald. 1998. *Disability, Difference, Discrimination*. Lanham, Md.: Rowman & Littlefield.
Simon, T. 2001. Group Rights, Wrongs, and Culture. In *Groups and Group Rights*, ed. C. Sistare, L. May, and L. Francis. Lawrence: University Press of Kansas.
Singer, P. 1972. Famine, Affluence, and Morality. *Philosophy and Public Affairs* 1, no. 3 (Spring): 229–43.
Sistare, C., L. May, and L. Francis, eds. 2001. *Groups and Group Rights*. Lawrence: University Press of Kansas.
Smith, T. A., and R. Tatalovich. 2003. *Cultures at War: Moral Conflicts in Western Democracies*. Peterborough, Ont.: Broadview Press.
Soroush, Abdolkarim. 2000. *Reason, Freedom, and Democracy in Islam: Essential Writings of Abdolkarim Soroush*. New York: Oxford University Press.
Steiner, H. 1999. Just Taxation and International Redistribution. In *Global Justice*, ed. I. Shapiro and L. Brilmayer. New York: New York University Press.
Stoler, Ann. 1989. Making Empire Respectable: The Politics of Race and Sexuality in Twentieth Century Colonial Cultures. *American Ethnologist* 16: 634–60.
Straetz, R. 1958. *PR Politics in Cincinnati*. New York: New York University Press.
Summers, R. S. 1982. *Instrumentalism and American Legal Theory*. Ithaca, N.Y.: Cornell University Press.
Swain, C. 1993. *Black Interests: The Representation of African Americans in Congress*. Cambridge, Mass.: Harvard University Press.
Tan, K.-C. 1998. Liberal Toleration in Rawls's Law of Peoples. *Ethics* 108: 73–89.
Taylor, C. 1992. *Multiculturalism and the Politics of Recognition: An Essay by Charles Taylor*. Princeton, N.J.: Princeton University Press.
———. 1997. Nationalism and Modernity. In *The Morality of Nationalism*, ed. R. McKim and J. McMahon. Oxford: Oxford University Press.
———. 1999. Conditions of an Unforced Consensus on Human Rights. In *The East Asian Challenge for Human Rights*, ed. J. R. Bauer and D. Bell, 101–19. Cambridge: Cambridge University Press.
Thernstrom, A. 1987. *Whose Votes Count? Affirmative Action and Minority Voting Rights*. Cambridge, Mass.: Harvard University Press.
Twine, France Winddance. 1997. Brown-Skinned White Girls: Class, Culture, and the Construction of White Identity in Suburban Communities. In *Displacing Whiteness: Essays in Social and Cultural Criticism*, ed. by Ruth Frankenberg. Durham, N.C.: Duke University Press.

Van den Berghe, Pierre L. 1981. *The Ethnic Phenomenon*. Elsevier.
Waldron, J. 1993. *Liberal Rights*. New York: Cambridge University Press.
Walzer, M. 1983. *Spheres of Justice*. New York: Basic Books.
Ware, Vron. 1992. *Beyond the Pale: White Women, Racism and History*. London: Verso.
Wasserman, D. 1998. Distributive Justice. In *Disability, Difference, Discrimination*, ed. A. Silvers, D. Wasserman, and M. Mahowald. Lanham, Md.: Rowman & Littlefield.
———. 2000. Stigma without Impairment: Demedicalizing Disability Discrimination. In *Americans with Disabilities: Exploring Implications of the Law for Individuals and Institutions,* ed. L. P. Francis and A. Silvers. New York: Routledge.
Weiler, P. 1983. Promises to Keep: Securing Workers' Rights to Self-Organization under the NLRB. *Harvard Law Review* 96 (June): 1769–1827.
Wellman, David T. [1977] 1993. *Portraits of White Racism*, 2d ed. Cambridge: Cambridge University Press.
———. 1997. Minstrel Shows, Affirmative Action Talk, and Angry White Men. In *Displacing Whiteness: Essays in Social and Cultural Criticism,* ed. by Ruth Frankenberg. Durham, N.C.: Duke University Press.
Welsh, C., and V. Leary, eds. 1990. *Asian Perspectives on Human Rights*. Boulder, Colo.: Westview.
Wendell, S. 1996. *The Rejected Body: Feminist Philosophical Reflections on Disability*. New York: Routledge.
Williams, Andrew. 2002. Dworkin on Capability. *Ethics* 113 (October): 23–39.
Wilson, W. J. 1987. *The Truly Disadvantaged: The Inner City, the Underclass, and Public Policy*. Chicago: University of Chicago Press.
Wohlgast, E. 1987. *The Grammar of Justice*. Ithaca, N.Y.: Cornell University Press.
Wright, J. 1986. Australian Experience with Majority-Preferential and Quota-Preferential Systems. In *Electoral Laws and their Political Consequences,* ed. Arend Lijphart and Bernard Grofman. New York. Agathon Press.
Young, Iris Marion. 1990a. *Justice and the Politics of Difference*. Princeton: Princeton University Press.
———. 1990b. *Throwing like a Girl and Other Essays in Feminist Philosophy and Social Theory*. Bloomington: Indiana University Press.
———. 2000a. Disability and the Definition of Work. In *Americans with Disabilities: Exploring Implications of the Law for Individuals and Institutions,* ed. L. P. Francis and A. Silvers. New York: Routledge.
———. 2000b. *Inclusion and Democracy*. Oxford: Oxford University Press.
Zack, Naomi. 1993. *Race and Mixed Race*. Philadelphia. Temple University Press.

Index

aboriginals. *See* Indians
Ackerman, Bruce, 11, 148, 153, 172n2
adjudication, 24, 30, 148, 153, 172n2
administration, 30–31, 226, 242
administrators, 4, 12–13, 21, 24, 26, 40, 121, 239
Adorno, Theodor, 97
affirmative action, 18, 26, 34, 58–60, 69–70, 89n19, 100–2, 105–8, 112, 130, 133, 190–94
Africa, 204–5
African Americans, 20, 24, 34, 42, 191; and racial identity, 56, 69, 77–78, 81, 84n7, 88n17, 89n18, 131–32; and racial redistricting, 127–35, 139–40, 142nn6–7. *See also* blacks
Afrikaners, 20, 23, 34, 56, 74, 187
Aid to Families With Dependent Children (AFDC), 114
Alba, Richard, 88nn17–18
Allen, Theodore, 59
American Constitution, the, 126-27
American Declaration of Independence, 7, 37–39
American Legal Realism. *See* legal realism
American Sign Language (ASL). *See* culture, deaf

Americans With Disabilities Act (ADA), 26, 34–35, 100–105
Ames, Roger, 226
Amish, the, 19, 44–45, 193–94
Amundson, Ronald, 115n4
Amy, Douglas, 138
Anderson, Eric, 194
An-Na'im, Abdullahi Ahmed, 223–24
antiracism, 20–21, 36, 55, 61, 63–64, 68, 70, 72, 91, 132–34, 222
Apel, Karl-Otto, 196–97
Appiah, K. Anthony, 61, 82n1
Arendt, Hannah, 16
Arneson, Richard, 108–10
Arrow, Kenneth, 120–21
Asian Americans, 85n7, 88n17, 89n18, 91

Balibar, E., 88n18
Bangkok Declaration, 33, 211–12
Barry, Brian, 219
Bauer, Bruno, 6–7
Beitz, Charles, 219, 233, 235, 238n5
Bentham, Jeremy, 123
Berghe, Peter van den, 65
Bickenbach, Jerome, 105
Biological Weapons Convention, 238n5
Black Power Movement, 56, 87n16

257

blacks, 55–56, 59–60, 63, 73, 83n2, 86n9, 86n11, 88n16, 89n19, 91, 93–95, 104, 222; Caribbean, 130. *See also* African Americans
Bohman, James, 223
Boorse, C., 115n4
Bourdieu, Pierre, 77
Brandeis, Justice Luis D., 173n7
Brock, Daniel, 109, 115n4
Buchanan, Allen, 217, 2236, 238n7
Buddhism, 223
Bush, George W., 24
Butler, Judith, 17, 62

Calabresi, G., 173n8
Calhoun, J., 142n9
Canada, 33
Canadian Charter of Rights and Freedoms, 33–34, 105, 163–66
capabilities, 2–3, 9–10, 13, 25, 27, 31, 92, 100, 109–10, 122, 124, 127, 185–86, 197, 202, 234, 241. *See also* disability; human rights
capitalism, 3–5, 11, 23–27, 33, 49, 80, 88n18, 96–99, 108, 120, 179; global, 204–6, 210–11, 229, 231–32, 234, 241–42; post-Fordist, 60; post-liberal, 53, 143–46, 149–54, 160, 164, 168, 171–72
Cardozo, Justice Benjamin, 157, 159
Carens, Joseph, 219, 229–30, 237n3
Cashinahua people, 36
Catholics, 57
Civil Rights Act, 34–35, 101–2
civil rights struggles, 6, 81
civil society, 7, 12–13, 24, 114, 145, 170
civility, 22, 31–32, 42, 44–46, 220
civilizations, clash of, 214, 242
class, economic, 3, 16, 22, 26, 50, 100, 105, 107, 178, 191, 225, 234, 240; and democratic representation, 120, 123–26, 130, 132–33, 138–39; Marx on, 9–10; and post-liberal capitalism, 144–48, 158, 168; and race, 5–6, 53, 59–60, 66, 89nn20–21

Clinton, President William Jefferson, 85n8
coalitions, 13, 122, 136, 138. *See also* labor
Coase, R., 173n8
Cohen, Felix S., 158
Cohen, Phil, 60
Cold War, 2, 188, 204, 242–43
colonialism, 231, 234, 243
communicative expectations, 10, 226
communism, 10
communitarianism, 27, 203, 207–9, 216, 229, 233
complexity, 10, 49, 188
Condorcet, Marquis de, 120
consensus, 11–13, 30, 41, 43, 46–48, 142n9, 161, 221, 225, 236, 240; overlapping, 22, 31, 45, 47–48, 200, 215, 218–223
Convention on the Rights of Children, 238n8
corporations, 16, 188, 209, 236
courts, 25, 102–4, 120–21
Crisp, Roger, 238n5
Critical Legal Studies Movement, 159, 165
critical theorists, 3–6, 11, 25, 92, 139, 165, 194, 239–40
critical theory, 3–4, 15, 17, 100, 187, 239–40
culture, 20, 22, 34, 55, 63–64, 192, 222, 225, 228; aspects of, 76; Christian, 27, 242, 244; clash, 27, 75, 213, 215, 221, 238n4; deaf, 6, 20, 23, 92–95; European, 61, 71, 75, 80, 203, 206; and global migration, 21, 23, 80–81, 203, 206–9, 216; Islamic, 2, 27, 216, 221, 223–25, 242–44; and mass (mono-)culture, 54, 80, 231; national, 216, 229; political, 4, 229, 231, 233, 238n5; popular, 4; societal, 18–19, 21; and tradition, 45–47, 73, 75, 81, 220–25; tribal, 231; white, 61, 71, 75, 80. *See also* ethnicity; groups; identity; multiculturalism; rights

Index

Dahl, Robert, 169
Dallmayr, Fred, 244
Daniels, Norman, 108–9, 115n4
d'Ans, Andre Marcel, 36
Davidson, Donald, 44, 238n4
democracy, 1–2, 9, 21, 114, 170, 223, 225; American, 24, 33; and autonomy, 12, 121–24, 128–30, 136–38, 141, 226, 240; and compromise, 12–13, 16, 25–26, 40, 48, 92, 121, 125; and computer technology, 50n2; and decision v. deliberation, 11–15, 31–32, 39–40, 49, 120–22, 125, 162, 240; deliberative, 11–15, 23–24, 26, 29, 48–49, 92, 119–26, 210, 213, 222, 240–42; and dialogue, 14, 28, 32, 45–47, 49, 101, 119–22, 128, 138, 140–41, 210–11, 220–25, 231, 239–44; direct, 124; discourse theory of, 14, 242; and equality, 3, 8, 12, 27, 121–23, 128–30, 136–37, 140–41, 217, 240; and fairness, 2, 8, 122, 128; formal v. informal processes of, 11–14, 24, 120–22, 242; global, 27–28, 33, 208, 210, 213, 227, 232, 234, 236–37, 241; ideals of, 3, 13, 35, 120–22, 143, 169, 244; institutions of, 4, 11, 120–122, 213; justification of, 14, 159, 197, 200; liberal, 27–28, 45, 57, 208, 215–19, 221, 233–37, 243–44; and majority rule, 57, 126; multivector model for evaluating, 12–13, 120–22, 142n1, 222; parliamentary rules of, 17, 121, 140; procedures of, 4, 11, 14–15, 21, 25, 49, 128; and public opinion, 4, 10, 12, 32, 49, 109, 120, 123–25; and reciprocity, 121–23, 128–29, 135, 136–38, 141, 240; representative, 122–26, 144, 154, 182; workplace, 8, 12–13, 24, 33, 41, 113, 145–49, 169, 171, 226, 232. *See also* elections; identity politics; representation; voting

democratization, 25, 49, 113, 210, 213, 215, 226
deontologism, 3, 100
dependency, 26, 107, 113–15, 182
Derrida, Jacques, 3, 160
Dewey, John, 25, 146, 156–59, 173n12, 181
Dicey, A. V., 150, 172n5
disability, 4–6, 9, 16, 22–23, 26–27, 42; and capabilities, 92, 96–98; and care giving, 112–115, 116n13; and deafness, 92, 111–112; definition of, 36, 92, 95–97, 99–103, 106, 111, 115n4; and identity, 92, 182; medicalization of, 98–100, 111. *See also* Americans with Disabilities Act; culture; justice; law; rights
discourse ethics, 22, 32, 46, 240–41; and rights, 196–97, 202, 215, 222, 225–28, 230–32. *See also* democracy, dialogue; ideal speech situation
discrimination, 6, 9, 14–15, 17–18, 20, 26, 30, 34, 36, 133, 139, 185, 189–90, 192, 232, 237; against the disabled, 93–95, 100–9, 111–12; racial, 68, 71, 78, 86n10, 88n17
dissidents, 19, 42, 193
domination, 2, 5 17, 50, 54–55, 58–59, 62, 75–77, 91, 98, 100, 120, 131, 191, 209–210, 240
Du Bois, W. E. B., 60, 69, 78, 87n16, 88n16, 133
Dubinin, N. P., 83n2
Dworkin, Ronald, 110, 159–63, 185

ecology, 208; and ecological consciousness, 223, 234, 237
economism, 5, 40
economy, market, 32, 40, 204, 207, 226–27, 235–36. *See also* capitalism
education, 4, 8, 12–13, 18, 96, 106, 125, 155, 185, 204; and the Amish, 19, 44–45, 192–93; and Quebec's language law, 33, 231–32 and race

and ethnicity, 62, 70, 87n14, 88n17, 89n20, 127–28, 130, 140, 142n9 and women, 205, 223,
elections, 4, 12, 17, 23, 120–22, 126, 136–41, 142n6
Electoral College, 127, 141. *See also* representation; voting
Eleventh Amendment, 103–4
enlightenment, 4, 153
Enlightenment, the, 98
equality, 2, 8–9, 15, 25, 35, 46, 70, 161–165, 168, 197, 199; of the disabled, 100, 106–8; global, 217, 226, 235, 237n1. *See also* democracy, equality
ethnicity, 4, 20, 23, 34, 53–55, 72–75, 80, 84n7, 91, 93, 132, 189; and clubs, 60–61, 71; new, 62–65
ethnocentrism, 46, 81, 210, 233
eudaimonism, 3, 5, 92, 96, 100
European Union (EU), 206, 211, 236
evangelicals, 57
exploitation, 54, 59, 203

Family and Medical Leave Act (FMLA), 113–115
Federal Reserve Board, 40, 154
Federal Trade Commission, 154
federalism, 33–35, 103, 121, 231
Feenberg, Andrew, 50n2
Feinberg, Joel, 182
feminists, 26, 107, 113
feudalism, 7
First Nation people, 163
Flandrin, J.-L., 90n21
Foucault, Michel, 3, 17, 50, 63, 77, 79, 98–99, 155, 173n11, 194
Fourteenth Amendment, 35, 104–5
France, 37–38, 187
Frank, Jerome, 143, 153, 157
Frankenberg, Ruth, 79, 84nn4–5
Frankfurt School, 25
Fraser, Nancy, 115
free trade, 211, 229, 232, 234–35

freedom, 1, 3–4, 7–10, 15, 19, 25, 27, 37– 39–40, 68, 113, 115, 123–24, 134, 158, 166, 169, 103–96, 207, 217, 235, 237n1, 239; of association, 4, 55; negative v. positive, 7, 31, 111, 177–78, 182, 194, 211–12, 243; of speech, 4, 45–46. *See also* democracy, autonomy; rights
French Declaration of the Rights of Man, 7, 37–39
French Revolution, 37
Fuller, Lon, 153

Gadamer, Hans-Georg, 28, 32, 46–47, 77
Garvey, John, 61
gender, 4–6, 17, 53, 62, 66, 96, 114, 132, 187, 224, 237
General Allotment Act, 57
Gewirth, Alan, 195–97
Gilligan, 113
Giroux, Henry, 20, 23, 55, 58, 61–65, 67–70, 72, 76–79
globalization, 50n2, 144–45, 198, 215, 223, 225, 236, 244 and immigration, 60, 80, 203–9. *See also* culture, global migration; capitalism; neoliberalism
Great Depression, 147
Gonzalez, Elian, 212
Gore, Al, 127, 137
Grodin, Michael, 93–95
Guinier, Lani, 24, 127, 129–132, 135, 138–40, 140nn4, 9
Gunther, Klaus, 174n14
groups, 3, 6–7, 9–10, 15–22, 26–27, 30–32, 35, 37, 43, 46, 101, 119, 122, 134; affinal v. aggregate, 16, 189; ethnic, 34, 62, 65, 71–72, 76, 78, 84n7, 85n8, 88n17, 90n23, 125; in-group v. out-group, 72, 89n21; legitimacy of, 9, 16, 19–20, 94, 130; plural interest, 53; racial, 76, 84n7, 85n8, 120, 125, 130, 142n6; religious, 189 rights of. *See* rights,

group structural, 16, 53–55, 58. *See also* African Americans; Amish; Asian Americans; blacks; disability; immigrants; Indians; Latinos; minorities; religion; subnationalities; whites; women; workers

Habermas, J., 4, 14, 22, 28, 32, 42, 145, 155, 159, 162, 165, 168, 173n11, 173nn14–15, 238n4; on adjudication, 163, 170; on democracy, 16, 47, 115, 146, 161, 166–71, 200, 215; on international law, 45, 210, 215–16, 232; on Quebec, 45–46, 231; on rights, 18, 25, 156, 158, 164, 168, 215–216, 221, 226–227. *See also* discourse ethics
Hacker, A., 129
Hall, Stuart, 55, 63–64
Hannaford, I., 90n21
happiness, 4, 18–19, 21, 123, 200, 239
Hardin, Garrett, 205
healthcare, 108–110, 204–5, 234
heavily indebted poor countries (HIPCS), 183, 204
Hegel, G. W. F., 79, 150, 223, 244
Heidegger, Martin, 77
Hirschfeld, Lawrence, 66–67, 82n1, 86nn12–13, 87n14, 90n22
Hispanics. *See* Latinos
Hitler, Adolf, 187
Hochschild, J., 127
Hohfeld, Wesley, 158, 181
Holmes, Justice Oliver Wendell (Jr.), 156–57, 172n6, 174n16
home schooling, 19, 194
hooks, bell, 61, 67–68, 70
Horkheimer, Max, 1–2, 97
Horsman, R., 59
Horwitz, Morton, 156, 171, 172n1, 172n4, 173nn9, 173n10,
human nature, 3–4, 7–10, 18, 37, 40, 96–97, 100, 108, 122, 178, 180, 202, 224, 226, 241

human rights, 15, 27, 178–80, 185, 188, 201–2, 237n2, 238n8, 239; and capabilities, 3, 92, 95–96, 178, 185–86, 197, 202, 228, 238n8, 239; Chinese conception of, 226–227; completeness (complementarity) of, 179–84, 212–14, 226, 228, 236; definition of, 10, 178, 197, 239; determinacy of, 30, 33–34, 41, 209–211, 214, 226, 228, 236; and the International Criminal Court (ICC), 200; justification of, 10–11, 194–202, 227; legitimacy of, 37, 194–202, 214–225, 227, 241; liberal interpretation of, 216–21, 237n1; perfection of, 177–86, 225–28, 236; ranking of, 33–34, 92, 200, 211–214, 227–28, 236; realization of, 27–28, 92, 177–86, 210, 215, 225, 237; third generation, 184; and the United Nations Universal Declaration of Rights, 11, 184, 211, 213, 226, 237n1; universality of, 3, 7, 37, 95–96, 203, 206, 210, 215–16, 236, 237n1, 242. *See also* rights
humanism, 3–4, 7, 9, 37, 44, 123, 223–24
Huntington, Samuel, 2, 214, 242–43

ideal speech situation, 42, 46
identity, 9, 64, 122; biological conception of, 26; black, 58, 79, 89n20, 91, 139; citizenship, 45, 70, 208, 218, 231–33; constitution of, 16–17, 22, 26, 43–44, 123, 139; crisis of, 31, 167; cultural, 43, 55, 57, 80–81, 86n10, 90n24, 91, 119, 219, 230–32, 241; ethnic, 23, 55, 63–64, 68, 72–75, 80–81, 85n8, 88nn17–18, 90n23, 94; gender, 17, 61–62, 219; group, 4, 53, 85n8, 86n10, 131–32, 142nn4–6, 186–91; Hispanic, 85n8, 86n11, 88n18; Jewish, 72; legitimacy of, 20, 23, 54, 64, 68, 119, 130–32, 230; national,

72, 132, 209, 224, 229–32; personal, 17, 43–44, 131, 209; postmodern, 4, 16, 55, 60, 63, 65, 72; racial, 20, 23, 54, 57, 68, 72–75, 88n18, 91, 94, 131, 230; religious, 70, 219; tribal, 57; white, 23, 55, 58, 89n20, 143. *See also* ethnicity; groups; identity politics; race
identity politics, 2, 4–6, 14–21, 53–54, 58, 86n10, 92–93, 126–128, 147, 149, 163–65, 177–79, 186–91, 194, 203, 209; and resentment, 26, 54, 101, 106, 115n4, 194; separatist-preservative (SP), 22–24, 26–28, 30–32, 42–46, 48–49, 55–57, 62–64, 68, 70–72, 80–81, 91, 93–94, 100–101, 111, 119–20, 130, 141, 179, 209–10, 216, 218, 220–22, 230–31, 239–40; syncretist-transformative (ST), 22–24, 26–28, 30–32, 42–46, 48–49, 55–56, 70, 72, 91, 107, 119–20, 123, 129, 136, 138–39, 141, 179, 209–10, 222, 227, 230–31, 241
ideology, 10, 12, 16, 131–33, 150, 204, 226, 230, 243
Ignatiev, Noel, 59, 61, 67–68, 70, 86n9
Illingworth, P., 112
immigrants, 28, 33, 152, 203–9, 228–32, 236; American ethnic, 59–60, 62–63, 73, 77, 79, 84n7, 85n7, 88nn17–18, 91, 112; justice for, 203–9, 228–32, 236
immigration, 56, 60, 66, 215, 219, 223, 228–32; causes of, 203–9
Indians, 20, 22–23, 33, 46, 55, 72, 80, 89n21, 119, 163, 184–85, 203, 208, 236. *See also*, Cashinahua people, First Nation people, Native Americans, New Mexico Pueblos, Seminoles
individualism, 8, 75, 89n20, 119, 153, 209, 223–24, 226, 229–30, 234
individuality, 3, 123, 178, 225

Ingram, David, 19, 57, 94, 121, 128, 163, 191, 198, 222
injustice, 3, 17, 30–31, 99, 107, 145, 239, 243; and differends, 13, 21–22, 25, 39–42, 49–50, 54, 100, 125, 144, 147, 221, 239; economic, 107, 114, 155, 167, 181, 225; electoral, 126–28
integration, 56, 80–81, 91, 99, 230–41
International Covenant on Civil and Political Rights, 211
International Covenant on Economic, Social, and Cultural Rights, 211
International Criminal Court (ICC), 200, 213, 238n8
International Monetary Fund (IMF), 183, 236, 242
Interstate Commerce Commission, 154
Iraq War, 1–2, 242
Islamic fundamentalism, 2, 242–43

Jackson, Jesse, 133
Jaffe, Louis, 173n10
James, Michael R., 142n1
Jamieson, Dale, 238n5
Jefferson, Thomas, 29, 37, 59,
Jewish question, the, 6
Jews, 72–73, 76, 85n7, 86n9
Johnson, Jim, 142n1, 240
judges, 4, 12–13
justice, 2, 4, 22, 24, 39, 42–43, 157, 170, 187, 202, 241; cosmopolitan v. communitarian approaches to, 203–9, 229, 233; distributive, 8, 21, 40, 92, 100, 106–115, 130, 154, 184, 207–8, 219, 229–30, 233–36, 238n5; economic, 217, 219, 229–30, 232–37, 238n5; feminist approaches to, 112–115; international, 203–39, 242–43; Rawls's theory of, 14, 107–8, 215–19, 229–30, 233–36, 237n1, 238n5

Kant, Immanuel, 40, 150, 195, 197, 215, 218, 243
Kavka, Gregory, 108

Kelman, Mark, 106, 173n13
Kennedy, Justice Anthony, 132,
Kinder, Donald, 78
Kirchheimer, Otto, 25, 155, 164, 174n15
Kittay, Eva, 107, 113
Klare, K., 172n2
Knight, Jack, 142n1, 240
Kohlberg, Lawrence, 198
Kraybill, D., 193
Kymlicka, Will, 18–20, 46
Kyoto Protocol, 238n8

labor, 5, 8–9, 22–23, 33, 41, 54–60, 96–98, 107, 112–115, 145, 147–49, 168, 205–7; alliance with environomental movement, 48, 50n2
Landis, J., 154, 173n10
Land Mine Treaty, 238n8
Lane, Harlan, 93–95
Langdell, Christopher C., 150
language games, 3, 38–39, 43; reflexivity of, 43–45
language laws (Quebecois), 23, 33, 45–46, 163, 231–32
Lassalle, Ferdinand, 8
Latinos, 85n8, 86n11, 88n17–18, 194
law, 8, 24, 154, 157, 159–60, 163, 199; anti-discrimination, 100–106, 133–34; common, 33, 42, 153; contract, 22, 33, 42, 59, 147, 150, 152, 165, 223; and democracy, 153, 162, 167–68, 239; and differends, 143–76, 239; and disability, 100–6, 115nn6–8, 116nn8–12; indeterminacy of, 24, 151, 240; and integrity, 25, 160, 162, 240; international, 2, 45, 93, 206, 211–12, 216–19, 232–34, 237, 238n8; interpretation of, 24, 154, 164; Islamic, 223–25; Jim Crow, 89n21, 160, 170, 187; and juridification of life, 155; labor, 25, 33, 35, 151; legitimation of, 14, 159–164, 239–40; natural, 10, 21, 37, 123, 151, 178, 201, 224; of Peoples, 216–19, 228, 237n2; property, 22, 33, 42, 149–50; rule of, 2, 21, 25, 150, 216, 239; tort, 22, 150; treaty, 33, 238n8; welfare, 155, 179. *See also* adjudication; affirmative action; ADA; human rights; legal paradigms; legal realism; legislation; rights
law and economics movement, 154
Lazare, Daniel, 127
League of Nations, 187
legal paradigms, 164, 171, 179, 186, 188, 206, 211, 221–22, 225, 239; formal-liberal, 22–24, 27, 31, 33, 35, 41, 49, 92, 101, 106–7, 111–13, 115, 124, 128, 145, 149, 152, 165, 207–12, 214–15, 243; participatory-democratic (reflexive), 22, 24, 26, 31, 33–35, 92, 101–3, 106–7, 109, 113, 115, 122, 124, 128, 166, 210–11, 214–15, 240; substantive-welfare, 22, 24, 26–27, 31, 33–35, 92, 101, 106–7, 111–113, 115, 124, 128, 148, 207–9, 212, 235
legal realism, 25, 149, 153, 156
legislation, 24, 30, 141, 142n9, 163
legislators, 12–13, 26, 30, 40, 142n9, 154, 166, 186
legitimation, 14–15, 21, 39, 41, 43, 46, 49, 50n1, 179, 198–99; crisis of, 11, 31–32, 167; of government, 2, 21, 217. *See also* groups; identity
liberalism, 25, 43, 47, 149, 220, 229, 243. *See also* political liberalism
Lijphart, A., 136
Llewelyn, Karl, 153, 155–56, 174n16
Locke, John, 7, 180
Lott, Tommy, 84n6, 88n16
Lowe, Lisa, 89n18
Lukacs, Georg, 145
Lupton, D., 98
Lyotard, Jean-Francois, 3, 13, 21–22, 25, 36–39, 41–43, 49, 50nn1–2, 144, 147

MacIntyre, Alasdair, 47, 196
Madison, James, 123
Mahowald, Mary, 107, 115n2
manifest destiny, 60
Marable, Manning, 85n7
Marcuse, Herbert, 96–97, 145
Marsh, James, 196
Marx, Karl, 5, 169, 191, 194, 240; on alienation, 3, 96–97; on rights, 6–10, 177–78
McCarthy, T., 226
medical establishment, 97–99, 102, 106
Memmi, Albert, 78, 82n1, 83n3, 90n21
Mead, George Herbert, 198
Medicaid, 109, 134
Mendieta, Eduardo, 88n18
Mezey, Susan, 103–4
Michaels, Walter Benn, 90n24
Middle East, 2, 38, 212, 243
Mill, John Stuart, 24, 122–26, 129, 132, 134, 144, 200, 229–30
Mills, Charles, 83n2
Milosovic, S., 213
minorities, 45, 104, 160, 166, 217, 232; and democracy, 120, 125–26, 130–31, 134, 141, 142nn6, 8, 9; ethnic and racial, 53–54, 60–1, 68–70, 77, 85n8, 91; and rights, 181–82, 189, 192. *See also* groups
Mohammad, 224, 244
multiculturalism, 2, 20–21, 28, 47, 58, 61–62, 74, 94, 208, 216, 231; and politics of recognition, 43–44, 48, 55–56, 62–63, 80, 86n10, 91
Muslims, 223–25, 243

NAACP, 85n8
Nader, Ralph, 127, 137
narratives: modern, 37–39, 50n1, 240; mythic, 36–37, 50n1; Nazi, 37
nation state, 216, 233, 235–36, 238n7
nationalism, 209, 232
Native Americans, 38, 42, 45, 142n8, 166; and race, 63, 80, 84n7, 85n7, 86n11, 87n17

needs, 5, 8–10, 35–36, 92, 106, 109–11, 115n2, 122, 166; and human rights, 8–10, 35–36, 92, 185, 195, 200, 228, 233, 238nn5, 7, 239
neo-liberalism, 231, 235, 242–43
neo-Malthusians, 205
Neumann, Franz, 25, 155, 165, 174n15
New Deal, 149, 153
New Mexico Pueblos, 19, 57
NGOs, 12, 14
Noble, David, 98
Noddings, N., 113
normalcy, standards of, 9, 96, 105, 108, 113, 115n4
Norman Yoke Doctrine, 60

O'Connor, Justice Sandra Day, 103, 130, 132
Oliphant, Herman, 158
oppression, 2, 5–6, 17, 62–63, 77–79, 100, 131, 139, 186, 191, 240
Oregon Health Plan, 109
Outlaw, Lucius, 65–66
Owen, David, 198

Pagden, A., 90n21
Palestinians, 208
Palestine/Israel, 230
Parks, Jennifer, 107, 113
Parmet, W. E., 112
patriarchy, 62, 114, 223
perspectivalism, 4, 25
Pitney, Justice Mahlon, 147, 172n7
pluralism, 16, 27, 47, 123–25, 140, 168, 215, 218–20, 224, 239–44
pluralist theory, 53
Pogge, Thomas, 108–9, 111–12, 219, 233, 235, 237n3, 238n5
political liberalism, 22, 45–47, 217
political parties, 16, 122, 133, 136–38, 140, 142n6; Democratic and Republican, 128, 130. *See also* representation, partisan
Posner, R., 173n8
postmodernists, 4, 151, 156, 181

power, 8, 10, 18, 36, 38, 49, 79, 83n4, 98–99, 154, 189, 191, 242–44
pragmatism, 3, 158, 167, 17–72, 180, 186, 201
presidential election 2000. *See* voting
private property, 7–8, 150–53. *See also* law, property
Protestant work ethic, 58, 74
public accountability, 45, 49, 120, 125, 134, 238n4
public sphere(s), 12–13, 120, 166–69, 202, 232

Quebecois, 18, 33, 42, 163, 231–32,

race, 4–6, 16, 35, 127, 132, 211, 222, 224–25; and biology, 54, 57, 65–67, 73–74, 82n1, 82n1, 83n2, 85n8, 90nn22–23; and census data, 67, 82n1, 85n8, 86n11, 88n17, 89n19; cognition of, 66–67, 70, 74, 82n1, 86nn12–13, 87n14; and disability, 22–23, 92–95, 100, 102, 104–5, 115n4, 119; history of, 89n21; and identity, 20, 53–89, 130, 229; mixed, 66–68, 82n1, 85n8, 96n11, 87nn14–15, 89n20, 91; and natural selection, 65, 74; Nazi criteria of, 82n1; permanency of, 62, 64–67; as social construct, 23, 36, 54, 65, 83n2, 85n8; systems of, 54, 67–68, 70, 82n2, 85nn7, 9, 88nn17–18, 89n21, 90n21; and whiteness, 20, 23, 55, 58–64, 68–70, 75–80, 83n4, 84n5, 91. *See also* ethnicity; identity; segregation; racism; white privilege
racism, 20, 58–62, 67–68, 70, 81, 90n21, 130–32, 134, 139, 160, 191, 206, 210, 212, 237 black, 69, 89n20 extrinsic v. intrinsic, 59, 61. *See* antiracism
rational choice theory, 12, 106–7, 120–21
Rawls, John, 27–28, 31, 200–201; on distributive justice, 106–8, 227, 229, 232–36, 238nn3, 5; on international law, 45, 47, 210, 215–21, 228–36, 237nn1, 2, 238nn3, 5; on justifying moral principles, 14, 111, 113, 218–19, 228, 238n4. *See also* consensus (overlapping); political liberalism
reason, political, 29, 30, 122, 242, 244
reason, public, 22, 42, 220
reasoning: a priori, 29; deductive, 32, 35, 39, 43, 49, 156; dialogic, 35–36, 38, 40–41, 49, 169; formal logical, 35–36, 38, 40–41, 150–51; fragmentation of, 29–32, 35–41; incommensurabilities of, 30, 32, 35–36, 38, 47, 239; instrumental, 125; levels of, 30, 32, 35–38, 49, 125; substantive-calculative, 35–36, 38, 40–41. *See also* democracy, dialogue
reciprocity, 10, 12, 25, 113, 161, 199. *See also* democracy
Reconstruction, 34
Rehabilitation Act, 101–3
Refugees, 204, 208, 210, 212, 229, 231
Rehnquist, Justice William, 116n11
religion, 6, 18–19, 23, 35, 44–46, 81, 132, 208, 223–25, 237n1, 238n6, 242–44. *See also* Amish; Buddhism; culture; evangelicals, fundamentalism, Islam, Jews, Muslims
representation, 142n4, 170, 182, 190; of African Americans, 133–34, 138–40, 142n6; interest v. descriptive, 24, 125, 133–35, 139–41; as mirroring, 124–25, 134; partisan, 131–33, 142n6; of preferences and perspectives, 12, 16, 54, 120–22, 125, 133–35, 139, 142nn7–8; proportional, 34, 122, 125–26, 131, 134, 136–38; and racial redistricting, 23–24, 34, 42, 74, 85n8, 89n19, 120, 128–35, 139–41, 142n6; reserved seat, 136; single seat v. multiple seat,

13, 15, 18, 23–24, 125–27, 129–30, 133–35, 138–41, 142n6; virtual, 125, 134, 181; of women, 125, 186. *See also* voting
representatives, 14, 24, 37, 145, 219, 227, 235, 238n6, 239; Mill on, 125–27; of racial minorities, 34, 42, 129–30, 133–35, 138–41, 142n6
revolution, 11, 101
rights, 2–3, 6, 53, 125, 158, 168, 171; to asylum, 212; to citizenship, 182, 208; of children, 221, 181–82, 193, 238n8; civil, 4, 7, 18–19, 33, 85n8, 100, 105, 130, 182, 211–12, 216, 224, 227, 232; claim. *See* rights, will theory of; constitutional, 11, 18, 103–5, 220; contractarian theory of, 28, 123, 148, 210, 215–19, 225–28, 236; to culture, 18, 23, 27, 33, 74, 184–85, 203, 206, 212, 214; of disabled persons, 26, 92, 100–12; discourse ethical theory of, 26, 196–98, 215–16, 225–228, 236; economic, 149, 212, 214, 225, 228, 233, 236, environmental, 228; familial, 193, 223; formal and substantive, 8–9, 25, 31, 35, 177–78, 182, 206, 212, 216, 237n1; of groups, 3, 9, 16–19, 22–23, 27, 31–32, 35, 43–45, 57, 124, 186–94, 216–217, 229, 231, 236, 237n2; of immigrants, 18, 203–9, 211–12, 229–32; interest theory of, 26, 179, 214; labor, 33, 212; to liberty, 7, 27, 29–30, 40, 107, 219, 227; to life, 29–30, 33, 40, 203, 219, 237n1; natural, 10, 123, 180, 203; political, 7, 18, 27, 33, 41, 181, 211–12, 216–17, 223, 227, 232; postmodern critique of, 3, 29, 39; property, 7–9, 33, 40, 145, 207–10, 212, 219, 223–24, 228, 237n1; to security, 27, 182, 206, 224, 227, 237n1; sovereignty, 18, 203, 206, 208–210, 215, 229–32; states, 104; to subsistence, 27, 29, 33, 184, 211–12, 225, 227–28, 237n1; treaty, 38, 45, 56; voting, 15, 42, 127–28, 223; welfare, 182, 184, 211, 237; will theory of, 26, 214; of women, 186–87, 223–25. *See also* freedom; human rights
Roediger, David, 59–60
Roosevelt, President Franklin Delano, 155, 173n7
Rousseau, Jean-Jacques, 7, 124–25, 154, 203
Rush, M., 131

Saint Augustine, 224
Sanders, Lynn, 78
Sartre, Jean-Paul, 188–89
Saxton, A., 59–60
Scheffler, Samuel, 235
Scheuerman, William, 174n15
Schmitt, Carl, 174n15
Schumpeter, Joseph, 169
Schweickart, David, 207
science, 99
Securities and Exchange Commission, 154
segregation, 13, 21, 23, 48, 54, 56, 74, 80–81, 98, 128, 131, 138, 143, 160, 241. *See also* voting
self-realization, 12, 18–19, 113, 123–25, 128, 226
Seminoles, 23, 34, 56–58, 72
Sen, Amartya, 110, 185, 206, 223
separation of powers, 10, 49, 121, 154, 224
sexism, 59, 191
sexual orientation, 17, 62, 185
Shari'a. *See* law, Islamic
Shiva, V., 208
Shue, Henry, 179, 195, 228
Silvers, Anita, 111–12
Simon, Thomas, 202n3
Singer, Peter, 207
slaves, 37–39, 56, 59, 127
Sleeter, Christine, 75, 90n24

Index

social contract theory, 28, 106–8, 123, 172n4, 200, 209–11, 216–219, 221, 225–26, 229–30. *See also* legal paradigms, formal-liberal; Rawls; rights, contractarian theory of
social evolution, 29
social movements, 13, 16, 62, 140
social roles, 36, 96, 114, 226
socialism, 5, 8–9, 41–42, 169, 207
solidarity, 4, 7–8, 16, 65–66, 73, 119, 140, 202, 208, 233
Soroush, Abdolkarim, 243–44
speech, 86n13; acts, 36, 43; hate, 15
stakeholder theory, 12, 168, 188, 210, 216
standpoint ethics, 4, 107, 240
Steiner, Hillel, 238n5
Stoler, A., 90n21
Stone, Justice Harlan Fiske, 148
Straetz, R., 138
subnationalities, 28, 84n7, 187
Summers, R. S., 172n3
Supreme Court, 34, 103–5, 131–33, 160, 165, 172n7

Taha, M. M., 224
Taft-Hartley Act, 148
Tan, K.-C., 217
Tatalovitch, Ray, 6
Taylor, Charles, 43, 45, 222, 226, 244
Temporary Assistance to Needy Families (TANF), 114
Tenth Amendment, 103–4
terrorism, 2, 184, 121, 237, 143
Thernstrom, Abigail, 134
Third World countries, 204–5, 207
Thomas, Justice Clarence, 133
Tocqueville, Alexis de, 122–23
toleration, 19–20, 22, 28, 30–31, 44–48, 201, 216–17, 224, 237, 242
totalitarianism, 11, 41
Twine, France Winddance, 89n20
tyranny, 11, 19, 21, 49, 123, 126, 163

unions, 5, 16, 53, 60, 103, 113, 147, 149, 212

United Nations (UN), 2, 5, 95–96, 186, 227; on human development, 204; and General Assembly, 210, 213, 236, 241; Security Council, 1, 236, 242
United States (US), 8, 13, 30, 33, 37–38, 48, 98, 114, 116n13, 123; international relations, 1–2, 38, 189, 204–6, 221, 235, 238n8, 242–43; race relations, 13, 20, 23–24, 34, 56, 62, 65–68, 77, 81, 82n1, 83n2, 88n17, 126, 138, 140–41, 142n8, 187
urban ghetto, 54, 81, 133–34, 139
US Court of Appeals, 148
US Department of the Interior, 57
US Department of Justice, 34, 128, 211
US State Department, 33, 211–13, 226–27, 238n8
utilitarianism, 106, 110, 123, 200, 207, 230
utopianism, 3, 5, 21, 96, 178, 227, 239,

Vienna Convention on Consular Rights, 238n8
voting, 8, 16, 120, 237n2, 238n8; and aggregation, 11–12, 15–16, 120–23, 127; alternative systems of, 18, 120–22, 135–41; Hare's system of, 126; ordinal, 126, 129, 137–38; plural, 13, 125–26, 129, 135, 138–41; and presidential election 2000, 24, 126–28, 137; tabulation of, 41, 126–28, 131, 137, 141, 142n6; and vote dilution, 127–30, 135, 138, 141, 142n9; Voting Rights Act, 35, 128, 142n3, 165–66

Wagner Act, 35, 147–49, 172n2
Waldron, Jeremy, 192
Wallerstein, Immanuel, 88n18
Walzer, Michael, 147, 229, 231
war crimes, 213
Ware, V., 59
Wasserman, David, 105, 108, 110
Weber, Max, 169, 174n15

welfare, 13, 25, 40, 100, 106, 112–115, 123, 134, 192, 194, 196; and American capitalism, 146, 154–55, 165–68; and disability, 100, 106, 112–115; and international justice, 204, 212, 225, 228, 234, 239
welfare state, 5, 49, 98
Wellman, David, 58–60
Wendell, Sharon, 95–96
white privilege, 5, 23, 54–55, 58, 60–61, 63. *See also* race, whiteness
white supremacism, 54–60, 63, 69, 76–77, 83n4, 91
whites, 54, 56–62, 64–65, 68–69, 70, 73–74, 76–79, 83n2, 86n9, 84n5, 86n11, 128–29, 131, 133–35, 140, 142n9, 222
wiggers, 61
Wilson, William Julius, 133
Wittgenstein, Ludwig, 77, 192
Wohlgast, Elizabeth, 181
women, 28, 30, 34, 53–54, 57, 69, 71, 87n14, 125, 142n8; and care giving, 96, 99, 107, 112–115, 116n13; global emancipation of, 205, 207, 223–25, 236; political empowerment of, 181–82, 186–87, 189, 191–92
workers, 30, 33, 41, 205–6; and disability, 91, 97–98, 113; as politically organized, 22, 24–25, 48, 125–26, 147–49, 152, 162, 181, 191; and racial politics, 54, 59–60
workfare, 5, 114
World Bank, 38, 204, 236
World Trade Organization, 38, 48, 211, 236
World War II, 85n7, 155, 187
Wright, J., 137

Young, Iris, Marion, 86n10, 96, 115n6, 142nn7–8, 230, 236

Zack, Naomi, 61, 68, 75, 83n2, 86n9, 90n21